End

OF MODERN CIVILIZATION & ALTERNATIVE FUTURE

Total Rethinking on How We Live, Work and Prosper.

By
Dr. Sahadeva dasa

B.com., FCA., AICWA., PhD
Chartered Accountant

Soul Science University Press

WorldCrisisSolutions.com

Modern Civilization
A Legacy of Dissatisfaction, Conflict & Pollution

Readers interested in the subject matter of this
book are invited to correspond with the publisher at:
SoulScienceUniversity@gmail.com   +91 98490 95990

To order a copy write to chandra@rgbooks.co.in
or buy online: at www.rgbooks.co.in

First Edition: December 2008

Soul Science University Press expresses its gratitude to the Bhaktivedanta
Book Trust International (BBT), for the use of quotes by His Divine
Grace A.C.Bhaktivedanta Swami Prabhupada.
Copyright Bhaktivedanta Book Trust International (BBT)

©Soul Science University Press
All rights reserved

ISBN 978-81-909760-1-5

Published by:
Dr. Sahadeva dasa for Soul Science University Press

Designed by : Sailesh Ijmulwar, Waar Creatives.

Printed in India : Rainbow Print Pack, Hyderabad

Dedicated to
His Divine Grace A.C. Bhaktivedanta Swami Prabhupada

> "This is not good civilization. It will not stay. There will be catastrophe, waiting. Many times it has happened, and it will happen because transgressing the law of nature, or laws of God, is most sinful."
> ~Srila Prabhupada (Lecture on Bhagavad-gita, Geneva, June 6, 1974)

End of Modern Civilization and Alternative Future

By The Same Author

Oil - Final Countdown To A Global Crisis And Its Solutions

To Kill Cows Means To End Human Civilization

Cow And Humanity - Made For Each Other

Capitalism Communism And Cowism - A New Economics For The 21st Century

Cows Are Cool - Love 'Em !

Wondrous Glories of Vraja

Modern Foods - Stealing Years From Your Life

Noble Cow - Munching Grass, Looking Curious And Just Hanging Around
Lets Be Friends - A Curious, Calm Cow
We Feel - Just Like You Do
(More information on availability at the back)

Contents

Preface

Section I : What Is Civilization — 1
- Civilization As A Broad Cultural Identity — 4
- Education - A Technique of Transmission — 6
- Civilizational Interaction — 8

Section II : Civilizations in Historical Perspective — 10
- One World - Many Civilizations — 11
- Models of Civilizations Collapse — 18
- Lost Cities — 20
- The Sentinelese - A Tale of Survival — 29

Section III : What Is Modern Civilization — 32

Section IV : Evolution of Modern Civilization — 35

Section V : Preindustrial Society — 45

Section VI : Theories on End of Modern Civilization — 49

Section VII : The Threats To Modern Civilization — 65
- Threat 1 - Food Insecurity — 66
- Threat 2 - Global Water Scarcity — 98
- Threat 3 - Resource Depletion — 131
- Threat 4 - Moral, Ethical, Spiritual Ruination — 155
- Threat 5 - Violence & Wars, Clash of Civilizations — 187
- Threat 6 - Resurgence of Diseases & Health Issues — 236
- Threat 7 - Brittle Economies — 258
- Threat 8 - Growing Cruelty and Desensitization — 278

Section VIII: The Alternative Future — 331
- Alternative Future 1 - A World Based on Proper Understanding of Self — 337
- Alternative Future 2 - Ecology of The Mind, Chanting of The Holy Name — 356
- Alternative Future 3 - Holy Cow: Land & Cow Subsistence — 385
- Alternative Future 4 - Enlightened Agriculture — 408
- Alternative Future 5 - From Artificial Necessities To Basics of Life — 428
- Alternative Future 6 - Living on Mother Nature's Gifts — 444

Preface

Saying goes that 'hope for the best and prepare for the worst'. Carl Jung, one of the fathers of modern psychology remarked that "people cannot stand too much reality." And one such reality is that end has come for many civilizations in the course of human history and the prophets of doom haven't been all wrong. In fact, it's safe to say that more civilizations have collapsed than have persisted. If we examine the reasons for their collapse, we find one or two like neglect of agriculture, moral degradation or lack of leadership. But in our present day civilization, all these factors with many more additional ones are operating. We better watch out!

Purpose of this work is not to create a scare but to give a caution to not take things for granted. Our universe works under finely balanced laws and making things topsy-turvy will not work to our advantage. Our best interest lies in following the universal scheme of things and not in defying the subtle laws of creation due to foolish arrogance.

Ours may as well add to that record of vanished civilizations, the primary difference being that it's global in scope and threatens the stability of the entire community of life. Civilizations have always been local and this is the first time in history that entire humanity shares a common fate. Keeping all our eggs in one basket is not a wise policy. One day we might have to pay dearly for our quest for globalization.

Directions we take now would decide our fate, for better or for worse. On many fronts, the crumbling of this colossal industrial setup is becoming apparent. Material world is a calamitous place but all the previous calamities were local in nature. Now we have to be prepared for disasters on global scale, thanks to our interdependence and interconnectivity. Earlier we suffered in isolation and now if we go down, we go down hand in hand, all together.

This book is an awakening call, a call to act before time runs out, before its too late. A stitch in time saves nine. We stand at the cross roads and time to act is now. .

Tony Blair, the former British Prime Minister, rightly put it in October 2006, "We have a window of only 10 to 15 years to take the steps we need to avoid crossing catastrophic tipping points."

Dr. Sahadeva dasa

End of Modern Civilization and Alternative Future

Section-I

What Is Civilization

"The true test of civilization is, not the census, nor the size of the cities, nor the crops, but the kind of man that the country turns out."
                                        –Ralph Waldo Emerson

End of Modern Civilization and Alternative Future

Civilization

Civilization is a kind of human society or culture; a sum total of the arts, customs, habits, beliefs, values, behavior and material habits that constitute a people's way of life. Specifically, a civilization is usually understood to be a complex society characterized by the practice of agriculture, settlements, a diverse division of labour and an intricate social hierarchy. The term civilization is often used as a synonym for culture and it also refers to society as a whole. Thus the term can mean "refinement of thought, manners, or taste".

As historians have often remarked, civilization is a word easier to describe than it is to define. The word civilization comes from the Latin word civilis, meaning a "citizen" or "townsman" governed by the law of his city. Civilizations have been distinguished by their means of subsistence, types of livelihood, settlement patterns, forms of government, social stratification, economic systems, literacy, and other cultural traits.

The *Oxford English Dictionary* defines civilization as "the action or process of civilizing or of being civilized; a developed or advanced state of human society."

All human civilizations have depended on agriculture for subsistence. Growing food on farms results in a surplus of food, which allows for specialized careers, division of labour and a more diverse range of human activity, a defining trait of civilizations.

Morton Fried, a conflict theorist, and Elman Service, an integration theorist, have classified human cultures based on political systems and social inequality. This system of classification contains four categories:

* Hunter-gatherer bands, which are generally egalitarian.
* Horticultural/pastoral societies in which there are generally two inherited social classes; chief and commoner.

* Highly stratified structures, or chiefdoms, with several inherited social classes: king, noble, freemen, serf and slave.
* Civilizations, with complex social hierarchies and organized, institutional governments.

Civilization As A Broad Cultural Identity

Every society, civilization or not, has a specific set of ideas and customs, and a certain set of items and arts, that make it unique. Civilizations have intricate cultures, including literature, professional art, architecture, organized religion, and complex customs associated with the elite.

Primitive Civilizations

Nevertheless, some tribes or peoples remained 'uncivilized' even to this day. These cultures are called by some "primitive," a term that is regarded by others as pejorative. "Primitive" implies in some way that these people do not have hierarchical governments, organized religion, writing systems or money. The little hierarchy that exists, for example respect for the elderly, is mutual and not instituted by force, rather by a mutual reciprocal and customary agreement.

Thus, the intricate culture associated with civilization has a tendency to spread to and influence other cultures, sometimes assimilating them into the civilization (a classic example being Chinese civilization and its influence on Korea, Japan, Vietnam, and so forth), all of them sharing the fact that they belong to an East Asian civilization, sharing Confucianism, Mahayana Buddhism. Many civilizations are actually large cultural spheres

" Civilization is social order promoting cultural creation. Four elements constitute it: economic provision, political organization, moral traditions and the pursuit of knowledge and the arts. It begins where chaos and insecurity end. For when fear is overcome, curiosity and constructiveness are free, and man passes by natural impulse towards the understanding and embellishment of life."   *– Will Durant,*

containing many nations and regions.

The civilization in which someone lives is that person's broadest cultural identity. A female of African descent living in the United States has many roles that she identifies with. However, she is above all a member of "Western civilization." In the same way, a male of Kurdish ancestry living in Iran is above all a member of "Islamic civilization."

Civilization As Internal Traits, Higher Faculties

The term has transitioned from denoting internals to expressing externals over a period of time. In its classic sense, "human" civilization may contrast sharply with conventional notions about "civilization." A "human" civilization, therein, would be an expression and extension of the two most basic pillars - connection with God and leading life on ethical and moral grounds. Everything else, whether technology, science, art, music, etc., is by this definition is considered supplementary. Indeed, to the degree the surface terrain of a human society, i.e., culture is considered "civilized," is to the degree the internal terrain (characteristics, personality or substance) of the people and leadership have evolved. The Biblically described Sodom, for instance, while being a society comprised of people with a culture, would by Jewish or Biblical standards of "civility" have been uncivilized. Ultimately, there is no true or lasting "civility" for any man in the absence of moral composure. In its

Dr. Patel: Sir, let us first describe what is civilization.
Prabhupada: Civilization means advancement from animal life. Civilization means not animal. Man, human being, must not be animal. This is the basic principle of civilization.
Dr. Patel: Primary all are animals. They have to advance from animal life to further up.
Prabhupada: Yes, that I say. So not to remain animal.
(Morning Walk — November 21, 1975, Bombay)

vedic sense 'human' civilization is distinguished from 'animal' civilization by the development and understanding of higher faculties of life and self-realization.

Civilization Is An Outcome Of Culture And Religion Of The Society

Strong cultural and religious growth play important role for a strong society, gives strong identity to one society which initiates other small societies to join or bigger population of same society who follow their ideology. Thus a strong and large society is established. So cultural and religious growth of the society in one era is civilization.

Measurement of the strength of the civilization is based on quality of life: behavior, art, ritual practices, faith, language, food habits, intelligence and economy etc.

Society's identity is its culture and religion. Each society has its own identity but when it weakens against the strong due to deficiency, people divert or merge with strong one. At present major population of the world is trying to follow western civilization which is technologically, financially and otherwise more powerful.

Education -A Technique of Transmitting Civilization

Man differs from the beast only by education, which may be defined as the technique of transmitting civilization.

Physical and biological conditions are only prerequisites to civilization; they do not constitute or generate it. Subtle psychological factors must enter into play. There must be political order. There must be some unity of language to serve as medium of mental exchange. Through church, or family, or school, or otherwise, there must be a unifying moral code, some rules of the

What is civilization? Civilization... The Aryans are called civilized. Why? Aryan means going forward. And what is the destination of going forward? The destination is to understand the original cause of creation, God. Janmady asya yatah.
-Srila Prabhupada (Bhagavad-gita 16.7 -- Tokyo, January 27, 1975)

game of life acknowledged even by those who violate them, and giving to conduct some order and regularity, some direction and stimulus. Perhaps there must also be some unity of basic belief, some faith — supernatural or utopian — that lifts morality from calculation to devotion, and gives life nobility and significance despite our mortal brevity. And finally there must be education — some technique, however primitive, for the transmission of culture. Whether through imitation, initiation or instruction, whether through father or mother, teacher or priest, the lore and heritage of the tribe — its language and knowledge, its morals and manners, its technology and arts — must be handed down to the young, as the very instrument through which they are turned from animals into men.

The disappearance of these conditions — sometimes of even one of them — may destroy a civilization. A geological cataclysm or a profound climatic change; an uncontrolled epidemic like that which wiped out half the population of the Roman Empire under the Antonines, or the Black Death that helped to end the Feudal Age; the exhaustion of the land or the ruin of agriculture through the exploitation of the country by the town, resulting in a precarious dependence upon foreign food supplies; the failure of natural resources, either of fuels or of raw materials; a change in trade routes, leaving a nation off the main line of the world's commerce; mental or moral decay from the strains, stimuli and contacts of urban life, from the breakdown of traditional sources of social discipline and the inability to replace them; the weakening of the stock by a disorderly sexual life, or by an epicurean, pessimist, or quietist philosophy; the decay of leadership through the infertility of the able, and the relative smallness of the families that might bequeath most fully the cultural inheritance of the race; a pathological concentration of wealth, leading to class wars, disruptive revolutions, and financial exhaustion: these are some of the ways in which a civilization may die.

For civilization is not something inborn or imperishable; it must be acquired anew by every generation, and any serious interruption in its transmission may bring it to an end.

Civilizational Interaction

There have existed many types of relations between civilizations, including economic relations, cultural exchanges, and political/diplomatic/military relations. These spheres often occur on different scales. For example, trade networks were, until the nineteenth century, much larger than either cultural spheres or political spheres. Extensive trade routes, including the Silk Road through Central Asia and Indian Ocean sea routes linking the Roman Empire, Persian Empire, India, and China, were well established 2000 years ago, when these civilizations scarcely shared any political, diplomatic, military, or cultural relations.

Many theorists argue that the entire world has now become integrated into a single "world system", a process known as globalization. Different civilizations and societies all over the globe are economically, politically, and even culturally interdependent in many ways.

Civilizations have shown an inclination towards conquest and expansion and they experience cycles of birth, life, decline and

---

If you want to know what is civilization, you have to learn here: dhiranam, gentle. In the Bhagavata the description is there. So Vedic civilization is meant for the most gentle, highly advanced, not for the cats and dogs.
So one should be trained from the very beginning how to become gentle. From the very beginning if one is taught to become ungentle, uncontrolled of senses, how at the end he can become gentle? And if the people are not gentle, how you can expect peace and prosperity? Therefore we see in your country, every house: "Beware of dog. Don't come here." Because... What is that? Because they cannot trust anybody. Anybody.
- Srila Prabhupada (Lecture, Srimad-Bhagavatam 1.3.13 -- Los Angeles, September 18, 1972)

death, being often supplanted by a new civilization. Networks of societies have expanded and shrunk since ancient times, and the current globalized economy and culture is a product of recent European colonialism.

From a Vedic perspective, the globalization is not a new phenomenon. Five thousand years ago, as proclaimed by vedic history, the world was ruled by the emperors based in Indraprastha, modern Delhi, and vedic culture was prevalent far and wide.

Section-II

Civilizations in Historical Perspective

One World, Many Civilizations

Civilizations - A historical perspective
One World, Many Civilizations

According to time, place and circumstances, various civilizations took birth in various parts of the world. They grew to the peak of their glory and then declined and went into oblivion. Following are some of the civilizations that the world has seen in last five thousand years.

African and Eurasian Civilizations of The "Old World"

Vedic civilization 3000 BC - present
Sumer 3000–2334 BC
Indus Valley and the Indian subcontinent 3200–1700 BC
Ancient Egypt 3200–343 BC
Elamite (Iran) (2700–539 BC)
Canaan (Mediterranean) (2350 BC -100 AD)
China 2200 BC–present
Greece 2000 BC–present
Korea c. 900 BC - present
Etruscans and Ancient Rome 900BC-500AD
Persia (Iran)(550 B.C -- 650 A.D)
Norte Chico 3000-1600 BC South America
Olmec(Mesoamerican) (New World) 1200–450 BC

Prehistoric Civilizations

Since the days of Plato there has been the suggestion at different times that there were in fact a number of additional ancient

Look back over the past, with its changing empires that rose and fell, and you can foresee the future, too.
- Marcus Aurelius

civilizations that disappeared. These include:

Atlantis: first spoken of by Plato, further supported by Ignatius L. Donnelly, and now part of the New Age movement.
Lemuria
Mu (Pacific)

Civilizations evolved independently, in many different places, at different times throughout the history. Karl Jaspers, the German historical philosopher, proposed that the ancient civilizations were affected greatly by an Axial Age in the period between 600 BCE-400 BCE during which a series of sages, prophets, religious reformers and philosophers, from India, China, Iran, Israel and Greece, changed the direction of civilizations forever.

Civilizations affected by these developments include
Mediterranean Civilizations of the Classical Period
Ancient Greece and Hellenic civilization
The Roman Empire
Phoenicia
Second Temple Judaism

Middle Eastern Civilizations
Iranian Civilization since the Archaemenids
Islamic Civilizations
Georgian and Armenian Civilizations

Indian Hindu and Buddhist Civilizations
Mauryan and Post-Mauryan Indian Civilization
Gupta Empire in North India
Chola Empire in South India
Civilizations of ancient Ceylon

East Asian Civilizations
The Mandarinate of Chinese Civilization
Pre-modern Korean Civilization

"If a path to the better there be, it begins with a full look at the worst,"
-Thomas Hardy

Pre-modern Vietnamese Civilization
Japanese Civilization

The Civilizations of South East Asia
Funan and Chen-la
Angkor Cambodia
Sri Vijaya, Shailendra and Majapahit Civilizations
Burmese, Thai and Lao Civilizations

Central Asian Civilization
Tibetan Civilization
Turkic and Mongol Civilizations

European Civilizations
Western Christendom
Byzantium and Eastern Orthodox Christendom
Russian and Ukrainian Civilization

Planetary Industrial World Civilization
Since the voyages of discovery by European explorers of the 15th and 16th century, another development has occurred whereby European forms of government, industry, commerce and culture have spread from Western Europe, to the Americas, South Africa, Australia, and through colonial empires, to the rest of the planet.

Dr. Patel: They say, sir, that the Aryan civilization, cradle of Aryan civilization near the North Pole, is somewhere in Russia. From there they started transmigrating. People went to Europe, from there to America, then south down to Iran, and then to India and all that. When they have such extreme cold they were able to civilize themselves to that extent.
Prabhupada: We don't say.
Dr. Patel: The Eskimos are not able to do it.
Prabhupada: No. Civilization means they must live in a nice place like India. That is civilization. The America in those days, they were neglecting. Nobody was living there. Gradually they advanced. Otherwise these tracts of land were rejected.
(Morning Walk -- November 21, 1975, Bombay)

Today it would appear that we are all parts of a planetary industrial world civilization, divided between many nations and languages.

Cradle of Civilization

The cradle of civilization is any of the possible locations for the emergence of civilization. Following were the places where civilizations developed.

Near East
India
Mesopotamia.
Egypt
China

The Americas
South America
Mesoamerica

Collapse of Civilization

Civilization collapse is the large scale breakdown or long term decline of the culture, civil institutions or other major characteristics of a society or a civilization, temporarily or permanently. The breakdown of cultural and social institutions is perhaps the most common feature of collapse. Societies may not end or die when they collapse. Instead, they may adapt and be born anew. Collapse may also result in  a degree of empowerment for the most disenfranchised sections of the collapsing society.

The most common factors contributing to the collapse of society are environmental, social and cultural. Usually civilization collapse results from the convergence of all three factors, but in many instances one factor may be the dominant cause. In many cases a

Surely the only sound foundation for a civilization is a sound state of mind.
~E. M. Forster

natural disaster (e.g. tsunami, earthquake, massive fire) may wreak such havoc on a culture that it can no longer sustain itself through past social processes and it undergoes massive change. In other instances significant inequity in the social structure may result in the lower classes rising up and taking power from a smaller wealthy elite. Civilization collapse may occur over a relatively short period of time, or as a result of an event or series of events which lead to significant depopulation (e.g. natural disaster, war, genocide, famine, pandemic). The groups which comprise a society may also make a deliberate or voluntary decision to disperse or relocate which in effect amounts to the "collapse" of that society, or presents to later archaeologists or researchers as a collapse.

Civilization collapse has recurred throughout history and is an aspect of the human condition which may await all human societies.

Manifestations of Civilization Collapse

Civilization collapse occurs in one of two ways:

1. Its adaptive capacity is reduced by social complexity, leading to a destabilization of social institutions and eventual massive shifts in population and social dynamics. In nearly all cases civilizations revert to less complex, less centralized and a more simple technological or socio-political forms. Examples of such societal collapse are: the Hittite Empire, the Mycenaean civilization, the Western Roman Empire, the Mauryan and Gupta states of India, the Mayas, the Angkor in Cambodia, and the Han and Tang dynasties in China.

Collapse By The First Method
Sumer
Hittite Empire
Mycenaean Greece

"Formerly, great civilizations flourished by promoting theistic values. The Vedic civilization of India is an example. It organized society in such a way that the citizens could take care of life's ordinary requirements with minimum anxiety. At the same time it encouraged people to concentrate on spiritual principles that might be considered esoteric in modern life." — *Sthita-dhi-muni dasa*

The Neo-Assyrian Empire
Indus Valley Civilization
Mauryan and Gupta states
Angkor civilization of the Khmer Empire
Han and Tang Dynasty of China
Anasazi
Etruscans
Western Roman Empire
Izapa
Maya
Munhumutapa Empire
Olmec

2. It may be gradually incorporated into a more dynamic, more complex inter-regional social structure. This happened in ancient Egypt and Mesopotamia, the Levantine cultures, the Eastern Roman Empire, the Mughal and Delhi Sultanates in India, Sung China, the Aztec and Inca cultures in Mesoamerica, and the modern civilizations of China, Japan, and India as well as many modern states in the Middle East and Africa.

Collapse By The Second Method
Ancient Egypt
Ancient Babylonia
Ancient Levant
Classical Greece
Eastern Roman Empire (Medieval Greek) of the Byzantines
Modern North East Asian civilizations, Hindu and Mughal India
Chin, Sung, Mongol and Manchu China
Tokugawa Shogunate of Japan
Aztecs and Incas

Apart from these two methods, Societal collapse may also manifests itself in various other ways:

> We shall require a substantially new manner of thinking if mankind is to survive.
> ~*Albert Einstein*

Complex societies stratified on the basis of class, gender, race or some other salient factor become much more homogeneous or horizontally structured. In many cases past social stratification slowly becomes irrelevant following collapse and societies become more egalitarian.

One of the most characteristic features of complex civilizations (and in many cases the yardstick to measure complexity) is a high level of job specialization. The most complex societies are characterized by artisans and tradespeople who specialize intensely in a given task. Indeed, the rulers of many past societies were hyper-specialized priests or priestesses who were completely supported by the work of the lower classes. During societal collapse the social institutions supporting such specialization are removed and people tend to become more generalized in their work and daily habits.

As power becomes decentralized people tend to be more self-regimented and have many more personal freedoms. In many instances of collapse there is a slackening of social rules and etiquette. Geographically speaking, communities become more parochial or isolated. For example, following the collapse of the Mayan civilization many Maya returned to their traditional hamlets, moving away from the large cities that had been the epicenters of the empire.

What do they know? Great civilizations were existing on this earth hundreds of thousands of years ago. They are thinking that everything begins with them, with cavemen or monkeys. But in ages past, Maharaj Bharat ruled the entire world, and there were great civilizations everywhere. Who can deny that Sanskrit is the mother of languages? So-called scholars are simply concocting nonsense, proposing theories. Their business is: 'You propose a theory, and I propose a greater theory.' But Bhagavad-gita is not theory. It is a fact. - Srila Prabhupada

Institutions, processes, and artifacts are all manifest in the archaeological record in abundance in large civilizations. After collapse, types of artifacts left or evidence of institutions changes dramatically as people are forced to adopt more self-sufficient lifestyles.

Societal collapse is almost always associated with a decline in population densities. In extreme cases, the collapse in population is so severe that the society disappears entirely, such as happened with the Greenland Vikings, or a number of Polynesian islands. In less extreme cases, populations are reduced until a demographic balance is reestablished between human societies and the depleted natural environment. A classic example is the case of ancient Rome which had a population of about 1.5 million during the reign of Trajan, but had only 15,000 inhabitants by the 9th century.

Models of Civilization Collapse

According to Joseph Tainter, in his book *The Collapse of Complex Societies* (1990), societies that inevitably collapse adhere to one or more of the following three models in the face of collapse:

1. **Dinosaur Model:** The best example is a large scale society in which resources are being depleted at an exponential rate and yet nothing is done to rectify the problem because the ruling elite are unwilling or unable to adapt to said changes. In such examples rulers tend to oppose any solutions that diverge from their present course of action. They will favor intensification and commit an increasing number of resources to their present plans, projects and social institutions.

2. **Runaway Train Model:** An example would be a society that only functions when growth is present. Societies based almost exclusively on acquisition, including pillage or exploitation, cannot be sustained indefinitely. The society of the Assyrians and the Mongols, for example, both fractured and collapsed when no new conquests were forthcoming. Tainter argues that Capitalism can be seen as an example of the Runaway Train model as it requires whole economies, individual sectors, and companies to constantly grow on a three month basis. Current methods of resource extraction and food production may be unsustainable, however,

the philosophy of consumerism and planned obsolescence encourage the purchase of an ever increasing number of goods and services to sustain the economy.

3. **House of Cards Model**: In this aspect of Tainter's model societies that grow to be so large and include so many complex social institutions that they are inherently unstable and prone to collapse.

Let us take an example of Easter Island to see how these factors operate in disintegrating a civilization. These factors do not necessarily act independently. Usually they are interconnected occurrences that reinforce each other. For example, leaders on Easter Island saw a rapid decline of trees but ruled out change (Dinosaur model). Timber was used as rollers to transport and erect large statues called *moai* as a form of religious reverence to their ancestors. Reverence was believed to result in a more prosperous future. It gave the people an impetus to intensify *moai* production (i.e. Runaway Train model). Easter Island also has a fragile ecosystem because of its isolated location (i.e. House of Cards model). Deforestation led to soil erosion and insufficient resources to build boats for fishing or tools for hunting. Competition for dwindling resources resulted in warfare and many casualties. Together these events led to the collapse of the civilization.

Toynbee's Theory of Decay

The British historian Arnold J. Toynbee, in his 12-volume magnum opus *A Study of History*, theorized that all civilizations pass through several distinct stages: genesis, growth, time of troubles, universal state, and disintegration.

Toynbee argues that the breakdown of civilizations is not caused by loss of control over the environment, over the human environment, or attacks from outside. Rather, it comes from the deterioration of the "Creative Minority," which eventually ceases to be creative and degenerates into merely a "Dominant Minority" (who forces the majority to obey without meriting obedience). He argues that creative minorities deteriorate due to a worship of their "former self," by which they become prideful, and fail to adequately address the next challenge they face.

He argues that the ultimate sign a civilization has broken down is when the dominant minority forms a "Universal State," which stifles political creativity. He states:

"First the Dominant Minority attempts to hold by force—against all right and reason—a position of inherited privilege which it has ceased to merit; and then the Proletariat repays injustice with resentment, fear with hate, and violence with violence when it executes its acts of secession. Yet the whole movement ends in positive acts of creation—and this on the part of all the actors in the tragedy of disintegration. The Dominant Minority creates a universal state, the Internal Proletariat a universal church, and the External Proletariat a bevy of barbarian war-bands."

He argues that in this environment, people resort to archaism (idealization of the past), futurism (idealization of the future), detachment (removal of oneself from the realities of a decaying world), and transcendence (meeting the challenges of the decaying civilization with new insight, as a Prophet). He argues that those who Transcend during a period of social decay give birth to a new Church with new and stronger spiritual insights, around which a subsequent civilization may begin to form after the old has died.

Toynbee's use of the word 'church' refers to the collective spiritual bond of a common worship, or the same unity found in some kind of social order.

Lost Cities

lost cities were real, prosperous, well-populated areas of human habitation that fell into terminal decline and whose location was

"There are many humorous things in the world; among them, the white man's notion that he is less savage than the other savages."
~ Mark Twain

later lost. Most known lost cities have been studied extensively by scientists. Abandoned urban sites of relatively recent origin are generally referred to as ghost towns. This chapter however includes places where people lived that were important local centres, without applying a specific test of size.

Lost cities generally fall into three broad categories: those whose disappearance has been so complete that no knowledge of the city existed until the time of its rediscovery and study, those whose location has been lost but whose memory has been retained in the context of myths and legends, and those whose existence and location have always been known, but which are no longer inhabited. The search for such lost cities by European adventurers in the Americas, Africa and in Southeast Asia from the 15th century onwards eventually led to the development of the science of archaeology.

Cities may become lost for a variety of reasons, including geographic, economic, social (e.g. war), others, or some combination of these.

There is a song in the Bengali language which states, "I constructed this home for happiness, but unfortunately there was a fire, and everything has now been burnt to ashes." This illustrates the nature of material happiness. Everyone knows it, but nonetheless one plans to hear or think something very pleasing. Unfortunately, all of one's plans are annihilated in due course of time. There were many politicians who planned empires, supremacy and control of the world, but in due time all their plans and empires—and even the politicians themselves—were vanquished. Everyone should take lessons from Prahlada Maharaja about how we are engaged in so-called temporary happiness through bodily exercises for sense enjoyment. All of us repeatedly make plans, which are all repeatedly frustrated.
-Srila Prabhupada (Srimad Bhagavatam 7.9.25)

Lost Cities By Continent

Lost Cities of Africa

Akhetaten, Egypt – Capital during the reign of 18th Dynasty pharaoh Akhenaten. Later abandoned and almost totally destroyed. Modern day el Amarna.

Canopus, Egypt – Located on the now-dry Canopic branch of the Nile, east of Alexandria.

Itjtawy, Egypt – Capital during the 12th Dynasty. Exact location still unknown, but it is believed to lie near the modern town of el-Lisht.

Tanis, Egypt – Capital during the 21st and 22nd Dynasties, in the Delta region.

Memphis, Egypt – Administrative capital of ancient Egypt. Little remains.

Avaris, capital city of the Hyksos in the Nile Delta.

Leptis Magna – Roman city located in present day Libya. It was the birthplace of Emperor Septimius Severus, who lavished an extensive public works programme on the city, including diverting the course of a nearby river. The river later returned to its original course, burying much of the city in silt and sand.

Dougga, Tunisia – Roman city located in present day Tunisia.

Carthage – Initially a Phoenician city, destroyed and then rebuilt by Rome. Later served as the capital of the Vandal Kingdom of North Africa, before being destroyed by the Arabs after its capture in AD 697.

Great Zimbabwe

Aoudaghost – Wealthy Berber city in medieval Ghana, sacked by mujahideen, location unknown.

Timgad - Roman city founded by the emperor Trajan around 100 AD, covered by the sand at 7th century.

Lost Cities of Asia

Far East Asia
Yamatai – Japan.

Southeast Asia
Sukhothai
Ayutthaya
Angkor and surrounds

South Asia
Vijayanagar
Poompuhar – Located in South India
Mohenjodaro – Located in Pakistan Sindh
Harappa – Located in Pakistan Punjab
Taxila – Located in Pakistan's Northwest Frontier Province
   Muziris
Dwarka – ancient seat of Krishna, hero of the Mahabharata. Now largely excavated. Off the coast of the Indian state of Gujarat.

Central Asia
Abaskun – Medieval Caspian Sea trading port
Ani – Medieval Armenian capital
Harappa – early city part of the Indus Valley Civilization
Mohenjo Daro – early city part of the Indus Valley Civilization
Niya – Located in the Taklamakan Desert, on the ancient Silk Road route.
Loulan – Located in the Taklamakan Desert, on the ancient Silk Road route.
Subashi – Located in the Taklamakan Desert, on the ancient Silk Road route.
Otrar – City located along the Silk Road, important in the

"Modern man is just ancient man... with way better electronics."
- unknown

history of Central Asia.
Karakorum – Capital of Genghis Khan.
Old Urgench – Capital of Khwarezm.
Mangazeya, Siberia
Turquoise - Mountain Capital of Afghanistan, destroyed in 1220
Sarai - Capital of the Golden Horde

Western Asia/Middle East
Akkad
Babylon
Catalhöyük – A Neolithic and Chalcolithic settlement, located near the modern city of Konya, Turkey.
Choqa Zanbil
Ctesiphon
Iram of the Pillars – Lost Arabian city in the Empty Quarter.
Kourion, Cyprus
Hattusa – Capital of the Hittite Empire. Located near the modern village of Bodazköy in north-central Turkey.

Lost Cities of South America

Inca cities
Machu Picchu – Possibly Pachacuti's Family Palace.
Vilcabamba – Currently known as Espiritu Pampa.
Paititi – A legendary city and refuge in the rainforests where Peru, Bolivia and Brazil meet.
Choquequirao - Considered to be the last bastion of Incan resistance against the Spainiards and refuge of Manco Inca Yupanqui.

Other
Chan Chan – Chimu. Located near Trujillo, in present day Peru.
Tiahuanaco – pre-Inca. Located in present day Bolivia.
Cahuachi – Nazca, in present day Peru.
Caral – An important center of the Norte Chico civilization, in present day Peru.
Ciudad de los Cesares - City of the Caesars, A legendary city in Patagonia, never found. Also variously known as City of the Patagonia, Wandering City, Trapalanda or Trapananda, Lin Lin or Elelín,

Santa Maria de la Antigua del Darien – First city in the mainland of the American continent, in the Darien region between Colombia and Panama. Founded by Vasco Nuñez de Balboa in 1510.

Lost City of Z - A city allegedly located in the jungles of the Matto Grosso region of Brazil, was said to have been seen by the British explorer Col. Percy Harrison sometime prior to World War I.

Kuelap - A massive ruined city still covered in jungle that was the capital of the Chachapoyas culture in Northern Peru.

Tayuna (Ciudad Perdida) located in present day Colombia

Lost Cities of North America

Mexico and Central America
Maya cities

Chichen Itza – This ancient place of pilgrimage is still the most visited Maya ruin.

Copán – In modern Honduras.

Calakmul – One of two "superpowers" in the classic Maya period.

Naachtun – Rediscovered in 1922, it remains one of the most remote and least visited Maya sites. Located 44 km (27 miles) south-south-east of Calakmul, and 65 km (40 miles) north of Tikal, it is believed to have had strategic importance to, and been vulnerable to military attacks by both neighbours. Its ancient name was identified in the mid-1990s as *Masuul*.

Palenque — in the Mexican state of Chiapas, known for its beautiful art and architecture

Tikal — One of two "superpowers" in the classic Maya period.

Olmec cities

La Venta – In the present day Mexican state of Tabasco.

San Lorenzo Tenochtitlán – In the present day Mexican state of Veracruz.

United States

The cities of the **Ancestral Pueblo** (or Anasazi) culture, located in the Four Corners region of the Southwest United States – The best known are located at Chaco Canyon and Mesa Verde.

Cahokia – Located near present-day St. Louis, Missouri. At its height Cahokia is believed to have had a population of between 40,000 and 80,000 people, making it amongst the largest pre-Columbian cities of the Americas. It is known chiefly for its huge pyramidal mounds of compacted earth.

Kennett, California was lost under 400 feet of water when Shasta Dam was built.

Kane, Wyoming was a city that was lost when the Yellowtail Dam was built.

Dana, Enfield, Greenwich, and Prescott, Massachusetts, were submerged beneath the Quabbin Reservoir in 1938.

Napoleon, Arkansas was a city along the Arkansas Delta wich was destroyed during a flood.

Lost counties, cities, and towns of Virginia

Pattenville, New Hampshire was flooded when the Moore Dam was built.

Pueblo Grande de Nevada a complex of villages, located near Overton, Nevada

Canada

L'Anse aux Meadows – Viking settlement founded around 1000.

Other

Aztlán - the ancient home of the aztecs

Izapa – Chief city of the Izapa civilization, whose territory extended from the Gulf Coast across to the Pacific Coast of Chiapas,

The Supreme Personality of Godhead said: Time I am, the great destroyer of the worlds, and I have come here to destroy all people. With the exception of you [the Pandavas], all the soldiers here on both sides will be slain.
Time is destruction, and all manifestations are to be vanquished by the desire of the Supreme Lord. That is the law of nature.
~Srila Prabhupada (Bhagavad gita 11.32)

in present day Mexico, and Guatemala.

Teotihuacan – Pre-Aztec Mexico.

Lost Cities of Europe

Akrotiri – On the island of Thera, Greece.

Atil, Tmutarakan, Sarai Berke – Capitals of the steppe peoples.

Attila's Fortified Camp, Romania – Probably the great ruins at Saden (Zsadany, Jadani, now Cornesti -jud. Timis) from or to which the Hun tribe Sadagariem took or gave their name.

Avars' Khan Fortified Camp, Romania - Probably the re-occupied city of Attila at Saden (Zsadany, Jadani, now Cornesti -jud. Timis).

Birka, Sweden

Biskupin, Poland

Calleva Atrebatum, Silchester, England - Large Romano-British walled city 10 miles south of present day Reading, Berkshire. Just the walls remain and a street pattern can be discerned from the air.

"*Not much is known about them. They apparently, had a highly advanced, thriving civilization. Then one August, everyone left the city and never returned.*"

Chryse Island in the Aegean, reputed site of an ancient temple still visible on the sea floor.

Damasia – Sank into the Ammersee, Germany.

Dunwich, England, United Kingdom – Lost to coastal erosion.

Hedeby, Germany

Helike, Greece on the Peloponese – Sunk by an earthquake in the 4th century BC and rediscovered in the 1990s.

Kaupang - In Viksfjord near Larvik, Norway. Largest trading city around the Oslo Fjord during the Viking age. As sea levels

"*America is the only country that went from barbarism to decadence without civilization in between.*"
 -Oscar Wilde

retreated (the shoreline is 7m lower today than in 1000) the city was no longer accessible from the ocean and was abandoned.

Kitezh, Russia - Legendary underwater city which supposedly may be seen in good weather.

Niedam near Rungholt

Ny Varberg, Sweden

Old Sarum, England, United Kingdom

Paestum - Greek and Roman city south of Naples, abandoned after attacks by Muslim pirates. Three famous Greek temples.

Pompeii and Herculaneum in Italy - buried by the eruption of Vesuvius in 79 AD and rediscovered in the 18th century

Roxburgh, Scotland - abandoned in the 15th century

Rungholt – Sunken in the Wadden Sea, Germany.

Saeftinghe, Netherlands - prosperous city lost to the sea in 1584.

Selsey, England, United Kingdom - mostly abandoned to coastal erosion after 1043.

Skara Brae, Scotland, United Kingdom - Neolithic settlement buried under sediment. Uncovered by a winter storm in 1850.

Sybaris, Italy - Ancient Greek colonial city of unsurpassed wealth utterly destroyed by its arch-rival Crotona in 510 BCE.

Teljä, Finland

Trellech, Wales, United Kingdom.

Uppåkra, Sweden

Vineta – Legendary city somewhere at the Baltic coast of Germany or Poland.

Winchelsea, East Sussex, UK Old Winchelsea, Important Channel port, pop 4000+, abandoned after 1287 inundation and coastal erosion. Modern Winchelsea, 2 miles inland, was built to replace it as a planned town by Edward I of England

Ys - Legendary city on the western coast of France.

Eternal time enters anywhere and everywhere, but it cannot enter the kingdom of god. There everything is in its original existence, free from the domination of time. Time cannot deteriorate or interfere with the conditions in the spiritual world. - Srila Prabhupada (Srimad Bhagavatam 8.12.44)

The Sentinelese - A Tale of Survival and A Lesson To The 'Civilized'
60000 Years And Still Going Strong

After citing a number of civilizations that could not withstand the test of time, let us take a look at the Sentinelese Tribe of Andaman Islands (India).

The Sentinelese are one of the Andamanese indigenous peoples of the Andaman Islands, located in the Bay of Bengal. They exclusively inhabit North Sentinel Island which lies westwards off the southern tip of the Great Andaman archipelago. They are noted for vigorously maintaining their independence and sovereignty over the island, and resisting attempts of contact by outsiders. By their long-standing separation from any other human society they are among the most isolated and unassimilated peoples on Earth, their social practices being almost entirely free of any recorded external influence.

The Sentinelese maintain an essentially hunter-gatherer society, obtaining their subsistence through hunting, fishing, and collecting wild plants.

Their dwellings are either shelter-type huts with no side walls and a floor sometimes laid out with leaves, which provide enough space for a nuclear family of 3 or 4 and their belongings, or larger communal dwellings which may be some dozen square meters and are more elaborately constructed, with raised floors and partitioned family quarters.

Sentinelese wear no clothes, but utilize leaves, fibre strings or similar material as decorations, and they fashion belts which are apparently worn to provide some protection to the groin during potentially dangerous activity such as hunting or when encountering potentially hostile strangers.

Their weaponry consists of javelins, and an excellent flatbow with high accuracy against human-sized targets up to nearly 100

If the Aborigine drafted an I.Q. test, all of Western civilization would presumably flunk it.
~Stanley Garn

meters. At least 3 varieties of arrows, apparently for fishing and hunting, and untipped ones for shooting warning shots have been documented.

Perhaps no people on Earth remain more genuinely isolated than the Sentinelese and are believed to have lived on their island home for 60,000 years.

Like so many isolated tribal people with a fearsome reputation, the Sentinelese are often inaccurately described as 'savage' or 'backward'. Their hostility to outsiders, though, is easily understandable, for the outside world has brought them little but violence and contempt.

In 1879, for example, an elderly couple and some children were taken by force and brought to the islands' main town, Port Blair. The colonial officer in charge of the kidnapping wrote that the entire group, 'sickened rapidly, and the old man and his wife died, so the four children were sent back to their home with quantities of presents.' Despite being responsible for the deaths of at least two people, and quite possibly starting an epidemic amongst the islanders, the same officer expressed no remorse, but merely remarked on the Sentinelese's 'peculiarly idiotic expression of countenance, and manner of behaving.'

The Sentinelese enjoy excellent health, unlike those Andamans tribes whose lands have been destroyed.

The islanders are clearly extremely healthy, alert and thriving, in marked contrast to the two Andaman tribes who have 'benefited' from Western civilization, the Onge and the Great Andamanese,

whose numbers have crashed and who are now largely dependent on state handouts just to survive.

Pressure from Survival and other organisations has led the Indian government to alter its policy towards the Sentinelese, from attempting to make contact, to recognising that similar policies have proved disastrous for other Andaman tribes, and accepting that they have the right to decide for themselves how they wish to live. Underpinning this shift is the simple acknowledgment that the people themselves are best placed to decide what is in their own interests.

Sentinelese Unaffected By Tsunami

In the days after the cataclysmic tsunami of 2004, as the full scale of the destruction and horror wreaked upon the islands of the Indian Ocean became apparent, the fate of the tribal peoples of the Andaman Islands remained a mystery.

It seemed inconceivable, above all, that the Sentinelese islanders could have survived, living as they did on a remote island directly in the tsunami's path.

Yet when a helicopter flew low over the island, a Sentinelese man rushed out on to the beach, aiming his arrow at the pilot in a gesture that clearly said, 'We don't want you here'. Alone of the tens of millions of people affected by the disaster, the Sentinelese needed no help from anyone.

> *And the wind shall say*
> *"Here were decent godless people;*
> *Their only monument the asphalt road*
> *And a thousand lost golf balls."*

Section-III

Modern (Techno-Industrial) Civilization

Modern Industrial civilization

Modern Industrial civilization refers to a society characterised by machine based industrial production and energized by fossil fuels. Modern civilization is a well organized social system with complex structure of police, army, civil service, agriculture, business, industry, education, means of communication, telecommunications, mass media, medicine, engineering, science, commerce, defense arrangements and so on.

The facilities of printing and publication have made possible the spread of modern culture all over the world and now we can find a common kind of ethos because of the free exchange of ides and writings, which the printing press and mass media have made possible.

The present society that we live in examplifies industrialism. Modern civilization is different from pre-industrial society which was mainly an agrarian one. Modern society evolved from technological innovations and discovery of dense fossil fuels, which resulted in development of large-scale energy and metallurgy production.

The Industrial Revolution was a major shift of technological, socioeconomic, and cultural conditions that occurred in the late 18th century and early 19th century in some Western countries. It began in western Europe and spread throughout the world, a

Then what is civilization? That is also said, tapo divyam putraka yena suddhyet sattvam [SB 5.5.1]. This is Rsabhadeva's instruction to His sons. "My dear boys, this life, this human form of life, is not meant for wasting like hogs and dogs, but tapasya, just have little restraint, self-control. Don't become hogs and dogs."
-Srila Prabhupada (Lecture, Srimad-Bhagavatam -- Paris, June 12, 1974)

process that continues till today as modernization. The onset of the Industrial Revolution marked a major turning point in human social history.

Industrial revolution is the successor to an agricultural revolution. Much of the pre-industrial world was based on simple life of subsistence farming. For example, in medieval Europe, 80% of the labor force was employed in subsistence agriculture and more so in other parts of the world.

Some salient features of industrial civilization are:

i) Amassing symbols of status

ii) Fear and suspicion of the other, both on individual and national level.'

iii) Fascination with new and shiny

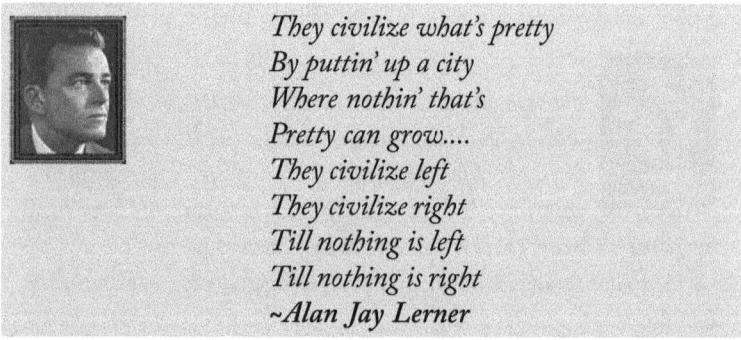

They civilize what's pretty
By puttin' up a city
Where nothin' that's
Pretty can grow....
They civilize left
They civilize right
Till nothing is left
Till nothing is right
~Alan Jay Lerner

Section-IV

Evolution of Modern Civilization

From Agrarian To Industrial Base

From A Firm and Secure Foundation To
A Greasy and Slippery Foundation

 *"It has become appallingly obvious that our technology has exceeded our humanity."*
–Albert Einstein

History (Evolution) of Modern Civilization

First Industrial Revolution

In the 16th and 17th century western Europe experienced a massive increase in agricultural productivity known as Agricultural Revolution, which freed up a significant percentage of the workforce, and thereby helped drive the Industrial Revolution. Before The Civil War (1861-66) America too was primarily a agricultural society of farmers and intensive cultivation methods led to surplus man power.

For the new manpower, there was apparently no need to dedicate to agriculture because the higher productivity resulted from mechanized farming allowed a single peasant to feed a bigger number of otherwise employed workers. On the other hands, new agriculture techniques raised the demand for machines and other hardware, traditionally provided by the urban artisans who then employed rural exodus' workers to increase their output and meet the country's needs. The growth of their business led to rationalization and standardization of the duties in the workshops, thus leading to division of work. The process of creating a product was divided into simple tasks, each one of them being gradually mechanized in order to boost the productivity, therefore the income. The accumulation of capital allowed investments in the conception

The average age of the world's greatest civilizations has been two hundred years. These nations have progressed through this sequence: from bondage to spiritual faith; from spiritual faith to great courage; from great courage to liberty; from liberty to abundance; from abundance to selfishness; from selfishness to complacency; from complacency to apathy; from apathy to dependence; from dependency back again to bondage and into oblivion. -Sir Alex Fraser Tytler

and application of new technologies, enabling the industrialization process to roll-on and self-sustain.

In this way, industrialization started with the mechanisation of the textile industries, the development of iron-making techniques and the increased use of refined coal. Once started, it spread. Trade expansion was enabled by the introduction of canals, improved roads and railways. The introduction of steam power (fuelled primarily by coal) and powered machinery (mainly in textile manufacturing) underpinned the dramatic increases in production capacity. The development of all-metal machine tools in the first two decades of the 19th century facilitated the manufacture of more production machines for manufacturing in other industries. The effects spread throughout Western Europe and North America during the 19th century, eventually affecting most of the world. The impact of this change on society was enormous.

Thus was laid the foundation for the first industrial revolution during the 18th and 19th centuries in western Europe.

The mechanization of production spread to the countries in western and northern Europe and to British colonies, making those areas the wealthiest since, and shaping what is now known as the Western world.

The first Industrial Revolution merged into the Second Industrial Revolution around 1850, when technological and economic progress gained momentum with the development of steam-powered ships, railways, and later in the nineteenth century with the internal combustion engine and electrical power generation.

Second Industrial Revolution

The Second Industrial Revolution denotes somewhat less dramatic changes which came about with the widespread availability of electric power, the internal-combustion engine and assembly lines. The Second Industrial Revolution saw the rise of various industrial powers such as Germany and the USA.

Several developments within the chemical, electrical, petroleum, and steel industries took place. Mass production of consumer goods also developed at this time, for the mechanization of manufacture of food and drink, clothing and transport and even entertainment with the early cinema, radio and gramophone both served the needs of the population and also provided employment for the increasing numbers. This increasing production, however, was a factor leading up to the Long Depression and 'new Imperialism'.

The second industrial revolution refers to the second phase of industrialization, since from a technological and a social point of view there is no clear break between the two. Indeed, it might be argued that it stems from the middle of the nineteenth century with the growth of railways and steam ships.

In the United States of America the Second Industrial Revolution is commonly associated with electrification and scientific management systems. Inventions and their applications were much more diffuse in this phase of revolution. This period saw the growth of machine tools in America capable of making precision parts for use in other machines. It also saw the introduction of the assembly line for the production of consumer goods.

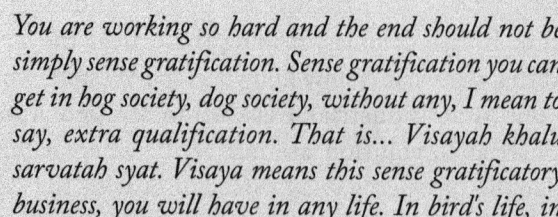

You are working so hard and the end should not be simply sense gratification. Sense gratification you can get in hog society, dog society, without any, I mean to say, extra qualification. That is... Visayah khalu sarvatah syat. Visaya means this sense gratificatory business, you will have in any life. In bird's life, in dog's life, in cat's life. So do you think that human life is also meant for that purpose? Then what is the meaning of civilization? Is that civilization? If the end of life is the same, just like cats and dogs, is it civilization? They do not know what is civilization.
- Srila Prabhupada (Room Conversation -- July 16, 1968, Montreal)

Salient Developments

Communication

One of the most crucial inventions for the communication of technical ideas in this period was the steam-powered rotary printing press from the previous decades of the revolution. This in turn had been developed as the result of the invention of the paper-making machine by Henry Fourdrinier at the beginning of the nineteenth century. The second industrial revolution also saw the introduction of mechanical typesetting with the Linotype and the Monotype. This encouraged the growth of journalism and periodicals by cheapening production costs.

Engines

The steam engine was developed during the 18th century and became popular in Europe and the rest of the world during the 19th century. Later internal-combustion engine appeared in several industrialized countries.

The internal-combustion engine was tried out as a motive force for primitive automobiles in France in the 1870s, but it never was produced in quantity. It was Gottlieb Daimler of Germany who really exploited the breakthrough of using petroleum instead of coal gas as a fuel, for the automobile a few years later. Then it was Henry Ford of the United States who, still later, made the internal combustion engine a mass market phenomenon with a tremendous effect on society. The two stroke petrol engine was initially invented by the British engineer Joseph Day of Bath, who later licensed it to American entrepreneurs whereupon it quickly became the 'poor man's power source', driving motor cycles, motor boats, pumps and becoming a cheap, reliable, driver of small workshops before the days of mainstream electricity.

What we call progress is the exchange of one nuisance for another nuisance.
~Henry Havelock Ellis

Industrial Workers

This period, akin to the First Industrial Revolution was marked by a significant number of transient urban workers engaged in industrial labor (or the pursuit thereof), relatively common unemployment and low wages. This period is also notable for an expanding number of white collar workers and increasing enrollment in trade unions.

Rise of Germany

The German Empire came to replace Great Britain as Europe's primary industrial nation during this period. This occurred as a result of three factors:

* Germany made use of the latest technological concepts, the British continued to use expensive and outdated technology and therefore were unable (or unwilling) to afford the fruits of their own scientific progress.

* In the development of science and pure research, the Germans invested more heavily than the British.

* The German cartel system (known as Torre Moore), being significantly concentrated, was able to make more efficient use of fluid capital.

Other Developed Countries

After the humiliation Japan suffered by the hand of the US Navy, illustrated by the terms of the Convention of Kanagawa, Japanese leadership decided to move forward its feudal status in order to being able of preserving its independence. The government strongly promoted technological and industrial development wich eventually brought Japan to became a modern wealth power.

In a similar way, after the stranger's invasion Russia suffered during its civil war, Soviet Union's centrally controlled economy decided to invest a big part of its resources to enhance its industrial production and infrastructures in order to assure its own survival, thus becoming a world superpower.

The other European communist countries followed all the same developing scheme, albeit with a less emphasis on heavy industry.

Southern Europe countries saw a moderate industrialization period during from fifties to the seventies, reached through a healthy integration of the European economy, though their level of development, as well as those of eastern countries, don't match the western standards.

The Third World

A similar state-led developing program was pursued in virtually all the third world countries during the Cold War, including socialist ones, but specially in Sub-Saharan Africa after the decolonization period. The primary scope of those projects was to achieve self-

India's civilization was based on village residence. They would live very peacefully in the villages. In the evening there would be bhagavata-katha. They will hear. That was Indian culture. They had no artificial way of living, drinking tea, and meat-eating and wine and illicit sex. No. Everyone was religious and satisfied by hearing -- what we are just introducing -- Bhagavatam, Bhagavad-gita, Puranas, and live simple life, keeping cows, village life as it is exhibited by Krsna, Vrndavana -Srila Prabhupada (Morning Walk -- Durban, October 13, 1975)

sufficiency through the local production of previously imported goods, the mechanization of agriculture and the spread of education and health care. However, all those experiences failed bitterly due to lack of realism: most countries didn't have a pre-industrial bourgeoisie able to  carry on a capitalistic development or even a stable and peaceful state. Those aborted experiences left huge debts toward western countries and fueled public corruption.

Petrol Producing Countries

Oil-rich countries saw similar failures in their economic choices. The oil being both important and expensive, regions with big reserves have huge liquidity income. However this was rarely followed by economic development. Experience shows that local elites are unable to reinvest the petrodollars obtained through oil export, and currency is wasted in luxury goods. This is particularly evident in the Persian Gulf states, where the per capita income is comparable to those of western nations, but where no industrialization has started. Apart from two little countries (Bahrain and United Arab Emirates), Arab states didn't diversify their economies, and no replacement for the upcoming end of oil reserves is envisaged.

Asia

A totally different pattern was followed in East Asia, which is experiencing accelerated industrialization. In the sixties a network of small private-owned factories spread across four small countries

"There is a spiritual hunger in the world today - and it cannot be satisfied by better cars on longer credit terms" - *Adlai E. Stevenson*

known as the Asian tigers, focusing their activities on the export to rich countries of low value added goods. This specialization, allowed by the existence of stable governments and well structured societies, was favoured by a low workforce cost, a favorable exchange rate, and low custom duties. Because the success of those initial policies, in recent years the Asian tigers are trying to stepping forward this stage and diversifying theirs economies.

This starting model was afterwards successfully copied in all eastern and southern Asian countries, included communist ones. The dimensions of this phenomenon leads to a huge wave of offshoring, that is, western factories or tertiary corporations choice to move their activities to poor countries where the workforce is less expensive and less collectively organized.

The Evolution Of Man

China and India, while roughly following this development pattern, were forced to adopt specific policies. China's government is actively investing in expanding its own infrastructures and securing its energy and raw materials supplying channels, is supporting its exports by financing the United States balance payment deficit through the purchase of US treasure bonds, and is strengthening its military in order to endorse a major geopolitical role. India's government is investing in specific vanguard economic sectors such as bioengineering, nuclear technology, pharmaceuticals, informatics or technologically-oriented higher education, openly overpassing its needs, with the goal of creating several specialization poles able to conquer foreign markets. China and India have also started to make huge investments in third countries, making them active actors of today's world economy.

Other Countries

In recent years, other countries like Mexico, Brazil or Turkey have experienced a moderate industrial growth, fueled by exports to bigger economies like United States, China or the European Union respectively. They are sometimes called newly-industrialized countries. Also most African and Latin American nations seem to follow a similar scheme. Despite this trend being artificially influenced by the oil price increases, the phenomenon is not entirely new nor totally speculative. Most analyst conclude in the next decades the whole world will experience industrialization at an increasing pace.

At the start of the 21st century the term "second industrial revolution" has also been used to describe the anticipated effects of hypothetical molecular nanotechnology systems upon society.

Current situation

In 2005, the USA was the largest producer of industrial output followed by Japan and China, according to International Monetary Fund.

Currently the "international development community" (World Bank, OECD, many United Nations departments and some other organisations) endorses development policies based on merely poverty reduction, and giving access to poor populations to basic services like drinkable water or primary education. It does not recognize traditional industrialisation policies as being adequate or beneficial in the longer term, with the perception that it could only create inefficient local industries unable to compete in a free-trade dominated world.

Various Revolutions Of The Last Two Centuries

* Industrial Agricultural Revolution/Neolithic Revolution
* Scientific Revolution
*Sexual revolution
* Digital Revolution
* Chemical Revolution
* Green Revolution
* Bio/Nano Revolution
*Atomic Age Revolution
*Space Age Revolution
*Information Technological Revolution

Section-V

Preindustrial Society

"God forbid that India should ever take to industrialism after the manner of the west... keeping the world in chains. If our nation took to similar economic exploitation, it would strip the world bare like locusts."   –Mahatma Gandhi

P re-industrial society refers to specific social attributes and forms of political and cultural organization that were prevalent before the advent of the Industrial Revolution.

Preindustrial life was easy on resources - both human and natural. Before capitalism, most people did not work very long hours. The tempo of life was slow, even leisurely; the pace of work relaxed.

In a vast number of ways and places, the biosphere of this planet is undergoing a great deal of damage. Parts of the environment have already been rendered uninhabitable through toxic wastes and nuclear power plant disasters, while systemic pollution, ozone holes, global warming, and other disasters are increasingly tearing the fabric on which all life depends. That such damage is wrought overwhelmingly by corporations in a competitive international market economy has never been clearer, while the need to replace

"Human prosperity flourishes by natural gifts and not by gigantic industrial enterprises. The gigantic industrial enterprises are products of a godless civilization, and they cause the destruction of the noble aims of human life. The more we go on increasing such troublesome industries to squeeze out the vital energy of the human being, the more there will be unrest and dissatisfaction of the people in general, although a few only can live lavishly by exploitation. The natural gifts such as grains and vegetables, fruits, rivers, the hills of jewels and minerals, and the seas full of pearls are supplied by the order of the Supreme, and as He desires, material nature produces them in abundance or restricts them at times."
-Srila Prabhupada (Srimad Bhagavatam 1.8.40)

the existing society with one such as social ecology advances has never been more urgent.

Modernization, the replacement of machines for muscle, is a universal social solvent. Even when resisted by traditional leaders, modernization erodes established social, economic patterns, and threatens ecosystems.

> *Our concern is not how to worship in the catacombs but how to remain human in the skyscrapers.*
> ~Abraham Joshua Heschel

Peasants and tribal members ultimately succumb to mechanisms yielding enhanced productivity. They rapidly scrap traditional practices in favor of those more materially productive.

Our ancestors may not have been rich, but they had an abundance of leisure. The contrast between capitalist and precapitalist work patterns is most striking in respect to the working year. The medieval calendar was filled with holidays. Official - that is, church - holidays included not only long "vacations" at Christmas, Easter, and midsummer but also numerous saints' and rest days. These were spent both in sober churchgoing and in feasting. In addition to official celebrations, there were often weeks' worth of ales -- to mark important life events. All told, holiday leisure time in medieval England took up probably about one-third of the year. And the English were apparently working harder than their neighbors. The ancient regime in France is reported to have guaranteed fifty-two Sundays, ninety rest days, and thirty-eight holidays. In Spain, travelers noted that holidays totaled five months per year. The peasant's free time extended beyond officially sanctioned holidays. A thirteenth-century study finds that whole peasant families did not put in more than 150 days per year on their land. Manorial records from fourteenth-century England indicate an extremely short working year - 175 days.

"It is not enough to be industrious; so are the ants. What are you industrious about?"
- Henry David Thoreau

Some attributes of the pre-industrial societies
* Limited production (i.e. artisanship and no mass production)
* Primarily an agricultural economy
* Limited division of labor - Capitalism needs a vast amount of specialized knowledge and skills due to the complex nature of industrial production. In pre-industrial societies, production was relatively simple and, thus, the number of specialized crafts was limited.
* Limited variation of social classes
* Parochialism- Communications were limited between human communities in pre-industrial societies. Few had a chance to see or hear beyond their own village. Knowledge was traditional and in most cases, amazingly authentic. For example, old sea maps used by early sailors were amazingly accurate and they can only be drawn from satellite pictures. So we do not yet know who made them and how they were drawn.
* Pre-industrial societies developed largely in rural communities as compared to modern civilization which has developed largely in urban areas.

"I have traveled across the length and breadth of India and I have not seen one person who is a beggar, who is a thief, such wealth I have seen in this country, such high moral values, people of such caliber (of noble character), that I do not think we would ever conquer this country............unless we break the very backbone of this nation which is her spiritual and cultural heritage."
-Lord MCLau, British colonial, on February 2, 1835

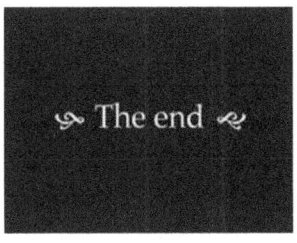

Section-VI

Theories on The End of Modern Industrial Civilization

"All our lauded technological progress — our very civilization - is like the axe in the hand of the pathological criminal."
-Albert Einstein

Industrial civilization, with its outrageous fortune, is killing the planet, plunging all life into a veritable sea of troubles. Our main modern problem is our (seemingly) inability to think about a future longer than say six months and our inability to work with each other to promote social and environmental reforms.

Pitfalls of industrial civilization mentioned here are something like cancer in the human body. At the beginning the symptoms may not appear to be very acute and it can pass off like something as minor as cold. As the cancer progresses it starts to reveal ever more serious effects, but by the time the victim does pay attention it is very often too late. The longer the failure to treat it, the greater the risk of it proving fatal.

We used to think about saving the planet, and though that's still essential, what's now really at stake is civilization itself. We have a growing backlog of unresolved problems: deforestation, collapsing fisheries, expanding deserts, falling water tables, deteriorating grasslands, melting icebergs, eroding soils, diminishing food. Nearly every one of these trends is getting worse and the fallout is becoming more difficult to manage, especially in developing countries. If allowed to continue unchecked there is nothing that will prevent us all being swept into history's dustbins,

There are four classes: lazy intelligent, busy intelligent, lazy foolish, and active foolish. The active foolish is a fourth-class man. So at the present moment they're very active, but they're all foolish. Therefore the world is in danger. Active foolishness. Foolish, if he stops, he does not work, it is better. But as soon as he becomes active he becomes more dangerous.
-Srila Prabhupada (Lecture, , Los Angeles, December 8, 1973)

like so many other civilizations. Now, to that list add the impact of climate change, population growth and peak oil.

Earth 2100

Earth 2100 is a television program that will be presented by the American Broadcasting Company (ABC) network and will be scheduled to air in March of 2009. Hosted by ABC journalist Bob Woodruff, the 2 hour special will explore the consequences of our future if humans do not take action on current or impending problems that could threaten our own society. The problems addressed in the program include climate change, overpopulation, and misuse of energy resources.

The program will include projections of the state of a dystopian Earth in the years 2015, 2050, 2070, and 2100 by leading scientists, historians, and economists.

EROEI and Societal Collapse Theory

Thomas Homer-Dixon has recently suggested that societal collapse occurs as a result of a reduction in the Energy Return on Energy Invested or EROEI. This is the measure of the amount of energy needed to secure a source of energy. Societal collapse occurs whenever the EROEI approaches 1:1. If it falls below 1:1, those attempting to harvest the energy source have insufficient energy

"Newspapers are unable, seemingly to discriminate between a bicycle accident and the collapse of civilization"
-George Bernard Shaw

to maintain themselves, and famine results. An EROEI of more than 1 is necessary to provide sufficient energy for socially important tasks, such as constructing buildings, maintaining infrastructure, and supporting the social elite upon which a society depends. The EROEI figure also determines the ratio between the number of people engaged in energy extraction compared to the total population. For example in the pre-modern world, it was often the case that 80% of the population was employed in agriculture to feed a population of 100%. In modern times, the use of fossil fuels with an exceedingly high EROEI has enabled 100% of the population to be employed with only 4% of the population employed in agriculture. Diminishing returns of an unsustainable EROEI, Homer Dixon proposes, leads to societal collapse.

The Olduvai Theory of Industrial Civilization
Sliding Towards The Post-industrial Stone Age

An Olduvai scenario of industrial society was envisioned by historian Henry Adams in 1893, quantified by architect Frederick Ackerman in 1932, and graphed by geophysicist King Hubbert in 1949.

The Olduvai Theory states that the life expectancy of industrial civilization is approximately 100 years: around 1930-2030. Energy production per capita *(e)* defines it.

This theory proposes four postulates:

Postulate 1: The exponential growth of world energy production would end in 1970 .

Postulate 2: Average *energy production* per capita will show no growth from 1979 through circa 2008.

Postulate 3: The rate of change of *energy production per capita* will go steeply negative around 2008.

"My idea of our civilization is that it is a shoddy, poor thing and full of cruelties, vanities, arrogances, meannesses and hypocrisies"
- Mark Twain

Postulate4: World population decline will follow roughly the same pattern of decline in Energy production per capita *(e)* resulting in a population of about two billion circa 2050.

Olduvai Gorge is an archaeological site in the eastern Serengeti Plains in northern Tanzania. The gorge is a very steep-sided ravine roughly 30 miles long and 295 ft. deep. Exposed deposits show rich fossil fauna, many hominid remains and items belonging to one of the oldest stone tool technologies, called Olduwan. The objects recovered date from 2,100,000 to 15,000 years ago.

The name of this premier site for studying the archaeology has been taken to label the theory that industrial civilization will soon collapse and send humankind into precipitous decline.

The proximate cause of the collapse of industrial civilization, if and when it occurs, will be that the electric power grids go down and never come back up.

Theory is based on the premise that there is no comprehensive substitute for oil in its high-energy density, ease of handling, myriad end-uses, and in the volumes in which we now use it. The peak of world oil production and then its irreversible decline will be a turning point in Earth history with worldwide impact beyond anything previously seen. And that event will surely occur within the lifetimes of most people *living today*.

'Social Steady State' and 'Social Change'

We shall define as a "social steady state" any society in which the quantity of energy expended per capita shows no appreciable change as a function of time. On the other hand a society wherein the average quantity of energy expended per capita undergoes appreciable change as a function of time is said to exhibit "social change." Upon this basis we can measure quantitatively the physical status of any given social system. The energy per capita equals the total amount of energy expended divided by the population. This

> *This civilization should be brought down as soon as possible in order to save the planet. So much damage has been done, that it's not a matter of if, but when.*
> *-Jensen*

End of Modern Civilization and Alternative Future

is known as Ackerman's Law and is expressed by the ratio: e = Energy/Population.

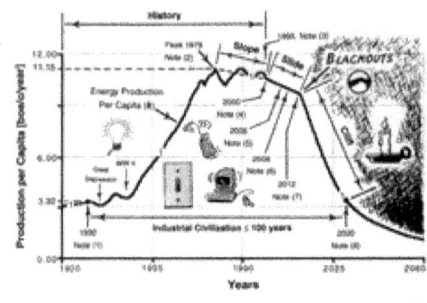

In 1949 King Hubbert noted that world energy consumption per capita, e, after historically rising very gradually from about 2,000 to 10,000 kilogram calories per day, then increased to a much higher level in the 19th century.

Electromagnetic Civilization

Electricity is the most versatile and convenient end-use energy ever put to use by humanity. But one catch is that electricity is "everywhere and nowhere."

Think of all the energized switches, outlets, and wires in an "empty" room plus the electromagnetic waves that pervade it at the speed of light (AM, FM, TV, cell phone, etc.). Then there is the vastly greater expanse of man-made electromagnetic energy that envelops the planet and radiates out into the space. Every power plant generates electromagnetic waves. From there they follow countless miles of high voltage wave guides (commonly called "wires" or "lines") at near the speed of light to numerous customer loads: heaters, motors, telephones, lights, antennas, radios, televisions, fiber-optic systems, Internet, etc. We constantly "swim" through this sea of electromagnetic energy just as fishes swim through water. And, like water to fishes, this ethereal energy is vital to modern civilization.

> "The big cities stand out as bright yellow-orange dots on NASA's satellite mosaics (i.e. pictures) of the earth at night. These planetary lights blare out "Beware," "Warning," and "Danger." The likes of Los Angeles and Chicago and Baltimore-to-Boston, London and Paris and Brussels-to-Berlin, Bombay and Hong Kong and Osaka-to-Tokyo are all unsustainable hot spots."

The second catch is that electricity is generated, transmitted, and distributed by a complex, far-flung, costly, and fragile infrastructure.

The electric power networks are the largest, most complex machines ever constructed. They have been built, rebuilt, and interconnected over many decades with a baffling variety of hardware, software, standards and regulations. The ravenous input nodes must be continuously fed with immense amounts of primary energy and then the output nodes deliver electromagnetic energy to myriad customer loads.

Between the input and output nodes are power plants, substations, and transmission and distribution lines and towers. Then there are power control centers that monitor and manage the generation, transmission, and distribution of electric power over local, regional, and super-regional areas. Each control center has numerous computers, databases, and special software to monitor and control the flow of power. Thoroughly trained and dedicated operators are essential to keep the grids going 24/7/365.

Permanent Blackouts - A Theoretical Possibility

The third catch, according to the Olduvai Theory, is that sooner or later the power grids will go down and never come back up. The reasons are many. The International Energy Agency (IEA, 2004) estimates that the cumulative worldwide energy investment funds required from 2003 to 2030 would be about $15.32 trillion allocated as follows:
1. Coal: $0.29T (1.9% of the total),
2. Oil: $2.69T (17.6%),
3. Gas: $2.69T (17.6%),
4. Electricity: $9.66T (63.1%).

Thus the IEA projects that the worldwide investment funds

The end of the human race will be that it will eventually die of civilization.
~Ralph Waldo Emerson

essential for electricity will be 3.7 times the amount needed for oil alone, and much greater than all of that required for oil, gas, and coal combined.

The Olduvai Theory says that the already debt-ridden nations, cities, and corporations will not be able to raise the $15.32 trillion in investment funds required by 2030 for world energy. (Not to mention the vastly greater investment funds required for agriculture, roads, streets, schools, railroads, water resources, sewer systems, and so forth.)

World Energy and Population

"During the last two centuries we have known nothing but exponential growth and in parallel we have evolved what amounts to an exponential-growth culture, a culture so heavily dependent upon the continuance of exponential growth for its stability that it is incapable of reckoning with problems of no growth." (M. King Hubbert, 1976)

The Olduvai Theory is based on time-series data of world energy production and population. We can rank the five sources of energy production by the duration of their intervals of exponential growth:

1. Coal grew exponentially for 209 years: 1700-1909.

2. Oil grew exponentially for 137 years: 1833-1970.

3. Natural gas grew exponentially for 90 years: 1880-1970.

4. Hydroelectric energy grew exponentially for 82 years: 1890-1972.

5. Nuclear-electric energy grew exponentially for 20 years: 1955-1975.

It is to be noted that none of the above five sources of primary energy production grew *exponentially* after 1975.

"That is the way of material civilization, too much depending on machine. At any time the whole thing may collapse and therefore we may not be self complacent depending so much on artificial life. The modern life of civilization depends wholly on electricity and petrol and both of them are artificial for man."
- Srila Prabhupada

There is the possibility that world coal and/or nuclear-electric energy production could grow exponentially for very brief periods in the future, but that option does not exist for oil, natural gas, or hydroelectric energy production.

World Total Energy Production And Energy Production Per Capita

By combining world oil, natural gas, coal, nuclear, and hydroelectric energy production, we get the world total energy production. World total energy production grew exponentially at about 4.6%/y from 1700 to 1909. Next it grew linearly at 2.2%/y from 1909 to 1930 and 1.5%/y from 1930 to 1945. Subsequently it surged exponentially at 5.5%/y from 1945 to 1970. This was followed by linear growth at 3.5%/y from 1970 to 1979. Thereafter world total energy production slowed to linear growth of about 1.5%/y from 1979 to 2003.

World population grew linearly at an average of 0.5%/y from 1850 to 1909; 0.8%/y from 1909 to 1930; 1.0%/y from 1930 to 1945; 1.7%/y from 1945 to 1970; 1.8%/y from 1970 to 1979; and 1.5%/y from 1979 to 2003 (UN, 2004)

Comparing the foregoing numbers: World total energy production easily outpaced world population growth from 1700 to 1979, but then from 1979 through 2003 total energy production and population growth went dead even at 1.5%/y each.

World total energy production per capita, e, grew exponentially at 3.9%/y from 1700 to 1909. Thereafter it grew at linear rates of 1.4%/y from 1909 to 1930; 0.5%/y from 1930 to 1945; 3.7%/y from 1945 to 1970; 1.7%/y from 1970 to 1979; and 0.0%/y (i.e., zero net growth, called the 'Plateau') from 1979 to 2003.

The Olduvai Theory Chronology - Seven Stages

i)**1930** - Olduvai theory takes this period as the real beginning of the Industrial civilization. (From 1930 to 1945 e shows irregular

> "The dinosaur's eloquent lesson is that if some bigness is good, an overabundance of bigness is not necessarily better."
> - Eric Johnston.

growth during the Great Depression and World War II.)

ii)**1945** - Very strong growth begins; (The strong growth from 1945 to 1970 correlates with the strong growth in world oil and natural gas production.)

iii)**1970** - Growth begins to slowdown. (The slowing growth of e from 1970 to 1979 reflects slackening oil production.)

iv)**1979** - The no-growth "Plateau" begins. (The rugged *Plateau* from 1979 to 2003 shows that energy production ran neck-in-neck with population growth.)

v)**2004** - The "Brink" begins. (The *Brink* from 2004 to circa 2008 represents the energy industry's struggle to keep up with rising demand.)

vi)**2008** - The "Cliff" begins. (The *Olduvai Cliff* from circa 2008 to 2030 correlates with a spreading epidemic of permanent blackouts) and

vii)**Circa 2030** - Industrial civilization ends. (From 2030 onward society approaches the agrarian level of existence.)

The most reliable leading indicator of the Olduvain Cliff event, if and when it happens, will be brownouts and rolling blackouts. As a result of permanent blackouts of electric power the industries of all civilized countries would stop working, so that, with millions unemployed and with a total cut in the production of goods, unprecedented and incurable misery would occur, killing perhaps three-quarters of the population, and leaving the rest in a *deplorable state*. (Thirring, 1956, p. 135). Thus the permanent blackouts will happen one-by-one, region-by-region, and spreading worldwide over time – will be the *proximate (direct, immediate)* cause of the collapse of industrial civilization.

Thus as per Olduvai Theory and what King Hubbert realized In 1949, the human population could collapse back to "the agrarian level of existence"

> *"In the end, cockroaches would prove to be more intelligent than humans if humans destroy themselves. Intelligence is really a survival skill for the entire species and that which survives proves intelligent on a species level."*

Millennium Ecosystem Assessment

The Millennium Ecosystem Assessment (MA) is a research program that focuses on ecosystem changes over the course of decades, and projecting those changes into the future. It was launched in 2001 with support from the United Nations by the UN Secretary-General Kofi Annan. It cost 24 million USD.

On March 30, 2005 it released the results of its first four-year study of the use and depredation of a variety of the planet's natural resources. The initial report warned that the world is degrading its natural resources across the board. "The harmful consequences of this degradation could grow significantly worse in the next 50 years," it continued.

The assessment demanded that changes be instituted firmly and quickly. It was recognized that, as humanity has the power and ability to prevent the damages to the planet, it is also our duty to do so. One of the most important issues brought up was the effects of environmental damage to the underdeveloped and poor people of the world. The report urged the nations of the world to work harder to achieve a sustainable future.

The bottom line of the MA findings is that human actions are depleting Earth's natural capital, putting such strain on the environment that the ability of the planet's ecosystems to sustain future generations can no longer be taken for granted. At the same time, the assessment shows that with appropriate actions it is possible to reverse the degradation of many ecosystem services over the next 50 years, but the changes in policy and practice required are substantial and not currently underway.

Findings

The MA is the most comprehensive survey of the ecological state of the planet. It concludes that the way society has caused irreversible changes that are degrading the ecological processes that support life on Earth. Some findings:

> *"Industrial society seems likely to be entering a period of severe stress, due in part to problems of human behavior and in part to economic and environmental problems"*

60% of world ecosystem services have been degraded

Of 24 evaluated ecosystems, 15 are being damaged

About a quarter of the Earth's land surface is now cultivated.

People now use between 40 percent and 50 percent of all available freshwater running off the land. Water withdrawals has doubled over the past 40 years.

Over a quarter of all fish stocks are overharvested.

Since 1980, about 35 percent of mangroves have been lost

About 20% of corals were lost in just 20 years; 20% degraded

Nutrient pollution has led to eutrophication of waters and coastal dead zones

Species extinction rates are now 100-1,000 times above the background rate

Collapse vs Planned Demolition

The one way to stop civilization from destroying the world is to bring it down as quickly as possible in a sort of planned demolition, like bringing down a condemned building.

Modern Civilization Is A Disease - Gandhi

Following is an interview of M.K. Gandhi conducted in 1909 and published in the book 'Hind swaraj'.

Reader: To what do you ascribe this state of England?

Gandhi: It is not due to any peculiar fault of the English people, but the condition is due to modern civilization. It is a civilization only in name. Under it the nations of Europe are becoming degraded and ruined day by day.

Reader: Now you will have to explain what you mean by civilization.

Formerly, men worked in the open air only as much as they liked. Now thousands of workmen meet together and for the sake of maintenance work in factories or mines. Their condition is worse than that of beasts. They are obliged to work, at the risk of their lives, at most dangerous occupations, for the sake of millionaires.
-Gandhi

Theories on End of Modern Civilization

Gandhi: It is not a question of what I mean. Several English writers refuse to call that civilization which passes under that name. Many books have been written upon that subject. Societies have been formed to cure the nation of the evils of civilization. A great English writer has written a work called Civilization: Its Cause and Cure. Therein he has called it a disease.

Reader: Why do we not know this generally?

Gandhi: The answer is very simple. We rarely find people arguing against themselves. Those who are intoxicated by modern civilization are not likely to write against it. Their care will be to find out facts and arguments in support of it, and this they do unconsciously, believing it to be true. A man whilst he is dreaming, believes in his dream. He is undeceived only when he is awakened from his sleep. A man laboring under the bane of civilization is like a dreaming man. What we usually read are the works of defenders of modern civilization, which undoubtedly claims among its votaries very brilliant and even some very good men. Their writings hypnotize us, and so, one by one, we are drawn into the vortex.

Reader: This seems to be very plausible. Now will you tell me something of what you have read and thought of this civilization?

Gandhi: Let us first consider what state of things is described by the word "civilization". Its true test lies in the fact that people living in it make bodily welfare the object of life. We will take sonic examples. The people of Europe today live in better-build houses than they did a hundred years ago. This is considered an emblem of civilization, and this is also a matter to promote bodily happiness.

Formerly, they wore skins, and used spears as their weapons. Now, they wear long trousers, and for embellishing their bodies,

they wear a variety of clothing and instead of spears, they carry with them revolvers containing five or more chambers. If people of a certain country, who have hitherto not been in the habit of wearing much clothing, boots etc., adopt European clothing, they are supposed to have become civilized out of savagery. Formerly in Europe, people ploughed their lands mainly by manual labor. Now one man can plough a vast tract by means of steam engines and can thus amass great wealth. This is called a sign of civilization.

Formerly, only a few men wrote valuable books. Now anybody writes and prints anything he likes and poisons people's minds. Formerly, men traveled in wagons. Now, they fly through the air in trains at the rate of four hundred and more miles per day. This is considered the height of civilization. It has been stated that, as men progress, they shall be able to travel in airship and reach any part, of the world in a few hours. Men will not need the use of their hands and feet. They will press a button, and they will have their clothing by their side. They will press another button, and they will have their newspaper. A third, and a motorcar will be in waiting for them. They will have a variety of delicately dished up food. Everything will be done by machinery.

Formerly, when people wanted to fight with one another, they

Gandhi wanted it... Village organization. He started that Wardha Ashram. But you have rejected. What Gandhi can do? That was good proposal -- to remain satisfied in one's own place. That was Gandhi's proposal. That "Don't go to the city, town, for so-called better advantage of life. Remain in your own home, produce your food, and be satisfied there." That was Gandhi's policy. The economic problem he wanted to solve by keeping cows, by agriculture, by spinning thread. "You want food, shelter and cloth? Produce here, and remain here. Don't be allured by the capitalists and go to cities and engage in industries." But Jawaharlal Nehru wanted, overnight, to Americanize the whole India. That is the folly.
-Srila Prabhupada (Room Conversation with Reporter from Researchers Magazine -- July 24, 1973, London)

measured between them their bodily strength; now it is possible to take away thousands of lives by one man working behind a gun from a hill. This is civilization. Formerly, men were made slaves under physical compulsion. Now they are enslaved by temptation of money and of the luxuries that money can buy. There are now diseases of which people never dreamt before, and an army of doctors is engaged in finding out their cures and so hospitals have increased. This is a test of civilization.

Formerly, people had two or three meals consisting of homemade bread and vegetables; now, they require something to eat every two hours so that they have hardly leisure for anything else. What more need I say'? All this you can ascertain from several authoritative books. These are all true tests of civilization. And if anyone speaks to the contrary, know that he is ignorant. This civilization takes note neither of morality nor of religion. Its votaries calmly state that their business is not to teach religion. Some even consider it to be a superstitious growth. Others put on the cloak of religion, and prate about morality. But after twenty years' experience, I have come to the conclusion that immorality is often taught in the name of morality. Even a child can understand that in all I have described above there can be no inducement to morality.

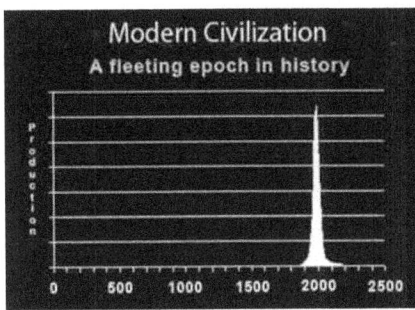

Civilization seeks to increase bodily comforts, and it fails miserably even in doing so. This civilization is irreligion, and it has taken such a hold on the people in Europe that those who are in it appear to be half mad.

They lack real physical strength or courage. They keep up their

This civilization is such that one has only to be patient and it will be self-destroyed.
-Gandhi

energy by intoxication. They can hardly be happy in solitude. Women, who should be the queens of households, wander in the streets or they slave away in factories. For the sake of a pittance, half a million women in England alone are laboring under trying circumstances in factories or similar institutions. This awful act is one of the causes of the daily growing suffragette movement.

This civilization is such that one has only to be patient and it will be self-destroyed. According to the teaching of Mohammed this would be considered a Satanic Civilization. Hinduism calls it a Black Age. I cannot give you an adequate conception of it. It is eating into the vitals of the English nation. It must be shunned. Parliaments are really emblems of slavery. If you will sufficiently think over this, you will entertain the same opinion and cease to to blame the English. They rather deserve our sympathy. They are a shrewd nation and I therefore believe that they will cast off the evil. They are enterprising and industrious, and their mode of thought is not inherently immoral. Neither are they bad at heart. I therefore respect them. Civilization is not an incurable disease, but it should never be forgotten that the English are at present afflicted by it.

In short, industrialism is over.
-Paul Hawken

Section-VII

The Threats To Modern Civilization

'The world is changed. I feel it in the water. I feel it in the earth. I smell it in the air. Much that once was, is lost, for none now live who remember it.'
— *Galadriel from Lord of the Rings*

End of Modern Civilization and Alternative Future

Threat - 1

Food Insecurity

The right time to eat is: for a rich man when he is hungry, for a poor man when he has something to eat.
-Mexican Proverb

Starving Billion - A Scandal For Humanity

According to the United Nations, around 950 million people are malnourished or starving in the world today and 1.1 billion people do not have access to safe drinking water.

Attention of mankind has been diverted from necessities to luxuries. There are thousands and millions of products like cars, computers, ipods, aeroplanes, TV channels, luxury yatchs, Caribbean vacations, palatial homes, video phones, designer clothes, designer drugs, cosmetic surgery, so on and so forth which are vying for our attention. In US, only 1% of population is engaged in agriculture. Agriculture everywhere else also is a pretty much neglected affair. The result is a serious global food crisis.

Food Crisis Looms Over 33 Nations

Thirty-three countries, mainly in Africa and Asia, are experiencing 'very serious' to 'grave' food supply problems. The German food relief group Welthungerhilfe and the International Food Policy Research Institute (IFPRI) have warned against neglecting the fate of starving people amidst the current financial crisis.

There is something called annual Global Hunger Index (GHI) which is prepared by the two aforesaid organizations. The GHI index lists 88 countries' food supply situation, with 33 countries chiefly from Asia and Africa in the lower positions. The country with the gravest food situation is Congo.

> *Food insecurity exists when all people, at all times, do not have physical and economic access to sufficient, safe and nutritious food to meet their dietary needs and food preferences for an active and healthy life."*

In view of the current financial crisis, it will be very difficult to mobilise long-term investments required for the urgently needed expansion of agriculture in developing countries. Current financial crisis is a very bad news for the world's hungry.

The GHI index is a compilation based on three chief criteria including the share of undernourished in the population, the number of children below the age of five who are underweight, and the mortality rate for children under five.

Africa May Be Able To Feed Only 25% Of Its Population By 2025

According to the experts present at an United Nations University (UNU) conference on desertification in Algiers, Africa may be able to feed just 25% of its population by 2025 if soil degradation on the continent continues at its current pace,

Karl Harmsen, Director of UNU's Ghana-based Institute for Natural Resources in Africa, said that should soil conditions continue to decline in Africa, nearly 75% of the continent could come to rely on some sort of food aid by 2025.

Harmsen's comments come as some 200 delegates from 25 countries convene at the December 17-19 meeting in Algiers to

They say that a worldwide survey was conducted by the United Nations. The only question asked was: "Would you please give your opinion about solutions to the food shortage in the rest of the world?" The survey was a massive failure, because:
in Africa, they didn't know what 'food' meant;
in Europe, they didn't know what 'shortage' meant;
in China, they didn't know what 'opinion' meant;
in the Middle East, they didn't know what 'solution' meant;
in South America, they didn't know what 'please' meant;
and in the United States, they didn't know what 'the rest of the world' meant.

discuss the causes and consequences of desertification, a threat that puts an estimated 2 billion people at risk of becoming "environmental refugees". The U.N. warns that climate change could worsen the situation by depriving populations living in arid regions of adequate water supplies. Christian Aid has estimated that an average global temperature increase exceeding 3°C could cause 182 million deaths in Africa this century and leave 750 million additional hungry people in Africa and Asia.

Thus looming desertification could spawn millions of environmental refugees

Food Rationing Confronts US, The Breadbasket of the World

Many parts of America, long considered the breadbasket of the world, in year 2008 confronted a once unthinkable phenomenon: food rationing. Major retailers across the country limited purchases of flour, rice, and cooking oil as demand outstripped supply. There were also reports of consumers panic buying and hoarding stocks.

In different parts of the US, frustrated shoppers were seen uttering expletives as they searched in vain for the large sacks of rice they usually buy.

Many shoppers seemed headed for disappointment, as they were being allowed to buy only one bag. Commotion was witnessed at many stores when clerks took away rice bags from customer who tried to exceed the one-bag cap. Several Wal-marts displayed the sign "Due

> *"Where's the rice? You should be able to buy something like rice. This is ridiculous."*
> -Yajun Liu *(engineer from Palo Alto, Calif. while shopping in Wal-mart)*

> *saka-mulamisa-ksaudra-*
> *phala-puspasti-bhojanah*
> *anavrstya vinanksyanti*
> *durbhiksa-kara-piditah*
> *Harassed by famine and excessive taxes, people will resort to eating leaves, roots, flesh, wild honey, fruits, flowers and seeds. Struck by drought, they will become completely ruined."*
> -Srimad Bhagavatam 12.2.9

to the limited availability of rice, we are limiting rice purchases based on your prior purchasing history."

Limits were also imposed on purchases of oil and flour. Bakery owners flocked warehouse stores when the price of flour from commercial suppliers doubled.

The curbs and shortages were tracked with concern by survivalists who viewed the phenomenon as a harbinger of more serious trouble to come.

Monster of Commercial Farms - Rising Out of Ashes of Small Farms

Family farms have been the core of agrarian culture for thousands of years, providing the opportunity to connect with the land and to live in tune with the seasons and the weather. Traditional farmers don't produce more than the carrying capacity of the land. They understand the condition of the soil and its ability to sustain various crops from season to season. They commonly produce and save their own seeds, a practice that has helped small farms maintain the integrity of crops, and allow hardier, diverse strains of plants to prosper. Contrasting this, industrial farms use a few strains of high yielding crops, an approach that threatens genetic diversity and often leads to chemical dependency.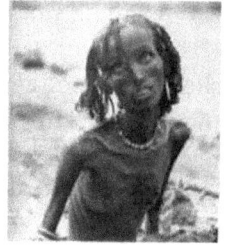

Small farms help to create close-knit communities and thriving local economies. Various rural institutions, ranging from banks to equipment and feed suppliers, are created to support farming, and family farmers support the local community by hiring and buying

 *They are now killing animal, but animal lives on this grass and grains. When there will be no grass, no grains, where they will get animal? They'll kill their own son and eat. That time is coming. Nature's law is that you grow your own food. But they are not interested in growing food. They are interested in manufacturing bolts and nuts.*
-Srila Prabhupada (Morning Walk — June 22, 1974, Germany)

inputs locally rather than contracting to an outside supplier. Family farm dollars paid to equipment dealers, grocery stores, and gas stations re-circulate throughout the local economy, strengthening it.

Large scale farms tend to bypass the local economy, buying their inputs and marketing their products largely outside of the community. Industrialized farming also negates the traditional sense of community - a place where people share values, interests and work. Rather than creating healthy, sustainable employment, these operations tend to create dangerous, low-paying jobs. The rise of factory farms, along with the decline of family farms, often signals the degradation of rural communities.

Short term efficiency and profitability, rather than long term sustainability drives the factory farming model. It externalizes costs, such as pollution clean up and health care services, onto others in the community. Neighbors of industrial operations have experienced health problems ranging from chronic asthma to neurological damage, and they have watched property values plummet.

Rising Temperatures - Threat To Food Security

It is being warned that the most dangerous threat to future food security is the rise in temperature. Among crop ecologists there is now a consensus that for each temperature rise of 1 degree Celsius above the historical average during the growing season, there can be a 10 percent decline in grain yields.

In recent years on many occasions, crop-withering heat waves have led to major crop losses. For example, India's wheat harvest

They that die by famine die by inches. –Matthew Henry

in 2007 dropped from 73 million tons to 68 million tons due to high temperatures during the crop's critical growth stage in January and February.

Great Wheat Panic of 2007

In 2007, India's massive purchase of nearly 800,000 tonnes of wheat in the international market at record prices attracted world attention — besides domestic controversy.

This panic purchase added to what agricultural experts are calling the great wheat panic of 2007. Wheat prices had already reached record levels ahead of the Indian move, thanks to falling or stagnating production in many countries — blamed on poor weather and crop diversion. Prices went going through the roof and India's transaction was almost stratospheric.

New Delhi paid $10.64 per bushel compared to the September 2006 price of $4.22 a bushel! For India it was a 'must-buy-to-build-buffer-stock' situation.

This trigger event pushed the world wheat trade into "full-panic mode". Egypt and Iraq followed the deal with large purchases, adding to price pressure at a time when global stocks were at a 30-year low. India has been an unlikely wheat importer. As the world's second largest wheat producer at around 75 million metric tonne annually (behind China's 96 million metric tonne), it was widely perceived to be self-sufficient in food production.

"We have got experience. Sometimes we find in mango season profuse mango supply. People cannot end it by eating. And sometimes there is no mango. Why? The supply is in the hand of Krsna through His agent, the material nature, this earth. The earth can produce profusely if people are honest, God conscious. There cannot be any scarcity. Therefore it is said that kamam vavarsa parjanyah [SB 1.10.4]. God gives. Eko yo bahunam vidadhati kaman. Nityo nityanam cetanas cetananam (Katha Upanisad 2.2.13). So God, Krsna, fulfills all our desires."
-SrilaPrabhupada (Srimad-Bhagavatam 1.10.4, Mayapur, June 19, 1973)

Green revolution which took place four decades back is now witnessing diminishing returns as the soil slowly dies from excessive use of chemicals. India's food production stagnated years ago and it is now coming down gradually. One editorial "Panic in wheat" (Business Line, March 20, 2007) noted that "India may well end up with an additional food subsidy of Rs 8,500 crore, including the Rs 3,400 crore spent on the import of 5 million tonnes."

As a result, major wheat exporters such as US (around 60 million metric tonne annually), Canada and Australia (25 million metric tonne each) have come into play. Coincidentally, all three are major voices in the nuclear suppliers cartel. The wheat crisis, in addition to similar squeeze in food products such as corn and milk in some countries, is so severe that the UN has warned of impending food-related social tensions and political upheaval.

Jacques Diouf, director-general of the UN's Food and Agriculture Organisation mentioned that surging prices for basic food imports such as wheat, corn and milk had the "potential for social tension, leading to social reactions and eventually even political problems." Diouf added that food prices would continue to rise because of a mix of strong demand from developing countries; a rising global population, more frequent floods and droughts caused by climate change; and the biofuel industry's appetite for grains.

Peak Grain - Forget Oil, Worry About Food

World is witnessing major price hikes in food, as 'peak grains' join the lineup of lifestyle-changing events along with peak oil and peak water. All societies more complex than hunter-gatherers depend on agriculture to survive. This fundamental fact is easily ignored in shopping centers of giant urban metropolises, but the advent of electronic technology, petroleum combustion and globalized economies does not reduce the need for someone, somewhere to grow the food that all of us eat.

Now that Peak Oil and climate change are no longer distant

Hunger is sharper than the sword.
-Francis Beaumont

concerns but are the reality of daily events, the impact of these twin crises upon the global food supply is an urgent situation without precedent in history. Peak Oil threatens to remove key energy inputs for industrial agriculture and climate change is starting to destabilize growing conditions that make large scale food production possible. This was experienced in 1973 when abysmally low inventories of wheat and an Arab-Israeli war sparked off an oil embargo, runaway global inflation, and upheavals that have scarred societies till today.

The world's is ever-decreasing number of farmers do not produce enough staple grains to feed the world. That is a crisis of quiet desperation over the past decade for the 15,000 people who die each day from hunger-related causes. It is also about to cause a problem for people who assumed that the sheer unavailability of food basics, usually seen as a problem of dire poverty, would never cause a problem for them. People in rich nations are also now waking up to possibilities of food shortages.

World Cupboard Has 57 Days Supply of Grains

Whenever there is a shortfall in the amount of food produced in any given year, it is possible to dip into an international cupboard or reserve of grains (wheat, rice and corn, for example) left over from previous years of good harvests. Tabs have been kept on the size of that reserve by the U.S. Department of Agriculture since the end of World War II but recent figures revealed that the international cupboard or "reserve" of grains (wheat, rice and corn, for example), is now at its lowest point since the early 1970s. This is the outcome of a nasty agriculture policy which is all about finding ways to raise prices by getting rid of farm surpluses and not about feeding people.

The world's grain reserves are now at its lowest point since the early 1970s. **There is enough in the cupboard to keep people**

"Modern agriculture is the use of land to convert petroleum into food. Without Petroleum we will not be able to feed the global population."
-Professor Albert Bartlett

alive on basic grains for 57 days. Two months of survival foods is all that separates mass starvation from drought, plagues of

locusts and other pests, or wars and violence that disrupt farming, all of which are more plentiful than food.

To put the 57 days in historical perspective, the world price for wheat went up six-fold in 1973, the last time reserves were this low. Then there are two other pressing demands for grains that were not as forceful during the 1970s, feedstock for ethanol and livestock feed. Wealthy nations are converting grains into fuel and meat while others are starving.

Historians will also recall that 1970s food prices went up alongside price hikes for oil, contributing to the runaway inflation that defined the decade's economic challenge. The 1970s experience shows that seemingly small blips in food reserves and availability can lead to major shocks in the economy and society.

Even modest price changes can carry a big wallop especially in a world that is already suffering from crisis-overload. For a third of the world is people who subsist on less than two dollars a day, pennies can make a life and death difference. A garden on top of every garage, a veggie stew in every pot, we might see this and more in the years ahead.

At the press conference in Hyderabad one reporter asked right away whether Srila Prabhupada was an advaita (monistic) or dvaita (dualist) philosopher. Srila Prabhupada scoffed at the question. "What is the point of discussing such things -- whether one is dvaita or advaita. Krsna says, annad bhavanti bhutani: 'All living beings subsist on food grains' Annad means grains. The people have no grains. Grains are produced from rain, and the rain from yajna (sacrifice).' So perform yajna. Become Krsna conscious. Dvaita or advaita you may be, but you still need grains.
-*Srila Prabhupada (Lecture, Hyderabad, India. April 19, 1974)*

Australia - Going Down On Droughts

Australia is one of the major producers of food and in recent years, reports suggest falling food production.

The latest report from a government forecasting body has described the nation's key winter crops of being in the grip of a severe drought, one which will whip more than $6 billion off farm production, and the bureau of agricultural and resource economics has made another substantial cut in its estimates of production from the nation's major crops of wheat, barley and canola, only one month after its last forecast.

The failure of the Australian grains crop further reduces the worlds food stock piles. The "drought" in Australia is a symptom of a major redistribution of rainfall within Australia. Rainfall has decreased in the South East in many areas by half.

Short-term, Frivolous Approach To The Crisis - A Case Study

Our shortsighted politicians have their own answers to the food crisis - irresponsible and frivolous political maneuvers.

Let us take the case of Andhra Pradesh, India. Average farmer is going through a harrowing time. Duty of political leaders in such situation is to help the farmers become more self-reliant, and make the agriculture a more viable and sustainable profession. Instead they have come out with their own solution - Rs 2 (4 cents) a kilo rice scheme. These gimmicks do nothing to help the situation because earth can not be fooled. Leaders, unable to rein in food prices, are utilizing the food crisis to serve their electoral populism.

> *"Hunger is the best pickle."*
> *-Benjamin Franklin*

Threat 1 - Food Insecurity

The Government has launched the subsidised rice scheme—offering a poor family 20 kg at Rs 2 a kilo—on Ugadi, Telugu New Year's Day, and it has been clearly done with an eye on the assembly elections less than a year away.

While the Chief Minister kickstarted the scheme in the backward Mahbubnagar district, his ministers, legislators, MPs and party leaders took up the baton at 41,884-odd fair price shops across the state. Legislators of other parties, too, participated in the launch in their constituencies as the Rs 2-a-kilo rice scheme is known to fetch rich political dividends as a potential vote grabber. The government directed the officials to ensure that the rice reached the eligible alone and did not get diverted to the open market.

The rival party was distraught by the government's move. "This is a publicity stunt to cover up the Government's failure in controlling prices and is bound to boomerang in the next elections," thundered the opposition leader.

Food Riots -The Worst Food Crisis in 45 Years

In 2008, Food riots erupted around the world. Protests occurred in Egypt, Cameroon, the Philippines, Burkina Faso, Ivory Coast, Mauritania and Senegal. One Senegalese demonstrator told new reporters: "We are holding this demonstration because we are hungry. We need to eat, we need to work, we are hungry. That's all. We are hungry." United Nations Secretary-General Ban Ki-moon convened a task force to confront the problem, which threatens, he said, "the specter of widespread hunger, malnutrition and social unrest on an unprecedented scale." The World Food Program called the food crisis the worst in 45 years, dubbing it a "silent tsunami" that would plunge 100 million more people into hunger.

> *The day is coming when a single carrot, freshly observed, will set off a revolution.*
> *-Paul Cezanne*

Food riots in Haiti killed six, injured hundreds and led to the ousting of Prime Minister Jacques-Edouard Alexis. One visiting dignitary wrote that, "hunger is on the march here. Garbage is carefully sifted for whatever food might be left. Young babies wail in frustration, seeking milk from a mother too anemic to produce it."

There was a global food crisis in 1946. Then, as now, the U.N. convened a working group to deal with it. At its meeting, the head of the U.N. Relief and Rehabilitation Administration, said, "Ticker tape ain't spaghetti." In other words, the stock market doesn't feed the hungry. His words remain true today.

Profiteers Squeeze Billions Out of Growing Global Food Crisis

Giant agribusinesses are enjoying soaring earnings and profits out of the world food crisis which is driving millions of people towards starvation and speculation is helping to drive the prices of basic foodstuffs out of the reach of the hungry.

The prices of wheat, corn and rice soared in 2008 driving the world's poor -- who already spend about 80 per cent of their income on food -- into hunger and destitution.

"What do you mean, you ate the survival manual?"

The World Bank says that 100 million more people are facing severe hunger. Yet some of the world's richest food companies are making record profits. Monsanto reported that its net income for the three months up to the end of February 2008 had more than doubled over the same period in 2007, from $543m (£275m) to $1.12 billion. Its profits increased from $1.44 billion to $2.22 billion.

Cargill's net earnings soared by 86 per cent from $553m to $1.030 billion over the same three months. And Archer Daniels Midland, one of the world's largest agricultural processors of soy, corn and wheat, increased its net earnings by 42 per cent in the first three months of 2008 from $363m to $517m. The operating profit of its grains merchandising and handling operations jumped 16-fold from $21m to $341m.

Similarly, the Mosaic Company, one of the world's largest fertilizer companies, saw its income for the three months ending 29 February 2008 rise more than 12-fold, from $42.2m to $520.8m, on the back of a shortage of fertiliser. The prices of some kinds of fertiliser have more than tripled over the past year as demand has outstripped supply. As a result, plans to increase harvests in developing countries have been hit hard.

The Food and Agriculture Organisation reports that 37 developing countries are in urgent need of food. And food riots are breaking out across the globe from Bangladesh to Burkina Faso, from China to Cameroon, and from Uzbekistan to the United Arab Emirates.

Benedict Southworth, director of the World Development Movement, called the escalating earnings and profits "immoral". He said that the benefits of the food price increases were being kept by the big companies, and were not finding their way down to farmers in the developing world.

The soaring prices of food and fertilisers partly come from increasing appetites for meat, especially in India and China;

If your energy is all engaged in manufacturing tires and wheels, then who will go to the... Actually I have seen in your country. Now the farmers' son, they do not like to remain in the farm. They go in the city. I have seen it. The farmers' son, they do not like to take up the profession of his father. So gradually farming will be reduced, and the city residents, they are satisfied if they can eat meat. And the farmer means keeping the, raising the cattle and killing them, send to the city, and they will think that "We are eating. What is the use of going to..." But these rascals have no brain that "If there is no food grain or grass, how these cattle will be...?" Actually it is happening. They are eating swiftly.

-Srila Prabhupada (Room Conversation with Dr. Theodore Kneupper — November 6, 1976, Vrndavana)

producing 1 pound of beef for example, takes 21 pounds of grain. World food stocks at record lows, export bans and a drought in Australia have contributed to the crisis, but experts are also fingering food speculation.

Moscow Considers Wheat Export Ban

Russia, the world's fifth largest wheat exporter, is concerned about rising local bread prices and inflation and is considering a ban on cereals exports in a move that exacerbates fears that wheat prices, already at an all-time high, could surge further on reduced supplies.

Moscow is contemplating either a partial ban on wheat exports or to introduce a prohibitive export tariff to rein in foreign sales. Moscow's concern comes as other food-exporting countries, such as Ukraine and Indonesia, try to rein in foreign sales amid rising prices.

Ukraine, the world's sixth largest wheat exporter, introduced in June prohibitive cereal export tariffs. Indonesia, the world's second largest palm oil exporter, recently raised to 10 per cent its export tariff on crude palm oil to cool domestic prices.

World Food Crisis Follows Decades of Imposed Import-Dependency

Decades back, it was the notion of 'self-sufficiency' that drove the food policy of the nations. Subsequently, as the economic boundaries melted down during the globalization era, countries fell for the dollar lure and agriculture was commercialized or made export oriented while nations grew dependent on import of cheap food. But now it is becoming obvious that it was not a wise trade-off. Import dependency in matters of food security is a death knell for a nation.

Global annual world grains output (grains of all kinds, including wheat, corn, barley, millet, rice, etc.) has stagnated, or declined, to around 1,900 million tons or less for the past five years , at a time when over 3,000 million tons of grains produced annually is required to ensure that dietary needs are met globally. There is something radically wrong when the total of the world's grains harvested stagnates, or drops.

The picture is even worse on a per-capita basis. For everyone to have decent daily rations, there needs to be well over 14 bushels of grains available in the world food chain per person, on average. But millions are without even their daily bread. For millions, there are fewer than 10 bushels of grain per capita in the food chain.

Production Is Below 1980s Level of Use

An indication of just how low annual grains output is, is that production is below the average utilization level of the 1980s. Today's global grains output of about 1,900 million tons a year, means that annual grains output is dropping below the level of yearly global grains utilization (for direct human consumption, livestock feed, seed, and all other uses) which existed for several years in the 1980s. This means that more and more people don't have the food they need. And whatever stocks of grains were on hand in recent years as carryover from harvest to harvest or reserves for emergencies, have been, relatively speaking, wiped out. Only in exceptional places, such as India, are there, at present, significant reserves.

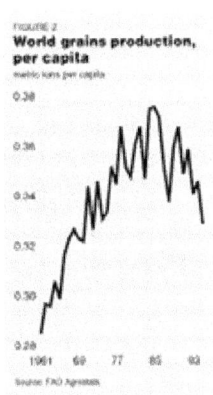

Today, world grains carryover stocks are at the same absolute levels they were 20 years ago. Stocks have dropped from 460-490 million metric tons in the late 1980s, down to less than 250 million tons projected for year-end 1995—the level of stocks in 1969.

The only reason that there are stocks reported at all is that consumption itself (for livestock feed, cereals consumption, etc.) is declining. This has been apparent for the past few years.

If this grains gap is obvious on the crude scale of world tonnage statistics, it is even more manifest at the local level, where there are millions of undernourished people at points of need around the globe.

Thus, the situation in grains production and shortages is a good marker of the overall food crisis. Dozens of countries, with millions of people, have gone from national self-sufficiency in basic grains, to dependency on imports or donated cereals aid. And now the grain isn't there. The adjacent figure shows the decline in annual global food aid in grains from the World Food Program over the past 10 years, from a peak of 15 million tons, down to little more than 7 million tons in 2008.

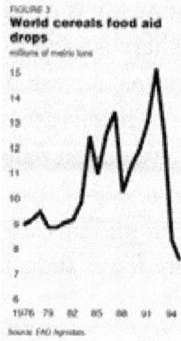

FIGURE 3
World cereals food aid drops
millions of metric tons
Source: FAO Agrostat

Decline in National Food Self-sufficiency

Most of the countries in the world are slipping from self-sufficiency into import dependency.

13 nations specified in National Security Study Memorandum 200 (NSSM-200), prepared under Henry Kissinger in 1974, were analyzed with regards to food self-sufficiency.

By 1990, there were significant drops in food self-sufficiency over the prior 27-year period. In 1963, Mexico was 100% self-sufficient in grains output; it was a grains-exporting nation. As of 1990, Mexico was only 79% self-sufficient, i.e., a grains importing nation. The situation is even worse today.

> *The Kali-yuga people will forget performing yajna. They will be busy in ghora-rupa activities, horrible and fierceful activities, not yajna. They will neglect yajna. So then how your these bolts and nuts and rubber tires will help you? Therefore there is scarcity of anna, food grains. That will increase more and more. It will so increase that now you are getting anna by paying high price, but time will come when even if you are prepared to pay price, there will be no more grains. That time is coming. Naturally, what people will eat? They will eat mamsa (meat) and roots and seeds. No milk. No sugar. No wheat.*
>
> *-Srila Prabhupada, (Lecture, Srimad-Bhagavatam 3.26.26 — Bombay, January 3, 1975)*

Elsewhere in the Western Hemisphere, Brazil was about 90% self-sufficient in cereals in 1963, but dropped to 76% self-sufficient in 1990. Colombia remained about the same, staying at only 86-87% self-sufficient. Other nations in Ibero-America saw drastic declines in basic grains self-sufficiency. For example, Haiti, in 1970, was close to 95% self-sufficient; but, as of 1990, self-sufficiency had dropped down to 45%.

In Africa, Egypt was 84% self-sufficient in cereals production in 1963, and only 62% self-sufficient in 1990. Ethiopia was over 100% self-sufficient in grains supply in 1963, and dropped down to 81% self-sufficient in 1990. Nigeria remained at 99% self-sufficiency in grains the entire period but grains declined markedly as a component of the daily diet. Other locations in Africa saw drastic declines in grain self-sufficiency. For example, Algeria was 76% self-sufficient in grains in 1970; in 1990, Algeria was only 44% self-sufficient.

On the Asian subcontinent, India, which has moved from 96% in 1963 to 93% sufficiency at present, and Pakistan, has stayed at the 93-95% level. Bangladesh has gone from 106% grains self-sufficiency in 1963, down to 87%, and is subject to wide swings from year to year in grains supplies.

In Southeast Asia, wide annual swings in staple grains are also now common. In 1963, Indonesia was 89% self-sufficient in cereals; in 1990, it was 100% self-sufficient. But in several years since then, it has fallen back to rely on imports. Similarly, the Philippines stayed at 80-83% self-sufficiency levels for 1963 and 1990, but in recent years has seen growing dependency because of shortfalls in rice. Thailand, from which the cartel trading companies export many kinds of commodities (corn, livestock feed, meat, processed foods, etc.), was 159% self-sufficient in cereals in 1963, and 131% in 1990.

The United States, Canada, Australia, France, South Africa, and Argentina, these six nations together are the origin for a large percentage of the total tonnages of food products that the commodities cartels control and use to dominate world trade and food supplies

Growing Disinterest in Agriculture

Over 70% of the work force of the majority of nations in the world were in the agricultural sector in 1963; and during the subsequent three-decade period of increasing world food import-dependency, and poorer diets, this percentage fell to about 58%. Moreover, for most countries, this does not reflect greater agricultural productivity gains, but rather a dispossession of farm populations, and their migration into the shanty camps of urban areas.

In the United States, the percentage of the work force in agriculture dropped from 5% in 1963 to under 3% by 1990. In the six export source nations overall, the percentage of workers in agriculture dropped from 11% in 1963, down to 4.5% by 1990.

Farmers' Suicides : Indications of A Failing Agriculture In India

According to Gandhi's vision of Gram-swaraj, villages and farmers were to be the main focus of any development plan in India. As years passed, agriculture as an industry lost its importance to policy makers. Over a time, this caused severe distress among the farmers leading to recent dramatic rise in the number of suicides among farmer community. Every day in national newspaper invariably there is some news related to farmers' suicides.

Now in black market you can get things, means eatables, rice, wheat. But if you don't take to Bhagavad-gita, there will be no more even if you pay black price. Just time it... That time is coming. There will be no more available. There will be no milk. There will be no more sugar. There will be no more rice. There will be no more wheat. No more fruits. Then you have to eat meat. Oh, beef shop. Then that will go on. Then human shop also. Gradually it will come. You have to eat the human being also. Cannibals. So it is therefore a great necessity that rajarsayo viduh, raja, those who are government men, they must study Bhagavad-gita. Otherwise don't give them vote.
-Srila Prabhupada (Lecture, Bhagavad-gita 4.2 — Bombay, March 22, 1974)

Threat 1 - Food Insecurity

India, consisting of 16% of world's population, sustains only on 2.4% of land resource. Agriculture sector is the only livelihood to the two-third of its population which gives employment to the 57% of work force and is a raw material source to large number of industries.

In 1990s, India woke-up to a spate of suicide among farmers community. The first state to report suicides was Maharashtra.

Since long time, Indian farmers have been facing a number of socioeconomic problems, such as harassment by moneylenders, inability to repay debts following crop losses, lack of health care etc. The problem is compounded by lack of support from banks especially in the face of inclement weather and market fluctuations. Economic plight of farmers might be illustrated with the fact that a farmer having as much as 15 acres of land and hence considered a well off farmer in Vidarbha, with an average income of Rs 2700 per acre per annum, had an income just little more than what he would have earned the legal minimum wage for all 365 days of the year.

In a country of 70 million farmers, 10 in every 100,000 are committing suicide. This is higher than the total national suicide rate. Over 16,600 farmer committed suicide in 2007 which work out to 2 suicides every hour. Farmer suicides in the country for the period 1997-2007 now total 182,936.

Distribution Lapses Leading To Chronic Hunger & Malnutrition - A Case Study

Many times, in spite of good crops, food fails to reach the needy due to distribution anomalies. In many parts of Africa, aid fails to reach the hungry due to corruption and war. In India, in spite of the significant progress that has been made in food production and sufficiency over the last 50 years, most rural populations/communities have had to deal with uncertainties of food security on a daily basis year after year, most often generation after generation. In aggregate, over one fifth of India's population suffers from chronic hunger.

This above fact makes the problem of food insecurity in India a complicated one. It highlights the fact that hunger in India is not necessarily a function of underproduction, bad monsoons or the fall in buffer stocks. In fact India finds itself in a paradoxical situation of having food grain stocks with the Food Corporation of India (FCI) standing at an all time high of 63.1 million tonnes in July 2002 (Patnaik, 2003). This exceeds the requirements for food security by about 20 million tonnes, yet above 200 million people go hungry and about 50 million are on the brink of starvation (Goyal, 2004). The existence of food stocks above buffer requirements has not translated into availability and in 2001, a per capita availability of 151 kg per annum was lower than the level in the late 30s and around the average for the time period corresponding to World War II, which included the Bengal famine of 1943 (Patnaik, 2003)

Diminishing Nutrition And Denaturing of Foods

By denatured foods we mean foods that have been so altered and impaired in the processes of manufacturing, bleaching, canning, cooking, preserving, pickling, etc., that they are no longer as well fitted to meet the needs of the body as they were in the state nature prepared them.

> Only Irish coffee provides in a single glass all four essential food groups: alcohol, caffeine, sugar, and fat." *- Alex Levine.*

In the Museum of Natural History (New York), is an exhibit showing the effects of soil deficiency on plant life. These plants, all of the same kind, were reared in soils lacking some element. The plants range in size from about three inches to about eighteen inches in height. Their color ranges from pale yellow to dark green. The leaves of some are broad, of others narrow. Some of the leaves are kinky. All of the plants except one is defective both in size, color and features and all except that one were raised in soil lacking some food element. For example, one was raised in a soil lacking iron, (the plant has "anemia"), another in a soil lacking potassium, another in a soil lacking nitrogen, etc.

Deficient soil means deficient food that grows on it. Humans and animals who consume such food also naturally become nutrient deficient. If essential food elements are lacking in their foods, they, like the plants in the experiments, fail and die. Ride along the highway with an experienced farmer and he will point out fertile soil and poor soil, by the vegetation growing thereon; therefore sickly and stunted children are the result of poor food.

The biggest problem with foods of the modern civilization is their so called refinement or purification. We have to eat them as the nature intended us to do. Experiments revealed that animals fed on a diet composed of purified proteins, purified starches, purified fats and inorganic salts, although they may live on these for a time, do not grow and in a short time develop various pathological conditions as a result of such "diet." If whey, or fruit juice, or vegetables are then added to the diet, the symptoms improve and the animals thrive better.

People now a days regularly consume breakfasts such as this one: a denatured cereal with white sugar and pasteurized cream, toast (white), pasteurized milk and, perhaps, bacon and eggs. Every article in this breakfast is denatured and altered chemically to a great extent. It is a predominantly acid forming breakfast and yet, the vitamin faddist will tell us only that it is lacking vitamin C or D. Our vitamin knowledge, where it is permitted to obscure all else, as is usually the case, certainly blinds so-called dietitians to some of the most important facts and principles of food science.

Except for the fresh fruits and vegetables we eat, practically everything we have on our table has had something done to it. Our milk is pasteurized, condensed, evaporated, boiled; Our sugar is the crystallized, refined and bleached sap of cane that has had all the minerals and vitamins removed from it. Our cereals are cracked, rolled, hammered, frittered, curled, flaked, ironed, roasted, twice roasted, boiled, and in other ways rendered useless. Wheat is milled, its minerals and vitamins removed, the flour is bleached and chemicalized. Its most important food elements are removed in the milling process. Our dried fruits are heated in drying, bleached with sulphur dioxide, stored for long periods of time and, finally, stewed and mixed with white sugar before being eaten.

The refining, preserving and cooking processes to which our foods are subjected destroy extraordinarily delicate and tender vital food factors. The refining and cooking processes rob foods of so much of their values that we add salt, sugar, spices, pepper and various other condiments and seasonings to them to make them palatable. Without the additions of such things they are dull, flat, insipid. Not so natural foods. Nature has placed delicate flavors and aromas in her foods that appeal to the senses of taste and smell.

A nation whose diet is made up almost wholly of such 'foodless' foods cannot possibly be well nourished. Why go to great lengths and much trouble to build up our soils and then take everything out of the foods that the 'improved' soils have put into them?

Over eighty years ago, Dr. Magendie, of Paris, starved one full pen of dogs to death by feeding them a diet of white flour and water, while another pen thrived on whole wheat flour and water. He fed another pen of dogs all the beef tea they could consume, and gave the dogs of another pen only water. The beef tea fed dogs all starved to death. The water fed dogs had lost considerable weight and would have starved also if the experiment had been continued; however, they were alive after those fed on beef tea were all dead. They were fed and all recovered.

Dogs fed on oil, gum or sugar died in four to five weeks. Dogs fed on fine (white) flour bread lived but fifty days. A goose fed on sugar in twenty-one days; two fed on starch died in twenty-four and twenty-seven days.

Eating Anything and Everything

The standard of eating all over the world is rapidly deteriorating. Global population is eating lessser quality foods then they did years back. The deterioration in the composition of the diet can be seen by looking in more detail at the constituent food groups that make up the diet. We can take the example of, let's say, Nigeria.

Figure shows the relative percentages of the different food groups that make up the total annual food utilized in the country, in 1963, and then in 1990.

The largest component is starchy roots, about 56% of the diet in 1963. In 1990, this has gone up to almost 67% of the diet. Mostly, this is cassava, which, along with a variety of companion foods, is part of West African cuisines. However, the increased use of cassava from 1963 to 1990 reflects not a dietary preference, but rather a forced reliance on the root vegetable as a heavy-bearing crop, on which people can subsist, i.e., it's filling, but not nutritious.

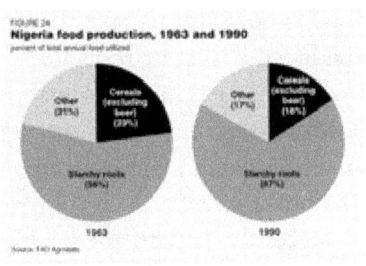

What is shown as the "other" segment on the Nigeria food charts, is the total of all 12 other food types. In 1990, this included 5.4% vegetables; 3.5% fruits; 2% peas and beans; 1.6% sugar crops; 1% meats, and even lesser amounts of the remaining food groups.

Death of Soil Is Death of Civilization

Bad soil is bad for global health, and the evidence is mounting that the world' soil is in trouble. We're dead without good soil. Soil holds minerals and organic compounds critical to life. Without good soil we have got nothing.

All over the world, more than seven and a half million acres of soil has been degraded. That's larger than the U.S. and Canada combined. What remains is ailing as a result of compaction, erosion and salination making it near impossible to plant and adding to greenhouse gases and air pollution. Soil degradation is putting the future of the global population is at risk according to a National Geographic article by Charles Mann.

Civil unrest in Latin America, Asia and Africa have been attributed to a lack of food and affordable food as a result of poor soil. *Currently, only 11-percent of the world's land feeds six billion people.*

Experts estimate that by 2030 the Earth's population will reach 8.3 billion. Farmers will need to increase food production by 40-percent. But not much soil remains.

Scientists don't know much and don't care either about this critical resource.

One Who Feeds The World - A Victim of Hunger : A Case Study

Farmers all over the world are in a sorry state. Farming, which is called the noblest profession, has lesser takers nowadays. People are shying away from this. This does not bode well for world's food supply. Let us take the example of Punjab (India) which is the bread basket of India.

When one thinks of Punjab, one imagines fields of golden wheat and rich farmers. But if we dig a little deeper, we will find that small farmers in the state are caught in the vicious cycle of debt and poverty.

Recently, Indian media highlighted the plight of Punjab's farmers. Harpreet Singh, a farmer's son was quoted as saying, "We want to eat delicious food like kheer and Dal but we don't get it. What we get is only saag. Sometimes we don't even get roti and have to sleep hungry. This happens twice or thrice a month,"

The last time Harpreet tasted kheer (rice and milk pudding) was at a wedding in a Gurdwara, a year ago. And as he spoke, his helpless father Harjit Singh couldn't stop crying. A landless farmer

So it is not that because there is overpopulation there is scarcity of food. No. That is not the cause. The cause is that as soon as people will become godless, the supply will be stopped. That time is coming.
-Srila Prabhupada (Srimad-Bhagavatam 5.5.1 — Bombay, December 25, 1976)

in Sangrur, Harjit managed to lease one acre of land for cultivation. But while he spent Rs 32,000 on rent and input costs, he earned just Rs 24,000 after selling his crop.

He had to borrow from the local moneylender at an exorbitant rate to make up for his losses. "I am not able to give more than two meals and at times not even that to my family. The produce is poor and if it rains, I can't even work as labourer. How do I earn and feed my family?" says Harjit.

Five years ago, Harjit Singh met with an accident. He couldn't afford treatment, leaving his arm deformed. His neighbour Malkiat Singh too can't afford treatment for his eyes even though he runs the risk of turning blind. Being the only earning member in his family, he can't afford a break either. "Doctor says I should get operated or otherwise I will go blind. But I don't have money to even properly feed my family. How do I get operated?" Malkiat said.

For a small farmer, it costs Rs 25,000 to 35,000 to till one acre of land. Input costs are anything between Rs 18,000 to 25,000. Also, the rent on the land ranges from Rs 10,000 to 15,000. So, small farmers often end up paying from his own pocket because he rarely makes a profit and the downturn has made the matters worse.

The standing crop looks beautiful, but the other side of the story -- that of the farmer -- is not that good. The small farmer is still caught in the vicious cycle of poverty and there is little he can do to get out of it. Ironically the one who feeds us, is himself a victim of poverty and hunger.

Agricultural Meltdown - The Last Straw That Would Break The Civilization's Back

Agriculture is our last frontier to get destroyed. The oil is going. Finances are in dire straits. Agriculture is next meltdown and looks like it is ripe.

UN Food and Agriculture Organization (FAO) Director-General Jacques Diouf has called on US President Barack Obama to make the eradication of world hunger a priority on his agenda and to host a world summit on the issue in the first half of this year.

In a message congratulating Obama on his election, Diouf said the US should, "in the first semester of 2009, take a leadership role in convening a World Summit on Food Security in order to reach a wide and common consensus on the definitive elimination of hunger from the world."

Heightened awareness of the plight of 923 million hungry persons as a result of the ongoing global food and financial crises created a "special window of opportunity for such an initiative," he added. FAO pointed out that the surge in food prices over the past year has increased the number of undernourished people in the world to an estimated 923 million, and this number could grow.

The GM genocide: Thousands of Indian Farmers Are Committing Suicide After Using Genetically Modified Crops

When Prince Charles claimed thousands of Indian farmers were killing themselves after using GM crops, he was branded a scaremonger. In fact, situation is even worse than he feared.

Beguiled by the promise of future riches, thousands of farmers are borrowing money in order to buy the GM seeds. But when the harvests fail, they are left with spiralling debts - and no income.

As already mentioned earlier, thousands of farmers have taken their own life as a result of the ruthless drive to use India as a testing ground for genetically modified crops. The crisis, branded the 'GM Genocide' by campaigners, was highlighted recently when Prince Charles claimed that the issue of GM had become a 'global moral question' - and the time had come to end its unstoppable march.

Official figures from the Indian Ministry of Agriculture do

indeed confirm that it is a huge humanitarian crisis, more than 1,000 farmers are killing themselves each month. The price difference is staggering: £10 for 100 grams of GM seed, compared with less than £10 for 1,000 times more traditional seeds.

But GM salesmen and government officials had promised farmers that these were 'magic seeds' - with better crops that would be free from parasites and insects. Indeed, in a bid to promote the uptake of GM seeds, traditional varieties were banned from many government seed banks.

India's economic boom means cities such as Mumbai and Delhi have boomed, while the farmers' lives have slid back into the dark ages. When crops failed in the past, farmers could still save seeds and replant them the following year.

But with GM seeds they cannot do this. That's because GM seeds contain so- called 'terminator technology', meaning that they have been genetically modified so that the resulting crops do not produce viable seeds of their own. As a result, farmers have to buy new seeds each year at the same punitive prices. For some, that means the difference between life and death. Thus the cost of the genetically modified future is murderously high.

Biofuels and Grains: Recipe for Disaster
Corn, Cows, Cars And Collapse

Malthus may have been right after all, though two centuries early. Mankind is outrunning its food supplies. As discussed earlier, hunger-- if not yet famine--is a looming danger for a long list of countries that are both poor and heavily reliant on farm imports, according to the Food Outlook of the UN Food and Agriculture Organisation (FAO).

The farm crunch has been creeping up on the world for 20 years but What has abruptly changed is the twin revolution of biofuel politics and Asia's switch to an animal-protein diet. Together, they have shattered the fragile equilibrium.

Asia Takes Up American Diet

The world's grocery bill has jumped 21pc this year to $745bn, hence the food riots ripping through West Africa, Morocco, Yemen, Bengal, and Indonesia.

Headlines have appeared like "Three people were killed this month in China at a cooking oil stampede in Chongqing. Mexico has imposed a ceiling on corn prices to quell a tortilla revolt....

Asian countries like China are replicating the switch to a diet of beef, pork, chicken, and fish that occurred in Taiwan and Japan when they became rich. The US Department of Agriculture says the Taiwanese eat nine times as much animal protein as the Chinese.

Why does it matter? Because it takes 16lb or so of animal feed- mostly soya or corn - to produce a single pound of animal flesh. It takes 50 times as much water.

Until last year, China was able to grow enough grain to supply its ubiquitous poultry and fish farms. It has now become a net importer of corn for the first time in its modern history.

Urban sprawl across China's eastern seaboard is stealing most the fertile land, and the water tables of northern China are drying up. The same trends are under way in India, Vietnam, and much of emerging Asia.

US And Europe - We Drive, Let The World Starve

Us aims to supply 20pc of total fuel needs from biofuels within a decade, up from 3.5 percent today. The US Department of Agriculture says reserves will reach the lowest in 35 years by 2008. The EU's vast silos are empty. Rich countries will not starve. But as Japan's Marubeni Institute warns, they may face a return to post-War food rationing long before the world population peaks in the middle of the century.

For bio-fuels, many countries have started growing Jatropha, a drought-resistant, poisonous weed that can be grown on marginal land; hence, the plant's image as an oilseed miracle crop. Critics in India and other countries, however, say jatropha grows best on good cropland and that large-scale commercial cultivation of the hardy perennial is likely to further reduce the amount of land that is available for growing food instead of fuel. Critics are also concerned about the effects of the plant's toxicity on humans and the unknown impact on fertile soil of a jatropha monoculture.

America's ethanol boom, which threatens the world with mass hunger, cannot be understood without first understanding the country's terribly destructive corn monoculture. The great corn fields of the American Midwest are not for corn on the cob - these monocultures primarily feed cows. These corn varieties are not very digestible for humans (and aren't good for cattle who love to eat grasses).

In 2006, more than a third of the US corn crop went to ethanol, nearly a 50 percent rise in one year alone. As the world corn price rose, prices of wheat and rice followed. As a result, mass hunger could result among those populations that are already at the edge of starvation.

Ethanol from corn is inefficient to boot. In contrast with sugarcane-based ethanol, which is made in Brazil, corn-based ethanol may actually use more energy than it produces while causing air pollution.

The foreign policy implications of US government mandated ethanol madness are plainly disturbing. In the name of energy independence and reducing greenhouse gas emissions, the US taxpayer is funding an industry that is contributing to food inflation and is likely to make life even more miserable than it presently is for the planet's poorest and most vulnerable people.

EU proposals will make it mandatory by 2020 for 10 per cent of all member states' transport fuels to come from biofuels. In order to meet the substantial increase in demand, the EU will have to import biofuels made from crops like sugar cane and palm oil from developing countries.

But the rush by big companies and governments in countries such as Indonesia, Colombia, Brazil, Tanzania and Malaysia to win a slice of the EU biofuel pie threatens to force poor people from their land, destroy their livelihoods, lead to the exploitation of workers and hurt the availability and affordability of food.

Robert Bailey, an Oxfam spokesperson says, "In the scramble to supply the EU and the rest of the world with biofuels, poor people are getting trampled. The EU proposals as they stand will exacerbate the problem. It is unacceptable that poor people in developing countries should bear the cost of questionable attempts to cut emissions in Europe."

Bio-fuels : A Crime Against Humanity

The United Nations' special reporter on the right to food, Jean Ziegler, called for the suspension of biofuels production: "Burning food today so as to serve the mobility of the rich countries is a crime against humanity." He's asked the U.N. to impose a five-year ban on food-based biofuels production. The Consultative Group on International Agricultural Research, a group of 8,000 scientists globally, is also speaking out against biofuels. The scientists are pushing for a plant called switchgrass to be used as the source for biofuels, reserving corn and other food plants to be used solely as food.

In a news conference, former US President Bush defended food-based ethanol production: "The truth of the matter is it's in our national interests that our farmers grow energy, as opposed to us purchasing energy from parts of the world that are unstable or may not like us." One part of the world that does like Bush and his policies are the multinational food corporations. International nonprofit group GRAIN has just published a report called "Making a killing from hunger." In it, GRAIN points out that major multinational corporations are realizing vast, increasing profits amid the rising misery of world hunger. Profits are up for agribusiness giants Cargill (86 percent) and Bunge (77 percent), and Archer Daniels Midland (which dubs itself "the supermarket to the world") enjoyed a 67 percent increase in profits.

"Plenty sits still, hunger is a wanderer"
- Proverb

Threat 1 - Food Insecurity

GRAIN writes: "Is this a price blip? No. A food shortage? Not that either. We are in a structural meltdown, the direct result of three decades of neoliberal globalization. ... We have allowed food to be transformed from something that nourishes people and provides them with secure livelihoods into a commodity for speculation and bargaining." The report states: "The amount of speculative money in commodities futures ... was less than $5 billion in 2000. Last year, it ballooned to roughly $175 billion."

The best choice for civilization is clear -- we need what Pat Murphy of Community Solution calls "Plan C" -- The Conserver Option : Curtailment, Cooperation, Community. Efficiency by itself will not be enough to solve the enormous challenges we all face, but it could buy us a little time for deeper shifts.

As global granaries pass "Peak Grain" the world must decide if the American diet is more important than addressing preventable world hunger. We will only be able to feed the expected nine billion people if we abandon factory farming as a basis for agriculture. Energy efficient diets are a critical part of any plans for a global powerdown scenario to bridge the gap of energy decline.

End of Modern Civilization and Alternative Future

Threat - 2

Global Water Scarcity

Sinking Water Table and Diminishing Rainfall

Thousands have lived without love, not one without water.   *- W.H. Auden*

Dawn of a Thirsty Century

In an age when man has forgotten his origins and is blind even to his most essential needs for survival, water along with other resources has become the victim of his indifference. By 2015, according to estimates from the United Nations and the United States government, at least 40 percent of the world's population, or about three billion people, will live in countries where it is difficult or impossible to get enough water to satisfy basic needs.

Water covers about two-thirds of the Earth's surface, admittedly. But most of it is too salty to use. Only 2.5% of the world's water is not salty, and two-thirds of that is locked up in the icecaps and glaciers. Of what is left, about 20% is in remote areas, and much of the rest arrives at the wrong time and place, as monsoons and floods. Humans have availability of less than 0.08% of all the Earth's water. Yet over the next two decades our use is estimated to increase by about 40%.

In 1999 the United Nations Environment Programme (UNEP) reported that 200 scientists in 50 countries had identified water

"That time is coming. It is predicted in the Srimad-Bhagavatam that anavrsti and kara-piditah. People gradually being godless, they will be suffering from these three principles. There will be no more rainfall. Therefore last time when I was in Europe -- I do not know what has happened now -- there was scarcity of rain, and England was making plan to import water. So this is scientist's program. There is enough water in the sea, but they cannot use it. So that is hand of God. Unless God helps, Krsna helps, mayadhyaksena prakrtih suyate sa-caracaram... [Bg. 9.10]. The vast ocean, although the water is there, you cannot use one drop. You are so controlled."

-Srila Prabhupada (Lecture on Srimad-Bhagavatam 5.5.1 -- Bombay, December 25, 1976)

shortage as one of the two most worrying problems for the new millennium (the other was global warming).

Water Is Life and Water Is Death

The direst, direct effects of water scarcity will undoubtedly be on health. The presence of water can be a bane as well as a benefit.

Waterborne diseases and the absence of sanitary domestic water are one of the leading causes of death worldwide. For children under age five, waterborne diseases are the leading cause of death. At any given time, half of the world's hospital beds are occupied by patients suffering from waterborne diseases. According to the World Bank, 88 percent of all diseases are caused by unsafe drinking water, inadequate sanitation and poor hygiene. Year 2025 forecasts state that two thirds of the world population will be without safe drinking water and basic sanitation services.

Waterborne illnesses, such as gastric infections leading to diarrhea, are caused by drinking contaminated water; vector-borne diseases, such as malaria and schistosomiasis, are passed on by the mosquitoes and small snails that use water to breed. Millions contract such diseases.

Water is one of the most basic of all needs -- we cannot live for more than a few days without it. And yet, most people take water for granted. We waste water needlessly and don't realize that clean water is a very limited resource. More than 1 billion people around the world have no access to safe, clean drinking water, and over 2.5 billion do not have adequate sanitation service. Over 4 million people die each year because of unsafe water, 10 times the number killed in wars around the globe - and most of them are children. *In*

"Of all the social and natural crises we humans face, the water crisis is the one that lies at the heart of our survival and that of our planet Earth."
-Koichiro Matsuura (the director general of Unesco)

fact a child dies every eight seconds from drinking contaminated water, and the sanitation trend is getting sharply worse, mostly because of the worldwide drift of the rural peasantry to urban slums.

For many of us, water simply flows from a faucet, and we think little about it beyond this point of contact. We have lost a sense of respect for the river, for the complex workings of a wetland, for the intricate web of life that water supports. Children of a culture born in a water-rich environment, many of us have never really learned how important water is to us and how the destruction of aquatic ecosystem health, and the increasing water scarcity, are some of the most pressing environmental problems facing humankind. Water is being depleted many, many times faster than nature can replenish it.

Water Crisis Closing In On Agriculture

It takes 1,000 tons of water to produce 1 ton of grain. As water becomes scarce and countries are forced to divert irrigation water to cities and industry, they will import more grain. As they do so,

Srimad-Bhagavatam instructs us solely on this subject from the very beginning to the end. Human life is simply meant for self-realization. The civilization which aims at this utmost perfection never indulges in creating unwanted things, and such a perfect civilization prepares men only to accept the bare necessities of life or to follow the principle of the best use of a bad bargain. Our material bodies and our lives in that connection are bad bargains because the living entity is actually spirit, and spiritual advancement of the living entity is absolutely necessary. Human life is intended for the realization of this important factor, and one should act accordingly, accepting only the bare necessities of life and depending more on God's gift without diversion of human energy for any other purpose, such as being mad for material enjoyment. The materialistic advancement of civilization is called "the civilization of the demons," which ultimately ends in wars and scarcity.
-*Srimad Bhagavatam 2.2.3 Purport*

water scarcity will be transmitted across national borders via the grain trade. Aquifer depletion is a largely invisible threat, but that does not make it any less real. Water deficits are already spurring heavy grain imports in numerous smaller countries, may soon do the same in larger countries, such as China or India. The water tables are falling in scores of countries (including Northern China, the US, and India) due to widespread overpumping using powerful diesel and electric pumps. Other countries affected include Pakistan, Afghanistan, and Iran. This will eventually lead to water scarcity and cutbacks in grain harvest. Even with the overpumping of its aquifers, China is developing a grain deficit. When this happens, it will almost certainly drive grain prices upward. Most of the 3 billion people projected to be added worldwide by mid-century will be born in countries already experiencing water shortages. After China and India, there is a second tier of smaller countries with large water deficits — Afghanistan, Algeria, Egypt, Iran, Mexico, and Pakistan. Four of these already import a large share of their grain. Only Pakistan remains largely self-sufficient. But it will also likely soon turn to the world market for grain.

Freshwater: Lifeblood of The Planet

Clean water is a necessity that we can no longer take for granted. Each year more people die of water related diseases than any other cause of death on this planet, with a higher rate of suffering and mortality than diabetes, cancer, high cholesterol, or war; or any two combined for that matter. An entire economy is growing around water.

To the naked eye, our oceans are beautiful. But scientists tell us

As we watch the sun go down, evening after evening, through the smog across the poisoned waters of our native earth, we must ask ourselves seriously whether we really wish some future universal historian on another planet to say about us: "With all their genius and with all their skill, they ran out of foresight and air and food and water and ideas," or, "They went on playing politics until their world collapsed around them."
~ U Thant

Threat 2 - Global Water Scarcity

that all of the world's fisheries will collapse by 2040, unless we change how we manage them. Water, like religion and ideology, has the power to move millions of people. Since the very birth of human civilization, people have moved to settle close to it. People move when there is too little of it. People move when there is too much of it. People journey down it. People write, sing and dance about it. People fight over it. And all people, everywhere and every day, need it. We can use our scientific knowledge to improve and beautify the earth, or we can use it to poison the air, corrupt the waters, blacken the face of the country, and harass our souls with loud and discordant noises. "Polluted Water—No Swimming" has become a familiar sign on too many beaches and rivers. A lake that has served many generations of men now can be destroyed by man in less than one generation. Robert F. Kennedy once said "We in Government have begun to recognize the critical work which must be done at all levels—local, State and Federal—in ending the pollution of our waters." Industrial agriculture now accounts for over half of America's water pollution.

If we're to have any hope of satisfying the food and water needs of the world's people in the years ahead, we will need a fundamental shift in how we use and manage water. A nation that fails to plan intelligently for the development and protection of its precious waters will be condemned to wither because of its shortsightedness. The hard lessons of history are clear, written on the deserted sands and ruins of once proud civilizations.

Water Water Everywhere, Nor Any Drop To Drink

The total amount of water available on earth has been estimated at 1.4 billion cubic kilometers, enough to cover the planet with a layer of about 3-km deep. About 97.5% of the earth's water is in

> *raso 'ham apsu kaunteya*
> *I am the taste of water.*
> *- Krishna (Gita 7.8)*

the oceans, which is unfit for human consumption and other use because of its high salt content. As mentioned earlier, only 0.8% of water is available as fresh water in rivers, lakes, and streams, which is suitable for human consumption. What is available, in lakes, rivers, aquifers (ground water) and rainfall runoff, is now increasingly coming under pressure from several directions at once. This highlights the significance of the need to preserve our fresh water resources.

A big difficulty with water is that, at least in the rich West, it is largely taken for granted. After all, it is the most widely-occurring substance, but reality is quite different.

Water Scarcity Is The Biggest Crisis of All - World Water Development Report By UN

Mankind's most serious challenge in the 21st century might not be war or hunger or disease or even the collapse of civic order, a UN report says; it may be the lack of fresh water.

Population growth, pollution and climate change, all accelerating, are likely to combine to produce a drastic decline in water supply in the coming decades, according to the World Water Development Report by UN. And of course that supply is already problematic for up to a third of the world's population.

At present 1.1 billion people lack access to clean water and 2.4

Commenting on Srila Prabhupada's mood in Mayapur, Bhavananda Goswami said if a water tap on the land was dripping only once every three hours, then Srila Prabhupada would come at exactly the time it dripped, see it, and say, "Just see, Krsna's energy is being wasted."

In Bhaktivedanta Manor one time, Srila Prabhupada complained of a dripping water faucet that disturbed him. The devotees searched and searched, but found nothing. Finally, they found the offending faucet. It was outside his room, down the hall, down a small block of stairs, down another small hall, and inside a closet in a place from which water was hardly ever taken. No one knew how he could possibly have heard it drip.

-From Srila Prabhupada Nectar (by Satsvarupa dasa Goswami)

billion lack access to proper sanitation, nearly all of them in the developing countries. Yet the fact that these figures are likely to worsen remorselessly has not been properly grasped by the world community, the report says. "Despite widely available evidence of the crisis, political commitment to reverse these trends has been lacking."

Faced with "inertia at the leadership level and a world population not fully aware of the scale of the problem", the global water crisis will reach unprecedented heights in the years ahead, the report says, with growing per capita scarcity in many parts of the developing world. And that means hunger, disease and death.

"IT'S NO MIRACLE — IT'S JUST SOLID INDUSTRIAL WASTE."

The report makes an alarming prediction. By the middle of the century, it says that, in the worst case, no fewer than seven billion people in 60 countries may be faced with water scarcity, although if the right policies are followed this may be brought down to two billion people in 48 nations.

The trouble with water—and there is trouble with water—is that they're not making any more of it. They're not making any less, mind, but no more either. There is the same amount of water in the planet now as there was in prehistoric times. People, however, they're making more of—many more, far more than is ecologically sensible—and all those people are utterly dependent on water for their lives (humans consist mostly of water), for their livelihoods, their food, and increasingly, their industry. Humans can live for a month without food but will die in less than a week without water. Humans consume water, discard it, poison it, waste it, and restlessly change the hydrological cycles, indifferent to the consequences: too many people, too little water, water in the wrong places and in the wrong amounts.
- Marq de Villiers

The report was intended as an alarm call, launched in advance of the World Water Forum meet which took place in Kyoto, Japan. It was hoped that governments and policy makers would make a new commitment to get to grips with the water problem internationally. That sadly did not happen as the United States and Britain had just invaded Iraq and the world was convulsed by war.

Non-conventional Demands & Pollution

Demand of course, comes not just from the need to drink, the need to wash and the need to deal with human waste, enormous though these are; the really great calls on water supply come from industry in the developed world, and in the developing world, from agriculture. Irrigating crops in hot dry countries accounts for 70 per cent of all the water use in the world.

Pollution, from industry, agriculture and not least, human waste, adds another fierce pressure. About two million tons of waste are dumped every day into rivers, lakes and streams, with *one liter of waste water sufficient to pollute about eight liters of fresh water*. Reports estimate that across the world there are about 12,000 cubic kilometers of waste water, which is more than the total amount contained in the world's 10 largest river basins at any given moment. Therefore, it suggests, if pollution keeps pace with population growth, the world will in effect lose 18,000 cubic kilometers by 2050 – almost nine times the amount all countries currently use for irrigation.

All that's bad enough. But increasing the stress on water supply still further will be climate change, which UN scientists calculate will probably account for about a fifth of the increase in water scarcity. While rainfall is predicted to get heavier in winter in high latitudes, such as Britain and northern Europe, in many drought-

Water and air, the two essential fluids on which all life depends, have become global garbage cans.
–Jacques Cousteau

prone countries and even some tropical regions it is predicted to decrease further; and water quality will worsen with rising pollution levels and water temperatures.

Production of biofuels will further deplete the world's water supply.

Water Under Pressure From Urban Living

Yet another difficulty will be the growing urbanization of the world: at present, 48 per cent of the Earth's population lives in towns and cities; by 2030 this will be 60 per cent. Urban areas often have more readily available water supplies than rural ones; their problem is that they concentrate wastes. Where good waste management is lacking, urban areas are among the world's most life-threatening environments.

Water & Environment - The Double-edged Sword

The world's soaring demand for fresh water is also causing increasing environmental stress; the stream flows of about 60 per cent of the world's largest rivers have been interrupted by dams and, of the creatures associated with inland waters, 24 per cent of mammals and 12 per cent of birds are threatened. About 10 per cent of freshwater fish species have been studied in detail and about a third of these are thought to be threatened.

Water picture is a distinctly gloomy one – of a vital but limited human resource subject to increasingly insatiable demands.

You may be great scientist and calculate so much hydrogen and so much oxygen, mixed up, there is water. Now mix up and bring water where there is no rain.
So these so-called scientists, philoso..., all of them are rascals.
-Srila Prabhupada (Lecture, Srimad-Bhagavatam 1.10.4 - Mayapura, June 19, 1973)

Water - China To California

China

About 300 million Chinese drink unsafe water tainted by chemicals and other contaminants according to a new report from the Chinese government. A leading government official said the greatest non-drought threat to China's water resources, is chemical pollutants and other harmful substances that contaminate drinking supplies for 190 million people.

California

At current rates, California's demand for water will increase by 40 percent over the next 25 years, warns a new study from the Public Policy Institute of California. The nonprofit group projects that California will add fourteen million more people by 2030, each of whom will be using 232 gallons a day. Much of the water will be used for landscaping, especially in the drier interior areas where much of the state's population growth is occurring. About half of all the water used by inland homeowners goes to irrigating yards.

Melting Glaciers

Global Warming is melting glaciers in every region of the world, putting millions of people at risk from floods, droughts and lack of drinking water. Glaciers are ancient rivers of compressed snow that creep through the landscape, shaping the planet's surface. They are the Earth's largest freshwater reservoirs, collectively covering an area the size of South America. Glaciers have been retreating worldwide since around 1850, but in recent decades glaciers have begun melting at rates that cannot be explained by historical trends.

Data from close to 30 reference glaciers in nine mountain ranges indicate that between the years 2004-2005 and 2005-2006 the average rate of melting and thinning more than doubled. The

"I have little need to remind you that water has become one of our major national concerns."
-- Ezra Taft Benson, U.S. Secretary of Agriculture

findings come from the World Glacier Monitoring Service (WGMS), a centre based at the University of Zurich in Switzerland and supported by UNEP.

Another report circulated at a conference on climate change by the International Centre for Integrated Mountain Development (ICIMOD) in Kathmandu says that global warming has pushed up the temperature of the Himalayas by up to 0.6 degrees Celsius in the past 30 years.

"It is extremely serious," said Surendra Shrestha, regional director at the United Nations Environment Programme for Asia and the Pacific. "It is going to change fundamentally the way we live. If the temperature continues to rise as it is, there will be no snow and ice in the Himalayas in 50 years."

Thousands of glaciers in the Himalayas are the source of water for nine major Asian rivers whose basins are home to 2.4 billion people from Pakistan to Myanmar, including parts of India and China. As per Andreas Schild, ICIMOD's director general, the disappearance of glaciers would mean a reduction in the mountains' natural water storage capacity.

Tsunami - From Up In The Mountains

Melting glaciers will have an adverse impact on biodiversity, hydropower, industries and agriculture and make Himalayan basin region dangerous to live in. The melting causes lakes to form at the base of glaciers, lakes which can subsequently burst their banks as temperatures continue to rise. This can have devastating effects downstream.

Now by your talent, you are producing nice food, but producing food, tilling the ground some way or other, by machine or by this way... But there must be rain, and so many other conditions. But time will come when there will be no rain. Then what you will do with your tractor and machine? You'll have to eat the tractor. (laughter)
That's all.
-Prabhupada (Srimad-Bhagavatam 1.16.22 -- Hawaii, January 18, 1974)

In the opinion of the International Centre for Integrated Mountain Development (ICIMOD), Kathmandu, if there is a small earthquake all that water is going to come down and because of the altitude it will pick up debris and speed... it is like a big bulldozer that wipes everything out. It is a silent tsunami.

Officials estimate that there are more than 3,200 glaciers in Nepal -- 14 of which have lakes which are at risk of bursting. According to Om Bajracharya, a senior Nepali government hydrologist, the Khumbhu glacier in the Everest region frequented by thousands of climbers and trekkers every year, receded by 30 meters between 1978 and 1995.

Rivers Might Bid Us Goodbye

According to another UN climate report, the Himalayan glaciers that are the sources of Asia's biggest rivers - Ganges, Indus, Brahmaputra, Yangtze, Mekong, Salween and Yellow - could disappear by 2035 as temperatures rise. Approximately 2.4 billion people live in the drainage basin of the Himalayan rivers. India, China, Pakistan, Bangladesh, Nepal and Myanmar could experience floods followed by droughts in coming decades. In India alone, the Ganges provides water for drinking and farming for more than 500 million people. The west coast of North America, which gets much of its water from glaciers in mountain ranges such as the Rocky Mountains and Sierra Nevada, also would be affected.

A Truly Global Problem: One In Three Faces Water Scarcity

One in three people is enduring one form or another of water scarcity, according to a new report from the International Water Management Institute (IWMI).

The assessment, carried out by 700 experts from around the world over the last five years, was released at World Water Week in Stockholm, a conference exploring the management of global water resources. The scarcity figures were higher than previous estimates.

> *"Water is life's matter and matrix, mother and medium. There is no life without water."*
> *~Albert Szent-Gyorgyi*

Desertification - Green Earth Turning Into Sand

Desertification is the degradation of land in arid areas, resulting primarily from human activities and influenced by climatic variations. A major impact of desertification is biodiversity loss and loss of productive capacity. Examples can be cited from various parts of the world. Semi-arid regions of southern California are turning into desert. In Madagascar's central highland plateau, 10% of the entire country has been lost to desertification due to slash and burn agriculture by indigenous peoples. In Africa, if current trends of soil degradation continue, the continent might be able to feed just 25% of its population by 2025, according to UNU's Ghana-based Institute for Natural Resources in Africa.

It is a common misconception that droughts by themselves cause desertification. While drought is a contributing factor, the root causes are all related to man's overexploitation of the environment. There is no geological evidence that deserts expanded significantly before the advent of civilization.

Human overpopulation is leading to destruction of tropical wet forests and tropical dry forests, due to widening practices of slash-and-burn and other methods of subsistence farming. A sequel to the deforestation is typically large scale erosion, loss of soil nutrients and sometimes total desertification. Examples of this extreme outcome can be seen on Madagascar's central highland plateau, where about seven percent of the country's total land mass has become barren, sterile land.

Marching Deserts And Advancing Oceans - Sandwiching Civilization

Our twenty-first century civilization is being squeezed between advancing deserts and rising seas. Measured by the land area that

A river is more than an amenity, it is a treasure.
- Oliver Holmes

can support human habitation, the earth is shrinking. Mounting population densities, are now also fueled by the relentless advance of deserts and the rise in sea level.

The newly established trends of expanding deserts and rising seas are both of human origin. The former is primarily the result of overstocking grasslands and overplowing land. Rising seas result from temperature increases set in motion by carbon released from the burning of fossil fuels.

Gobi Desert Has Marched To Within 150 Miles of Beijing

The heavy losses of territory to advancing deserts in China and Nigeria, the most populous countries in Asia and Africa respectively, illustrate the trends for scores of other countries. China is not only losing productive land to deserts, but it is doing so at an accelerating rate. From 1950 to 1975 China lost an average of 1,560 square kilometers of land to desert each year. By 2000, nearly 3625 square kilometers were going to desert annually.

A U.S. Embassy report entitled "Desert Mergers and Acquisitions" describes satellite images that show two deserts in north-central China expanding and merging to form a single, larger desert overlapping inner Mongolia and Gansu provinces. To the west in Xinjiang Province, two even larger deserts—the Taklimakan and Kumtag—are also heading for a merger. Further east, the Gobi Desert has marched to within 150 miles (241 kilometers) of Beijing, alarming China's leaders. Chinese scientists report that over the last half-century, some 24,000 villages in northern and western China were abandoned or partly depopulated as they were overrun by drifting sand.

> *nityam udvigna-manaso durbhiksa-kara-karsitah*
> *niranne bhu-tale rajan anavrsti-bhayaturah*
> *In the age of Kali, people's minds will always be agitated. They will become emaciated by famine and taxation, my dear King, and will always be disturbed by fear of drought.*
> -Srimad Bhagavatam 12.3.39

All the countries in central Asia—Afghanistan, Kazakhstan, Kyrgyzstan, Tajikistan, Turkmenistan, and Uzbekistan—are losing land to desertification. Kazakhstan has abandoned nearly half of its cropland since 1980.

In Afghanistan, a country with a population of 31 million, the desert is migrating westward, encroaching on agricultural areas. A UN Environment Programme (UNEP) team reports that "up to 100 villages have been submerged by windblown dust and sand." In the country's northwest, sand dunes are moving onto agricultural land, their path cleared by the loss of stabilizing vegetation from firewood gathering and overgrazing. The UNEP team observed sand dunes nearly 50 feet high blocking roads, forcing residents to establish new routes. More than 80% of Afghanistan's and Pakistan's land could be subject to soil erosion and desertification.

Iran, which has 70 million people and 80 million goats and sheep, the latter the source of wool for its fabled rug-making industry, is also losing its battle with the desert. Mohammad Jarian, who heads Iran's Anti-Desertification Organization, reported in 2002 that sand storms had buried 124 villages in the southeastern province of Sistan-Baluchistan, forcing their abandonment. Drifting sands had covered grazing areas, starving livestock and depriving villagers of their livelihood.

*When I first went to Hyderabad they said that for three, four years there was no rain. Is it not? But since Hare Krsna mantra is being chanted, there is rainfall. So they do not know the secret of rainfall. Yajnad bhavanti parjanyah. If you perform yajna, then there will be cloud. Parjanyad anna-sambhavah. Annad bhavanti bhutani parjanyad anna-sambhavah [Bg. 3.14]. This prescription is there. As soon as you stop performing yajna -- you take pleasure in sporting, no yajna... Now big, big cities, they have got big, big Olympian sporting, but no yajna performance. So why there shall not be scarcity of rain? And as soon as there is scarcity of rain, there is scarcity of food grains.
-Srila Prabhupada (Srimad-Bhagavatam 7.12.5 -- Bombay, April 16, 1976)*

Africa, too, is plagued with expanding deserts. In the north, the Sahara Desert is pushing the populations of Morocco, Tunisia, and Algeria northward toward the Mediterranean. In a desperate effort to halt the advancing Sahara, Algeria is geographically restructuring its agriculture, replacing grain in the south with orchards and vineyards.

In countries from Senegal and Mauritania in the west to Sudan, Ethiopia, and Somalia in the east, the growing human and livestock demands are converting land into desert.

Nigeria, slightly larger than Texas, is losing 3510 square kilometers of rangeland and cropland to desertification each year. With the food needs of its people forcing the plowing of marginal land and the forage needs of livestock exceeding the carrying capacity of its grasslands, the country is slowly turning to desert.

In Latin America, deserts are expanding in both Brazil and Mexico. In Mexico, with a large share of arid and semiarid land, the degradation of cropland now forces some 700,000 Mexicans off the land each year in search of jobs in nearby cities or in the United States. In scores of countries, the growth in human and livestock numbers that drives desertification is continuing unabated.

While deserts are now displacing millions of people, rising seas promise to displace far greater numbers in the future given the concentration of the world's population in low-lying coastal cities and rice-growing river deltas. During the twentieth century, sea level rose by 15 centimeters. In its 2001 report, the Intergovernmental Panel on Climate Change projected that during this century seas would rise by 10 to 85 centimeters. Since 2001, record-high temperatures have accelerated ice melting making it likely that the future rise in sea level will be even greater.

> *"When the Well's dry, we know the Worth of Water."*
> Benjamin Franklin

Rising Sea Levels

The earth's rising temperature is raising sea level both through thermal expansion of the oceans and the melting of glaciers and ice sheets. Scientists are particularly concerned by the melting of the Greenland ice sheet, which has accelerated sharply in recent years. If this ice sheet, a mile thick in some places, were to melt entirely it would raise sea level by 23 feet, or 7 meters.

Even a one-meter rise would inundate vast areas of low-lying coastal land, including many of the rice-growing river deltas and floodplains of India, Thailand, Viet Nam, Indonesia, and China. A World Bank map shows a one-meter rise in sea level inundating half of Bangladesh's rice land. Some 30 million Bangladeshis would be forced to migrate, either internally or to other countries.

Hundreds of cities, including some of the world's largest, would be at least partly inundated by a one-meter rise in sea level, including London, Alexandria, and Bangkok. More than a third of Shanghai, a city of 15 million people, would be under water. A one-meter rise combined with a 50-year storm surge would leave large portions of Lower Manhattan and the National Mall in Washington, D.C., flooded with seawater.

If the Greenland ice sheet should melt, the resulting 23-foot rise in sea level would force the abandonment of thousands of coastal cities and communities. Hundreds of millions of coastal residents would be forced to migrate inland or to other countries, spawning conflicts over land and living space. Together, rising seas and desertification will present the world with an unprecedented flow of environmental refugees—and the potential for civil strife.

During this century we must deal with the effects of the trends—advancing deserts and rising seas—that we set in motion during the last century. The rising atmospheric concentrations of carbon dioxide that are destabilizing the earth's climate are driven by the burning of fossil fuels.

Chad - A Shrinking African Lake

Lake Chad, once one of Africa's largest freshwater lakes, has shrunk dramatically in the last 40 years. Two researchers from the

University of Wisconsin, have been working to determine the causes.

In 1963, the lake covered about 9,700 square miles (25,000 square kilometers). Today it is one-twentieth of that size. In a report published in the Journal of Geophysical Research, they conclude that human activities are to blame for the shrinking of Lake Chad.

The lake's decline probably has nothing to do with global warming, report the two scientists, who based their findings on computer models and satellite imagery made available by NASA. They attribute the situation instead to human actions related to climate variation, compounded by the ever increasing demands of the population.

Humans in the system are the big actors here and what has happened to Lake Chad may be an illustration of where we're heading. Lake Chad is in the Sahel, a vast savanna bordered by the rain forests of the west coast of Africa on one side and the Sahara desert to the north. Chad, Niger, Nigeria, and Cameroon are neighboring countries.

The lake is probably at least 20,000 years old and has shrunk and expanded over thousands of years. But the recent decline is by far the greatest.

Corporations: Cashing In On Water Crisis

Multinational companies now run water systems for 7 per cent of the world's population and analysts say that figure could grow to 17 per cent by 2015. Private water management is estimated to be a $200 billion business, and the World Bank projects it could be worth $1 trillion by 2021. The potential for profits is staggering: in May 2000 Fortune magazine predicted that water is about to become 'one of the world's great business opportunities', and that 'it promises to be to the 21st century what oil was to the 20th'.

Global water consumption rose sixfold between 1900 and 1995 - more than double the rate of population growth - and goes on growing as farming, industry and domestic demand all increase. Here the issue seems to be not overpopulation but overconsumption.

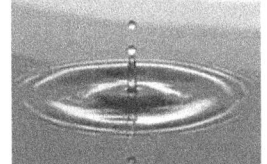

As important as quantity is quality - with pollution increasing in some areas, the amount of usable water declines. And the wider effects of water shortages are just as chilling as the prospect of having too little to drink. Seventy percent of the water used worldwide is used for agriculture.

And consumption will soar further as more people expect Western-style lifestyles and diets - one kilogram of grain-fed beef needs at least 15 cubic meters of water, while a kilo of cereals needs only up to three cubic meters.

Bottling The World Up

Corporations like Coke, Nestle, and Pepsi have manufactured demand for bottled water through years of misleading advertising – building a market by eroding confidence in public tap water. In reality, many times the tap water is just as good or better and doesn't generate billions of pounds of plastic waste.

It has become trendy to walk around with or sip on Fiji water to show that you are truly fashionable, but its time we stop to think about the repercussions of such actions. Most of the time, bottled water is just tap water with a really fancy label because laws all over world do not require bottled water to go through a vigorous testing process. In fact, by law, bottled water only has to be as "good" as tap water to be acceptable - legally speaking. Most bottle are also made out of crude oil - over 1.5 million tons of crude oil go to making plastic bottles. Scary fact is that almost 80% of water bottles do not get recycled. Its quite silly to pay $4 for a small bottle of water labeled Fiji.

In India, Coke promotes its brand with the slogan "can't live without it." Ironically, Coke continues to pump millions of gallons in drought stricken areas for marketing in cities, where agriculture and people's lives depend on local water resources – resources that are now drying up.

'Flow' - A film

Flow is a passionate and fact-filled film portraying issues facing the planet's water today. Focusing on human rights, environmental destruction and corporate greed, 'Flow' shows how many communities are fighting back for control over their most essential resource. Set in countries across the globe, the film is an inspiration and a call to action.

Water Wars

This is a term devised by environmentalists for a type of conflict (most probably a form of guerrilla warfare) due to an acute shortage of water for drinking and irrigation. About 40 per cent of the world's population is already affected to some degree, but climate change and rise in living standards will worsen the situation: the UN Environment Agency warns that almost 3 billion people will be severely short of water within 50 years. Possible flash points have been predicted in the Middle East, parts of Africa and in many of the world's major river basins.

There are approximately 260 different river systems worldwide, where conflicts exist crossing national boundaries. While Helsinki Rules help to interpret intrinsic water rights among countries, there are some conflicts so bitter or so related to basic survival that strife and even warfare are inevitable. In many cases water use disputes are merely an added dimension to underlying border tensions founded on other bases.

The Tigris-Euphrates River System is one example where

annad bhavanti bhutani
parjanyad anna-sambhavah
yajnad bhavati parjanyo
yajnah karma-samudbhavah
All living bodies subsist on food grains, which are produced from rains. Rains are produced by performance of yajna [sacrifice], and yajna is born of prescribed duties.   -*Bhagavad-gita 3.14*

differing national interests and withdrawal rights have been in conflict. The countries of Iran, Iraq and Syria each present valid claims of certain water use, but the total demands on the riverine system surpass the physical constraints of water availability. As early as 1974 Iraq massed troops on the Syrian border and threatened to destroy Syria's al-Thawra dam on the Euphrates.

In 1992 Hungary and Czechoslovakia took a dispute over Danube River water diversions and dam construction to the International Court of Justice. This case represents a minority of disputes where logic and jurisprudence may be the path of dispute resolution. Other conflicts involving North and South Korea, Israel and Palestine, Egypt and Ethiopia, India and Pakistan, may prove more difficult tests of negotiation. International leaders, notably former Czech President Vaclav Havel, have suggested that the supply of clean water for drinking and sanitation is essential for peace in the Middle East.

War over water would be an ultimate obscenity. And yet, unfortunately it is conceivable. Water has been a source, over so many years, of erosion of confidence, of tension, of human rights abuses.

While draught and desertification are intensifying around the world, the water wars of the twenty-first century may match, or even surpass, the oil wars of the twentieth century.

Mostafa Tolba, former head of the United Nations Environment Program says, "We used to think that energy and water would be the critical issues for the next century. Now we think water will be the critical issue." Last few decades have witnessed hundreds of violent conflicts over water sharing issues.

Kenyan Tribes Battling Over Water

The battle for water in the drought-hit north of Kenya has sparked tribal conflicts leaving hundreds dead with mounting death toll.

Fierce national competition over water resources has prompted fears that water issues contain the seeds of violent conflict.
- Kofi Annan (UN Chief)

On the arid northern plains, strewn with the decomposing carcasses of cattle, people are preparing for a battle. There are plenty of weapons in this remote corner of the country: homemade spears, bows and arrows, and guns smuggled in from southern Sudan. And now, there is a motive too. Kenya is suffering a severe drought that has dried up watering holes and turned grazing lands into sand. More than 70 per cent of the region's 260,000 cattle have died, devastating the thousands of nomadic communities that depend on them for wealth, milk and food.

Watery Issues For Nuclear Armed India & Pakistan

In November 2008, Pakistan Indus Water Commissioner Jamaat Ali Shah accused India of trying to make Pakistan a barren land in the next six years by blocking its water through construction of dams in violation of the Indus Water Treaty. Shah said India had constructed dams at various rivers and continued doing so in violation of the Indus Water Treaty.

As per Pakistan, the Treaty allowed New Delhi to generate electricity on the flow of the river but water to Pakistan cannot be stopped. India, on the other hand claimed that it had stopped Pakistan's water only for a week in August but Pakistani side rubbished this claim.

Sharing of rivers' water remains a bone of contention for the two heavily armed nations and time will tell where it will lead them to.

Catastrophic Floods

Poorly planned water management and deforestation is responsible for rising incidents of floods all over the world. Many a times, dams are ill-conceived. The number of people displaced by dams is estimated at between 40 million and 80 million, most of them in China and India. Some designed to reduce flooding

> *Water is the only drink for a wise man.*
> *-Henry David Thoreau*

have made it worse, and there were many unexpected environmental disadvantages. Half the world's wetlands have been lost because of dams.

Recently in Bihar, India, a breach developed in Kosi dam and the resulting floods killed thousands and displaced many millions. Many dams have been constructed due to financial and political considerations and they are time-bombs ticking away. One such example is Tehri dam in Himalayas. Indian government ignored the opinion of many experts and constructed a massive dam in an earthquake prone area. If ever it cracks, India's capital New Delhi will be wiped out.

In America, more than 5,500 large dams impede running waters, leaving less than 2 percent of the country's 3.1 million miles of rivers and streams flowing free. In the wake of these river alterations trails a record list of endangered aquatic species.

Damage To Biodiversity

Vegetation and wildlife are fundamentally dependent upon adequate freshwater resources. In the case of wetlands, considerable area has been taken from wildlife use to feed and house the human population. But other areas have suffered reduced productivity from gradual diminishing of freshwater inflow, as upstream sources are diverted for human use. In seven states of the U.S. over 80 percent of all historic wetlands were occupied by 1980.

In Europe extensive loss of wetlands has also occurred with resulting loss of biodiversity. On Madagascar's central highland plateau, a massive transformation occurred that eliminated virtually all the heavily forested vegetation in the period 1970 to 2000. The slash and burn agriculture eliminated about ten percent of the total country's native biomass and converted it to a barren wasteland. Adverse effects included widespread erosion that in turn produced heavily silted rivers that "run red" decades after the deforestation. This eliminated a large amount of usable fresh water and also destroyed much of the riverine ecosystems. Several fish species have been driven to the edge of extinction and some coral reef formations in the Indian Ocean are effectively lost.

'Water Police' Crack Down In Australia

Australia is in the grip of its worst-ever drought. In several of its cities, we can find cars which at first glance look like a police car – a white vehicle with a black-and-yellow checkerboard stripe but when we read black bold lettering across its trunk: "Water Restrictions" its purpose becomes clear. Yes, this is 'Water Police' trying to enforce water conservation measures as country endures a long drought made worse by global warming.

Under strict water-conservation measures in force in several cities, cars must not be washed with hoses, only buckets. Watering lawns and gardens with hoses or drip-irrigation systems is allowed on two days a week. A special permit is required to fill a swimming pool. Breaking any of these  rules incurs a spot fine of A$220 for householders and A$500 for businesses. Profligate shower-takers may find their water supply cut to a trickle.

The water crisis is no longer about desperate farmers watching their crops wither or cattle perish. Over the past six years, it has extended its grip to the cities and is changing the way Australians regard a resource they once took for granted. The water Police cars cruise city streets around the clock, every day of the week, sniffing out water wastage.

Climate scientists agree that Australia's drought is linked to global warming. Director of the Australian Research Centre for Water in Society says, "There's a lot of climate-model evidence that says that the drought is, at least in part, human-induced."

 *I'm coming from London, Paris, and Tehran. All fields yellow. And Europe, so much scorching heat and sunshine, I never seen. Especially in London. This time I saw everything has become yellow. Greenness gone.*
-Srila Prabhupada (Morning Walk — August 14, 1976, Bombay)

Data from the Australian Bureau of Meteorology show that, since 1970, rainfall has increased in the barely developed northwestern corner of the continent. But it has decreased in the densely populated east and southeast, the areas where it matters most.

Australians are increasingly bombarded with pleas to conserve their most precious resource. *Last year, the government asked people to refrain from singing, daydreaming, and engaging in other "nonessential activities" in the shower to save power and water.*  Exhortations range from installing a rainwater tank in the backyard to eating less meat, on the grounds that rearing livestock requires far more water than growing crops.

Ghost Cities of Future
Perth: The World's First Ghost City?

Ghost city refers to a city which has been abandoned for some reasons. The Australian of the year 2007, environmentalist Tim Flannery, has predicted that Perth in Western Australia could become the world's first ghost metropolis, its population forced to abandon the city due to lack of water.

Perth is likely to become a ghost city within decades as rising global temperatures turn the wheatbelt into a desert and drive species to the brink of extinction.

According to Tim Flannery, Perth is a city on the edge - isolated, dependent on energy and declining water supplies and more likely to feel the effects of global warming. This assertion has forced the city to wake up to the fact its water is running out and that it can no longer rely on its natural supply.

A metropolis of two million residents, Perth prides itself on being a garden city and is quickly draining its underground aquifers to keep its lawns green. "There is a joke doing the rounds : the good news is we'll all soon be drinking recycled sewage. The bad news is there will not be enough to go around.

India Facing A Drier Future

The drinking water crisis in many Indian cities is reaching alarming proportions. Urban population is suffering from irregular water supply, sometimes leading to clashes among them. A recent joint study conducted by United Nations International Children Education Fund (UNICEF) and the World Wide Fund (WWF) for Nature revealed the alarming situation of fresh water depletion in the country. They opined that the fall in the quality and quantity of available water resources is due to the following reasons:

- Pollution of water sources
- Improper water resources management
- Shortcomings in the design and implementation of legislation and regulations, which address these problems.

More number of similar cases can be expected from many of the developing countries. The per capita water availability in India is projected to decline to about 1,000 cubic meters by 2025 from 1,820 cubic meters per year recorded in 2001, the Intergovernmental Panel on Climate Change (IPCC) has stated in a report. The fall in the per capita water supply would be the result of both climate change and changing life style.

The warning comes at a time when the country is already recording a spate of water wars between different states. Indian government has done little to address the massive water shortage problem and its impact on overall infrastructure of the nation.

India's famous Keoladeo National Park at Bharatpur in Rajasthan is facing de-recognition from the list of Unesco's world

> *By God's arrangement one can have enough food grains, enough milk, enough fruits and vegetables, and nice clear river water. But now I have seen, while traveling in Europe, that all the rivers there have become nasty. In Germany, in France, and also in Russia and America I have seen that the rivers are nasty. By nature's way the water in the ocean is kept clear like crystal, and the same water is transferred to the rivers, but without salt, so that one may take nice water from the river. This is nature's way, and nature's way means Krsna's way.*
> *-Srila Prabhupada (Teachings of Queen Kunti 23)*

heritage site after a two-member team of the world organisation pointed out the persistent water crisis in the sanctuary. Unesco has pointed out repeatedly in the last five years that Indian Government is neglecting the water management and augmentation schemes. The irrigation is getting affected. Soil erosion is high. Drinking water contamination is spreading spreads disease as common people settle for contaminated water.

If there is a big drought, which is cyclically very probable in the next five years, Indian irrigation can collapse. The impact on the economy will be very severe.

A Parched Punjab - Case Study

The water table in 66% of Punjab has declined drastically during the past 25 years in the aftermath of Green Revolution, which made the state self-sufficient in food grains but at the same time, led to a huge decline in the water level and depletion of soil nutrients.

Situation is particularly grim in many districts where the water table is falling at an alarming rate of 40 cm per year. Punjab Agriculture University experts point out that the primary reason for extraction of groundwater is agriculture, particularly water-intensive crops such as wheat and rice. About 60 to 70% of the total cultivated land in Punjab is under wheat-rice cultivation. The dependence on groundwater is alarming. The PAU projections are that by 2010, entire central Punjab will have a water table below 16 m depth. And to add to the problems, a number of mega housing projects are coming up in the state, which would further tax the ground water.

Delhi's Water Crisis Set To Explode

A new study by the Associated Chambers of Commerce and Industry (Assocham) has warned that water is becoming a scarce commodity in the Indian capital that is home to some 16 million people and the crisis is going to worsen in the coming years, leading to more conflicts and pollution.

The nation's capital is perpetually in the grip of a water crisis, more so in the dry season, when the situation gets particularly worse. The study also points out that despite the current shortage of water, the city also sees huge wastage of water, estimated at over 40 percent, against 10-20 percent in cities of other developing countries.

The distribution losses are due to leakages in a network of nearly 9,000-km-long main water supply chains and theft through unauthorized connections.

The study says that water pollution is another area of concern even though the water in Yamuna reaches the national capital relatively clean after its 395-km descent from the Himalayas. As it leaves the city, the river becomes the principal drain for Delhi's waste as residents pour about 950 million gallons of sewage into it each day. Coursing through the capital, the river becomes a noxious black thread.

Let alone drinking, fecal coliform in the Yamuna (a measure of filth) is 20 percent, or 100,000 times the safe limit for even bathing, with raw sewage floating on top and methane gas gurgling on the surface.

Thus water availability, both in terms of quality and quantity, has declined to such an extent that many parts of India, rural and urban, today face a drought-like situation. And when drought actually sets in, as it did in Gujarat and other parts of the country most recently in the year 2000, scarcity takes on a frightening visage.

The Terrible Impact of Meat Diet On Water

Water experts calculate that currently half of the available fresh water on the planet is being appropriated by humans and nearly half of the total water usage in developed nations is used to raise animals for food. Producing food for a meat based diet requires much more water than it does to produce food for a vegetarian diet. It takes 2500 gallons of water to produce a pound of meat, but only 60 gallons of water to produce a pound of wheat. A plant based diet requires a total of 300 gallons of water per day, while a meat based diet requires more than 4000 gallons of water per day. Thus livestock sector is a key player in increasing water use.

Animals raised for food produce 130 times more excrement than the entire human population put together, for a total of 87,000 pounds per second. This enormous quantiy of waste products from livestock production exceeds the capacity of the planet to absorb it. The U.S. Environmental Protection Agency estimates that livestock waste has polluted more than 27,000 miles of rivers.

It is probably the largest sectoral source of water pollution, contributing to eutrophication, "dead" zones in coastal areas, degradation of coral reefs, human health problems, emergence of antibiotic resistance and many others. The major sources of pollution are from animal wastes, antibiotics and hormones, chemicals from tanneries, fertilizers and pesticides used for feedcrops, and sediments from eroded pastures.

A Thirsty World Resorting To Desalination And Sewage Recycling

Desalination is removal of salt and other impurities from sea water to make it drinkable.

A January 17, 2008, article in the Wall Street Journal states,

"Worldwide, 13,080 desalination plants produce more than 12 billion gallons of water a day, according to the International Desalination Association." However, given the energy intensive nature of desalination, with associated economic and environmental costs, desalination is generally considered a last resort.

A Tall, Cool Drink of ... Sewage?

Many cities of the world are establishing sewage recycling plants to provide potable water to the residents. Bangalore in India, is spending Rs. 1800 crores on one such plant. Should ongoing feasibility tests prove successful, Vivendi Water has plans to start commercial production of recycled sewerage water in Malaysia using membrane technology. The French water giant, already involved in more than a dozen local projects.

World's Largest "Toilet-to-Tap" System

The Orange County Sewage Recycling System in California is the largest of its type in the world. It cost $480 million to build. It works in this way. When some one flushes in Santa Ana, the waste makes its way to the sewage-treatment plant nearby in Fountain Valley, then flows not to the ocean but to a plant that filters the liquid until it is clean. The "new" water is then pumped 13 miles north and discharged into a small lake, where it percolates into the earth. Local utilities pump water from this aquifer and deliver it to the sinks and showers of 2.3 million customers. It is now drinking water. Depending on the mind set, some call it indirect potable reuse, while others call it toilet to tap.

"Brush your teeth with the best toothpaste, then rinse your mouth with industrial waste."
~ Tom Lehrer

It's Time To Drink Toilet Water

For decades, cities throughout the world have used recycled wastewater for nonpotable needs, like agriculture and landscaping but now the pressure is building up to use it for drinking and shower purposes as well.

A public outcry against toilet-to-tap in 2000 forced the city of Los Angeles to shut down a $55 million project that would have provided enough water for 120,000 homes. Similar reluctance among San Diego residents led Mayor Jerry Sanders to veto the city council's approval in November of a pilot program to use recycled water to supplement that city's drinking water.

But San Diego is in the midst of a severe water crisis. The city imports 90 percent of its water, much of that from the Colorado River, which is drying up. The recent legal decision to protect the ecosystem of the San Joaquin Delta in Northern California—San Diego's second-leading water source—will reduce the amount coming from there as well. Add to that rising population and an ongoing drought, and the situation looks quite bleak: 3 million people in a region that has enough water, right now, for 10 percent of them. Water supplied even right now  contains several contaminants, including ibuprofen, the bug repellents and the anti-anxiety drug meprobamate.

Looks like if we don't learn to deal with drinking toilet water, people are going to be mighty thirsty. The Ogallala Aquifer—North America's largest, stretching from Texas to South Dakota—is steadily being depleted. And Americans water footprint has been estimated to be twice the global average.

Despite the public's concerns, quite a few U.S. cities have already started to use recycled wastewater to augment drinking water. In El Paso, Texas, indirect potable reuse supplies 40 percent of the city's drinking water; in Fairfax, Va., it supplies 5 percent. Elsewhere in several places in the world like the African nation of Namibia, this system is already in use.

It is said that in several European countries, it was a common practice to make prisoners drink toilet-water and several of them who did so decided to leave the continent. Thus America's forefathers embarked on a perilous journey across the sea and settled in a wild land so that they would not have to drink poop water ever again. But the history seems to be repeating itself.

With the demand for water growing, water tables dropping faster than they are replenished, glaciers thinning and climate change predicted to make dry places even drier, water managers around the world are contemplating similar schemes. However revolting it may sound, turning sewage into drinking water is where lies our cities' future .

Travelling Spiritual Performers Bring Rain To Australia
For the last six years Australians have suffered the worst drought in a thousand years, say leading agriculturalists. As a result the price of food has nearly doubled in some areas. Water conservation schemes are mandated by local governments across the predominantly arid continent. Declared by politicians to be a national crisis, the situation is a recurring theme in the media and in citizens' minds.
Is it just coincidence that one of the longest uninterrupted streaks of wet weather broke at the same time Indradyumna Swami and his traveling spiritual festival team arrived on Australian shores?
Billed as 'Le Carnaval Spirituel' this vivid stage performance brings forth the timeless spiritual wisdom of ancient India's Vedic art and culture; culminating in a rousing full audience participation kirtana (call and response chanting of the Hare Krishna mantra). The European troupe of performing artists present eastern spirituality fused with a twist of the contemporary. Le Carnaval Spirituel, established in France in 1979, has for many years entertained audiences in Europe's largest music festival "Woodstock" which annually attracts crowds in excess of 250,000 people.
(From The West Australian)

Threat - 3

Resource Depletion

My candle burns at both ends; it will not last the night...
~St. Vincent Millay

What Is Resource Depletion

Resource depletion is an economic term referring to the exhaustion of raw materials within a region. Resources are commonly divided between renewable resources and non-renewable resources. Use of either of these forms of resources beyond their rate of replacement is considered to be resource depletion.

Resource depletion is most commonly used in reference to the farming (water, land fertility, soil nutrition), fishing, mining, and fossil fuels. Normally, resources will not become totally exhausted at some particular moment, but rather will diminish until the price of continued exploitation becomes so high that it is no longer economical to extract those resources. According to Hubbert peak theory, the rate of exploitation follows a sort of bell-shaped curve. The Hubbert peak theory discusses predictions for some resources.

Estimates for when various resources will run out if exploitation continues at present rates are somewhat controversial, but for some resources, the estimated time left is rather short.

The Deadly Scramble for the World's Last Resources

By Julian Brookes

For better or worse, a lot of the things we humans like about the way we live now – from electric lighting and indoor plumbing to global travel, advanced medicine, flat-screen TVs, and iPhones – depend on our ability to suck, scrape and blast stuff out of the earth. And not just obvious stuff, like oil, coal, and natural gas; modern life, with all its wonders and comforts, is brought to you

> *'The most successful and long lasting human cultures are those which have lived on nature's income rather than nature's capital.'*

by a huge array of natural resources, from metals like copper (used in electrical wiring) and iron ore (steel), to minerals like lithium (batteries) and tantalum (cell phones), to so-called "rare earth elements" (lasers, fiber optics, hybrid car engines, iPads and more). Some are more important than others, of course, but if even a few of them were to run out, we'd be in bad shape.

Well, here's the thing: These critical resources are running out. Virtually all of them.

The world is hurtling towards what author Michael Klare calls "a crisis of resource depletion." In a new book, Klare drops the stunning news that the earth's easily accessible supplies of oil, coal, gas, metals, minerals, rare earths and even water and food are disappearing fast, plunging governments and corporations into a balls-to-the-wall "race for what's left." And what's left is, above all, hard to get at – it's under the Arctic ice, deep below the ocean floor, in tar sands and shale, and in war zones,

A society concerned only with manufacturing new cars and new skyscrapers every year and then breaking them to pieces and making new ones — may be technologically advanced, but it is not a human civilization. A human civilization is advanced when its people follow the catur-varnya system, the system of four orders of life. There must be ideal, first-class men to act as advisors, second-class men to act as administrators, third-class men to produce food and protect cows, and fourth-class men who obey the three higher classes of society. One who does not follow the standard system of society should be considered a fifth-class man. A society without Vedic laws and regulations will not be very helpful to humanity. As stated in this verse, dharmam te na param viduh: such a society does not know the aim of life and the highest principle of religion.
-Srila Prabhupada (Srimad Bhagavatam 6.7.13)

like Afghanistan and the Democratic Republic of the Congo. Getting at it is becoming more and more dangerous, both environmentally – we can expect to see more Gulf-style disasters as companies breach the "final frontiers" of resource extraction – and politically, as countries clash more and more over who gets what.

Holy crap, right? But there's a (somewhat) hopeful part: For some of these resources, there are substitutes, and if we pick up the pace in developing them, we won't have to plunder the planet quite so much; in other cases, we'll just need to learn to do more with less (conservation, efficiency). The essential thing, says Klare, whose new book is called The Race for What's Left, is to start figuring this stuff out right now.

Rolling Stone recently got Michael Klare on the phone to talk about "peak everything," the mad scramble for the world's last resources, and our stark choice of futures.

You say we're facing a "crisis of resource depletion." Are we there yet? Are these must-have resources already disappearing?

They're not disappearing, but many of them are facing rapid decline and depletion. Virtually all of the easily accessible resources are now gone, so were going to need to replace them with new sources of supply.

How can you be sure we're at "the final frontiers," as you put it, of resource extraction?

When you look at what's being developed today, whether it's the deep oceans or the Arctic or shale gas and shale oil, you're seeing levels of investment costs and danger that are unprecedented, and levels of environmental risks that are unlike anything we've seen before. You wouldn't go to these lengths if easier resources were available.

If I read you right, conflict is pretty much inevitable as countries compete to scoop up as much of what's left as they can. Is this already happening?

> "The world has enough for everyone's need, but not for everyone's greed."
> -Mahatma Gandhi

There have been some testy moments. Russia and Norway have had some naval show of force up in the Bering Sea, but they've resolved that for the time being. The East China Sea and the South China Sea, where you have disputed off shore oil and gas fields, are exceedingly tense; we've seen naval clashes between Japan and China and between China and Vietnam and the Philippines. And now President Obama has said that the U.S. is going to become more deeply involved in those areas.

And things could get pretty hairy up in the Arctic.
The Arctic has been totally neglected up until now, but it's seen as the most promising future source of oil and natural gas, so suddenly it has become valuable real estate. Suddenly, national boundaries that nobody cared about before are becoming very important. Ironically, this is partly because the ice sheet is shrinking thanks to climate change, and so you can drill more of the year. Russia claims almost half of the entire Arctic region as its national territory and is seeking to dominate as much of the region as possible. Russian President Vladimir Putin has said he's going to build up Russia's military capabilities in the Arctic in years 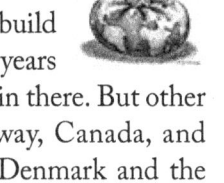 ahead to protect it against anybody else coming in there. But other countries also have claims in the area: Norway, Canada, and Greenland, which is ultimately controlled by Denmark and the United states, so you could have a very intense geopolitical competition for control over these future resources.
(By Julian Brookes for The Rolling Stone)

Extravagance And Inefficacies of Modern Living

From the earliest times, humans have interpreted, shaped and altered their environments in an attempt to improve the quality of their lives. In the process, technologies have evolved and been developed to the extent that, today, they have an impact on most

> *Our culture is like an algae bloom. We are consuming all available resources and then we are going to drown in our own waste.*
> *- Sam Webster*

aspects of our daily lives. But there is an important distinction - technologies in harmony with nature and technologies conflicting with nature. Most of the technologies in vogue today, coupled with our overconsumption, lie at the heart of resource depletion crisis. Overpopulation is not a problem, overconsumption is.

For example, the People's Republic of China has an area comparable to that of the United States of America. China's population density is 4.7 times higher than that of the USA, but its per capita energy consumption is nine times lower than that of the USA, so that in spite of its larger population, China uses only half the amount of energy consumed by the USA.

Americans constitute less than 5% of the world's population, but produce 25% of the world's CO_2, consume 25% of world's resources, including 26% of the world's energy, although having only 3% of the world's known oil reserves, and generate roughly 30% of world's waste. Americans' impact on the environment is at least 250 times greater than a Sub-Saharan African.

More than one century of industrial development, economic growth and intensive exploitation of nature has led us to a world where we can travel cheaply to anywhere in the world, import food,

Because they have no other business. Punah punas carvita-carvananam [SB 7.5.30]. Chewing the chewed. Make a car, break it, and again melt it and again make another car. That's all. This is their civilization, car-making civilization. No spiritual idea, no ambition for spiritual life. But they'll do. They'll do something. So therefore they are making, breaking more. Make the car; break the car; again make the car; again break the car.
-Prabhupada (Lecture, S.B. 2.1.1-5 — June 28, 1977, Vrndavana)

clothes and materials from any country, yet we are slowly destroying the very earth which keeps us alive. Despite increase in automation, we are working harder and harder, and neglecting our lives, both internal and external, to fulfil the demands of industry. The brave new world promised to us by technology has not arrived. Instead it has led to an increased gap between rich and poor within most countries and between countries. Cultures once unique and distinct are slowly merging into variations of Western popular culture. Languages and species are dying out.

The outlook is gloomy! We have a very strong responsibility to the future which we will create. If we wish to improve the situation, we will thus have to modify our ways of life and our manner of consuming because all resources crunch is due to overindulgence. The uneven distribution of food in the world is due not to food shortages but mainly to greed. Much too much land is being exploited for cash crops-junk foods, exports, tobacco, alcohol. Agribusiness is destroying small farms, food prices are soaring, and soil and forests are disappearing fast.

Earth's Resources are Limited and Human Greed is Unlimited
Finite Resources, Infinite Demands

We use things up as though they were infinite. That's bad mathematics. Resources could be considered as Natural Capital. This is capital which cannot be restored. That is, what is labeled by economists as ordinary capital can be restored from depreciation and maintenance funds by spending money. The natural resources of the earth cannot be.

Exact amount of resources available can be considered a debatable subject but there is no doubt that they are finite. If we do not wake up now, our civilization will go the way of Nineveh, Greece and Rome.

In 1972, a report called 'The Limits to Growth' was published.

> "More than 5,000 species become extinct every year - a rate 10,000 times faster than pre-human extinction rates. Half of the forests that originally covered 46% of the Earth's land surface are gone."

It marked the beginning of modern environmental policy. The report highlighted the impossibility of sustaining exponential economic growth and its associated Resource Depletion. Many of the resources that drive our economies are limited and will therefore one day be exhausted, if we continue to use them at current rates.

Thirty-five years after "Limits to Growth," the focus of environmental policy has shifted to other policy fields. For example, we have realised that, in spite of fairly abundant world resources of coal, the limits imposed by the risks of Climate Change will not allow their full exploitation.

The Great Squeeze - A Film

'The Great Squeeze: Surviving the Human Project' is the latest film from Colorado-based Tiroir a Films. This sequel to their 2006 offering, Energy Crossroads: The Burning Need to Change Course, looks to dig deeper into how the concurrent processes of resource depletion, climate change, ecosystem destruction and our consumption-oriented economic model are threatening to destroy both our planet and possibly our very civilization.

Collapse Due To Resource Depletion - A Case Study

On Easter Island (an island in the South Pacific, west of Chile), man-induced resource depletion caused the collapse of a entire civilization. This was caused by a competition by the islanders inhabiting it to build large statues. The statues were carved from the Easter island palm, which they also used to make their boats and to obtain food (fruit, honey and palmwine). As more statues were build and as competition rose, more trees were chopped and due to the recent arrival and infestation of rats from the colonials, the tree was soon extinct. The islanders had less food (they still grew taro, sweet potatoes and bananas) and could no more build

> "Americans throw out nearly twice as much stuff as they did 50 years ago, and twice as much as their European counterparts do today. Ninety-nine percent of the things they buy end up in the landfill within six months of their purchase."

boats to fish. Fish was extremely important part of their diet. Soon, rebellions arose, and fighting was initiated between several clans. Famine then arose and the caste of priests was destroyed. Only a small percentage of the original population survived, and their culture/technological advancement was swept away.

Chopping Down The Branch We Sit On

Many industrialized nations are now growing rapidly and placing ever-greater demands on world resources. Many of those resources come from the presently underdeveloped countries. What will happen when the resource-supplying countries begin to withhold resources because they foresee the day when their own demand will require the available supplies?

Will the developed nations stand by and let their economies

> *The Western civilization is a nasty civilization, artificially increasing the necessities of life. For example, take the electric light. The electric light requires a generator, and to run the generator you need petroleum. As soon as the petroleum supply is stopped, everything will stop. But to get petroleum you have to painstakingly search it out and bore deep into the earth, sometimes in the middle of the ocean. This is ugra-karma, horrible work. The same purpose can be served by growing some castor seeds, pressing out the oil, and putting the oil into a pot with a wick. We admit that you have improved the lighting system with electricity, but to improve from the castor-oil lamp to the electric lamp you have to work very hard. You have to go to the middle of the ocean and drill and then draw out the petroleum, and in this way the real goal of your life is missed. You are in a precarious position, constantly dying and taking birth in various species of life. How to get free of this cycle of birth and death — this is your problem. And this problem is meant to be solved in the human life. You have advanced intelligence for self-realization, but instead of using your advanced intelligence for self-realization, you are utilizing it to improve from the castor-oil lamp to the electric lamp. That's all.*
> *- Srila Prabhupada*

decline while resources still exist in other parts of the world? Will a new era of international conflict grow out of pressures from resource shortage? This will probably be the most important question of 21st Century.

Given our propensity as a species to act in a short term, acquisitional based manner, we will continue to pillage this planet until sheer Malthusian geometry overwhelms our resources, our bio defenses or our collective `sanity'. There seems to be no limits to man's greed. Advertising so easily convinces us that we are not sufficient unto ourselves- that if we will buy `x', we will be happy.

Historically speaking, western colonials killed, raped, tortured, imprisoned, starved, forcibly expelled natives or otherwise forced them to change their lifestyle against their will, all because of insatiable greed. Question remains whether history will repeat itself, that too in a world well-armed with lethal weapons.

Addictive Consumption - An Infectious Disease

Our cultural compulsion towards consumption is addictive and infectious in nature. This has been proven by the design of a model by Benjamin Alamar and Stanton A. Glantz of University of California. Basically the authors have proven that consumption pattern follows the pattern of infectious diseases and craze for a product spreads like an infectious disease too.

Some psychologists have termed this phenomenon as Chronic Shopping Disorder (CSD) and an Obsessive Fixation on Brands.

The dominant model of addictive consumption in economics is the theory of rational addiction. The addict in this model chooses how much they are going to consume based upon their level of addiction (past consumption), the current benefits and all future costs. Several empirical studies of consumer product sales and price data have found a correlation between future prices and

"I would rather have my people laugh at my economies than weep for my extravagance"
~ Oscar II of Sweden

consumption and current consumption. These studies have argued that the correlation validates the rational addiction model and invalidates any model in which future consumption is not considered. An alternative to the rational addiction model is one in which addiction spreads through a population as if it were an infectious disease, as supported by the large body of empirical research of addictive behaviors. In this model an individual's probability of becoming addicted to a substance is linked to the behavior of their parents, friends and society. In the infectious disease model current consumption is based only on the level of addiction and current costs. Price and consumption data from a simulation of the infectious disease model showed a qualitative match to the results of the rational addiction model.

If We All Were To Live Like Americans
Five or Six Earths Would Be Required

The overconsuming, overdeveloped lifestyles and industries of the minority developed world have depended upon the military

My Guru Maharaja used to say that "I don't find any scarcity within this world, except Krsna consciousness."... Actually, that is the fact. There is no scarcity all over the world. In India there may be scarcity, but outside India still there are so much vacant places, especially in Africa, in America, in Australia, in New Zealand, that ten times of the population of the whole world can be fed. Still. There is so much potency of producing food grains, milk, and other things. Profusely. In America, they throw away so many grains and vegetables daily. It is simply mismanagement. Otherwise, there is no question of scarcity or poverty. There is no question. It is simply propaganda. Because they cannot manage, the foolish people, they present the population has increased and the foodstuff is not properly supplied. Foodstuff is always sufficient. But when there are demons, the supply is restricted by nature.
-Srila Prabhupada (Srimad-Bhagavatam 1.2.10 -- Vrndavana, October 21, 1972)

and economic oppression of labour and ecosystems of majority world. For everyone on this planet to 'enjoy' the materialistic lifestyle of the average American or Australian, we would currently need five to six Earths in order to supply the necessary raw materials, handling of consumer and industrial wastes, and life-sustaining services such as clean air and water. Asians and others are waking up to American dream and there is simply not enough resources to facilitate this.

So far, we have only one usable planet. The astronauts are trying

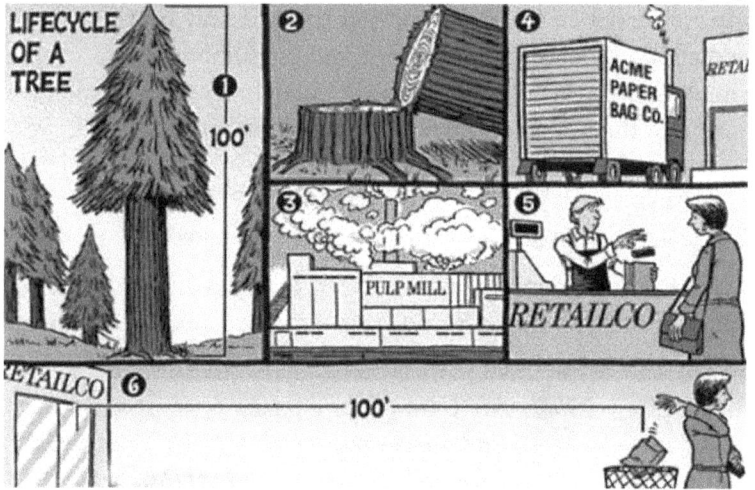

to discover if there are any planets out there that are suitable for humans to live on. This has not produced results. This leaves us to face the fact that the 6.5 billion humans on this rocky sphere are dependent on the natural resources that exist on our planet. Unfortunately, we are using those resources in an unsustainable way right now. Within 100 years, we will have to feed, clothe, and

 *"This cradle to grave flow relies on brute force (including fossil fuels and large amounts of powerful chemicals). It seeks universal design solutions ("one size fits all"), overwhelming and ignoring natural and cultural diversity. And it produces massive amounts of waste – – something that in nature does not even exist." - McDonough*

provide electricity and transportation and water to, around 10 billion humans. 850 million humans go hungry today out of which 220 million are children. 1 in 5 humans have no access to clean drinking water. By 2050, 85% of all humans will be living in developing countries. One third of the world's visible land is affected by desertification, the degradation of productive but fragile lands which have insufficient rainfall and has been damaged by unsustainable development. We are using resources 30% faster than the ability of those resources to renew themselves.

Self-centered Mentality - Me And Mine

Resource depletion originates from a degraded self-centered mentality of me and mine. On individual, social and national level, more than ever before, we have become more self-centered. I should be fine and rest of the world can go to dogs. President Bush is more concerned about the cough of his dog than the death of a million Iraqis. This phenomenal selfishness, apathy and unconcern is responsible for uneven distribution of resources and irresponsible exploitation of the same.

"The richest billion people in the world have created a form of civilization so acquisitive and profligate that the planet is in danger," says Alan Durning of the Worldwatch Institute. "The lifestyle of this top echelon car drivers, beef eaters, soda drinkers, and throwaway consumers-constitutes an ecological threat unmatched in severity."

Instead of wasting our energy to supply ourselves with so many facilities and modern amenities, we should apply intelligence to understand who and what we are. We do not like to suffer, but we should understand why suffering is being forced upon us. By so-called knowledge we have simply succeeded in manufacturing the atomic bomb. Thus the killing process has been accelerated. We are so proud to think that this is advancement of knowledge, but if we can manufacture something that can stop death, we have really advanced in knowledge.
-Srila Prabhupada (On The Way To Krishna)

We are Sailing In The Same Boat

When you think of the world as a system, you understand that air pollution from North America affects air quality in Asia, and that pesticides sprayed in Argentina could harm fish stocks off the coast of Australia. Therefore every individual, community or nation has to realize that its destiny is inextricably connected to the rest of the world. If we are to float, we will float together, if we were to sink, we will sink together.

worlds apart

Nature is one complex system and no nation can isolate itself from it.

Over-mining of Metal Resources

It is not a question of if but just a question of when. How long can we go on extracting natural wealth. Since its all finite in quantity, there will come a day when resources get exhausted.

Lets take the example of platinum. The catalytic converters that keep exhaust pollutants from cars, trucks and buses down to an acceptable level all use platinum. Platinum is a vital component not only of catalytic converters but also of fuel cells - and supplies are running out. It has been estimated that if all the 500 million vehicles in use today were re-equipped with fuel cells, operating losses would mean that all the world's sources of platinum would be exhausted within 15 years. Unlike with oil or diamonds, there is no synthetic alternative: platinum is a chemical element, and once we have used it all there is no way on earth of getting any more.

> 'Civilizations have a tendency to grow and to pursue complexity. Complexity is subject to diminishing returns and we have passed the point of diminishing returns.'

It's not just the world's platinum that is being used up at an alarming rate. The same goes for many other rare metals such as indium, which is being consumed in unprecedented quantities for making LCDs for flat-screen TVs, and the tantalum needed to make compact electronic devices like cellphones. How long will global reserves of uranium last in a new nuclear age? Even reserves of such commonplace elements as zinc, copper, nickel and the phosphorus used in fertiliser will run out in the not-too-distant future. So just what proportion of these materials have we used up so far, and how much is there left to go round? Recently, even coal prices have also gone up threefold internationally.

Resource Depletion Damages Third World - World Bank

According to a new World Bank study, resource depletion is draining the net "savings" of the world's poorest countries and could cripple future generations.

According to it, a new measure of wealth - which goes beyond the traditional gross domestic product yardstick - showed many developing countries were sinking deeply into the red. Accounting for the actual value of natural resources, including resource depletion and population growth, shows that net savings per person are negative in the world's most impoverished countries, particularly in sub-Saharan Africa.

Resource Depletion In Third World - A Case Study

Third world is being ravaged and pillaged to satisfy the consumer greed in North America and western Europe.

Let us take the case of Papua New Guinea (PNG). If it can properly be described as a 'nation', it is a nation which seems to consist entirely of 'indigenous peoples' - or what Papua New Guineans themselves would rather call 'customary landowners' - whose collective sovereignty resides in what was once described as

He who is extravagant will quickly become poor; and poverty will enforce dependence, and invite corruption. — Samuel Johnson

a 'parliament of a thousand tribes. For thousands of years, these indigenous people have led a natural and simple life but just in last few decades, the glare of dollars has led them become passive spectators to destruction of their home land by greedy foreign companies.

At the forefront of destruction are the mining and petroleum projects. But not much has been written about the local social impact of logging or forestry projects.

Nowhere have these shortcomings been more painfully evident than in the forestry sector. In the wake of a 1979 white paper which recommended an increase in log exports as a means of raising government revenues, a dubious array of foreign logging companies descended on the nation's shores, and most were allowed to operate without regard to the Environmental Planning Act.

In April 1987 the Prime Minister, Paias Wingti, appointed an Australian lawyer, Tos Barnett, to conduct a Commission of Inquiry into what Barnett himself later described as the 'heavy odour of corruption, fraud and scandal arising from the timber industry'. Two years of investigations revealed a scene of 'rampage and pillage' in many lowland areas.

Operations were being commenced illegally; forest working plans, if submitted at all, were being widely ignored; logging tracks were being pushed through at the discretion of the bulldozer driver; hillsides and river banks were being logged; and the immature forest resource was being bashed and trampled in the reckless haste to

> Bhagavan: (car screeches as passing by) So fast and they go nowhere.
> Prabhupada: He is proud that "How fast I can drive!" Just see. And where you are going? "I am going to hell, that's all. Never mind." That is described in the Bhagavad-gita. Just like the flies. They are coming very forcefully. Where? In the fire. Pat! Pa! Pa! Pa! Pa!" They are very busy. And as soon as on the fire, finished. Just see. Very busy. Without inquiring, "Where I am going so forcefully?" But they are going to the fire.
> -Srila Prabhupada

get the logs down to the waiting log ships. The dazed and disillusioned forest owners stood watching in disbelief as foreign operators removed their trees before moving on to the next area, leaving environmentally disastrous logged-over hillsides, temporary gravel/mud roads and rotting log bridges to erode and cave in to clog the watercourses.

In order to gain access to the timber, foreign operators misled and bribed local leaders, set up 'puppet' native landowner companies, bribed provincial government premiers or ministers and gave gifts or bribes to national ministers or members of the national parliament or took such people into some form of partnership with them.

China - A Hub of Illegally Felled Timber

Consumer demand in Europe, Japan and the US for reasonably priced furniture and other Chinese wood products is feeding a growing appetite in China for imports of illegally felled timber.

According to the report by US-based Forest Trends and the Beijing-based Centre for Chinese Agricultural Policy, China has become the world's biggest wood workshop in less than a decade. Chinese manufacturers account for 30 per cent of the world's furniture trade, with the value of China's exports of forest products rising from $3.6bn in 1997 to $17.2bn last year. Big markets such as the US and European Union have increased imports of Chinese wood products by 900 per cent over the same period.

Until now a lot of the focus has been on China's role as a destination market for illegally harvested timber. One of the key messages coming out of this report is that China is right in the middle of a global commodity chain that is driven in large part by consumers in North America and Europe.

In the meantime we are pushing up against some definite limits here, and in the short run we can only see the problem getting worse.

Profuseness is a cruel and crafty demon, that gradually involves her followers in dependence and debt; that is, fetters them with irons that enter into their souls. — *Samuel Johnson*

A State Turning Into A Barren, Toxic Wasteland By Indiscriminate Mining - All In The Name of Tribal Development
A Case Study of Orissa (India)

Orissa, a state in eastern India, is having the largest number of tribal groups in the country and they constitute about a third of the state's population. Government of Orissa has undertaken a number of 'development projects' for the welfare of the indigenous tribals over the last two decades and the net outcome of which has been distress migration, malnutrition, drought and crop failures.

These tribals have taken up arms to protect their lands and their agriculture. The state government's first brush with tribals took place in December 2000, when it pushed for an aluminium project. Several tribals where killed in clashes with police which came to evict them.

There is also a proposed steel industry which requires more than 30,000 hectares of land which is densely populated by the tribals. Conservative estimates reveal that at least 15,000 families will be evicted losing their homes. 60,000 more will lose their land and livelihood. Also, a large number of families will be occupationally displaced. For this reasons they have become more vicious. Lately, all this has led to arise in Maoist militancy in the state's tribal belt.

Prtyush Piyush, a tribal lifestyle research scholar mentions, "If this type of industrialisation continues in the state, we will not see our rich culture, heritage and tradition, even it will not be available in the museums." Orissa, like rest of India, has a predominantly agrarian population. The several memorandums of understanding that have been signed with various industrialists have already caused much dissent and dissatisfaction in different parts of the state.

Narendra Maharana, an NGO worker says, "The work is proceeding with blatant disregard for human life. From Kasipur to Lanjigad and Kalinganagar everywhere state police crack upon

If humanity has the will, it has the ways to live within the means of the planet.
- James Leape

villagers, using *lathis*, threats and even sexual abuse. Innocent villagers now have serious legal charges against them. Many have been served non-bailable warrants. For the 'development' of the tribal people, a large-capacity jail has been planned near the proposed industrial town!"

Another activity causing havoc in Orissa is bauxite mining, which is one of the most environmentally-destructive processes known. The slag to ore ratio is 3:1, which means that for every tonne of alumina produced, there will be three tonnes of highly caustic slag. This will be dumped as red mud in downstream areas, destroying agricultural land, surface and sub-soil water, and causing unnamed diseases and ailments.

Environmental activist Biswajit Mohanty says, "The state government has adopted a myopic and self-destructive policy of exhausting the entire stock of 3,120 million tonnes of iron ore and 1,626 million tonnes of bauxite within 20 to 25 years. This will result in massive environmental degradation as the region's carrying capacity to absorb and assimilate effluents and wastes produced due to such gigantic production facilities, which will soon be exhausted several times over, within a very short time period."

With the quantum of steel and aluminium extraction that is planned for Orissa, the state will turn into a barren, toxic wasteland. The processing of all metals, steel and aluminium particularly, requires huge quantities of water and leaves behind a toxic waste stream. What rivers remain after the catchments have been cleared will run full of toxins, unfit for human or animal use. This is not some doomsday, far-in-the-future scenario, it as has already happened in the case of the Damodar River in Jharkhand (coal mining) and the Bhadra River in Karnataka (iron ore).

Almost all major concentrations of coal, bauxite and iron ore are concentrated in forest areas. The same areas that are home to the country's dwindling indigenous cultures and biodiversity.

Wisdom seldom consorts with extravagance.
- Menedemus

Peak Oil - A Silent Tsunami Approaching Humanity

Oil is the lifeblood of modern civilization. Choke off the oil and it quickly seizes.

With no viable alternatives in sight, human society is facing a great crisis of unprecedented scale. All the previous calamities were local in nature. Oil crisis would be a global disaster because the world today shares a common fate.

Before the present lull, the headlines were blaring like "Shell chief fears oil shortage in seven years", "Spectre of food rationing hits US amidst global food crisis ", "Futures Market Traders Bet On $200/Barrel Oil In 2008", "Oilcos plan to ration fuel supply", "British truckers protest rising fuel prices", " Oil shock: Airlines cut flights, expansion plans" etc.

Stopgap solutions can not help as the nature and environment can not be cheated. In trying to do so, we end up cheating our ownselves. We have to get to the root of the problem which is an unsustainable life style, life style with hardly any reverence towards nature and its creator.

Our Lives Our Utterly Dependent on Cheap Oil

We have allowed oil to become vital to virtually everything we do. Ninety per cent of all our transportation, whether by land, air or sea, is fuelled by oil. Ninety-five per cent of all goods in shops involve the use of oil. Ninety-five per cent of all our food products require oil use.

Thus the three main purposes for which oil is used worldwide are food, transport and heating. In the near future the competition for oil for these three activities will be raw and real. But still reliable supplies of cheap oil and natural gas underlie everything we identify as the necessities of modern life - not to mention all of its comforts and luxuries: central heating, air conditioning, cars, airplanes, electric

The entire world economy rests on the consumer; if he ever stops spending money he doesn't have on things he doesn't need — we're done for.
~Bill Bonner

lights, inexpensive clothing, recorded music, movies, hip-replacement surgery, national defense - you name it.

Imagine a day of your life without oil! Well its almost impossible to escape oil's influence for even a single day in our lives. Did you wake up to a plastic alarm clock after a restful night? Thank petroleum for the mosquito repellent, both bottle and liquid. And did you put on your eye glasses? Then you started your this day with petroleum too. The frame and plastic lens owe their origin to oil. When you get ready to shave, your shaving cream, razor body and deodorant contain petroleum products as important ingredients. Your bathroom pvc door and toilet seats, where do they come from? You guessed it right. Then comes toothbrush, an outright petroleum based product and toothpaste, with petrochemical-enhanced artificial coloring and mineral oils. You are living with oil in your mouth if you are wearing dentures. After shower when you put your lip balm, you have used a petroleum product once again.

> *Poverty is often concealed in splendor.*
> *–Samuel Johnson*

While still in shower, you rush to answer a phone call and it is all oil based plastic. Suddenly your tiny tot requires a change of diapers and its linings are fathered by petroleum too. After shower, when you put on your formals, you are again draped in oil because all synthetic fabrics originate therefrom. And when you put on your leather shoes with synthetic soles, once again you step into the realms of oil. Then as you quickly spray perfume, you have sprayed oil. Then to avoid drizzle, you put on your raincoat. Lo and behold! You have added another layer of oil on your existence.

But what about streets. You guessed it right! Streets are paved with asphalt, a sticky byproduct remaining after refining crude oil.

> *And whatever produce they get, sometimes they dump tons of it into the ocean to keep the prices high. And I have heard here in Geneva that when there was excess milk production, some of the people wanted to slaughter twenty thousand cows just to reduce the milk production. This is what is going on in people's brains. Actually, they have no brains.*
> — *Srila Prabhupada*

End of Modern Civilization and Alternative Future

Of course no need to discuss what goes in your car to run and lubricate it. In your office canteen, your breakfast comes off a non stick pan and this too is a petroproduct. Of course food production and transport is also at the mercy of petroleum because most of the fertilizers and pesticides are harvested from oil. Then as you insert a CD or DVD, you have handled oil once again. So is with your credit and debit cards, bunch of which your wallet holds. And yet same again with your wallet whether it is leather or rexine. Leather too requires petrochemicals for tanning and processing. Well if all this is beginning to give you a headache and you would like to pop in an aspirin, guess where it comes from. Answer again would be the same.

"We Shell not EXXONerate Saddam Hussein for his actions. We will Mobilize to meet this threat to vital interests in the Persian Gulf until an [Amo]ble solution is reached. Our best strategy is to BP repared. Failing that, we ARCO ming to kick you

Petroleum follows you when in the evening you head for a round of golf. Yes the ball is practically oil solidified. We are merged or shall we say drowning, from toe to head, in an ocean of oil. Unfortunately this ocean is limited in its dimensions and full of fearsome waves of uncertain supplies.

Thus almost every current human endeavour from transportation, to manufacturing, to electricity to plastics, and especially food production is inextricably intertwined with oil and natural gas supplies.

World Energy Forecasts - Bleak Future

At present the heavily industrialized United States, with only 5% of the world's population, is using more than 30% of the world's

> *If we don't change our course, we'll end up where we're headed.*
> *- Chinese proverb*

energy output. But how long can this situation last? To catch up to the United States, the rest of the world is racing to industrialize, but the world's limited energy reserves make the end of the energy bonanza inevitable.

There is a saudi proverb which says, " My father rode a camel; I drive a car; my son flies a jet; his son will ride a camel."

Reality is that we have to bid good bye to oil one day. Its not a question of what or if, but just a question of when. And the thing is we don't have to run out of oil to start having severe problems with industrial civilization and its dependent systems. We only have to slip over the all-time production peak and begin a slide down the arc of steady depletion. In other words, we won't have to run completely out of oil to be rudely awakened. The panic starts once the world needs more oil than it gets. The key event in the Petroleum Era is not when the oil runs out, but when oil production peaks. Just like they thought that the Titanic was unsinkable. The upcoming end of cheap oil seems to have surprised markets. The exponential increase in demand for fossil fuels seems to have come as an unpleasant surprise. The alternative sources of power: solar, wind, nuclear, tidal, etc. are not as energy dense, portable, or as readily usable as fossil fuels.History tells us that complete development of new energy sources (coal and oil in the past) takes a long time, at least about half a century. The peak in fossil energy extraction will expose the fallacy of limitless growth.

Recently in US, the National Petroleum Council, a body of 175 authorities that reports to the US government, presented a 420-page report which is considered the most comprehensive study ever carried out into the industry and includes the heads of the world's big oil companies including ExxonMobil, Chevron, ConocoPhillips, Occidental Petroleum, Shell and BP. The report concludes that the global supply of oil and natural gas may run short by 2015.

Many of our short sighted politicians and officials are simply

Extravagance is its own destroyer.
- Zeno

busy filling their coffers and we can not expect any concrete measures from them. This is the time to build a mass opinion to save our planet, to save our resources. It is surprising that so little awareness exists about this cataclysm and so little is being done about a problem which can choke the very life line of our civilization, both on official as well as grassroot levels. People are going about their chores, driving around in SUVs, hopping about in jets as if nothing has happened and as if the government will just handle everything. Reality is that we can no longer take cheap energy for granted and on national and international levels and energy planning has to percolate down into our lives. Every short walk, every cycling scuttle, every switching off a light or turning off a tap will give extra lease of life to human society.

> *He who buys what he needs not, sells what he needs.*
> *-Japanese Proverb*

Threat - 4

Moral, Ethical and Spiritual Ruination

Technological revolution that we witnessed in the last century has gone so far for our human moral to catch up with.
~Hun Sen

Arnold J. Toynbee in the mid-twentieth century, explored civilization processes and traced the rise and, in most cases, the decline of 21 civilizations. Civilizations generally declined and fell, according to Toynbee, because of moral or religious decline, rather than economic or environmental causes. Many other scholars also see sobering parallels between the decadence of ancient civilizations in their decline and the decadence of World culture today.

One of the significant developments of the last 50 years has been the dramatic shift away from ethical-religious values that provide the foundation of any civilization. Older generations wonder why this is happening and where it will lead. Younger people seem oblivious to the concern. While some analysts realize why this is occurring, most have no idea where these changes will lead to.

Media which controls the popular mind set has become increasingly callous and hostile to ethical-religious values. Public schools today demand value-neutrality. Religious leaders are increasingly prone to ambiguity and compromise in vital areas of doctrine and morals and are disregarding universal principles of goodness. State has outlawed God in public places while claiming that 'In God We Trust'.

The result has been a surge in divorce, cohabitation, sexual promiscuity, perversion, teen pregnancy, abortions, child abuse, drug

> *Popular culture has been infected by nonsense - nonsense about truth and reality, nonsense about self, nonsense about thought and feeling. These false views have had a devastating effect on peoples lives leading to the breakdown of the family, self-indulgence, and undermining the pursuit of excellence.*
> *~Vincent Ruggerio*

abuse, rape, cheating, shoplifting, embezzling, bankruptcy, incivility, and violent crime—the very things God prophesied would happen to nations that forsake His laws.

The intellectual elite of the world - academics, writers, filmmakers, television producers, liberal politicians and theologians are promoting "do-your-own-thing morality". Over several decades they have waged an all-out assault on common sense and the common traditional values and we thus appear to be witnessing the gradual abdication of tradition and culture. Even religious authorities who are supposed to protect and strengthen the moral fabric of society, have taken a hike by downplaying sin and the importance of marriage while condoning promiscuity, easy divorce and homosexuality. All this being done at a time when people need strong moral and spiritual guidance more than ever before.

The Immorality Explosion
Moral Standards Falling Fast And Inexorably To Barbarity

Our moral standards are in steep decline. What's worse is that as older generations pass away, fewer and fewer of present generation are even aware of the decline. Younger class probably think that today's standards have always been so.

Now a days for vast majority of the people, the qualities of honesty, sincerity, having high moral standards are no longer valued, rather for them these are meaningless qualities which have no relevance in the present day world. People are increasingly mired in selfishness, corruption, knavery and other wrong doings. Today one can do anything to meet his or her narrow ends. The pace at

In ancient Egypt, Carthage, Greece and Rome, the collapse of society began each time with a period of obvious moral decay. Every one of the symptoms of decline are present in this nation today... to ignore such lessons is to court disaster
-Black

which people are giving up their values, future of human society remains a debatable topic.

Proud To Be Immoral And Adulterous

North America has television shows like 'Jerry Springer', 'Jenny Jones', 'Ricki Lake' and 'Montel Williams'. These programs feature guests telling detailed stories of deviant behaviour, such as mothers sleeping with their daughter's boyfriend, kids who curse and threaten their parents, parents who teach their kids how to shoplift and incest stories at times. It seems as though acceptance or rejection of their deviant behavior is measured by the applause of a degraded audience. Deviancy and immorality are not new in human history.

30% of American women and 60% of men have extramarital affairs, while 66% of both believe that they will go to heaven.

What's new is the willingness of people to put bizarre lifestyles on display to millions of strangers. Even worse is the relative absence of social sanction. Years ago, people would have

So similarly, when people will be so much degraded that they will not be able to understand anything about God... That time is coming gradually. Already the time is there. People are not at all interested in God's business. In your Western world all the churches are vacant. Nobody is interested now in church. Especially in Europe, we have seen... In your country also. So people are being degraded, godlessness. Because godless means animal. What is the difference between animal and man? The animal cannot be instructed anything about God. It is not possible for them to understand. But a man, however degraded he may be, if he is trained up, he can understand about God.
-Srila Prabhupada (Srimad-Bhagavatam 1.3.25 — Los Angeles, September 30, 1972)

Threat 4 - Moral, Ethical, Spiritual Ruination

been personally ashamed if others knew about their corrupt lifestyles. They'd try to hide it rather than go on national television or radio to broadcast it. Now various other countries are copying these American programs.

Decency, Chastity Gone Down Under

Sexual overtones permeate every aspect of modern society. Media is filled up and based upon sex. It has become the guiding principle in people's lives. Products and services are marketed on the basis of sex appeal.

Then there are television advertisements featuring female personal-hygiene products, with pictures and descriptions that leave little room for the imagination. Discretion is a thing of the past. Years ago, for example, sanitary napkins were discretely sold and wrapped in plain brown paper. Condoms were sold with similar discretion. Decency is a thing of past.

Most of human behavior cannot and should not be regulated by law. Informal codes of conduct and moral standards provide the glue that holds society together. When these codes and standards, sometimes called traditional values, are ignored, trivialized or forgotten, we take another step toward barbarism and incivility.

Hari-sauri: The whole civilization is completely crazy.
Prabhupada: Kartikeya told me. After many years he went to see his mother, and mother was going to ball dance. And mother said, "Wait, I am coming back." And he was surprised. He told me. Son has come home after many years, and she could not talk with him. She was going to ball dance.
-Srila Prabhupada (Room Conversation -- July 4, 1976, Washington D.C.)

The Dot Net Generation - A Generation of Undisciplined Barbarians?

Modern entertainment is so saturated with sex, violence and anarchy that normal relationships, respect for law and order and the value of human life are disappearing—especially in the young. Many young people today have no sense of discipline, no goals, no direction and they are kind of lost in their ownselves.

All over world, there is reemergence of a "pagan mentality" that believes "there is no fixed truth, no final good, no ultimate meaning or purpose, and that the concept of God is a primitive illusion.

Great nations like United States, Germany, France, Great Britain, Canada and Australia are finally entering a 'post-Christian' age.

Teen Pregnancy & Abortion

Teen pregnancy is a major issue to many people all across the globe. Many efforts are being made to educate youth about sexual activities and birth controlling methods but there is hardly any education on abstinence or self control.

This is also an important cause for the spread of AIDS. Early and rapid exposure to sex, early marriages and rise in sexual abuse are some of the reasons for the rise in teen pregnancy, which usually occurs between the age group of 16-19.

Most of the teen mothers drop out of school are physically weak and are not economically self-sufficient. The children of teen mothers are more likely to have developmental delays, may get involved in anti-social activities and if the child is illegitimate it may be ill-treated by the society.

Nearly 1 million teens in US alone and nearly 6 million worldwide become pregnant each year; 78% of these pregnancies are unintended.

In US, every year 3 million teens - about 1 in 4 sexually

The gross heathenism of civilization has generally destroyed nature, and poetry, and all that is spiritual.
~John Muir

experienced teens - acquire a sexually transmitted infection. Approximately half of all new HIV infections in the US occur among young people under age 25.

And as far as abortion is concerned, in year 2008 alone, nearly 42 million babies were killed in the womb all over the world. Put simply, per day, 115,000 babies were killed in 2008. This translates into 80 babies every minute.

Evil Is Good, Good Is Evil
The Deviant Is Normal And The Normal Is Deviant

Public today is condoning or at least is nonjudgmental about behavior long considered disgraceful and immoral.

What about personal character? Take the example of a former US President who had his lawyers seeking an out-of-court settlement on charges of indecent exposure, not to mention presiding over a scandal-a-day administration. Yet he received high approval ratings from the general population.

Clinton's moral lapses say little about the man himself. He's just one among thousands of men who have cheated on their wives or have been charged with indecent exposure. The fact that he became president, was re-elected and retains a high approval rating does say something about the new standards people have for what's acceptable conduct. This is probably the first time in history that a open womanizer could have been elected and re-elected president, and, in the face of one scandal after another, get high public-approval ratings.

Then there is French President Nicolas Sarkozy, who is living with a former model Carla Bruni. When he was touring Asia, some of the hosting leaders were in a fix and they feared public backlash as cohabiting is considered prostitution in their cultures.

 *"If a man walks in the woods for love of them half of each day, he is in danger of being regarded as a loafer. But if he spends his days as a speculator, shearing off those woods and making the earth bald before her time, he is deemed an industrious and enterprising citizen."*
-Henry David Thoreau

Sensing trouble, the President dumped his partner from the tour.

A nude photograph of Carla, France's first lady, has been auctioned for $91,000. To top it all, in what is being called in diplomatic circles as an unprecedented and dangerous move, she,

France's first lady, has stripped for a pay-per-view special and given the proceeds to Somalian kidnappers in order to secure the freedom of their hostages aboard a French-owned cruise ship just off the coast of Africa.

Bedlam erupted in the security council chamber of the United Nations as furious diplomats took the government of France to task when the 'Breasts for Hostages' campaign was finally uncovered. It seems that leaders of countries within the southern hemisphere were seen as having no qualms about using their wives in such a manner.

Child Abuse

Child abuse is the physical, psychological or sexual maltreatment of children. Most child abuse happens in a child's home, with a smaller amount occurring in the organizations, schools or communities they interact with. There are four major categories of child abuse: neglect, physical abuse, psychological/emotional abuse, and sexual abuse.

Many children today are unwanted and uninvited arrivals, resulting from uncontrolled passions. Naturally they become subjected to abuse in various forms. According to a UNICEF report on child well-being, the United States and the United Kingdom ranked highest among first world nations with respect to the

 *It is related that someone asked the late President Kruger whether there was gold in the moon. He replied that it was highly unlikely because, if there were, the English would have annexed it. Money is their God.   -Gandhi*

maltreatment of their children. This study also found that child neglect and child abuse are far more common in single-parent families than in families where both parents are present.

Children with a history of neglect or physical abuse are at risk of developing psychiatric and physical health problems. Also they have higher criminal tendencies. Approximately 15% to 25% of women and 5% to 15% of men were sexually abused when they were children. The WHO estimates that 150 million girls and 73 million boys under 18 have experienced forced sexual intercourse or other forms of sexual violence involving physical contact, though this is certainly an underestimate.

Most sexual abuse offenders are acquainted with their victims; approximately 30% are relatives of the child, most often fathers, uncles or cousins; around 60% are other acquaintances such as friends of the family, babysitters, or neighbors; strangers are the offenders in approximately 10% of child sexual abuse cases *(Family Research Laboratory, US)*. In India, a report by Ministry of Women and Child Development says that in a Government conducted survey, 53.22% children in 13 states reported having faced one or more forms of sexual abuse.

Political instability and other internal disturbances, including conditions of insurgency in many countries are also creating major problems, with increasing number of child soldiers, refugee children, trafficked children and children on the streets.

According to the report published in 2005 on 'Trafficking in Women and Children in India', India is a major source and destination country for trafficked children from within India and adjoining countries and it has by conservative estimates, three to five lakh girl children in commercial sex and organized prostitution. (Sen, S & Nair P. M., 2005)

We have created an industrial order geared to automatism, where feeble-mindedness, native or acquired, is necessary for docile productivity in the factory; and where a pervasive neurosis is the final gift of the meaningless life that issues forth at the other end.
~Lewis Mumford

Child sexual abuse became a public issue in the 1970s and 1980s. Prior to this point in time sexual abuse remained rather secretive and socially unspeakable. Studies on child molestation were nonexistent until the 1920s and the first national estimate of the number of child sexual abuse cases was published in 1948 in US. By 1968, 44 out of 50 U.S. states had enacted mandatory laws that required physicians to report cases of suspicious child abuse. Legal action began to become more prevalent in the 1970s with the enactment of the Child Abuse Prevention and Treatment Act in 1974 in conjunction with the creation of the National Center for Child Abuse and Neglect. Since the creation of the Child Abuse and Treatment Act, reported child abuse cases have "increased" dramatically.

Nudity Explosion

In the opinion of Darwin, humans have come from monkeys and for Darwin's followers it is only appropriate to display monkeyism of nudity.

In today's world, an outfit is rarely considered beautiful if the wearer does not bare a little flesh. Necklines are plunging deeper and wider and because so much is bared, a normal cleavage no longer arrests attention. To get attention, some women go the extra mile leaving nothing to imagination.

> *Srila Prabhupada: Human life is meant for cultivating God consciousness. But in the modern so-called advanced civilization, instead of cultivating God consciousness people are cultivating nudity. Isn't it so? So nature will punish them:*
> *"All right, you want to be nude? Then become a tree and remain standing naked for five thousand years." Trees sometimes live up to five thousand years. I've seen them in a park near San Francisco.*
> *Devotee: But they argue that if God wanted us to wear clothes. He would have made us with clothes.*
> *Devotee: We could argue with the nudists that by their logic, if God had wanted us to have food He would have made us with food, too. Just as you have to work for your food, you also have to work for your clothes.*
> *(Conversation)*

Threat 4 - Moral, Ethical, Spiritual Ruination

So much has been bared that these days, men get impatient with little or no exposure at all. For you to be noticed, you have to bare a lot. Why are a lot of older women involved in this practice they see as fashion? A woman blamed the development on the problems created by younger women. "What do you want the housewife to do when her husband is busy looking at younger women who wear skimpy clothes and display their firm bodies?

"How many women like what they see when they stand in front of the mirror?" A lot of women after having children, feel uncomfortable with their bodies. So, when they are able to get their bodies 'lifted', mainly through plastic surgery, they want to flaunt what they've got. The competition is very raw and stiff.

So much for clothing and its complications. Now public nudity is becoming more common with nude sporting and other activities being held. These include naked hiking, nude canoeing, naked skating, the World Naked Bike Ride, Solstice Cyclists, and modern art movements and nude news on TV. No general public outcry has accompanied these events.

In many countries and in some US states, public nudity is legal and protected as free speech, as long as there is no "intent to arouse". In many other countries, police can only 'invite' a nude person to dress up but can not force. All over the world, many nudist resorts have come up. Nudity at many beaches is legal and common. If you work in a restaurant in New York City, the chances are you've seen a lot more shocking things than a room full of naked diners.

As the twenty-first century dawns, American culture is in a mess... the system has lost its moorings, and, like ancient Rome is drifting into a dysfunctional situation.
~Morris Berman (The Twilight of American Culture)

Yoga classes across America are encouraging participants to expose their 'inner selves'. There you have to obey two rules - leave your clothes behind, and bring your own mat. Its easier than ever before to get lost in an 'attire-optional' crowd. As the saying goes, 'if you've got it flaunt it.'

Nudity in media, advertising and films is on the rise. Portrayal of body is becoming more explicit. They cannot make any TV program or film that does not incorporate some 'demented instinct driven human primates rutting every episode, four times an hour.'

Promiscuity & Perversion

To say that we are living in times heavily saturated with sex and the myriad ways by which it is being expressed and experienced is an understatement. It is virtually impossible to go through a day without being exposed to images and language which bluntly remind us that God's sacred gift of sexuality has been disgraced, distorted, abused, misused, and perverted!

"Sexting," sending nude or partially nude photos via cell phone, is becoming more and more common among high school students. Twenty-two percent of 13 to 19-year-old girls and 18 percent of

Due to their extraordinary materialistic way of life, the so-called "civilised" human society has degraded to the position of the animals. They are now dancing naked on the public stage and so-called "respectable" persons are going to enjoy such performances. The animals wander here and there naked, the monkeys walk naked; even the aborigines in the jungles, they also cover their private parts by some skin or tree or leaf. I do not know how the so-called "civilised" men are gliding to the stage of animal life, and still they are proud of their advancement of education and civilisation. So the disease of human society is becoming more and more acute, and Lord Caitanya desired that the Indians should preach this cult for the benefit of human society. Unfortunately, the present generation of Indians is more attracted to technological knowledge than this cult of Krishna consciousness. Their position is very precarious.
-Srila Prabhupada (Letter to Bali-mardana, January 1970)

13 to 19-year-old boys have taken or electronically sent nude pictures of themselves, according to The National Campaign to Prevent Teen and Unplanned Pregnancy's survey in US.

Sexting usually begins with a young girl taking a picture of herself and sending it to her boyfriend. When they break up, the boy will send the picture to all his friends. To prevent teen sexting, many high schools are planning to teach texting safety.

Then there is mass mooning, an act of displaying one's bare buttocks by removing clothing, usually bending over. Mooning is being used to express protest, scorn, disrespect or provocation but also being done for shock value or fun. In 2006, a Maryland USA court of appeal determined that mooning is a form of 'artistic expression' protected by the United States constitutional right of freedom of speech!

The Annual Mooning of Amtrak is a long-running annual tradition in California, U.S.A, where many people spend all day mooning at Amtrak trains; some even ride the trains on that day just so they can witness the event. This mooning has spawned a chain of "train moonings" throughout the entire country. In July 2008, 8,000 people participated in the 'festivities'.

In June 2000, a mass mooning event was organised outside of Buckingham Palace in the United Kingdom by the Movement Against the Monarchy (MAM). The idea was for anti-monarchists to show their dislike of the British monarchy by performing a mass mooning at their home.

"In those days, it was easy to tell a prostitute from a decent lady through her dressing. When young girls strayed from decency, their parents, particularly their mothers immediately whipped them back on line. Today, the story is so different. You can barely differentiate decent and indecent ladies via their dressing. Housewives are dressing no different from prostitutes. What is happening? There is a shift in values and prostitution is relocating to homes and family life."
~Pastor Enoch Adeboye

Rising Crime

The definition of what constitutes a crime depends on the social and political factors in a particular society, and the nature of crime can change over time. For example thirty five years ago, abortion was a crime in almost all countries of the world including US but today it is perfectly legal to kill babies in the womb. Same goes with homosexuality etc.

Since 1960, per capita crime rates have more than tripled, while violent crime rates have nearly quintupled. By any measure, we live in a world much less safe than that in which our parents grew up. US Department of Justice estimated that 83 percent of all Americans are victims of violent crime at least once in their lives. About a quarter would be victims of three or more violent crimes.

Increasing crime rate means more murders, rapes, robberies, aggravated assaults, burglaries, and auto thefts. At about 50 per 100,000, Washington DC has the highest murder rate in the developed world, more than a hundred times that of the capital of the European Union, Brussels. The highest murder rate for a large city in Europe is in Moscow, 15 per 100,000 per year.

Violence is also increasing among teenagers and other youths. Crime is not a function of poverty but the overall moral fabric of the society. The total number of prisoners in the United States increased from 319,000 in 1980 to 1.3 million in 1999. Another 523,000 people were also in jail. This translates into 1 in every 150 Americans being in prison or jail. The present ratio of the population in prison is more than four times what it was in the

"There is something even more valuable to civilization than wisdom, and that is character"
~ Henry Louis Mencken

mid 1970s, five times the rate of imprisonment in Britain, eight times the rate in France and 14 times the rate in Japan. This is disturbing for a society perceived as law abiding and which inscribes its currency with "In God We Trust." Crime and a godly society are not compatible.

Since 1980, the United States has engaged in the largest jails buildup of any country in the history of the world. So much money and man-hours are required for just the fingerprinting, photography and paperwork involved. Stuffed into police files are about 50 million criminal records—enough to represent nearly one-fifth of the entire U.S. population. One would think the extraordinary expansion of the criminal justice system

Formerly the kings were so... The king himself used to judge. A criminal was brought before the king, and if the king thought it wise, he would take his own sword, immediately cut his head. That was the duty of king. Even not many, about hundred years ago in Kashmir, the king, as soon as a thief was caught, he would be brought before the king, and if he is proved that he was a thief, he has stolen, immediately the king will cut off his hands personally, chopped off. Even hundred years ago. So all other thieves warned, "This is your punishment." This one example will stop millions of thieves not to commit stealing. So there was no thieving. There was no stealing, no burglary in Kashmir. Even somebody lost something on the road, it will lie there. Nobody will touch it. The order was, king's order was, "If something is lying on the street uncared for, you cannot touch it. The man who has left it, he would come; he will collect. You cannot take." Even hundred years ago. So this capital punishment is required. Nowadays the capital punishment is excused. Murderers are not hanged. This is all mistake, all rascaldom. A murderer must be killed. No mercy. Why a human killer? Even an animal killer should be immediately hanged? That is kingdom. The king should be so strict.
- Srila Prabhupada (Bhagavad-gita 2.3 -- London, August 4, 1973)

would have made at least a small dent in the crime rate! But no. Almost two thirds of those released are convicted again for committing new crimes. It has been estimated that one quarter of all inmates are victims of sexual assault each year during incarceration. The overall rate of confirmed AIDS cases for prisoners in 1995 was more than six times the rate for the general population.

Porno Plague

As technology progressed with development of photography, wire and tape recording, motion pictures, video cameras and camcorders, so did the industry that sought to exploit human sexuality make great strides forward as well. Businesses sprang up throughout the countries whose sole purpose was the marketing of a variety of literary and visual materials focusing on every conceivable kind of sexual indulgence!

It was the icing on the cake — a double scoop of gravy on the potatoes — the long awaited bonus — it was the conquering of the Mt. Everest of human sexuality with the advent of the internet.

It is not without exaggeration to say that with the rapid expansion of home computer purchases with the fringe benefit of home privacy and the establishment of the internet, "all hell broke loose!"

As with a fast growing deadly cancer, so the immoral exploitation of human sexuality quickly became a multi billion dollar business enterprise whose tentacles reached out to persons of all ages through an incalculable number of websites.

Commercialization Of Human Sexuality

Sex sells. If you want to be successful in your business of selling goods and services, then use scantily dressed (or undressed) young women in your ads. Whether you are selling toothpaste, soap powder, motor oil, pizza, or advertising your air-conditioning and

> "At the present time we have reached the bottom of the abyss — we have gone about as low as it is possible to go — we can't dig the pit any deeper — there is no way we can further express as a culture our total rejection of our Creator's guidelines for sane, sensible, and healthy living."

plumbing business, you need to inject sexuality into your marketing strategy.

Widespread Incest

Incest refers to any physical relationship between closely related persons, often within the immediate family. Some societies consider it to include only those who live in the same household, or who belong to the same clan or lineage; other societies consider it to include blood relatives; other societies further include those related by adoption or marriage.

Incestuous societies simply cannot exist and the effective prohibition of incest is linked with the functioning of every society. One important distinction between human culture and animal culture is abolition of incest. Levi-Strauss says, "the prohibition of incest can be found at the dawn of culture... It is culture itself."

How prevalent and common incest is, can be judged from the authoritative figures mentioned below:

* In US, incidents of mother-son and father-daughter incests are reported to as high as 20%. Brother-sister incests are rated anywhere between 30% to 35%.

* In India, a government survey of 12,500 children and parents in 13 of 29 states found that over 53% of children between the ages of 5 and 18 have been sexually abused. Most surveyed said they knew the abuser. (Ministry of Women and Child Welfare, United Press International, April 2007)

* In Barbados, a national survey of women and men aged 20 to 45 found that 33 per cent of women and 2 per cent of men reported

> *"After my death you will become utterly corrupt, and turn aside from the way I have commanded you. And evil will befall you in the latter days"* ~Moses (Deuteronomy 31:29)

having been sexually abused during childhood. (UNFPA)

* A review of victim reports in 3 states in the US in 1992 revealed that 46% of rape victims under age 12 had a family relationship with the perpetrator, and 20% were raped by their fathers. (Bureau of Justice Statistics)

* One of every seven victims of sexual assault reported to law enforcement agencies were under age 6. (Bureau of Justice Statistics, US)

* In a 1992 report from Canada, 17% of girls under the age of 16 had experienced incest. (J. Holmes and E. Silverman, 1992, We're Here, Listen to Us: A Survey of Young Women in Canada)

* A random survey of 2,627 women and men conducted by the Los Angeles Times found that 27% of the women and 16% of the men had been incestuously abused as children (By Silence Betrayed, John Crewsdon, Little Brown, 1988).

* In Australia, based on a range of behaviours where children are used for someone's sexual gratification, the prevalence rate is 1 in 3 women and 1 in 6 men. (Fergussen and Mullen, 1999)

*According to a 1989 study, one out of every eight women in New Zealand has had an experience of incest (Otago Women's Health Study, 1989)

* According to New Zealand's Rape Crisis Auckland 2003 statistics, 43% of cases of childhood sexual abuse were perpetrated by a family member.

* In Malaysia, there are approximately 300 cases of incest

There is a story that one man was drinking. So, drinking in India is a great sin. So his friend advised that "You are drinking. You'll go to hell." So he said, "Oh, my father also drinks." So he said, "Your father also will go to hell." "Oh, my brother also drinks." "Oh, he also will go to hell." In this way, he continued to say, "My father, my brother, my sister, my this, my that..." So... And he was replying, "Yes, he will also go to hell." Then the drunkard replied,"Oh, hell is heaven. Because we're all drinking here and we will drink there. So what is that hell? That is heaven.
-Srila Prabhupada (Lecture, Los Angeles, June 27, 1972)

reported each year. Unreported cases are hundreds of times more. (Women's Center for Change, Panang).

* In Serbia's Belgrade Incest Trauma Center statistics for 2005, the average duration of incest and sexual abuse of a minor was 5 years, 8 months. In 28% of the cases, the minor was abused by two or more offenders.

* Even though there are no reliable statistics for most European countries, a recent flurry of books, articles and telephone "hotlines" has begun to reveal widespread sexual molestation. A recent BBC "ChildWatch" program asked its female listeners - a large sample - if they remembered sexual molestation, and, of the 2,530 replies analyzed, 83 percent remembered someone touching them, 62 percent of the full sample recalling complete incest. Official estimates of German children sexually abused and raped each year now number over 300,000, and sexual abuse hot lines are becoming more widespread.

* Over 70% of sexual assaults are not reported to police. Only 6% of rapists will ever spend a day in jail.

Focus On Self And Self-imagery

For lot many people today, the world is shrinking to within themselves. Care and concern for others, even own family members and friends seems to be evaporating. More for me is the mantra or the guiding principle in life and let the world go to hell. The younger generation is confined to cell-phones and internet and they are living in a phantasmagoria, with very little touch of ground realities of life. It appears that a whole generation is simply floating in air and they suffer nervous breakdown when they come crashing on the ground. Other than technology, things like fine arts, poetry, culture, spirituality, community life, contemplation, introspection etc. seem to have lost relevance. Materialism is commanding more

"Civilization has gotten further and further from the so-called 'natural' man, who uses all his faculties: perception, invention, improvisation."
~ Robert Green Ingersoll

attention than ever before and preoccupation with latest trends and fashions is sapping the vital energy.

Clinical psychologist Oliver James claims in his new book 'The Selfish Capitalist: Origins of Affluenza', that "selfish capitalism" is making us sick, literally. Owning too much stuff drives us into a spiral of sadness. He says the emergence of selfish capitalism has led to a "startling increase in the incidence of mental illness".

Alcohol & Drug Abuse

Experimentation with alcohol and drugs during adolescence is becoming common. Doctors are seeing rising numbers of patients in their late teens and early 20s with severe alcohol-related disease, many of them women. Teenagers are using a variety of drugs, both legal and illegal. Legally available drugs include alcohol, prescribed medications, inhalants (fumes from glues, aerosols, and solvents) and over-the-counter cough, cold, sleep, and diet medications. The most commonly used illegal drugs are marijuana (pot), stimulants (cocaine, crack, and speed), LSD, PCP, opiates, heroin, and designer drugs (Ecstasy). The use of illegal drugs is increasing. The average age of first marijuana use is 14, and alcohol use can start before age 12. The use of marijuana and alcohol in high school has become common.

> *Now this civilization has spread in the Western countries -- they want to remain naked. There are so many nudie clubs. So next life they'll be given chance to become tree, to stand naked for thousands of years. This is laws of nature. They do not know how they're getting chance, different types of body for different types of enjoyments, material enjoyment.*
> *-Srila Prabhupada*
> *(Srimad-Bhagavatam 1.2.31 -- Vrndavana, November 10, 1972)*

Threat 4 - Moral, Ethical, Spiritual Ruination

Whereas before most hospital consultants and rehabilitation centers would have seen patients in their fifties or sixties in the past, they now describe seeing patients in their early twenties with alcohol-related hepatitis, and women whose livers are permanently damaged with the disease known as cirrhosis by the time they are 30.

In the United States and Canada, approximately 40% of adults will use an illegal drug at some time during their lives. This does not include the use of alcohol or prescription medicines. There is a strong connection between the use of drugs and alcohol and high-risk sexual behaviors. This increases a person's chance of getting sexually transmitted diseases (STDs), hepatitis C, and human immunodeficiency virus (HIV). Alcohol abuse causes over 100,000 deaths in the United States and Canada each year, mostly in automobile accidents.

In developing countries, more and more people are resorting to alcohol these days. Thanks to the destruction of traditional values, easy spending power and wide availability of brands to choose from...a modernized Third world is saying cheers.

In India, around 15 to 20 per cent of Indians consume alcohol and over the past twenty years, the number of drinkers has increased considerably. According to a survey done by The Hindustan Times, an estimated 5 per cent of Indians can be classified as alcoholics which projects that at least fifty million people in India are addicted to alcohol.

Prior to British colonization, cannabis, marijuana and light country liquor were the major intoxicants in the third World but their consumption was extremely low. Use of alcohol was limited to the upper echelon of society. British rulers propagated alcohol and opened liquor shops.

In India, it became fashionable among Indians to use and offer alcohol at their western style parties. The use of alcohol started

A great civilization... is on the edge of extinction and... we have very little time to save it.
~ Peter Hitchens (The Abolition of Britain)

among educated and middle class. Gandhi was opposed to alcohol consumption and on his insistence, the constitution of India incorporated a directive principle of State policy stating that the State shall endeavour to bring about prohibition of the consumption of intoxicating drinks. In 1977, India imposed total prohibition that lasted two years. But despite all this, alcohol has become the in thing, a sign of social sophistication and a symbol of prestige. Just a century ago it was condemned and regarded as something alien to local culture.

Due to its large population, India has been identified as the potentially third largest market for alcoholic beverages in the world which has attracted the attention of multinational liquor companies. Sale of alcohol has been growing steadily at 6% and is estimated to grow at the rate of 8% per year.

In developing countries, barely three decades ago, less than 1% of the cases in psychiatric wards were admitted for alcohol-related problems; now the number exceeds 30% in most of the major psychiatric centres.

Dealing with drunkenness and with alcohol-related accidents, crime, violence, and disturbances consumes more resources than any other aspect of police operations, while the health consequences of alcohol abuse add enormously to national health care costs. Illegal drugs are more rapidly addicting than alcohol and have a more powerful effect on human behavior, but the alcohol consumption is many times greater than the level of illegal drug use. Normalisation of heavy drinking is putting a whole generation at risk from a silent killer.

"Industrial man --a sentient reciprocating engine having a fluctuating output, coupled to an iron wheel revolving with uniform velocity. And then we wonder why this should be the golden age of revolution and mental derangement."

Threat 4 - Moral, Ethical, Spiritual Ruination

Divorce And Break Down of Family

The institution of marriage is turning into a joke. The "live-in lovers" avenue is heavily traveled — in fact, the traffic volume is steadily increasing as young males and females decide to set up housekeeping together without getting married. When older parents voice their objections to this ever increasing practice of "living together" by the younger generation, usually the "old fashioned" folks who are "out of touch" in today's world are told that it's none of their business, old fogeys should not try to interfere. Peaceful married life is a thing of past.

Divorce rate continues to escalate with 2 of every 3 marriages ending in divorce in developed countries and 1 out of 4 in developing countries. This is the result of infidelity — with the chat room mess on the internet and websites featuring married women and men who desire to have a sexual encounter — just a "one night stand" with some one, why should there be any surprise that the divorce rate continues to accelerate.

Purposeless Life

Making things, buying things and selling things is not the goal of life. This is not the purpose of life. Human life is not meant for 'shopping culture' but for cultivation of 'spiritual culture'. Material things don't bring peace and happiness. Today billions of people have got things which even Kings did not have in the past. Car, computer, television, fridge, telephone - no King ever had these things but people are still restless and unhappy, more than ever before.

"Beware of the dog. Beware of the revolver." This is your culture. And when you go to the airport everyone is searched out, pocket. So who is gentleman? Is that gentleman? There is no gentleman in the world. All rogues and thieves, cheaters, bluffers. Here is the proof. If we are gentleman, why we are being checked in the airport? Hm? This is the proof. There is no gentleman and therefore you can not trust anyone.
-Srila Prabhupada (Morning Walk -- April 9, 1976, Vrndavana)

In Greed We Trust
Corruption & Loss of Integrity

The history of corruption goes back to the history of civilization. Although corruption existed in all societies and at all times, the problem seems to be more prominent in the context of modern civilization.

Moreover, gradually corruption is becoming more and more institutionalised involving policy-making authorities. Colonial and neo-colonial backgrounds of a large number of present day developing countries had also contributed in flourishing corrupt practices.

Black's Law Dictionary, one of the premier legal resources, defines corruption as "The act of an official or fiduciary person who unlawfully or wrongfully uses his station or character to procure some benefit for himself or for another person, contrary to duty and the rights of others." Gradually, over the periods, the concept has expanded to include all areas of life such as private business, religion, culture and so on.

With passage of time the concept has widened significantly. In modern world, corruption is evident in every sphere of life. **Political corruption** (involving governments or the policy-making bodies of a country) seems to be the major concern of developing countries whereas **Corporate corruption** is increasingly becoming a problem in industrialised rich nations. A long list of activities that include taking bribes, neglect of duties, profiteering activities, lavish living, gambling and visiting prostitutes, smuggling and so on can be included in the definition of corruption.

The political corruption has become so widespread that certain practices are no longer considered as illegal or unethical. Political

> *In light of the coarseness and vulgarity of our time, there are just too many signs of decivilization; that is, civilization gone rotten*
> *~Black*

donation at election times with expectations of favour in future is one of the most common practices in all democratic systems in the world.

There are two structures of corruption exists in practice in governments – **top-down** and **bottom-up** (Waller et al, 2002). Under the top-down structure, decisions are made at the highest level of the hierarchy and lower-level officials get whatever is given to them. Bottom-up structure is decentralised. Lower-level officials collect bribes and the highest ranking official is just one of the recipients.

The structure of corruption has changed from top-down level (in former USSR) to bottom-up level in present Russia, and the problem has become much more acute.

Developing countries like India, China, Indonesia, Cambodia and various Afrcan nations have very high levels of decentralized corruption.

In some nations, the corruption is as basic as greasing the palms of a telephone company clerk to expedite installation of a phone line or get away from violation of traffic laws. In other cases, corruption means millions in payoffs, often to secret foreign-bank accounts, where development funds are siphoned that should have been used to expedite roads, schools, bridges or basic health and sanitary facilities. Also if you get caught accepting bribe by anti-corruption Bureau, you can get away by paying bribe.

Corruption occurs in all countries, irrespective of whether they are rich or poor, socialist or capitalist, dictatorship or democracies etc. Only the form of corruption and its extent might be different.

The corruption issue assumed a very serious dimension with technological development in early 1980s and with globalisation

"In the modern techno-industrial culture, it is possible to proceed from infancy into senility without ever knowing manhood"
~Edward Abbey

of production factors. From late 1980s it has become a very serious global issue.

India's Holy text, Srimad Bhagavatam foresees this phenomenon five thousand years ago, "In Kali-yuga, wealth alone will be considered the sign of a man's good birth, proper behavior and fine qualities. And law and justice will be applied only on the basis of one's power. (SB 12.2.2)

Degenerate Art and Music

Art and music are the windows of a society. We get a peek into a society by its art and music. Over the decades, art and music has turned crude and foul. Fineness is gradually vanishing.

One painting in an European museum was hanging upside down without any one noticing any thing wrong until the painter visited and had it put up straight. No one could make out head or tail of the painting. Music is also turning gross and louder. Fine and tasteful literature is becoming a thing of past.

Sex has become an obsession in media and music. A new study shows a "significant" increase in sexual content on TV over the last 2 years. The number of episodes with sexual content increased from 56% in the 1997-1998 season to 68% of all episodes in the 1999-2000 season.

Jayapataka: That was published in the Bombay Illustrated Weekly, that the prostitutes are having difficulty because women are so freely available that no one is coming to pay for them.
Prabhupada: Because everyone is prostitute...So the whole civilization at the present moment they want to live like pig, and to live like pig they are working like an ass. And that is civilization, working like ass to become a pig.
-Srila Prabhupada (Morning Walks -- January 22-23, 1976, Mayapur)

Loss of Religious And Traditional Values

Godlessness is bad and also bad is fanaticism without philosophical understanding. Godlessness in the last days, the description is sounding not too unfamiliar.

Mark this: There will be terrible times in the last days. People will be lovers of themselves, lovers of money, boastful, proud, abusive, disobedient to their parents, ungrateful, unholy, unforgiving, slanderous, without self-control, brutal, not lovers of the good, treacherous, rash, conceited, lovers of pleasure rather than lovers of God— having a form of godliness but denying its power. They will be loaded down with sins and are swayed by all kinds of evil desires, always learning but never able to acknowledge the truth. Opposing the truth, they will be men of depraved minds. That's a prediction about current times made long ago. Sounds familiar?

Srimad Bhagavatam predicted five thousand years ago, "Then, O King, religion, truthfulness, cleanliness, tolerance, mercy, duration of life, physical strength and memory will all diminish day by day because of the powerful influence of the age of Kali.(SB 12.2.1)

Atheism was almost nonexistent, something like one out of every 7,000 people on the planet, in 1900. But situation is vastly different today.

A new survey in the U.S. shows that the number of 18-25 year olds who are atheist, agnostic or nonreligious has increased from 11 percent in 1986 to 20 percent today. Also The proportion of Americans reporting "no religious preference" doubled from 7 percent to 14 percent between 1991 and 2000. This doubling of no religion preference is significant because for the 17-year period from 1974 to 1991, there was no significant change in religious preference, but "no religion" responses have accelerated since 1991.

The industrial revolution has tended to produce everywhere great urban masses that seem to be increasingly careless of ethical standards.
    ~Irving Babbitt

End of Modern Civilization and Alternative Future

One good thing is that some of the religious dissenters are distancing themselves from the church and not from God. They may consider themselves 'spiritual' yet not 'religious.' They pray but do not attend service. They detach themselves from organized religion, not God.

In general, people are becoming too lazy to get into religion and more concerned with self imagery. No one wants to be known as the "Jesus freak". It's not like they are actually sitting down and thinking about it to make the choice to be atheist. The whole societal and cultural mould is designed on Godless ethos. Atheism and non-belief in general are proportionate to industrial and economic prosperity. The developing countries are tasting economic prosperity and rise in hedonism as well.

"Dude, it's nice to know we're not the only ones skipping out on church."

In a survey of eleven industrial democracies with population over twenty million, it was found that the non-religious were making more converts between 1990 and 2000 and the atheists

> *This gambling, drinking, meat-eating, these things were all unknown in India. They did not know how to drink. These Britishers introduced. There is still a lane, a street, Porterly Street. There was a woman of suspicious character. She was supplied big bottles of wine, and she used to canvass rich men's son to take wine, and it was distributed free. In this way wine was distributed, and people began to drink, gradually. And I have seen a tea committee. They... Advertising tea, preparing tea nicely. "You take this tea, you'll not feel hungry, you'll be cured from malaria...," and so many things. And people come and take tea in this way. Now any man is taking tea. In the morning they'll gather in the tea stall. You see. So people, they did not know what is gambling, what is drinking, what is meat-eating. So these things were introduced gradually.*
> *-Srila Prabhupada*
> *(Lecture on Srimad-Bhagavatam 5.5.2 - London, September 17, 1969)*

Threat 4 - Moral, Ethical, Spiritual Ruination

had net gains through conversion. Atheism is headed toward a long term recovery. With the fall of communism, coerced atheism has fallen rapidly. But voluntary atheism and other forms of voluntary non-belief are clearly on the rise.

In many places in Europe, to visit a church you need to pay 5 Euros as less people are visiting there, so they need money to maintain churches. Many churches in Europe and America have been sold or rented to other denominations or being used as warehouses. Looking back at the history two centuries ago, we find that people were remembering God. There was a place of worship in almost every small town and city of the world.

Spiritual life prevents people from going mentally down. As we are shifting from spirituality to atheism, we can see social disintegration. An example would be divorce rate of 85% in California alone. Every third person in US is consulting a psychiatrist at some point in his or her life.

Rise in bigotry and dogmatism is another bad news. People are more concerned with getting stamped as christians or hindus rather than understand and seriously follow their respective tenets. There is less need to try to make others think like you think. Christians are going out of their way to convert the whole world to their belief. Better they find peace within themselves and their own beliefs, live by example, and they'll have a much better chance of convincing others that their chosen path is the correct one. There was an old 60's quote, came out of Berkeley and the free speech movement "A man without Jesus is like a fish without a bicycle.

Political scientist Ronald Inglehart, in a 1998 survey gives us a ray of hope when he says, "Although church attendance is declining in nearly all advanced industrial societies, spiritual concerns more

Our trajectory continues downward... we are on the road to cultural disaster.
~Bork

broadly defined are not. In fact, in most industrial societies, a growing share of the population is spending time thinking about the meaning and purpose of life."

Spirituality has the answers to the ills afflicting modern man. The desire for sex out side of marriage has caused man to rape little babies, the desire for money has caused man to overtake countries killing thousands, the desire for solace has caused man to take his own life. The society is changing. These are the critical stages it is passing through and naturally it does produce a creeking noise.

Overspending & Indebtedness

On the surface, we seem better off than earlier generations. We might live more comfortable and stuff-filled lives than our forefathers did, but Oliver James, a Clinical psychologist, believes the rise of materialism has come with a high price tag attached - widespread anxiety and depression.

In the past, having a TV was seen as an indicator of wealth and class. Now, according to a study carried out by marketing and information group CACI, the average UK home has 4.7 television sets. Also, seven out of 10 children have a TV in their rooms and half of them have a DVD player too.

Can it really be the case that as we've become more comfortable, we've also become mentally ill? Yes, unfortunately it is the case. Average person's 'real' wage has broadly remained the same since

> *The Western, the Britishers were for two hundred years and they preached. Their policy was to kill the Indian culture. Because that report of Lord McCauley, after studying Indian situation, the report was to the Parliament that "If you keep India as Indian, then you will not be able to rule over them," so therefore there was regular policy to kill Indian civilization. And because they were on the governing power, they could do it. Therefore India lost its own culture and victimized by the Western culture. This is the position. Just they are learning how to eat meat, how to drink wine, how to dress them with coat and pant, how to go to the hotel, illicit sex.*
> *-Srila Prabhupada (Morning Walk - Durban, October 13, 1975)*

the 1970s, he or she is now constantly bombarded with messages to buy, buy, buy, and aspire to a posh and high flying life.

The media, advertising, reality TV shows and so on, they give people unrealistic aspirations that they simply cannot meet with their wages and living standards. As a result, people get sucked into competitiveness and workaholism....and indebtedness.

People end up tirelessly striving for material wealth and valuing it over family and friendships. This really heaps pressure on people, damaging their health.

Yet consumerism can be seriously addictive for some. Some experts believe 10% of Men and possibly 20% of British and American women, are manic, compulsive shoppers whose condition can lead to family break-ups, depression and in some instances suicide. Rest of the world is trying to walk in their footsteps. An American pharmaceutical firm is developing a pill to help wean shopaholics off their addiction.

In a book titled Stop Me Because I Can't Stop Myself, a compulsive shopper called "Gloria" describes how she shopped online for six to eight hours a day, ending up in $80,000 of debt. She lost her job and split from her husband and checked into a psychiatric institution after "shopping ruined my family".

It is time we valued what is truly important rather than focusing society around competitiveness and consumption.

The power of accurate observation is frequently called cynicism by those who don't have it.
~George Bernard Shaw

83 Percent British Believe UK's Moral Standards Are Falling - A Survey

According to BBC's The Big Questions programme, a vast number of people believe that Britain is experiencing a moral decline. The poll found that four out of five or 83 per cent Britons believe that moral standards in Britain are falling, while only 9 per cent disagreed that the country was in moral decline.

"When I turned the other cheek, it surprised him ... and that's when I let him have it."

Religion still kept its place of significance, with 62 per cent agreeing that religion was an important moral guide for the nation, while only 29 per cent disagreed that faith was important in shaping a nation's morals.

Real civilization is not concerned simply with man's animal needs but with enabling man to understand his relationship with God, the supreme father. One may learn about his relationship with God by any process - through Christianity, through the Vedic literatures or through the Koran - but in any case it must be learned.

—Srila Prabhupada (Matchless Gift 6)

Threat - 5

Violence and Wars
Clash of Civilizations

 *"I know not with what weapons World War III will be fought, but World War IV will be fought with sticks and stones."*
— *Albert Einstein*

20th Century - The Bloodiest Century In Human History
Industrialization of War & Violence

Savagery, much attributed to the 'old world' is not entirely absent in the 'new world' but rather it is more prevalent than ever before. Western civilization has made the 20th century the bloodiest century in human history. This civilization witnessed, besides the two most brutal World Wars, the worst acts of barbarism - holocaust, Gulag concentration camps, genocides and atomic bombing of Hiroshima and Nagasaki. Industrialization of wars and violence in this century led to killing of more than 350 million people, directly and indirectly. Science and technology led to discovery and mass usage of many lethal weapons. Usage of petroleum expanded the war zone to include several continents. Localized battles of 'old world' turned into global World wars.

But world wars haven't stopped for a moment. World has not seen respite from war. Since second World war, the list of nations invaded and occupied by the US is long, the list of nations with governments overthrown is longer. Latest in the news is a place called Iraq and prison systems that includes places like Guantanamo Bay.

There is an arsenal of more than 50,000 nuclear missiles that can destroy the planet several times over. Industrial Society is

... no nation is rich enough to pay for both war and civilization. We must make our choice; we cannot have both."
-Abraham Flexner

collectively making millions of tonnes of weapons and explosives of all kinds every year – and then it wonders why there is so much violence in this world. Well, if we make millions of tonnes of weapons and explosives on earth they are going to be used on earth – they are not going to be used on Mars.

If we honestly apply the definition of terrorism, we would find that the entire industrial society is a terrorist, the entire military-industrial-complex, with accompanying science and technology is a terrorist. So called terrorists are small time terrorists and dons of military-industrial complex are big time terrorists, but terrorists none the less. Just like when Alexander invaded India, his soldiers caught hold of a thief. He was duly produced before Alexander. On being charged, the thief enquired, "what is the difference between you and me? I am a small thief and you are a big thief. I operate alone and you operate with an army of thousands." Alexander had to agree with him and set him free.

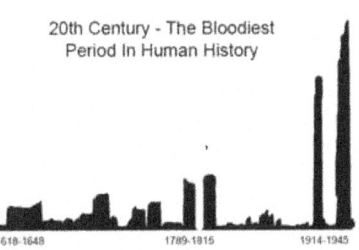

It was not possible to have world wars 1000 years ago where you could kill 50 million innocent citizens. World Wars became possible only when science and technology developed aeroplanes, ships and other carriers which could transport millions of troops and millions of tonnes of weapons from one corner of the globe to the other.

And today one doesn't even need all these paraphernalia to fight

Just like great scientists have discovered the atom bomb, by scientific research. What is the effect? Now by one drop you can kill many millions of people. That is his advancement of science. "Oh, why don't you create something that people will not die?" That is not... "I can assure death, but I cannot save death. That is not in my power." Then what kind of scientist you are?
-Srila Prabhupada (Bhagavad-gita 7.1-3 -- London, August 4, 1971)

a war. One just needs to move finger-tips to launch missiles that can destroy the planet several times over.

Right at this moment there are several countries fighting wars with one another. There is internal war going on in almost half of the countries in the world. All these wars are being fuelled and sustained by billions of tonnes of weapons produced by the Military-industrial complex every year. An impressive array of chemical, biological and nuclear weapons are waiting to be dropped on our heads. What has been produced at great cost and is being stored with great care, is certainly meant for use and will be used one day.

The Five Minute Decision That Averted Nuclear War
Cold War's Riskiest Moment

On January 19, 2006, a forgotten soldier, Stanislav Petrov was honored at a special ceremony held at the United Nations in New York City. Stanislav Petrov spoke at the UN and was presented with a World Citizen Trophy for his heroic decision in 1983 that has earned him the title of "The Man Who averted nuclear War."

This refers to the incident on September 26, 1983, when Lieutenant Colonel Petrov was the duty officer at Serpuk-hov-15, the Soviet Union's main command bunker just south of Moscow. He was in charge of 120 men with the responsibility of monitoring incoming signals from satellites when suddenly nightmare became reality as the warning system reported the soviet union was under attack by US Inter-Continental Ballistic Missiles.

It's important to note that this was a period of high tension between the United States and the Soviet Union. President Ronald Reagan was calling the Soviets the "Evil Empire." The Russian military had shot down a Korean passenger jet just three weeks before this incident and the United States and North Atlantic

> *If you kill one person they call it murder.*
> *If you kill a few hundred they call it terrorism.*
> *If you kill a few million they call it war.*
> *~Unknown*

Treaty Organization (NATO) were organizing a joint military exercise in Europe.

In an interview, held the day after the UN award ceremony, Petrov talked about that fateful night when the red button beamed "sTarT" along with flashing lights and a huge map of the united states with a US base lit up showing that the missiles had been launched.

Petrov's duty was to report the attack to command head-quarters, where an immediate counterattack could have been initiated. For five minutes, however, in the midst of chaos and the prospect of total destruction, petrov held a phone in one hand and an intercom in the other as the lights on his console continued to flash that a missile attack was on the way. Petrov believed in his heart that, contrary to what the high tech equipment was reporting, this alarm was an error. Petrov then made his historic decision and called his Kremlin liaison to report that it was a false alarm.

But Colonel petrov didn't know for certain this was a false alarm. He later said, "I made a decision and that was it." It was only after fifteen to twenty agonizing minutes passed, as he waited to detect if US missiles were incoming, that Petrov's decision proved correct. It was a system error that had signaled the attack. In his interview with the British Daily Mail newspaper, Petrov said that in principle "a nuclear war could have broken out, the whole world could have been destroyed."

Dr. Bruce Blair, president of the Center for Defense information, a leading expert on nuclear weapons and a former Minuteman

The nexus between modern science and violence is obvious from the fact that eighty per cent of all scientific research is devoted to the war industry and is frankly aimed at large-scale violence. In our times, this violence is directed not only against enemy fighting forces but also against civilian populations. I argue that modern science is violent even in peaceful domains such as, for example, health care and agriculture, where the professed objective of scientific research is not violence but human welfare.
-Vandana Shiva

End of Modern Civilization and Alternative Future

missile launch officer said: "I think this is the closest we've come to accidental nuclear war."

The catastrophic danger Petrov faced in 1983 is still with us today as four thousand US and Russian nuclear warheads are on hair-trigger alert, ready for launch on a few minutes notice and would destroy both countries in an hour. Such a doomsday scenario could result from an accidental missile launch, a system error, or a miscalculation.

Global Trends 2025 - A Dangerous World
121 Page Presidential Report Predicts Global Catastrophe

The use of nuclear weapons will grow increasingly likely by 2025, US intelligence warned in a report on global trends that forecasts a tense, unstable world shadowed by war.

Called 'Global Trends 2025 - A Transformed World', the 121-page report was produced by the National Intelligence Council, a body of analysts from across the US intelligence community.

The report says, "The world of the near future will be subject to an increased likelihood of conflict over scarce resources, including food and water, and will be haunted by the persistence of rogue

Prabhupada : So here the time is coming. ... The atom bomb is ready. You have got, I have got. I drop on you, and you drop on me. Both of us, we finish. This is going to be happening. People are so degraded. So unless one takes to Krsna consciousness, there is no possibility of being saved. There is example, that grinding mill... You know, grinding mill?
Prof. Regamay: Yes.
Prabhupada: Yes, and the grains are put within it and they are all smashed. But one grain who takes shelter of the center, the pivot, it is not smashed. Similarly the modern civilization is such that everyone will be smashed. And one takes the central point shelter, Krsna consciousness, he will not be. Kaunteya pratijanihi na me bhaktah pranasyati [Bg. 9.31].
-Srila Prabhupada
(Room Conversation with Prof. Regamay, June 4, 1974, Geneva)

states and terrorist groups with greater access to nuclear weapons. Widening gaps in birth rates and wealth-to-poverty ratios, and the uneven impact of climate change, could further exacerbate tensions.

The Report continues, "Some African and South Asian states may wither away altogether, organised crime could take over at least one state in central Europe; and the spread of nuclear weapons will heighten the risk that they will be used. The likelihood that nuclear weapons will be used will increase with expanded access to technology and a widening range of options for limited strikes."

The report adds, " There is perceived risk of a nuclear arms race in the Middle East where a number of countries are thinking about developing or acquiring technologies that would be useful to make nuclear weapons. Over the next 15-20 years, reactions to the decisions Iran makes about its nuclear program could cause a number of regional states to intensify these efforts and consider actively pursuing nuclear weapons. This will add a new and more dangerous dimension to what is likely to be increasing competition for influence within the region. It was not certain that the  kind of deterrent relationships that existed for most of the Cold War would emerge in a nuclear armed Middle East. Instead, the possession of nuclear weapons may be perceived as "making it safe" to engage in low intensity conflicts, terrorism or even larger conventional attacks. Terrorism would likely be a factor in 2025."

Report has been briefed to the President Barack Obama. Thomas Fingar, deputy director of US National Intelligence says, "In one sense, a bad sense, the pace of change that we are looking at in 2025 occurred more rapidly than we had anticipated. One overarching conclusion of the report is that "the unipolar" world is

"You can't say civilization doesn't advance... in every war they kill you in a new way."

~ Will Rogers

over, or certainly will be by 2025. But with the "rise of the rest," managing crises and avoiding conflicts will be more difficult, particularly with an antiquated post-World War II international system. The potential for conflict will be different then and in some ways greater than it has been for a very long time,"

The Nuclear War that Almost Happened More Than 20 Times
Next Time We May or May Not Be So Lucky

To err is human and in case of nuclear war, we can err only once. Ever since the two adversaries in the Cold War, the USA and the USSR realized that their nuclear arsenals were sufficient to do disastrous damage to both countries at short notice, the leaders and the military commanders have thought about the possibility of a nuclear war starting without their intention or as a result of a false alarm. Increasingly elaborate accessories have been incorporated in nuclear weapons and their delivery systems to minimize the risk of unauthorized or accidental launch or detonation. A most innovative action was the establishment of the "hot line" between Washington and Moscow in 1963 to reduce the risk of misunderstanding between the super powers.

Despite all precautions, the possibility of an inadvertent war due to an unpredicted sequence of events remained as a deadly threat to both countries and to the world.

On the American side many "false alarms" and significant accidents have been listed, ranging from trivial to very serious, during the Cold War. Probably many remain unknown to the public and the research community because of individuals' desire to avoid blame and maintain the good reputation of their unit or command. No doubt there have been as many mishaps on the

What is the advancement over the dogs? This destruction of another nation by nuclear bombs is the dogs' mentality. Sometimes, even when chained by their respective masters, two dogs will fight as soon as they meet. Have you seen it? It's no better than that.
-Srila Prabhupada (Lecture, Melbourne, Australia)

Threat 5 - Violence & Wars, Clash of Civilizations

Soviet side.

The risks are illustrated by the following selection of mishaps. If the people involved had exercised less caution, or if some unfortunate coincidental event had occurred, escalation to nuclear war could easily be imagined.

On this subject, there is a carefully researched book, 'The Limits of Safety' by Scott D. Sagan.

The following selections represent only a fraction of the false alarms that have been reported on the American side. Many probably remain unreported, or are hidden in records that remain classified. There are likely to have been as many on the Soviet Side which are even more difficult to access.

Following abbreviations have been used
NORAD - North American Aerospace Defense Command
SAC HQ - Strategic Air Command Headquarters
NATO - North Atlantic Treaty Organization
BMEWS - Ballistic Missile Early Warning Sites
DEFCON - The Defense Readiness Condition
ICBM - Inter-continental Ballistic Missile

"Oh, we are advancing. Advancement of knowledge." By advancement of knowledge, we have manufactured atom bomb so that killing process can be accelerated. People are dying, and that dying process is accelerated, and we are proud. Advancement of knowledge. Oh, manufacture something which will stop death; then you will have advancement of knowledge. Killing is there. What advancement? Killing is there and you are facilitating, you are making more killing at one drop. This is not knowledge. This is called mayayapahrta-jnana, "the knowledge taken by the illusory energy.
-Srila Prabhupada (Bhagavad-gita 7.11-16 -- New York, October 7, 1966)

1) November 5, 1956: Suez Crisis Coincidence

British and French Forces were attacking Egypt at the Suez Canal;. The Soviet Government had suggested to the U.S. that they combine forces to stop this by a joint military action, and had

There is a very nice story. One rat, he was troubled with cat. So he came to a saintly person: "My dear sir, I am very much troubled." "What is the difficulty?" The rat said, "The cat always chases. So I'm not in peace of mind." "Then what do you want?" "Please make me a cat." "All right, you become a cat." After few days, the same cat again came to the saintly person, says, "My dear sir, I am again in trouble." "What is that?" "The dogs are chasing me." "Then what do you want?" "Make me a dog." "All right, you become a dog." Then after few days, again he comes. He says, "I am again in trouble, sir." "What is that?" "The foxes are chasing me." "Then what do you want?" "To become a fox." "All right, you become a fox." Then again he comes. He says, "Oh, tigers are chasing me." "Then what do you want?" "I want to become a tiger." "All right, you become a tiger." And when he became a tiger, he began to stare his eyes on the saintly person: "I shall eat you." "Oh, you shall eat me? I have made you tiger, and you want to eat me?" "Yes, I shall eat you." Oh, then he cursed him, "Again you become a rat." So he became a rat.

So our human civilization is going to be like that. The other day I was reading in your -- what is called? -- World Almanac. In the next hundred years people will live underground like rats. So our scientific advancement has created this atomic bomb to kill man, and it will be used. And we have to go underground to become again rat. From tiger, again rat. That is going to be. That is nature's law. Daivi hy esa gunamayi mama maya duratyaya [Bg. 7.14]. If you defy the laws of your state and you are put into difficulty, similarly if you continue to defy the authority, the supremacy of the Supreme Lord, Personality of Godhead, then the same result: again you become rat. As soon as there is atomic bomb, everything, all civilization on the surface of the globe will be finished.

-Prabhupada (Lecture to College Students -- Seattle, October 20, 1968)

warned the British and French governments that (non-nuclear) rocket attacks on London and Paris were being considered. That night NORAD HQ received messages that:

(i) unidentified aircraft were flying over Turkey and the Turkish air force was on alert

(ii) 100 Soviet MIG-15's were flying over Syria

(iii) a British Canberra bomber had been shot down over Syria

(iv) the Soviet fleet was moving through the Dardanelles.

It is reported that in the US General Goodpaster himself was concerned that these events might trigger the NATO operations plan for nuclear strikes against the USSR.

The four reports were all shown afterwards to have innocent explanations. They were due, respectively to:

(i) a flight of swans

(ii) a routine air force escort (much smaller than the number reported) for the president of Syria, who was returning from a visit to Moscow

(iii) the Canberra bomber was forced down by mechanical problems

(iv) the Soviet fleet was engaged in scheduled routine exercises.

2) November 24, 1961: BMEWS Communication Failure

On the night of November 24, 1961, all communication links went dead between SAC HQ and NORAD. The communication loss cut off SAC HQ from the three Ballistic Missile Early Warning Sites (BMEWS) at Thule (Greenland), Clear (Alaska) and Fillingdales (England). There were two possible explanations facing SAC HQ: either enemy action, or the coincidental failure of all the communication systems, which had redundant and ostensibly

There is as yet no civilized society, but only a society in the process of becoming civilized. There is as yet no civilized nation, but only nations in the process of becoming civilized. From this standpoint, we can now speak of a collective task of humankind. The task of humanity is to build a genuine civilization.
~Felix Adler

independent routes, including commercial telephone circuits. All SAC bases in the United States were therefore alerted, and B-52 bomber crews started their engines, with instructions not to take off without further orders. Radio communication was established with an orbiting B-52 on airborne alert, near Thule. It contacted the BMEWS stations by radio and could report that no attack had taken place.

The reason for the "coincidental" failure was the redundant routes for telephone and telegraph between NORAD and SAC HQ all ran through one relay station in Colorado. At that relay station a motor had overheated and caused interruption of all the lines.

3) August 23, 1962: B-52 Navigation Error

On August 23, 1962, a B-52 nuclear armed bomber crew made a navigational error and flew 20 degrees too far north. They approached within 300 miles of Soviet airspace near Wrangel island, where there was believed to be an interceptor base with aircraft having an operational radius of 400 miles.

Because of the risk of repetition of such an error, in this northern area where other checks on Navigation are difficult to obtain, it was decided to fly a less provocative route in the future. However, the necessary orders had not been given by the time of the Cuban

> *Students' prayers 24 hours a day desiring the war should stop is useless. God cannot be their order supplier. First of all they act sinfully, and when there is reaction of war, pestilence, famine, and so many other nature's disturbances, they pray to God for stopping them. This is not possible. Just like a criminal first of all commits theft, burglary and debauchery, and when he is captured, by the police force, if he prays to the government to stop, that is not possible. So they are engaged in all sinful activities, and by natures' law, there must be reaction. I am encouraging now cow killing or animal killing, and when by nature's law, the turn comes upon me to be killed, if I pray I want to stop it, how it can be stopped?*
> *-Srila Prabhupada, (Letter to: Satsvarupa -- Seattle 9 October, 1968)*

missile crisis in October 1962, so throughout that crisis the same northern route was being flown 24 hours a day.

4) August-October, 1962: U2 Flights into Soviet Airspace

U2 high altitude reconnaissance flights from Alaska occasionally strayed unintentionally into Soviet airspace. One such episode occurred in August 1962. During the Cuban missile crisis on October of 1962, the U2 pilots were ordered not to fly within 100 miles of Soviet airspace.

On the night of October 26, for a reason irrelevant to the crisis, a U2 pilot was ordered to fly a new route, over the north pole, where positional checks on navigation were by sextant only. That night the aurora prevented good sextant readings and the plane strayed over the Chukotski Peninsula. Soviet MIG interceptors took off with orders to shoot down the U2. The pilot contacted his U.S. command post and was ordered to fly due east towards Alaska. He ran out of fuel while still over Siberia. In response to his SOS., U.S. F102-A fighters were launched to escort him on his glide to Alaska, with orders to prevent the MIG's from entering U.S. airspace. The U.S. interceptor aircraft were armed with nuclear missiles. These could have been used by any one of the F102-A pilots at his own discretion.

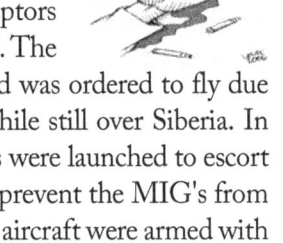

5) October 24, 1962- Cuban Missile Crisis: A Soviet Satellite Explodes

On October 24, a Soviet satellite entered its own parking orbit, and shortly afterward exploded. Sir Bernard Lovell, director of the Jodrell Bank observatory wrote in 1968: "The explosion of a Russian spacecraft in orbit during the Cuban missile crisis... led the US to believe that the USSR was launching a massive ICBM

Is there any man, is there any woman, let me say any child here that does not know that the seed of war in the modern world is industrial and commercial rivalry?
~Woodrow Wilson

End of Modern Civilization and Alternative Future

attack." The NORAD Command Post logs of the dates in question remain classified, possibly to conceal reaction to the event. Its occurrence is recorded, and U.S. space tracking stations were informed on October 31 of debris resulting from the breakup of the satellite.

6) October 25, 1962- Cuban Missile Crisis: Intruder in Duluth

At around midnight on October 25, a guard at the Duluth Sector Direction Center saw a figure climbing the security fence. He shot at it, and activated the "sabotage alarm." This automatically set off sabotage alarms at all bases in the area. At Volk Field, Wisconsin, the alarm was wrongly wired, and the Klaxon (alerting device) sounded which ordered nuclear armed F-106A interceptors to take off. The pilots knew there would be no practice alert drills while DEFCON 3 (highest alert) was in force, and they believed World War III had started.

Immediate communication with Duluth showed there was an error. By this time aircraft were starting down the runway. A car raced from command center and successfully signaled the aircraft to stop. The original intruder was a bear.

7) October 26, 1962- Cuban Missile Crisis: ICBM Test Launch

At Vandenburg Air Force Base, California, there was a program of routine ICBM test flights. When DEFCON 3 was ordered all the ICBM's were fitted with nuclear warheads except one Titan

Now if you are willingly killing cows and so many animals, so how much we are being responsible? Therefore at the present moment there is war, and the human society becomes subjected to be killed in mass massacre -- the nature's law. You cannot stop war and go on killing animals. That is not possible. There will be so many accidents for killing. The wholesale kill. When Krsna kills, He kills wholesale. When I kill -- one after another. But when Krsna kills, they assemble all the killers and kill.
-Srila Prabhupada (Srimad-Bhagavatam 6.1.8-13 -- New York, July 24, 1971)

missile that was scheduled for a test launch later that week. That one was launched for its test, without further orders from Washington, at 4 AM on the 26th.

It must be assumed that Russian observers were monitoring U.S. missile activities as closely as U.S. observers were monitoring Russian and Cuban activities. They would have known of the general changeover to nuclear warheads, but not that this was only a test launch.

8) October 26, 1962- Cuban Missile Crisis: Unannounced Titan Missile Launch

During the Cuba crisis, some radar warning stations that were under construction and near completion were brought into full operation as fast as possible. The planned overlap of coverage was thus not always available.

A normal test launch of a Titan-II ICBM took place in the afternoon of October 26, from Florida to the South Pacific. It caused temporary concern at Moorestown Radar site until its course could be plotted and showed no predicted impact within the United States. It was not until after this event that the potential for a serious false alarm was realized, and orders were given that radar warning sites must be notified in advance of test launches, and the countdown be relayed to them.

9) October 26, 1962- Cuban Missile Crisis: Malstrom Air Force Base

When DEFCON 2 was declared on October 24, solid fuel Minuteman-1 missiles at Malmstrom Air Force Base were being

Pakistan, since the beginning of Pakistan they could not make any economic condition very sound. But when the people are too much agitated, they declare war with India. The whole attention is... And they have been educated in such a way that India is their strongest enemy. Anything Indian, they dislike in Pakistan. So this is going on by the politicians. They are creating situation because they are not honest, they are not clean.
-Srila Prabhupada (Room Conversation with Richard Webster, chairman, Societa Filosofica Italiana — May 24, 1974, Rome)

prepared for full deployment. The work was accelerated to ready the missiles for operation, without waiting for the normal handover procedures and safety checks. When one silo and missile were ready on October 26 no armed guards were available to cover transport from the normal separate storage, so the launch enabling equipment and codes were all placed in the silo. It was thus physically possible for a single operator to launch a fully armed missile at a SIOP (Single Integrated Operational Plan) target.

During the remaining period of the Crisis the several missiles at Malstrom were repeatedly put on and off alert as errors and defects were found and corrected. Fortunately no combination of errors caused or threatened an unauthorized launch, but in the extreme tension of the period the danger can be well imagined.

10) October, 1962- Cuban Missile Crisis: NATO Readiness

It is recorded on October 22, that British Prime Minister Harold Macmillan and NATO Supreme Commander, General Lauris Norstad agreed not to put NATO on alert in order to avoid provocation of the U.S.S.R. When the U.S. Joint Chiefs of Staff ordered DEFCON 3, Norstad (A NATO General) was authorized to use his discretion in complying. Norstad did not order a NATO alert. However, several NATO subordinate commanders did order alerts to DEFCON 3 or equivalent levels of readiness at bases in West Germany, Italy, Turkey, and United Kingdom. This seems largely due to the action of General Truman Landon, Commander in Chief, US Air Forces Europe, who had already started alert

> *The modern civilization has got everything, but without God consciousness, any moment it will be finished. And there are symptoms... Any moment. At the present moment, this godless civilization, as soon as there is declaration of war, the America is prepared to drop atom bomb, Russia is... The America will be finished and Russia will be finished. That is the position. So you may make advancement of civilization, scientific improvement, economic development, but if it is godless, at any moment it will be finished.*
> *- Prabhupada (Srimad-Bhagavatam 1.15.21 -- Los Angeles, December 1, 1973)*

procedures on October 17 in anticipation of a serious crisis over Cuba.

11) October, 1962- Cuban Missile Crisis: British Alerts

When the US SAC went to DEFCON 2, on October 24, Bomber Command (UK) was carrying out an unrelated readiness exercise. On October 26, Air Marshall Cross, commander in chief of Bomber Command, decided to prolong the exercise because of the Cuba crisis, and later increased the alert status of British nuclear forces, so that they could launch in 15 minutes.

It seems likely that Soviet intelligence would perceive these moves as part of a coordinated plan in preparation for immediate war. They could not be expected to know that neither the British Minister of Defense nor Prime Minister Macmillian had authorized them.

12) October 28, 1962- Cuban Missile Crisis: Moorestown False Alarm

Just before 9 am, on October 28, the Moorestown, New Jersey, radar operators informed the national command post that a nuclear attack was under way. A test tape simulating a missile launch from Cuba was being run, and simultaneously a satellite came over the horizon.

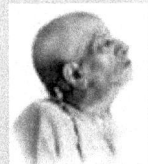

But we want to stop these killing houses. It is very, very sinful. Therefore in Europe, so many wars. Every ten years, fifteen years, there is a big war and wholesale slaughter of the whole human kind. And these rascals, they do not see it. The reaction must be there. You are killing innocent cows and animals. Nature will take revenge. Wait for that. As soon as the time is ripe, the nature will gather all these rascals, and club, slaughter them. Finished. They will fight amongst themselves, Protestant and Catholic, Russian and France, and France and Germany. This is going on. Why? This is the nature's law. Tit for tat. You have killed. Now you get killed. Amongst yourselves. They are being sent to the slaughterhouse. And here, you'll create slaughterhouse, "Dum! dum!" and be killed.
-Srila Prabhupada (Room Conversation -- June 11, 1974, Paris)

Operators became confused and reported by voice line to NORAD HQ that impact was expected 18 miles west of Tampa at 9:02 am. The whole of NORAD was reported, but before irrevocable action had taken place it was reported that no detonation had taken place at the predicted time, and Moorestown operators reported the reason for the false alarm.

During the incident overlapping radars that should have confirmed or disagreed were not in operation. The radar post had not received routine information of satellite passage because the facility carrying out that task had been given other work for the duration of the crisis.

13) October 28, 1962- Cuban Missile Crisis: False Warning Due to Satellite

At 5:26 p.m. on October 28, the Laredo radar warning site had just become operational. Operators misidentified a satellite in orbit as two possible missiles over Georgia and reported by voice line to NORAD HQ. NORAD was unable to identify that the warning came from the new station at Laredo and believed it to be from Moorestown, and therefore more reliable. Moorestown failed to intervene and contradict the false warning. By the time the commander in chief, NORAD had been informed, no impact had been reported and the warning was "given low credence."

14) November 2, 1962: The Penkovsky False Warning

In the fall of 1962, Colonel Oleg Penkovsky was working with the Soviets as a double agent for the CIA. He had been given a code by which to warn the CIA if he was convinced that a Soviet attack on the United States was imminent. He was to call twice, one minute apart, and only blow into the receiver. Further

The great masses of the people ... will more easily fall victims to a big lie than to a small one.
~Adolf Hitler

information was then to be left at a "dead drop" in Moscow.

The pre-arranged code message was received by the CIA on November 2, 1962.

It was known at the CIA that Penkovsky had been arrested on October 22. Penkovsky knew he was going to be executed. It is not known whether he had told the KGB the meaning of the code signal or only how it would be given, nor is it known exactly why or with what authorization the KGB staff used it. When another CIA agent checked the dead drop he was arrested.

15) November, 1965: Power Failure and Faulty Bomb Alarms

Special bomb alarms were installed near military facilities and near cities in the USA, so that the locations of nuclear bursts would be transmitted before the expected communication failure. The alarm circuits were set up to display a red signal at command posts the instant that the flash of a nuclear detonation reached the sensor and before the blast put it out of action. Normally the display would show a green signal, and yellow if the sensor was not operating or was out of communication for any other reason.

During the commercial power failure in the NE United States, in November 1965, displays from all the bomb alarms for the area should have shown yellow. In fact, two of them from different cities showed red because of circuit errors. The effect was consistent with the power failure being due to nuclear weapons explosions, and the Command Center of the Office of Emergency Planning went on full alert. Apparently the military did not.

16) January 21, 1968: B-52 Crash near Thule

On January 21, 1968, a fire broke out in the B-52 bomber on airborne alert near Thule. The pilot prepared for an emergency landing at the base. However the situation deteriorated rapidly, and the crew had to bale out. There had been no time to communicate with SAC HQ, and the pilotless plane flew over the

> *Civilization: a thin veneer over barbarianism.*
> *~John Shanahan*

Thule base before crashing on the ice 7 miles offshore. Its fuel and high explosive component of its nuclear weapons exploded, but there was no nuclear detonation.

At that time, the "one point safe" condition of the nuclear weapons could not be guaranteed, and it is believed that a nuclear explosion could have resulted from accidental detonation of the high explosive trigger. Had there been a nuclear detonation even at 7 miles distant, all communication methods would have given an indication consistent with a successful nuclear attack on both the base and the B-52 bomber. The bomb alarm would have shown red, and the other two communication paths would have gone dead. It would hardly have been anticipated that the combination could have been caused by accident, particularly as the map of the routes for B-52 airborne flights approved by the President showed no flight near to Thule. The route had been apparently changed without informing the White House.

17) October 24-25, 1973: False Alarm During Middle East Crisis

On October 24, 1973, when the U.N. sponsored cease fire intended to end the Arab-Israeli war was in force, further fighting started between Egyptian and Israeli troops in the Sinai desert. US intelligence reports and other sources suggested that the USSR was planning to intervene to protect the Egyptians. President Nixon was in the throes of Watergate episode and not available for a conference, so Kissinger and other U.S. officials ordered

Formerly the war was declared — the leader of the war, if he is killed, then the other party is victorious. Not that unnecessarily killing the civil citizens, no. This was nonsense. If there was fight between two kings, the citizens, they were unaffected, not that there is fight now between two parties, there is immediately siren, (imitates siren:) gaw, gaw, gaw, gaw, now bomb and the civil..., the most uncivilized way of war. In those days -those days means at least five thousand years ago - they selected a place, and "Let us fight and decide our fate," ksatriyas. Why the public should suffer?
-Srila Prabhupada (Town Hall Lecture, Auckland, April 14, 1972)

DEFCON3. The consequent movements of aircraft and troops were of course observed by Soviet intelligence. The purpose of the alert was not to prepare for war, but to warn the USSR not to intervene in the Sinai. However, if the following accident had not been promptly corrected then the Soviet command might have had a more dangerous interpretation.

On October 25, while DEFCON 3 was in force, mechanics were repairing one of the Klaxons (alert systems) at Kinchole Air Force Base, Michigan, and accidentally activated the whole base alarm system. B-52 crews rushed to their aircraft and started the engines. The duty officer recognized the alarm was false and recalled the crews before any took off.

18) November 9, 1979: Computer Exercise Tape

At 8:50 a.m. on November 9, 1979, duty officers at 4 command centers (NORAD HQ, SAC Command Post, The Pentagon National Military Command Center, and the Alternate National Military Command Center) all saw on their displays a pattern showing a large number of Soviet Missiles in a full scale attack on the U.S.A. During the next 6 minutes emergency preparations for retaliation were made. A number of Air Force planes were launched, including the President's National Emergency Airborne Command Post, though without the President! The President had not been informed, perhaps because he could not be found.

No attempt was made to use the hot line either to ascertain the Soviet intentions or to tell the Soviets the reasons for U.S. actions. This seems to me to have been culpable negligence. The whole purpose of the "Hot Line" was to prevent exactly the type of disaster that was threatening at that moment.

With commendable speed, NORAD was able to contact PAVE PAWS, an Air Force Space Command radar system, and learn that no missiles had been reported. Also, the sensors on the satellites were functioning that day and had detected no missiles. In only 6 minutes the threat assessment conference was terminated.

The reason for the false alarm was an exercise tape running on the computer system. US Senator Charles Percy happened to be in NORAD HQ at the time and is reported to have said there was absolute panic. A question was asked in Congress. The General Accounting Office conducted an investigation, and an off-site testing facility was constructed so that test tapes did not in the future have to be run on a system that could be in military operation.

19) June, 1980: Faulty Computer Chip

The Warning displays at the Command Centers mentioned in the last episode included windows that normally showed

0000 ICBMs detected 0000 SLBMs detected

At 2:25 a.m. on June 3, 1980, these displays started showing various numbers of missiles detected, represented by 2's in place of one or more 0's. Preparations for retaliation were instituted, including nuclear bomber crews starting their engines, launch of Pacific Command's Airborne Command Post, and readying of Minutemen missiles for launch.

While the cause of that false alarm was still being investigated 3 days later, the same thing happened and again preparations were made for retaliation. The cause was a single faulty chip that was failing in a random fashion. The basic design of the system was faulty, allowing this single failure to cause a deceptive display at several command posts.

This particular one could have hardly brought nuclear retaliation.; but there are still 30,000 nuclear weapons deployed, and two nuclear weapon states could get into a hostilities status again.

20) January, 1995: Russian False Alarm

On January 25, 1995, the Russian early warning radars detected an unexpected missile launch near Spitzbergen. The estimated flight time to Moscow was 5 minutes. The Russian President, the Defense Minister and the Chief of Staff were informed. The early warning and the control and command center switched to combat mode.

> *Not all criminals are in prison and not all crimes are indictable under the law.*
> *~-Ruth Minshull*

Within 5 minutes, the radars determined that the missile's impact would be outside the Russian borders.

The missile was Norwegian, and was launched for scientific measurements. On January 16, Norway had notified 35 countries including Russia that the launch was planned. Information had apparently reached the Russian Defense Ministry, but failed to reach the on-duty personnel of the early warning system.

These 20 incidents are only tip of an iceberg. Many far more serious incidents are locked up in Governments' classified files. Russian data is even more inaccessible. But this small sample does show us the gravity of the issue at hand. To err is human and erring with nukes will happen only once. As long as nukes are stockpiled, we run the risks of accidents which will prove very costly for the humanity.

Nukes Might End Up In Wrong Hands

The biggest fear of US administration is regarding Pakistan's nuclear arsenal falling into wrong hands, including through some groups which may try to provoke an Indo-Pak confrontation hoping that it would help them seize Islamabad's atomic arms.

To this effect an alarming stream of intelligence has begun circulating in international military circles. Many foreign-trained Pakistani scientists who harbour sympathy for radical Islamic causes, are returning to Pakistan to seek jobs within the country's nuclear infrastructure - presumably trying to burrow in among the 2000

> *But they are engaged in manufacturing atom bomb, duskrtinah. Atom bomb means killing. But discover something by which man will not die. That they are dying -- so you have discovered some instrument to die quickly. So that is duskrtinah. Merit, he has got merit, but misuse the merit. The death is there. He would have lived for, say, sixty years, and you drop atom bomb -- in ten years or twenty years finished. You cannot increase the duration of life. Therefore the so-called scientific advancement, what is that? Duskrtinah, no benefit for the human society.*
> *-Srila Prabhupada (Srimad-Bhagavatam 3.26.18 -- Bombay, December 27, 1974)*

or so people who have critical knowledge of the Pakistani nuclear infrastructure. Also there are steadfast efforts of different extremist groups to infiltrate the labs and put sleepers and so on in there.

Some groups are trying to provoke confrontation between Pakistan and India in the hope that Pakistani military would transport tactical nuclear weapons closer to the front lines, where they would be more vulnerable to seizure. The United Nations Terrorism Prevention Branch estimated that as many as 130 terrorist groups could pose a nuclear threat, due to the increase in the smuggling of radioactive material. In the first three months of 2001 alone there were 20 confirmed incidents of nuclear smuggling, including thefts from Germany, Mexico, Romania, and South Africa. The rate of incidents in 1999-2000 was double the rate in 1996.

India-Pakistan Relations : Seeds of Conflict And Destruction

India and Pakistan have fought three wars since independence in 1947, two of them over the disputed territory of Kashmir. In 1998, both countries conducted nuclear tests and in 1999 went to the brink of war over the incursion of armed Jehadis in the Kargil area of Indian-controlled Jammu and Kashmir.

On several occasions, the world has seen heavy builtup of troops along Indo-Pak border with tensions mounting high and it all just needs a spark to start a full fledged war which can easily translate into nuclear exchange.

In December 2001, A group of terrorists attacked Indian Parliament and Indian government, holding Pakistan responsible for their training and shelter, ordered heavy built up of forces along the border. Pakistan denied any involvement in the attack and, at least initially, implied that India may have "stage-managed" the incident for its own political purposes. Pakistan responded with its own built up and arsenal was moved to front lines. The US and

"I do not believe that civilization will be wiped out in a war fought with the atomic bomb. Perhaps two-thirds of the people of the earth will be killed."
Albert Einstein

European countries evacuated its citizens and issued warnings against travelling to these two countries. Threat of war and subsequent nuclear exchange was very real.

In the midst of all that, Indian Army Chief's plane, while flying in the front areas, was fired at when it allegedly strayed into Pakistani side. It did not even carry any flares to dodge the heat seeking missiles. Anyways God saved him and possibly the world.

Cyber Wars & Terrorism

20th century battle field boundaries are shifting. Battles have moved under water, in air and across continents. Now it is in the realm of computers because computers control every aspect of our life. Jamming a country's computers would mean choking its life air and ripping it apart.

Computers control our basic amenities like power, water and communication. Break down of computer infrastructure would instantly incapacitate a country.

Therefore, Cyber warfare (also known as cybernetic war, or cyberwar) is the use of computers and the Internet in conducting warfare in cyberspace.

Jeff Green, senior vice president of McAfee Avert Labs, says, "Cybercrime is now a global issue. It has evolved significantly and is no longer just a threat to industry and individuals but increasingly to national security. Future attacks are predicted to be even more sophisticated. Attacks have progressed from initial curiosity probes to well-funded and well-organized operations for political, military, economic and technical purposes."

There are several methods of attack in cyber warfare:

* Attacking critical infrastructure: Power, water, fuel, communications, commercial and transportation are all vulnerable to a cyber attack.

* Cyber Espionage: Cyber espionage is the act or practice of obtaining secrets (sensitive, proprietary of classified information) from individuals, competitors, rivals, groups, governments and enemies also for military, political, or economic advantage using illegal exploitation methods on internet, networks, software and or computers.

* Web vandalism: Attacks that deface web pages, or denial-of-service attacks. This is normally swiftly combated and of little harm.

* Propaganda: Political messages can be spread through or to anyone with access to the internet.

* Gathering data: Classified information that is not handled securely can be intercepted and even modified, making espionage possible from the other side of the world.

* Distributed Denial-of-Service Attacks: Large numbers of computers in one country launch a DoS attack against systems

* Equipment disruption: Military activities that use computers and satellites for coordination are at risk from this type of attack. Orders and communications can be intercepted or replaced, putting soldiers at risk.

* Compromised Counterfeit Hardware: Common hardware used in computers and networks that have malicious software hidden inside the software, firmware or even the microprocessors.

Reported Threats

The Internet security company McAfee stated in their 2007 annual report that approximately 120 countries have been developing ways to use the Internet as a weapon and targets rival country's financial markets, government computer systems and utilities.

In activities reminiscent of the Cold War, which caused countries to engage in clandestine activities, intelligence agencies are routinely testing networks looking for weaknesses. These techniques for probing weaknesses in the internet and global networks are growing more sophisticated every year.

The report further says that China is at the forefront of the cyber war. China has been accused of cyber-attacks on India and Germany and the United States.

The term terrorism is used by the great powers simply to refer to forms of violence of which they disapprove.
~Chomsky

Known Attacks - Examples

* The United States had come under attack from computers and computer networks situated in China and Russia.
* On May 17, 2007 Estonia came under cyber attack. The Estonian parliament, ministries, banks, and media were targeted.
* On first week of September 2007, The Pentagon and various French, German and British government computers were attacked by hackers of Chinese origin.
* In the second week of April hackers hacked the Indian MEA (Ministry of External Affairs) computers.
* Georgian and Azerbaijani sites were attacked by hackers during the 2008 South Ossetia War.

The intelligence groups are coming to grips with the challenge of cyber warfare intelligence. Much of the advanced infrastructure used in traditional warfare, like satellite imagery, is ineffective in the realm of cyber. New techniques and technologies are required for intelligence agencies to operate in this field.

Cyber Wars : India Vs Pakistan, China Vs India - A Case Study

China's cyber warfare army is marching on and has mounted almost daily attacks on Indian computer networks, both government and private.

According to senior government officials, these attacks are not isolated incidents of something so generic or basic as "hacking" — they are far more sophisticated and complete — and there is a method behind the madness. The core of the assault is that the Chinese are constantly scanning and mapping India's official networks. This gives them a very good idea of not only the content but also of how to disable the networks or distract them during a conflict. This, officials say, is China's way of gaining "an asymmetrical advantage" over a potential adversary.

China's biggest attacks in the last few months include an attack on NIC (National Infomatics Centre), National Security Council, and on the Ministry of External Affairs.

There are three main weapons in use against Indian networks — BOTS, key loggers and mapping of networks. According to sources in the government, Chinese hackers are acknowledged experts in setting up BOTS. A BOT is a parasite program embedded in a network, which hijacks the network and makes other computers act according to its wishes, which, in turn, are controlled by "external" forces.

The controlled computers are known as "zombies" in the colourful language of cyber security, and are a key aspect in cyber warfare. According to official sources, there are close to 50,000 BOTS in India at present — and these are "operational" figures.

What is the danger? Simply put, the danger is that at the appointed time, these "external" controllers of BOTNETS will command the networks, through the zombies, to move them at will.

Exactly a year ago, Indian computer security experts got a glimpse of what could happen when a targeted attack against Estonia shut that country down — it was done by one million computers from different parts of the world — and many of them were from India! That, officials said, was executed by cyber terrorists from Russia, who are deemed to be more deadlier.

National security adviser M K Narayanan has set up the National Technology Research Organization, which is also involved in assessing cyber security threats.

Now with regards to India vs Pakistan, cyberspace is rampant with incidents of Pakistani and Indian hackers playing a game of one upmanship with repeated reports of hacking of government oriented websites.

In the latest incident, the website of the Andhra Pradesh CID website was hacked by a Pakistani hackers group in retaliation to a hack of the Pakistan's Oil and Gas Regulatory Authority's (OGRA) website by a group of Indian hackers.

There is a group in Pakistan called Pakistan Cyber Army (PCA) which recently hacked the web site of the Indian Institute of Remote Sensing (IIRS) (www.iirs.gov.in), Centre for Transportation Research and Management (www.ctram.indianrail.gov.in).

Dangerous Weapons of Mass Destruction (WMDs)

Weapons of mass destruction can wipe out life from this planet in matter of hours which has sustained itself for millions of years. Following are some of the modern weapons of mass destruction.

Hydrogen bomb

A much more powerful weapon than the atom bomb, the hydrogen bomb relies on the release of thermonuclear energy by the condensation of hydrogen nuclei to helium nuclei (as happens in the Sun). The first test detonation was at Enewetak in the Pacific Ocean in 1952 by the USA.

Neutron bomb or enhanced radiation weapon (ERW)

The neutron or ERW bomb is a very small hydrogen bomb that has relatively high radiation but relatively low blast, designed to kill (in up to six days) by a brief neutron radiation wave that leaves buildings and weaponry intact.

Intercontinental Ballistic Missiles

ICBMs refer to missiles which can strike across the continents. These are equipped with clusters of warheads (which can be directed to individual targets) and are known as multiple independently targetable re-entry vehicles (MIRVs). The 1980s US-designed MX (Peacekeeper) carries up to ten warheads in each missile. Each missile has a range of about 6,400 kms and eight MIRVs (each nuclear-armed) capable of hitting eight separate targets within about 240 kms of the central aiming point.

Biological or Germ Warfare

Biological weapons can be released in a number of ways, both from air and ground and even clandestinely. These germs can kill many millions in matter of hours. Most feared germs of biological warfare include: Anthrax, Smallpox, Botulism, Ebola, Q Fever, Plague. Venezuelan Encephalitis, Yellow Fever, Tularemia etc.

Chemical Warfare

Chemical warfare involves using the toxic properties of chemical substances to kill, injure or incapacitate an enemy. About 70 different chemicals have been used or stockpiled as Chemical Weapons (CW) agents during the 20th century. These chemicals are in liquid, gas or solid form and blister, choke and affect the nerves or blood. Chemical warfare agents are generally classified according to their effect on the organism and can be roughly grouped as: Nerve Agents, Mustard Agents, Hydrogen Cyanide, Tear Gases, Arsines, Psychotomimetic Agents, Toxins etc.

We can cite the example of Mustard which is an oily liquid with a garlic-like smell. Mustard gas was first used as a chemical-warfare agent during WWI, when it was responsible for about 70% of the million-plus gas casualties. Both in vapour and in liquid form its effect is to burn any body-tissue which it touches. Taken into the body, it can act as a systemic poison. Its burning effects are not normally apparent for some hours after exposure, whereupon they build up into the hideous picture of blindness, blistering and lung damage.

Agent orange, a dangerous chemical was extensively used by America in Vietnam war for defoliating and its ill effect on local population is visible even today.

The Electromagnetic Bomb (E-bomb)

An e-bomb (electromagnetic bomb) is a weapon that uses an intense electromagnetic field to create a brief pulse of energy that affects electronic circuitry without harming humans or buildings. At low levels, the pulse temporarily disables electronics systems; mid-range levels corrupt computer data. Very high levels completely destroy electronic circuitry, thus disabling any type of machine that uses electricity, including computers, radios, and ignition systems in vehicles. Although not directly lethal, an e-bomb would devastate any target that relies upon electricity: a category encompassing any potential military target and most civilian areas of the world as well. According to a CBS News report, the United States deployed an experimental e-bomb on March 24, 2003 to knock out Iraqi satellite television and disrupt the broadcast of propaganda. In a matter of seconds, a big enough e-bomb could thrust an entire city back 200 years or cripple a military unit.

The concept behind the e-bomb arose from nuclear weaponry research in the 1950s. When the U.S. military tested hydrogen bombs over the Pacific Ocean, streetlights were blown out hundreds of miles away and radio equipment was affected as far away as Australia.

Clash of Civilizations

The Latest Phase Of The Evolution Of Conflict In The Modern World.

By Samuel P. Huntington

World politics is entering a new phase, in which the great divisions among humankind and the dominating source of international conflict will be cultural. Civilizations - the highest cultural groupings of people - are differentiated from each other by religion, history, language and tradition. These divisions are deep and increasing in importance. From Yugoslavia to the Middle East to Central Asia, the fault lines of civilizations are the battle lines of the future. The primary axis of conflict in the future would be along cultural and religious lines.

The Clash of Civilizations theory is proposed by Samuel P. Huntington, a political scientist and it says people's cultural and religious identities will be the primary source of conflict in the post-Cold War world. His warnings that the Western civilization may decline is inspired by Arnold J. Toynbee, Carroll Quigley, and Oswald Spengler.

Iranian leader Mohammad Khatami introduced the idea of Dialogue Among Civilizations as a response to the theory of Clash of Civilizations. The term "Dialogue among Civilizations" became more known after the United Nations adopted a resolution to name the year 2001 as the year of Dialogue among Civilizations.

During the Cold War, the world was divided into the First, Second and Third Worlds. Those divisions are no longer relevant. It is far more meaningful now to group countries not in terms of their political or economic systems or in terms of their level of economic development but rather in terms of their culture and civilization.

A Divided World Along The Civilizational Lines

Huntington divided the world into the following "major" civilizations in his thesis :

Western Civilization

Western civilization is centered on Australasia, Northern America, and Europe (excluding most of Eastern Europe and the Balkans). Whether Latin America and the former member states of the Soviet Union are included, or are instead their own separate civilizations, will be an important future consideration for those regions.

Latin America includes Central America (excluding Belize), South America (excluding the Guianas), Cuba, the Dominican Republic, and Mexico may be considered a part of Western civilization, though it has slightly distinct social and political structures from Europe and Northern America. Many people of the Southern Cone, however, regard themselves as full members of the Western civilization.

It also includes the Orthodox world of the former Soviet Union (excluding most of Central Asia, the Baltic states, and Azerbaijan), the former Yugoslavia (excluding Slovenia and Croatia), Bulgaria, Cyprus, Greece, and Romania.

The Eastern World

The Eastern world is the mix of the Buddhist, Sinic, Hindu, and Japonic civilizations.

The Buddhist areas of Bhutan, Cambodia, Laos, Mongolia, Myanmar, Sri Lanka, and Thailand are identified as separate from other civilizations, but they do not constitute a major civilization in the sense of international affairs.

Then there is the Sinic civilization of the China, Koreas, Singapore, Taiwan, and Vietnam. This group also includes the Chinese diaspora, especially in relation to Southeast Asia.

Hindu civilization, located chiefly in India and Nepal, and is

The West in effect is using international institutions, military power and economic resources to run the world in ways that will maintain Western predominance, protect Western interests and promote Western political and economic values.
-Huntington

culturally adhered to by the global Indian diaspora.

Japan is considered a hybrid of Chinese civilization and older Altaic patterns.

The Muslim world of the Greater Middle East

The Muslim world of the Greater Middle East (excluding Armenia, Cyprus, Ethiopia, Georgia, Greece, Israel, Kazakhstan, Malta, Sudan, and Turkey), also includes northern West Africa, Albania, Bangladesh, Brunei, Comoros, Indonesia, Malaysia, and Maldives.

Sub-Saharan Africa Civilization

The civilization of Sub-Saharan Africa is located in Southern Africa, Middle Africa (excluding Chad), East Africa (excluding the Horn of Africa, Comoros, Kenya, Mauritius, and Tanzania), Cape Verde, Côte d'Ivoire, Ghana, Liberia, and Sierra Leone.

Lone Countries

Instead of belonging to one of the "major" civilizations, Ethiopia, Haiti, and Turkey are labeled as "Lone" countries. Israel could be considered a unique state with its own civilization, but one which is extremely similar to the West. Anglophone Caribbean, former British colonies in the Caribbean, constitutes a distinct entity.

Torn Countries

There are also others which are considered as "Torn countries" since they do not belong to a single civilization. Examples include India ("torn" between Hindu and Islam), France (torn between South American, in the case of French Guiana; and the West), Benin, Chad, Kenya, Nigeria, Sudan, Tanzania, and Togo (all torn between Islam and Sub-Saharan Africa), Guyana and Suriname (torn between Hindu and South American), China (torn between Sinic, Buddhist, in the case of Tibet; and the West, in the case of Hong Kong and Macau), and the Philippines (torn between Islam, in the case of Mindanao; Sinic, and the West).

Why Civilizations Will Clash

Huntington feels that civilization identity will be increasingly important in the future, and the world will be shaped in large measure by the interactions among seven or eight major civilizations. These include Western, Confucian, Japanese, Islamic, Hindu, Slavic-Orthodox, Latin American and possibly African civilization. The most important conflicts of the future will occur along the cultural fault lines separating these civilizations from one another.

The Reasons For Clash

1) Differences among civilizations are not only real; they are basic. Civilizations are differentiated from each other by history, language, culture, tradition and, most important, religion. The people of different civilizations have different views on the relations between God and man, the individual and the group, the citizen and the state, parents and children, husband and wife, as well as differing views of the relative importance of rights and responsibilities, liberty and authority, equality and hierarchy. These differences are the product of centuries. They will not soon disappear. They are far more fundamental than differences among political ideologies and political regimes. Differences do not necessarily mean conflict, and conflict does not necessarily mean violence. Over the centuries, however, differences among civilizations have generated the most prolonged and the most violent conflicts.

2) The world is becoming a smaller place. The interactions between peoples of different civilizations are increasing; these increasing interactions intensify civilization consciousness and awareness of differences between civilizations and commonalities within civilizations. North African immigration to France generates hostility among Frenchmen and at the same time increased receptivity to immigration by "good" European Catholic Poles. Americans react far more negatively to Japanese investment than to larger investments from Canada and European countries.

> *"We are facing a need and a movement far transcending the level of issues and policies and the governments that pursue them. This is no less than a clash of civilizations -- the perhaps irrational but surely historic reaction of an ancient rival against our Judeo-Christian heritage, our secular present, and the worldwide expansion of both."*
> *-Bernard Lewis (The Roots of Muslim Rage)*

Similarly, as Donald Horowitz has pointed out, "An Ibo may be an Owerri Ibo or an Onitsha Ibo in the Eastern region of Nigeria. In Lagos, he is simply an Ibo. In London, he is a Nigerian. In New York, he is an African." The interactions among peoples of different civilizations enhance the civilization-consciousness of people that, in turn, invigorates differences and animosities stretching or thought to stretch back deep into history.

3) The processes of economic modernization and social change throughout the world are separating people from long-standing local identities. They also weaken the nation state as a source of identity. In much of the world religion has moved in to fill this gap, often in the form of movements that are labeled "fundamentalist." Such movements are found in Western Christianity, Judaism, Buddhism and Hinduism, as well as in Islam. In most countries and most religions the people active in fundamentalist movements are young, college-educated, middle-class technicians, professionals and business persons. The "unsecularization of the world," George Weigel has remarked, "is one of the dominant social factors of life in the late twentieth century." The revival of religion provides a basis for identity and commitment that transcends national boundaries and unites civilizations.

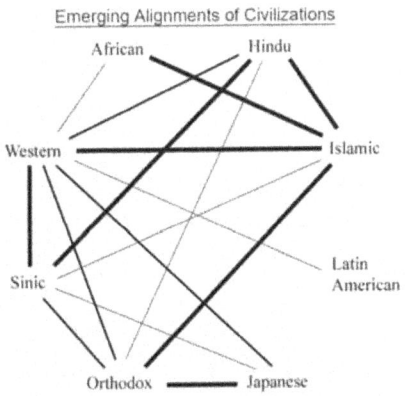

Greater Line Thickness Represents More Conflict in the Civilizational Relationship

4) The growth of civilization-consciousness is enhanced by the dual role of the West. On the one hand, the West is at a peak of power. At the same time, however, and perhaps as a result, a return to the roots phenomenon is occurring among non-Western civilizations. Increasingly one hears references to trends toward a turning inward and "Asianization" in Japan, the end of the Nehru

legacy and the "Hinduization" of India, the failure of Western ideas of socialism and nationalism and hence "re-Islamization" of the Middle East, and now a debate over Westernization versus Russianization in Boris Yeltsin's country. A West at the peak of its power confronts non-Wests that increasingly have the desire, the will and the resources to shape the world in non-Western ways.

In the past, the elites of non-Western societies were usually the people who were most involved with the West, had been educated at Oxford, the Sorbonne or Sandhurst, and had absorbed Western attitudes and values. At the same time, the populace in non-Western countries often remained deeply imbued with the indigenous culture. Now, however, these relationships are being reversed. A de-Westernization and indigenization of elites is occurring in many non-Western countries at the same time that Western, usually American, cultures, styles and habits become more popular among the mass of the people.

5) Cultural characteristics and differences are less mutable and hence less easily compromised and resolved than political and economic ones. In the former Soviet Union, communists can become democrats, the rich can become poor and the poor rich, but Russians cannot become Estonians and Azeris cannot become Armenians. In class and ideological conflicts, the key question was "Which side are you on?" And people could and did choose sides and change sides. In conflicts between civilizations, the question is "What are you?" That is a given that cannot be changed. And as we know, from Bosnia to the Caucasus to the Sudan, the wrong answer to that question can mean a bullet in the head. Even more than ethnicity, religion discriminates sharply and exclusively among people. A person can be half-French and half-Arab and simultaneously even a citizen of two countries. It is more difficult to be half-Catholic and half-Muslim.

A new cold war is under way between China and America.
~Deng Xaioping

5) Economic regionalism is increasing, opines Huntington. The proportions of total trade that are intraregional rose between 1980 and 1989 from 51 percent to 59 percent in Europe, 33 percent to 37 percent in East Asia, and 32 percent to 36 percent in North America. The importance of regional economic blocs is likely to continue to increase in the future. On the one hand, successful economic regionalism will reinforce civilization-consciousness. On the other hand, economic regionalism may succeed only when it is rooted in a common civilization. The European Community rests on the shared foundation of European culture and Western Christianity. The success of the North American Free Trade Area depends on the convergence now underway of Mexican, Canadian and American cultures. Japan, in contrast, faces difficulties in creating a comparable economic entity in East Asia because Japan is a society and civilization unique to itself. However strong the trade and investment links Japan may develop with other East Asian countries, its cultural differences with those countries inhibit and perhaps preclude its promoting regional economic integration like that in Europe and North America.

One cartoonist dividing the globe

Common culture, in contrast, is clearly facilitating the rapid expansion of the economic relations between the People's Republic of China and Hong Kong, Taiwan, Singapore and the overseas Chinese communities in other Asian countries. With the Cold War over, cultural commonalities increasingly overcome ideological differences, and mainland China and Taiwan move closer together. If cultural commonality is a prerequisite for economic integration, the principal East Asian economic bloc of the future is likely to be centered on China. This bloc is, in fact, already coming into existence. Despite the current Japanese dominance of the region, the Chinese-based economy of Asia is rapidly emerging as a new epicenter for industry, commerce and finance. This strategic area contains substantial amounts of technology and manufacturing capability (Taiwan), outstanding entrepreneurial, marketing and services acumen (Hong Kong), a fine communications network (Singapore), a tremendous pool of financial capital (all three), and very large endowments of land, resources and labor (mainland China).... From Guangzhou to Singapore, from Kuala Lumpur to Manila, this influential network -- often based on extensions of the traditional clans -- has been described as the backbone of the East Asian economy. *(Murray Weidenbaum, Greater China: The Next Economic Superpower?)*

Culture and religion also form the basis of the Economic Cooperation Organization (ECO), which brings together ten non-Arab Muslim countries: Iran, Pakistan, Turkey, Azerbaijan, Kazakhstan, Kyrgyzstan, Turkmenistan, Tadjikistan, Uzbekistan and Afghanistan. One impetus to the revival and expansion of this organization, founded originally in the 1960s by Turkey, Pakistan and Iran, is the realization by the leaders of several of these countries that they had no chance of admission to the European Community.

As people define their identity in ethnic and religious terms, they are likely to see an "us" versus "them" relation existing between themselves and people of different ethnicity or religion. The end of ideologically defined states in Eastern Europe and the former Soviet Union permits traditional ethnic identities and animosities to come to the fore. Differences in culture and religion create differences over policy issues, ranging from human rights to immigration to trade and commerce to the environment.

Most important, the efforts of the West to promote its values of democracy and liberalism to universal values, to maintain its military predominance and to advance its economic interests engender countering responses from other civilizations. Decreasingly able to mobilize support and form coalitions on the basis of ideology, governments and groups will increasingly attempt to mobilize support by appealing to common religion and civilization identity.

The clash of civilizations thus occurs at two levels. At the micro-level, adjacent groups along the fault lines between civilizations struggle, often violently, over the control of territory and each other. At the macro-level, states from different civilizations compete for relative military and economic power, struggle over the control of international institutions and third parties, and competitively promote their particular political and religious values.

The Fault Lines Between Civilizations

The Fault Lines between civilizations are replacing the political and ideological boundaries of the Cold War as the flash points for crisis and bloodshed. The Cold War began when the Iron Curtain divided Europe politically and ideologically. The Cold War ended with the end of the Iron Curtain. As the ideological division of Europe has disappeared, the cultural division of Europe between Western Christianity, on the one hand, and Orthodox Christianity and Islam, on the other, has reemerged. The most significant dividing line in Europe, as William Wallace has suggested, may well be the eastern boundary of Western Christianity in the year 1500. This line runs along what are now the boundaries between Finland and Russia and between the Baltic states and Russia, cuts through Belarus and Ukraine separating the more Catholic western Ukraine from Orthodox eastern Ukraine, swings westward separating Transylvania from the rest of Romania, and then goes through Yugoslavia almost exactly along the line now separating Croatia and Slovenia from the rest of Yugoslavia. The peoples to the north and west of this line are Protestant or Catholic; they are generally economically better off than the peoples to the east; and they may now look forward to increasing involvement in a common European economy and to the consolidation of democratic political systems. The peoples to the east and south of this line are Orthodox or Muslim; they historically belonged to the Ottoman or Tsarist empires and were only lightly touched by the shaping events in the rest of Europe; they are generally less advanced economically; they seem much less likely to develop stable democratic political systems. The Velvet Curtain of culture has replaced the Iron Curtain of ideology as the most significant dividing line in Europe.

As the events in Yugoslavia show, it is not only a line of difference; it is also at times a line of bloody conflict.

Conflict along the fault line between Western and Islamic civilizations has been going on for 1,300 years. From the eleventh to the thirteenth century the Crusaders attempted with temporary success to bring Christianity and Christian rule to the Holy Land. From the fourteenth to the seventeenth century, the Ottoman Turks reversed the balance, extended their sway over the Middle East and the Balkans, captured Constantinople, and twice laid siege to Vienna. In the nineteenth and early twentieth centuries as Ottoman power declined, Britain, France, and Italy established Western control over most of North Africa and the Middle East.

After World War II, the West, in turn, began to retreat; the colonial empires disappeared; first Arab nationalism and then Islamic fundamentalism manifested themselves; the West became heavily dependent on the Persian Gulf countries for its energy; the oil-rich Muslim countries became money-rich and, when they wished to, weapons-rich. Several wars occurred between Arabs and Israel (created by the West). France fought a bloody and ruthless war in Algeria for most of the 1950s; British and French forces invaded Egypt in 1956; American forces returned to Lebanon, attacked Libya, and engaged in various military encounters with Iran; Arab and Islamic terrorists, supported by at least three Middle Eastern governments, bombed Western planes and installations and seized Western hostages. This warfare between Arabs and the West culminated in 1990, when the United States sent a massive army to the Persian Gulf to defend some Arab countries against aggression by another.

This centuries-old military interaction between the West and Islam is unlikely to decline. It could become more virulent. Many Arab countries, in addition to the oil exporters, are reaching levels of economic and social development where autocratic forms of government become inappropriate and efforts to introduce democracy become stronger. Some openings in Arab political systems have already occurred. The principal beneficiaries of these openings have been Islamist movements.

Threat 5 - Violence & Wars, Clash of Civilizations

Those relations are also complicated by demography. The spectacular population growth in Arab countries, particularly in North Africa, has led to increased migration to Western Europe. In Italy, France and Germany, racism is increasingly open, and political reactions and violence against Arab and Turkish migrants have become more intense and more widespread since 1990.

On both sides the interaction between Islam and the West is seen as a clash of civilizations.

Historically, the other great antagonistic interaction of Arab Islamic civilization has been with the pagan and now increasingly Christian black people. It has been reflected in the on-going civil war in the Sudan between Arabs and blacks, the fighting in Chad between Libyan-supported insurgents and the government, the tensions between Orthodox Christians and Muslims in the Horn of Africa, and the political conflicts, recurring riots and communal violence between Muslims and Christians in Nigeria. The modernization of Africa and the spread of Christianity in Nigeria. The modernization of Africa and the spread of Christianity are likely to enhance the probability of violence along this fault line. Symptomatic of the intensification of this conflict was the Pope John Paul II's speech in Khartoum in February 1993 attacking

the actions of the Sudan's Islamist government against the Christian minority there.

On the northern border of Islam, conflict has increasingly erupted between Orthodox and Muslim peoples, including the carnage of Bosnia and Sarajevo, the simmering violence between Serb and Albanian, the fragile relation between Bulgarians and their Turkish minority, the tense relations between Russians and Muslims in Central Asia, and the deployment of Russian troops to protect Russian interests in the Caucasus and Central Asia. Religion reinforces the revival of ethnic identities and restimulates Russian fears about the security of their southern borders.

The conflict of civilizations is deeply rooted elsewhere in Asia. The historic clash between Muslim and Hindu in the subcontinent manifests itself now not only is the rivalry between Pakistan and India but also in intensifying religious strife within India between increasingly militant Hindu groups and India's Muslim minority. The destruction of the Ayodhya mosque in December 1992 brought to the fore the issue of whether India will remain a secular democratic state or become a Hindu one. In East Asia, China has outstanding territorial disputes with most of its neighbors. It has pursued a ruthless policy toward the Buddhist people of Tibet, and it is pursuing an increasingly ruthless policy toward its Muslim minority. With the Cold War over, the underlying differences between China and the United States have reasserted themselves in areas such as human rights, trade and weapons proliferation. These differences are unlikely to moderate.

The same phrase has been applied to the increasingly difficult relations between Japan and the United States. Here cultural difference intensifies economic conflict. People on each side allege racism on the other, but at least on the American side the antipathies are not racial but cultural. The basic values, attitudes, behavioral patterns of the two societies could hardly be more different. The economic issues between the United States and Europe are no less serious than those between the United States and Japan, but they do not have the same political salience and emotional intensity because the differences between American culture and European culture are so much less than those between American civilization and Japanese civilization.

The interactions between civilizations vary greatly in the extent to which they are likely to be characterized by violence. Economic competition clearly predominates between the American and European subcivilizations of the West and between both of them and Japan. On the Eurasian continent, however, the proliferation of ethnic conflict, epitomized at the extreme in "ethnic cleansing," has not been totally random. It has been most frequent and most  violent between groups belonging to different civilizations. In Eurasia the great historic fault lines between civilizations are once more aflame. This is particularly true along the boundaries of the crescent-shaped Islamic bloc of nations from the bulge of Africa to central Asia. Violence also occurs between Muslims, on the one hand, and Orthodox Serbs in the Balkans, Jews in Israel, Hindus in India, Buddhists in Burma and Catholics in the Philippines. Islam has bloody borders.

The West Versus The Rest

The West is now at an extraordinary peak of power in relation to other civilizations. Its superpower opponent has disappeared

 *The West's next confrontation is definitely going to come from the Muslim world. It is in the sweep of the Islamic nations from the Meghreb to Pakistan that the struggle for a new world order will begin."*
~M. J. Akbar

from the map. Military conflict among Western states is unthinkable, and Western military power is unrivaled. Apart from Japan, the West faces no economic challenge. It dominates international economic institutions. Global political and security issues are effectively settled by a directorate of the United States, Britain and France, world economic issues by a directorate of the United States, Germany and Japan, all of which maintain extraordinarily close relations with each other to the exclusion of lesser and largely non-Western countries. Decisions made at the U.N. Security Council or in the International Monetary Fund that reflect the interests of the West are presented to the world as reflecting the desires of the world community. The very phrase "the world community" has become the euphemistic collective noun (replacing "the Free World") to give global legitimacy to actions reflecting the interests of the United States and other Western powers. Through the  IMF and other international economic institutions, the West promotes its economic interests and imposes on other nations the economic policies it thinks appropriate.

Almost invariably Western leaders claim they are acting on behalf of "the world community." One minor lapse occurred during the run-up to the Gulf War. In an interview on "Good Morning America," Dec. 21, 1990, British Prime Minister John Major referred to the actions "the West" was taking against Saddam Hussein. He quickly corrected himself and subsequently referred to "the world community." He was, however, right when he erred.

Western domination of the U.N. Security Council and its decisions, tempered only by occasional abstention by China, produced U.N. legitimation of the West's use of force to drive Iraq out of Kuwait and its elimination of Iraq's sophisticated weapons and capacity to produce such weapons.

That at least is the way in which non-Westerners see the new world, and there is a significant element of truth in their view. Differences in power and struggles for military, economic and institutional power are thus one source of conflict between the

West and other civilizations. Differences in culture, that is basic values and beliefs, are a second source of conflict. V. S. Naipaul has argued that Western civilization is the "universal civilization" that "fits all men." At a superficial level much of Western culture has indeed permeated the rest of the world. At a more basic level, however, Western concepts differ fundamentally from those prevalent in other civilizations. Western ideas of individualism, liberalism, constitutionalism, human rights, equality, liberty, the rule of law, democracy, free markets, the separation of church and state, often have little resonance in Islamic, Confucian, Japanese, Hindu, Buddhist or Orthodox cultures. Western efforts to propagate each ideas produce instead a reaction against "human rights imperialism" and a reaffirmation of indigenous values, as can be seen in the support for religious fundamentalism by the younger generation in non-Western cultures. The very notion that there could be a "universal civilization" is a Western idea, directly at odds with the particularism of most Asian societies and their emphasis on what distinguishes one people from another. Indeed, the author of a review of 100 comparative studies of values in different societies concluded that "the values that are most important in the West are least important worldwide." In the political realm, of course, these differences are

Because in the material world, for the maintenance of equilibrium of the society, sometimes killing is necessary. Just like fight, war. When the enemy has come to your country, you cannot sit idly; you must fight. But that does not mean that you are allowed to kill everyone as you like. That is a special circumstances when fighting must be there.
-Srila Prabhupada (Conversation with Professors -- June 24, 1975, Los Angeles)

most manifest in the efforts of the United States and other Western powers to induce other people to adopt Western ideas concerning democracy and human rights. Modern democratic government originated in the West.

The central axis of world politics in the future is likely to be, in Kishore Mahbubani's phrase, the conflict between "the West and the Rest" and the responses of non-Western civilizations to Western power and values. Those responses generally take one or a combination of three forms. At one extreme, non-Western states can, like Burma and North Korea, attempt to pursue a course of isolation, to insulate their societies from penetration or "corruption" by the West, and, in effect, to opt out of participation in the Western-dominated global community. The costs of this course, however, are high, and few states have pursued it exclusively. A second alternative, the equivalent of "band-wagoning" in international relations theory, is to attempt to join the West and accept its values and institutions. The third alternative is to attempt to "balance" the West by developing economic and military power and cooperating with other non-Western societies against the West, while preserving indigenous values and institutions; in short, to modernize but not to Westernize.

The Future

Differences between civilizations are real and important; civilization-consciousness is increasing; conflict between civilizations will supplant ideological and other forms of conflict as the dominant global form of conflict; international relations, historically a game played out within Western civilization, will increasingly be de-Westernized and become a game in which non-Western civilizations are actors and not simply objects; successful political, security and economic international institutions are more

When you map WMD and terrorism, all roads intersect in Pakistan.
  ~Graham Allison

likely to develop within civilizations than across civilizations; conflicts between groups in different civilizations will be more frequent, more sustained and more violent than conflicts between groups in the same civilization; violent conflicts between groups in different civilizations are the most likely and most dangerous source of escalation that could lead to global wars; the paramount axis of world politics will be the relations between "the West and the Rest"; the elites in some torn non-Western countries will try to make their countries part of the West, but in most cases face major obstacles to accomplishing this; a central focus of conflict for the immediate future will be between the West and several Islamic-Confucian states.

For the relevant future, there will be no universal civilization, but instead a world of different civilizations, each of which will have to learn to coexist with the others.
(Copyright - Samuel P. Huntington)

Impact of Nuclear War

Nuclear bombs wreak far greater damage than conventional explosives. They owe their greater destructive power to immediate blast, heat, and radiation, and to the lingering effects of radioactive fallout. A study presented at the annual meeting of the American Geophysical Union in December 2006 asserted that even a small-scale, regional nuclear war could produce as many direct fatalities as all of World War II and disrupt the global climate for a decade or more. In a regional nuclear conflict scenario where two opposing nations in the subtropics would each use 50 Hiroshima-sized nuclear weapons (ca. 15 kiloton each) on major populated centers, the researchers estimated fatalities from 2.6 million to 16.7 million per country. Also, as much as five million tons of soot would be released, which would produce a cooling of several degrees over

Civilization... wrecks the planet from seafloor to stratosphere. ~Richard Bach

large areas of North America and Eurasia, including most of the grain-growing regions. The cooling would last for years and could be "catastrophic" according to the researchers.

The combined effects of the Hiroshima bomb killed over half of city residents, turned the lives of many survivors into a lifelong nightmare, and leveled the entire city. Owing to its greater yield, the effects of a typical contemporary bomb are expected to be far greater. Although the aftermath of an all-out nuclear war among major nuclear powers cannot be described with certainty, it would surely be the greatest catastrophe in recorded history. By the late 1960s the number of ICBMs and warheads was so high on both 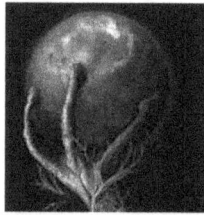 sides that either the USA or USSR was capable of completely destroying the other country's infrastructure. Thus a balance of power system known as mutually assured destruction (MAD) came into being. It was thought that any full-scale exchange between the powers could not produce a victorious side and thus neither would risk initiating one.

In any combatant country, it may kill half the people, afflict many survivors with a variety of radiation-induced diseases, destroy industrial and military capabilities, and contaminate vast tracts of land. Such a war might also lower the quality of the human genetic pool, damage the biosphere, cause a breakdown of national and international economic systems, destroy the health care and prevention system, and move surviving societies in unpredictable directions. Although extinction of the human species is unlikely, it cannot altogether be ruled out. History, psychology, and common sense strongly suggest that nuclear war is more probable than most of us would like to believe. This, and the cataclysmic quality of nuclear war, imply that humanity can scarcely afford another half a century in the shadow of a nuclear holocaust.

Nuclear Winter

Nuclear winter is a term that describes the predicted climatic effects of nuclear war. Severely cold weather and reduced sunlight for a period of months or years would be caused by detonating large numbers of nuclear weapons, especially over flammable targets such as cities, where large amounts of smoke and soot would be injected into the Earth's stratosphere.

The nuclear winter scenario predicts that the huge fires caused by nuclear explosions (particularly from burning urban areas) would loft massive amounts of dark smoke and aerosol particles from the fires into the upper troposphere / stratosphere, at 10-15 kilometers (6-9 miles) above the Earth's surface, the absorption of sunlight would further heat the smoke, lifting it into the stratosphere, a layer where the smoke would persist for years, with no rain to wash it out, and would block out much of the sun's light from reaching the surface, causing surface temperatures to drop drastically.

* A minor nuclear war (such as between India and Pakistan or in the Middle East), with each country using 50 Hiroshima-sized atom bombs as airbursts on urban areas, could produce climate change unprecedented in recorded human history. This is only 0.03% of the explosive power of the current global arsenal.

* A nuclear war between the United States and Russia today could produce nuclear winter, with temperatures plunging below freezing in the summer in major agricultural regions, threatening the food supply for most of the planet.

Not like this, where a sudra is elected as president, he is not fighting, he is in a safe place, and he is simply directing, "You go and fight. Let me see how you are fighting." No. The king, the ksatriya, he will come forth in the front of fight. That was fight. The king was on the front. The other party, he was also in front. The king is fighting with king, and the soldiers are fighting with soldier. So when the king is killed, then the other party becomes victorious. That was the process of war, not that releasing atomic bomb from the sky and kill so many innocent persons. No, that is not war. So war, if it is fought on principle, on religious principle, that is called dharma-yuddha.
-Srila Prabhupada (Bhagavad-gita 2.13 -- Manila, October 12, 1972)

End of Modern Civilization and Alternative Future

Threat - 6

Resurgence of Diseases
And Health Issues

Industrialisation has spawned its own health problems. Modern stressors include noise, air, water pollution, poor nutrition, dangerous machinery, impersonal work, isolation, poverty, homelessness, and substance abuse. Health problems in industrial nations are as much caused by economic, social, political, and cultural factors as by pathogens. Industrialisation has become a major medical issue worldwide.

Formerly problems were shortages of castor oil for night lamps, horse crap in city streets, and farm produce that could not be transported to the nearest city. Television, genetics, satellites, tiny personal computers, Google, refrigerators, aluminum, organ transplants, the new physics of nanoparticles, and so on and on... these things were not imagined. Well, we have increased these 'facilities' but at the same time we have increased our problems.

Lethal Viruses and Diseases of Industrial Era

In pre-industrial society there were diseases caused by viruses and bacteria. In modern society, in addition to viral and bacterial diseases, there are hundreds of lifestyle diseases - cancer, stroke, diabetes, hypertension, obesity, multiple organ failures etc. Science has miserably failed as far as containment of diseases is concerned. With the progress of modern science, the general health of masses has only degraded. Of late, several dangerous strains of viruses have surfaced and thanks to global interconnectivity, in matter of days millions can get infected if there is a global outbreak.

Let us take the case of Uganda. This country is gripped by

The hospitals are increasing, beds are increasing, and the diseases are increasing. Then what can you do?
-Srila Prabhupada (Morning Walk — April 1, 1974, Bombay)

terror over a new strain of one of the world's most deadly diseases, Ebola haemorrhagic fever, which spreads by touch and kills between 50% and 90% of victims. Ugandan President has asked people to stop shaking hands, MPs have called for an end to public gatherings, market vendors wear gloves and Roman Catholic priests no longer give the communion wafers and wine by hand.

After an incubation period of up to 21 days, Ebola patients develop terrible symptoms: high fever, headache and joint pains, then vomiting and diarrhoea, and in some cases bleeding from the mouth, nose, eyes and ears. In most cases, multiple organ failure, haemorrhaging or shock brings death. This new strain is feared to kill more slowly than previously, leaving more time for the disease to spread. There is no vaccine and no cure. The only hope is to contain the lethal virus, but Ebola moves fast and is hard to track. If just one infected person boards a plane, this could become a global outbreak.

"For the time being people should resort to jambo [waving]. If I don't shake your hand, it doesn't mean I don't like you," President Yoweri Museveni has told his people. America's Centres for Disease Control and Prevention (CDC) in Atlanta, Georgia has confirmed the fears with Ebola that it can move very quickly to different parts of the world.

Now we move back to day to day diseases like cancer. The claim that science can cure cancer is an irony because modern scientific living is the cause of cancer. Mostly Cancer is caused by toxic chemicals - carcinogens. Industrial Society has flooded the ecosystem and food chain with toxic chemicals. Most of the farm land has been poisoned with pesticides due to industrial agriculture. The Land, air, water, the entire food chain is contaminated with

Most of the tools a doctor used 25 years ago fitted into a small black bag. Today the typical American physician owns or has access to $250,000 worth of diagnostic equipment. Whenever one tries to link the development of new technology with any improvement in healing, the empirical response is the same: there is none.
- Dr. William Knaus

thousands of man-made toxic chemicals which did not exist before modernization. Out of millions of cases, a small percentage is treated successfully with surgery, radiation and chemotherapy etc. but the environmental toxicity, the cause of cancer, is ever present in life.

Tuberculosis: Dangerous New Incurable Strains

Many people think of tuberculosis as being a disease from the past. The truth is far from it: Tuberculosis is mutating into dangerous new strains for which there is no known cure.

One of the most frightening strains is XDR-TB, which stands for extensively drug-resistant TB. Unlike less virulent strains, XDR-TB does not respond to the antibiotics that are usually used to treat TB. The disease is virtually incurable and threatens to become a pandemic.

About 40,000 new cases of XDR-TB are emerging every year, the World Health Organization (WHO) estimates. Award-winning photojournalist James Nachtwey, who has chronicled the death and devastation the disease is bringing to many countries around the world, describes XDR-TB as "a merciless, man-eating predator lurking in the shadows." He warns: "If it's not contained, the consequences could be dire."

Nachtwey, who has been covering humanitarian crises for more than 30 years, was awarded a TED prize in 2007 which gave him $100,000. His wish centered on spreading awareness of this deadly form of TB and the images are borne out of Nachtwey's frustrations with the underreporting of what is potentially a global health crisis.

> *Because of all these self-destructive practices and the powerful influence of time, the average life span (ayur) is decreasing. Modern scientists, seeking to gain credibility among the mass of people, often publish statistics supposedly showing that science has increased the average duration of life. But these statistics do not take into account the number of people killed through the cruel practice of abortion. When we figure aborted children into the life expectancy of the total population, we find that the average duration of life has not at all increased in the age of Kali but is rather decreasing drastically.*
> *-Srila Prabhupada (Srimad Bhagavatam 12.2.1)*

His photos tell the grim stories of impending death. In one, a man's suffering is so palpable that it is almost impossible to tear your eyes away from him. Another image shows a woman in a Thai hospital staring vacantly, as if resigned to the fact that death is soon approaching.

Nachtwey traveled to seven different countries, including Cambodia, South Africa, Swaziland and Siberia, and used his photography to tell the story of a disease that primarily afflicts developing nations, but has been found elsewhere worldwide.

His work is documented at XDR-TB.org, a Web site solely dedicated to telling the story of the disease through his powerful images. Health experts say that the tragic thing about XDR-TB is that it should not exist.

Growing Cholera Epidemic - Zimbabwe

Zimbabwe's government has recently pleaded for international help after declaring a cholera epidemic that has killed thousands of people a national emergency and admitting that hospitals are no longer working.

The government and doctors say that hospitals need medicines and equipment and even money to pay salaries and water treatment chemicals as the country's economic crisis bites ever harder. According to the government and World Health Organisation, thousands have died in the cholera epidemic and many more cases recorded.

Health Minister says, "The emergency appeal will help us reduce the morbidity and mortality associated with the current socio-economic environment."

Sexually Transmitted Infections (STIs) Sweeping The World

The term Sexually Transmitted Infections (STIs), formerly known as venereal diseases, covers more than 25 infections passed

> *In 1996, WHO estimated that more than 1 million people were being infected daily with Sexually Transmitted Infections. An estimated 340 million new cases of syphilis, gonorrhea, chlamydia and trichomoniasis occurred throughout the world in 1999. (WHO)*

from one person to another primarily during sexual contact. In 1996, WHO estimated that more than 1 million people were being infected daily with STIs. About 60% of these infections occur in young people less than 25 years of age. An estimated 340 million new cases of syphilis, gonorrhea, chlamydia and trichomoniasis occurred throughout the world in 1999.

More than 15 million people in the United States become infected with one or more STIs every year. The United States has the highest STI rate in the industrialized world—roughly half of all Americans (50% population) become infected with an STI before the age of 35.

Every year in the UK alone, over 700,000 new STI cases are diagnosed and children as young as eleven are contracting gonorrhoea, genital warts and other STIs in increasing numbers.

In the 1970s, only two STIs were common, and both were curable. Now as many as 25 STIs have been identified, and several are incurable. In the 1980s, first genital herpes and then AIDS emerged into the public consciousness as sexually transmitted diseases that could not be cured by modern medicine.

The latest figures from the National Centre in HIV Epidemiology and Clinical Research on sexually transmitted infections in Australia show a major increase in the rates of syphilis, gonorrhoea and chlamydia and that syphilis bug has changed its infectiousness.

Despite the prevalence of STIs, studies show that many people are unaware of their risks for contracting an STI or the serious, and sometimes deadly, health consequences that may result from an untreated infection. Some STIs, such as gonorrhea or chlamydia, may cause no symptoms. People who do not know they are infected risk infecting their sexual partners and, in some cases, their unborn children. If left untreated, these diseases may cause debilitating pain or may destroy a woman's ability to conceive.

Roughly half of all Americans (50% of the population) become infected with an STI before the age of 35.
~MSN Encarta

Two thirds of people with STIs are under 25 years old. STIs are transmitted by infectious agents—microscopic bacteria, viruses, parasites, fungi, and single-celled organisms called protozoa—that thrive in warm, moist environments in the body, such as the genital area, mouth, and throat.

Reason For STI Endemic

- Sexual morals are changing. The society no longer values self-restraint and character.

- Easy and widespread availability of contraceptives, both oral and otherwise, have eliminated traditional sexual restraints.

-Both patients and physicians and have difficulty dealing openly and candidly with sexual issues. Many patients are unaware that they have a sexually transmitted infection and they keep spreading it to their partners. Many of the new STIs show symptom only in later stages but meanwhile the infection spreads to the partners.

-Additionally, development and spread of drug-resistant bacteria (e.g., penicillin-resistant gonococci) is making some STIs harder to cure.

-Globalization and the effect of travel is most dramatically illustrated by the rapid spread of the AIDS virus (HIV) from Africa to Europe and the Americas in the late 1970s.

Scary Trends In STIs

At any time in history, the prevalence and significance of different STIs mirror changes in science and society. For example, in many countries of the world, the incidence of STIs increased during and immediately after World War II (1939-1945), when soldiers spending extended periods of time away from home engaged in unprotected physical relations with different partners,

Results from a study reported in 2008 showed that one in four young women in the United States between the ages of 14 and 19 were infected with at least one of four diseases monitored: HPV, chlamydia, genital herpes, and trichomoniasis.
~ Centers for Disease Control and Prevention (CDC), Detroit

many of whom carried STIs. When the antibiotic penicillin became widely available in the following years, the same countries experienced dramatic reductions in STI incidence. Beginning in the 1950s, however, the STIs began to rise as American sexual culture changed. Strains of the disease developed resistance to penicillin, and by the 1970s and 1980s the disease reached epidemic proportions in young adult populations. Introduction of HIV into the human population led to an international AIDS crisis that began in the 1980s.

Cases of STIs are increasing despite higher rates of condom use since the onset of the AIDS epidemic. Results from a study reported in 2008 showed that one in four young women in the United States between the ages of 14 and 19 were infected with at least one of four diseases monitored: HPV, chlamydia, genital herpes, and trichomoniasis. Public health officials believe that many factors are probably responsible for the increase in STIs, among them trends in sexual behavior. In the last several decades, the age at which people have sex for the first time has shifted downward, while the average number of partners a person has sex with during his or her lifetime has increased. Together, these trends increase the risk of exposure to an STI.

Human Papilloma Virus (HPV)

Human Papilloma Virus (HPV) causes 90% of all cervical cancer cases. It is the most common viral disease and can cause genital warts, which are often very difficult to treat. Warts are spread through skin-to-skin contact. The CDC (Center for Disease Control and Prevention) estimates that there are 5.5 million new cases of genital warts in the United States each year. HPV is incurable and condoms are of only limited use. Not everyone who comes into contact with the virus will develop symptoms, which include itchiness, white small lumps or larger cauliflower shaped

"In the last several decades, the age at which people have sex for the first time has shifted downward, while the average number of partners a person has sex with during his or her lifetime has increased. Together, these trends increase the risk of exposure to an STI."

lumps on the genital area. Warts develop in the mouth also. It usually takes between 1-3 months from infection for the warts to appear, but it can take much longer. Treatment can be uncomfortable and take a long time, and most people will have a recurrence of warts that will need further treatment. It is the second most common form of cancer in women under 35 years of age.

> "In the UK, one out of every two sexually active people have HPV."

Chlamydia

It is estimated that in developed countries, 1 in 6 teenage girls and one in five teen boys has chlamydia. Three million people become infected with chlamydia each year in US alone. It is a very common infection and also one of the most serious. There are very often no symptoms, and an infected person might never know until serious complications develop. In those women who have symptoms, they might notice increased discharge, frequent or painful urination and/or irregular periods. Men, who are more likely to notice symptoms, might see discharge and pain/burning on urination. It is one of the causes of pelvic pain and inflammation and also a major cause of infertility in women. Even the eyes can become infected in which case both men and women may experience painful swelling and irritation. Recent evidence indicates that it might also play a role in the development of cervical cancer.

Syphilis

According to Centers for Disease Control and Prevention (CDC), there are an estimated 86,000 new cases of syphilis in the United States each year. From 1990s many urban communities in developed countries are experiencing a resurgence in syphilis cases. In the UK, Syphilis is the most rapidly spreading STI. If left undetected, it can result in brain damage, heart disease and/or death. It can be spread by skin-to-skin contact alone. The first signs are

> *In the United States, one in five individuals over the age of 12 is infected with HSV (herpes simplex virus) type 2, and the vast majority of those infected—about 90 percent—do not know they have the disease.*
> *~CDC, Detroit*

painless sores, which are followed by flu-like symptoms. In pregnancy, syphilis can cause miscarriage or stillbirth and it can be passed from mother to unborn child in the womb

Gonorrhoea

Closer to 650,000 people are infected annually with this disease in US. Gonorrhoea can cause widespread infection of the joints and skin. It is becoming increasingly resistant to treatment with antibiotics. Like chlamydia, it can cause infertility and serious health problems if left untreated. In women, it can lead to pelvic inflammatory disease which can in turn cause fever; pain and can lead to infertility. Man are much more likely to notice symptoms than women, but many who are infected have no symptoms at all. In women, symptoms include pain or burning sensation when passing urine, irritation and/or discharge from the anus, and/or increased discharge which could be of a yellow or greenish colour with increased odour. In men, symptoms may include a yellow or white discharge, irritation and/or discharge from the anus and/or inflammation of the prostate gland and testicles.

HIV and AIDS

Visnujana: In this country they have the venereal disease. One out of ten men is suffering gonorrhea.
Prabhupada: Yes. Long ago one professor, medical professor, he said, he was Englishman -- that in our country, 75% students are suffering from venereal disease. Colonel Megor. Yes. Colonel Megor. There must be venereal disease because sex life is so cheap. There must be venereal disease. And venereal disease, once infected, it brings so many other diseases, one after another, one after another. The cancer is also due to that. Madness. Yes. And the Vedic civilization knew it. Therefore first restriction: sex. Brahmacari. First beginning, brahmacari. No sex life. You see? Just to save. This venereal disease is mentioned in the Ayur-veda. It is called phirangamaya. Phiranga means "white Europeans." It is diseased... And medical science also says that it was begun from dog. The girls, they have ....dog and there is the beginning of venereal disease.
-Srila Prabhupada (Morning Walk - December 31, 1973, Los Angeles)

Center for Disease Control and Prevention (CDC) estimates that there are 60,000 new cases of HIV each year in the United States and that two million Americans overall have HIV infection. All over the world, more than 33 million people are infected with this disease. HIV leads to Acquired Immune Deficiency Syndrome (AIDS), which is fatal. AIDS attacks the body's immune system, leaving victims unable to fight off even the mildest infections. There is no available vaccine against HIV, and many people with HIV look and feel healthy for a long time.

Trichomoniasis

Trichomoniasis causes burning, itching, and discomfort in the private parts. The CDC estimates that 5 million Americans become infected with trichomoniasis each year.

Trichomonas Vaginalis (or TV for short) often has no symptoms but can cause discharge and painful urination.

Pubic lice/crabs

There is no protection against crabs/pubic lice, which are tiny insects that live on the skin, often infecting the hairy areas of the body. Contracted through skin-to-skin contact, they cause persistent itching, and it may be possible to see droppings from the lice in underwear and eggs from the lice in pubic hair.

They are usually sexually transmitted but can occasionally be transmitted by close physical contact or by the sharing of sheets or towels with an infected person.

Scabies

Scabies also appears in the form of an itchy rash. Caused by a female mite laying her eggs beneath the surface of the skin, the main symptom of scabies is an itchy rash on hands, elbows, breasts, genitals, wrists and buttocks. Any close physical contact can spread the infection.

Non-specific Urethritis

Non-specific urethritis only infects men and symptoms may

"Every year in the UK alone, over 700,000 new STI cases are diagnosed and Children as young as eleven are contracting gonorrhoea, genital warts and other STIs in increasing numbers."

include inflammation of the urethra, causing a burning sensation or pain when passing urine, discharge and/or frequent urination. Several different types of infection can cause NSU, but often it is caused by chlamydia.

Genital Herpes

In the United States, one in five individuals over the age of 12 is infected with HSV (herpes simplex virus) type 2, and the vast majority of those infected—about 90 percent—do not know they have the disease.

Genital herpes causes painful sores on and around the genitals. Symptoms include itching or tingling sensation in the genital or anal area, small fluid filled blisters which burst and leave painful sores, pain when urinating if the urine passes over the sores, and a flu-like illness, swollen glands, backache, headache or fever. One can catch herpes just from kissing an infected partner. HSV cannot be eradicated from the body, there is no known cure.

> *More than 15 million people in the United States become infected with one or more STIs every year. (CDC)*

Hepatitis B

Hepatitis B is one hundred times more contagious than HIV. Hepatitis B (HBV) is very common throughout the world and it is passed on through sex, sharing of contaminated needles or piercing instruments, from an infected blood transfusion and/or from an infected mother to her baby. Some people have no symptoms. Symptoms, if manifest, can include nausea, diarrhoea, loss of appetite, weight loss, jaundice, itchiness, fatigue and a short flu-like illness. In most cases hepatitis B is incurable, but arduous

"There has been a preoccupation with AIDS and more recently bird flu, but diabetes has been escalating. It's a timebomb. In Australia, 170 million dollars (US$123 million) has been committed to tackle a bird flu epidemic which may or may not happen, but we have a huge diabetes problem and there may be five million dollars spent annually. It's completely disproportionate."
-Professor Paul Zimmet

chemotherapy can eliminate the virus in some patients.

Hepatitis C virus (HCV) can be spread in the same way as Hepatitis B. Current evidence indicates that treatments clear only about 20% of those infected by HCV. The other 80% will remain infected and can pass it onto other people. After some years, they could develop liver cirrhosis, liver cancer or chronic hepatitis

The Myth of Safe Sex
Abstinence – 100% Failsafe Contraception

Several organizations, such as the CDC and the World Health Organization, monitor and research the prevalence and transmission of STIs on an international level in an effort to prevent local outbreaks from reaching global, epidemic proportions.

Unlike many serious diseases, simple measures can prevent STIs. The most effective prevention method is abstinence—that is, refraining from sex completely. No sexual contact means no risk of developing an STI. Practicing monogamy, in which two partners do not have sexual relations with anyone but each other, also greatly reduces the risk of spreading and contracting STIs.

Many speak of 'safe' sex, as if there is such a thing. Yet the only safe sex is sex between two people who are uninfected. Still, the myth, perpetuated by the manufacturers and those in the industry, is that condoms result in safe sex, which in turn leads to a false

> *This is the condition at the present moment. This is called Kali-yuga. The first symptom is: our span of life is very short, decreasing. With the advancement of Kali-yuga, our duration of life is decreasing. Everyone knows that. My father lived so many years, my grandfather lived so many years, but it is certain I am not going to live so many years. And then my son is not... Gradually, it is reduced. Reducing, reducing, reducing. By the end of Kali-yuga, the duration of life from twenty years to thirty years will be considered very, very old age, very, very old. If a man is living for twenty-five years, he will be considered a very grand old man. Yes. That is coming gradually.*
> -Srila Prabhupada (Sri Caitanya-caritamrta, Adi-lila 1.15 — Dallas, March 4, 1975)

sense of security. A false sense of security will in many cases lead to more acts of intercourse occurring.

It is becoming increasingly clear that condom promotion not only hasn't worked (since STIs are continuing to rise at an alarming rate) but is also a questionable approach. In fact, condoms have little or no benefit in preventing many STIs like HPV. More people are dying from cervical cancer caused by HPV than from AIDS.

The World Health Organisation has stated that the best way to avoid catching an STI is to stay faithful to one person for life whom you know is uninfected. Actually, this is also not entirely true. Since we cannot always know for sure that someone is uninfected, the best way to avoid catching an STI is by practicing sexual abstinence – which is also the only 100% failsafe contraception around!

Lifestyle Diseases of New Age

Lifestyle diseases (also called diseases of civilization) refer to ailments which have emerged from modern industrialized life style and diet in last few decades. These include Cancer, Hypertension, Obesity, Heart Disease, Diabetes, Alzheimers, Parkinsons, Osteoporosis, Osteoarthritis, Cirrhosis, Nephritis, Stroke, Asthma, Depression etc.

The increase in the incidence of the above-mentioned diseases is associated with supposed improvements in people's lives. People's lives have got better yet they've become more susceptible to some of the most devastating diseases known to man.

Main culprit has been the deterioration in nutrition levels of food. More high fat and high sugar foods; food preservation

> *In Kali-yuga, the duration of life is shortened not so much because of insufficient food but because of irregular habits. By keeping regular habits and eating simple food, any man can maintain his health. Overeating, over-sense gratification, overdependence on another's mercy, and artificial standards of living sap the very vitality of human energy. Therefore the duration of life is shortened.*
> *Srila Prabhupada (Srimad Bhagavatam 1.1.10)*

techniques have all contributed in one way or another to the lack of proper levels of nutrition in food. Refined and processed foods to satisfy commercial needs rather than seasonal fresh foods are greatly responsible for this phenomenon.

Sudden vs Slow Death

Earlier death was caused by sudden onset conditions. Sudden onset conditions are more easily handled by medicine. Lifestyle diseases are a result of an inappropriate relationship of people with their environment. The onset of these lifestyle diseases is insidious, they take years to develop, and once encountered do not lend themselves easily to cure.

In 1900, the top three causes of death were pneumonia / influenza, tuberculosis, and diarrhea/enteritis. Back then communicable diseases accounted for about 60 percent of all deaths. In 1900, lifestyle diseases like heart disease and cancer were ranked number 6 and 8 respectively. Since the 1940's, most deaths have resulted from heart disease, cancer, and other lifestyle diseases. And, by the late 1990's, lifestyle diseases accounted for more than 60 percent of all deaths.

Epidemiological Transition - From Infectious To Man Made Diseases

This is a largely unremarked change in the history of human health. The infectious diseases that have traditionally killed the people are starting to recede. Instead, people are beginning to die of the chronic and life style diseases. This change is known as the "epidemiological transition".

The epidemiological transition was first described in 1971 by Abdel Omran, a professor at the University of North Carolina. Writing in a Quarterly, he drew a map of disease through human history in which he charted this gradual replacement of infectious with chronic, degenerative and man-made diseases.

> "One quarter of what you eat keeps you alive and three quarter of what you eat keeps your doctor alive."

Threat 6 - Resurgence of Diseases & Health Issues

The epidemiological transition from infectious to chronic diseases began in western countries in the early 1900s. Today people are dying more of the chronic "western" diseases than infectious ones.

In 2005, about 58 million people died of life-style diseases around the world. By 2020, it's projected that lifestyle diseases will be responsible for seven out of every 10 deaths in the world. In Mexico, for example, three-quarters of all deaths are already in this category.

Third World Catching Up With The Diseases Of The Rich

These diseases often hit people at the peak of their economic productivity. Developing countries are adopting the least healthy habits of the west. This is particularly true of urban and wealthier classes. In China, where business relationships are often cemented with gifts of packets of cigarettes, with each brand having its own connotation, the great scourge is tobacco. The same unhealthy behaviours cause diseases in the same way across the globe. Today, only half of new cancer cases occur in developing countries, but as their citizens start smoking more and westerners smoke less, the developing world's share of new cancer victims will inevitably exceed those of the west.

Elsewhere the problem is often obesity. On a shopping street in Kampala or Johannesburg or Hyderabad today, you will find people as fat as those you'd see in a midwestern American mall. That wasn't the case 10 years ago. But now, many formerly poor people can afford to gorge on calories, often in new fast-food restaurants. Many now drive instead of walk and spend hours watching television or sitting behind computer screens.

Bacteria vs Social Network

The obesity epidemic blurs the distinction between infectious and chronic diseases: the way obesity spreads might actually mirror the transmission of infectious disease such as cholera. Whereas cholera is passed on through bacteria, obesity "travels" through social networks. A US study repeatedly weighed a network of 12,067 people over a period of 32 years. It concluded that a person's chance of becoming obese rose as those close to him became obese.

Hidden Cost of Development

The obesity epidemic is now spreading rapidly in many poor countries. One consequence is the global increase in hypertension – high blood pressure – which can cause heart disease or strokes. In African and Asian cities, the prevalence of hypertension in adults now approaches the levels of high-income countries.

In India today, the big problem is diabetes. Not long ago, public health officials considered this a disease of relatively minor importance. That has changed, mainly as people have become fatter. A diabetes epidemic typically follows an obesity epidemic with a lag of about 10 years. Already in 2000, there were about 171 million diabetics on the planet, or four to five times as many as those living with HIV. India now has perhaps 32 million diabetics, many of whom do not know that they have the condition; China has 40 million. An extreme case is the Pacific island of Nauru, where half a century ago diabetes was almost unknown. Now 40 per cent of adults have it.

Diabetes is very much a disease of the cities. It is rife in India's boomtown like Hyderabad. Make the slow, laborious drive out of the clogged-up city into the neighbouring villages, and the much thinner rural population is less likely to be diabetic. The problem is only partly the traditional Hyderabad biryani dish, made with meat, rice and lots of oil or ghee. Rich Indians now get a far larger proportion of their energy from fat than poor Indians do. A national survey found that by 2000, 12 per cent of urban Indians over the age of 20 already had diabetes.

It's not just that people in poor countries are adopting unhealthy habits. Once ill, they are much less likely than those in rich countries to see a doctor and receive treatment. A survey in Egypt

One third of your populations will die by pestilence and famine, one third by the sword and one third scattered to the wind. (Ezekiel 5:12;

published in 2000, for instance, showed that one in three people with very severe hypertension didn't even know they had the condition. Even if they knew, they struggled to find doctors. In Uganda, there is only one doctor of any kind for every 20,000 people, compared with one for 500 in the UK.

Modern diseases have a racial pattern. For instance, hypertension appears to affect Africans more severely than sufferers on other continents. South Asians seem to develop heart disease four to five years earlier than their white counterparts, and their diabetes seems to be more aggressive. The reasons for this are still unclear.

Decreasing Life Expectancy

After much hype of increase in life expectancy, we now have several documented episodes of declines in life expectancy. And some of them may be a terrifying warning for the developing world.

- The first decline occurred in Africa after Aids. By 2002, 22 million people had died of the disease. Life expectancy in southern Africa fell by as much as 10 years: in Botswana it dropped from 59 in 1995 to 49 in 2005.

- The second decline in life expectancy is alarming for today's Chinese, Indians and urban Africans. Chronic diseases are afflicting these populations. Life expectancy in these regions is likely to fall as the poor in these countries start to smoke, overeat and stop physical work and at the same time not having access to doctors.

We have discussed in the previous verse that we are decreasing the span of life. The scientists will say, "No, we are making arrangement so that by science we shall make man immortal." When a man becomes mad, he speaks so many nonsense. Like a child. A child also speaks so many nonsense things, and the parents enjoy it. Similarly, the so-called scientist, when he says that "By scientific method, we shall stop death," so there is no evidence in the history of the human society that a man has not died. That cannot be. Hiranyakasipu, he was also atheist and materialistic. He also tried to become immortal.
- Srila Prabhupada (Srimad-Bhagavatam 2.3.18-19 — Los Angeles, June 13, 1972)

— This was the decline that hit eastern Europe after the Soviet Union's collapse. Health services and established social structures fell apart, and stress and depression increased. One result was that alcoholism soared. By 1992, some of the new kiosks along Moscow's boulevards sold a liquid advertised as "100 per cent alcohol". The average Russian man's life expectancy had been 64 years. By 2005, it was just 59.

Dual Burden

For the first time in history, poor countries are now facing a dual burden of infectious and chronic diseases. While third world governments are funding cash and devising plans to prevent a possible flu pandemic, little is being done to tackle these big killers such as cancer, diabetes and respiratory and heart disease.

India has planned to import equipments worth $215 Billion to diagnose and treat lifestyle diseases in next 5 years. Renowned cardiologist Dr. R.R. Kasliwal has said that lifestyle diseases pose a greater threat to ordinary Indians than HIV/AIDS.

Digital Age Diseases

Sitting in front of a computer screen and typing on a keyboard whole day has given rise to serious ailments like Repetitive Stress Injury and Carpel Tunnel Syndrome. The fingers are not created to move so many times as they do on a keyboard. This damages their muscles and nerves. Other than physiotherapy, there is no known cure for these ailments.

Modern Economics : Earn Money And Lose Health, Then Lose Money To Gain Health

A study by the Indian Council for Research on International Economic Relations says that although India's IT boom has brought spiralling corporate profits and higher incomes for employees, it has also led to a surge in workplace stress and lifestyle diseases. The health minister, Anbumani Ramadoss, says, "IT is the fastest-growing industry in our country, but it is most vulnerable to lifestyle diseases. Its future growth could be stunted if we don't address the problem now."

India's rapid economic growth could be slowed by a sharp rise in the prevalence of heart disease, stroke and diabetes, and the successful information technology industry is likely to be the hardest hit. So-called lifestyle diseases are estimated to have wiped $9bn off the country's national income in 2005, but the cost could reach more than $100bn over the next 10 years if corrective action is not taken soon.

Long working hours, night shifts and a sedentary lifestyle make people employed at such companies prone to heart disease and diabetes. There have also been growing reports of depression and family breakdown in the industry.

Infosys Technologies, India's second-largest software exporter, has a 24-hour hotline for employees suffering from depression to contact psychiatrists. A company director says "We must have prevented at least 30 deaths from suicide because of this hotline." In Bangalore the psychiatrists say their Saturdays are reserved for marriage counselling for the IT sector.

Highest Outbreak of New Diseases In 1980s

Researchers from the Zoological Society of London, the Wildlife Trust and Columbia University have analysed databases of outbreaks and found 335 cases of emerging diseases between 1940 and 2004. Of these, 60.3% were infections which also affected animals, and 71.8% were known to have triggered disease in humans after spreading from wildlife.

Major outbreaks of disease have become more common around the globe in the past 40 years, according to the largest ever investigation into emerging infections. Diseases such as Ebola and Sars, which originally spread from animals, are an increasing threat to human health, and many infections have now become resistant to antibiotics.

The international team of scientists have warned that tropical regions are likely to become a future hotspot for new diseases, and called for early warning systems to be set up in countries to spot outbreaks before they become unmanageable.

Europe and North America have experienced high numbers of

outbreaks, but much of that is because those regions have invested heavily in detecting early signs of disease. Other countries, scientists fear, are less able to spot new diseases as they arise.

More diseases emerged in the 1980s than any other decade, according to the study. The great majority of outbreaks were triggered by bacteria and viruses, with 20% caused by antibiotic-resistant microbes while several others transmigrating from animals and birds. Preserving wildlife-rich areas could help to protect people from new diseases.

Cruelty Diet Leading To Unprecedented Health Hazards

Plant foods improve human health, while animal 'foods' degrade it. The most comprehensive study to date regarding the relationship between diet and human health found that the consumption of animal-derived 'food' products was linked with "diseases of affluence" such as heart disease, osteoporosis, diabetes, and cancer. T. Colin Campbell's landmark research in The China Project found a pure vegetarian (i.e. vegan) diet to be healthiest. Dr. Campbell estimates that "80 to 90% of all cancers, cardiovascular diseases, and other degenerative illness can be prevented, at least until very old age - simply by adopting a plant-based diet.

Deaths from foodborne illnesses have quadrupled in the last 15 years in the US. The Centre for Disease Control (CDC) estimates that there are 76 million food-related illnesses (1 out of 3 Americans), 325000 hospitalizations, and 10000 deaths from food poisoning every year.

The meat, poultry, dairy and egg industries employ technological short cuts— as drugs, hormones, and other chemicals — to maximize production. Under these conditions, virulent pathogens that are resistant to antibiotics are emerging. These new 'supergerms,' whose evolution is traceable directly to the overuse of antibiotics in factory farming, have the potential to cause yet unknown human suffering and deaths.

Peculiar new diseases have been amplified by aberrant agribusiness practices. For example, "Mad Cow Disease" (bovine spongiform encephalopathy or BSE), a fatal dementia affecting cattle, spread throughout Britain when dead cows were fed to living cows. When people ate cows with "Mad Cow Disease," they got Creutzfeldt-Jakob Disease (CJD), a fatal dementia that afflicts humans.

Another farm animal disease beginning to jeopardize human health is avian influenza. In Hong Kong, where scores of people have died from the so-called "bird- flu," over one million chickens have been destroyed in the panic to stop the spread of the disease. In India, so far, more than 45 million birds have been killed due to bird-flu scare.

Millions of Americans are infected, and thousands die every year from contaminated animal 'food' products. Despite repeated warnings from consumer advocates, the USDA's meat inspection system remains grossly inadequate, and consumers are now being told to "expect" animal products to be tainted.

Meanwhile, the agribusiness industry, rather than advising consumers to curtail their intake of animal products, has devised extreme measures (overcooking, antibiotics, etc.) to help consumers circumvent the hazards of animal products and maintain their gross over-consumption of meat and dairy.

Threat - 7

Brittle Economies

The massive inefficiencies of industrialism are not more apparent because they are masked by a financial system that gives improper information.

~Paul Hawken

World Economy : A House of Cards

There are limits to growth and the world economy has crossed those limits. In last 5 decades, world economy has been globalized and its not the best thing to have happened to our finances. The economic system built on a need for constant growth obviously can't last long in a finite world. Small is beautiful...and sustainable.

The world has always hoped against the hope..until the reality stares in its face. There are important lessons to be learnt from the history but more often than not we fail to do so.

John Maynard Keynes said in 1927."We will not have any crashes in our time." Dr Irving Fisher, another distinguished economist, said on October 17, 1929. "Stock prices have reached what looks like a permanently high plateau." US Treasury Secretary and Harvard Economic Society, among others, publicly shared their confidence.

They were reflecting on the state of the economy that was booming. It was a time when drivers and window cleaners evesdropped on the conversations of their patrons to collect tips on shares. The DJ Index doubled from little less than 200 when Keynes

> *The merchants of the earth will weep and mourn over her because no one buys their cargoes anymore–cargoes of gold, silver, precious stones and perils; fine linen, purple, silk and scarlet cloth; every sort of citron wood, and articles of every kind made of ivory, costly wood, bronze, iron and marble; cargoes of cinnamon and spice, of incense, myrrh and frankincense, of wine and olive oil, of fine flour and wheat; cattle and sheep; horses and carriages; and bodies and souls of men.*
> *~ Revelation 18:11–13*

made his prediction to almost 400 when Dr Fisher announced the high plateau of the state of the market. Within two weeks of Dr. Fisher's forecast, it had crashed by over 50% to reach 200 again. All those who had invested their savings from 1927 to 1929 were impoverished overnight. Several of them committed suicide. By 1933, the DJ Index lost 90% of its value from the day of Dr. Fisher's 'high plateau' proclamation to reach 40. Industrial production declined by two-thirds. The prices of farm land collapsed to nothing. The United States imposed high trade barriers, inviting retaliation by 25 other countries. Since Europe was dependent on exports to pay its World War I debts and Japan to be able to import the most basic necessities of life, high trade barriers devastated their economies. The Germans elected Hitler, a failed artist, to lead them. In Japan, too, nationalist extremism grew at a fast pace. The World War II followed from 1939 to 1945. History shows that bad finances and wars are the twins.

Ominous Headlines

The history is trying to repeat itself in last two quarters. Headlines are blaring - Financial markets in a free-fall, Chaos on Wall St, International markets in a tailspin, European bailout, More banks to fail, Investors shy away amidst growing fears, Congress approves bailout, 51 Million to loose jobs, China goes down in first quarter.

These foreboding headlines are indications of something coming out way, if we are willing to listen.

Financial system is a farce and it has become exponentially more so as Treasury/Federal Reserve bailouts in the financial sector become the rule rather than the exception.

Six years ago the Federal Reserve adopted unprecedented monetary extravagance, leading to what can only be described as the largest and most pervasive global financial bubble in history. The inevitable result, as is becoming increasingly clear, is that the cleanup in the aftermath of this bubble when all is said and done, will have the largest price tag, indeed the largest destruction of wealth, in history. Bursting of a bubble always has disastrous consequences, as is painfully evident today.

There is no greater testament to this carnage than the fact that major Wall Street institutions, many of which have been around for over a century (having even survived the Great Depression) are now falling like flies one after the other, almost overnight.

America - A Dubious Financial World Leader

America's unquenchable materialistic appetite is the machine that fuels a global economy. Japan's economy would collapse if it were not for the billions of dollars per year gained in trading with America. When America goes into a recession, the world follows. When America's economy is booming, the world's economy also booms.

America devours, yet is never satisfied. Running out of money, she tells the waiter to supply it on credit. He gladly complies making a tidy profit from the interest. He cannot serve her quick enough. The more she eats, the hungrier she becomes. As time passes, less goes to paying for food and more is needed to pay for the huge debt she is accumulating. Finally, all of her resources are used up in paying for the interest she owes. America falls crashing to the ground in economic ruin, so suddenly, it sends shock waves throughout the world. She is incapable of paying for her massive imports. Merchant ships sit offshore, heavy laden with cargo, weeping and wailing in horror.

In A Pit of Debts

In 1929, the debt ratio in relation to the America's Gross National Product stood at a healthy 16%. In 2008, the national debt has increased to an alarming 70% of the GNP. The total debt

> *They Say So*
> *When NASA first started sending up astronauts, they quickly discovered that ballpoint pens would not work in zero gravity.*
> *To combat the problem, NASA scientists spent a decade and $100 million to develop a pen that writes in zero gravity, upside down, underwater, on almost any surface including glass and at temperatures ranging from below freezing to 300 C.*
> *The Russians used a pencil.*

of America is greater than the combined external debts of all the nations of the world.

America's current debt is $10 trillion - $145,000 per American, or $350,000 for every full-time worker. Of course everyone is tossing around the words million, billion and trillion. Have we become numb to the numbers?

Number' itself can be pronounced as 'number' or 'numb-er.' And maybe in this case, the latter is a better pronunciation. Until now such big numbers were never heard that often.

To provide some perspective on just how big a trillion dollars is, think about it like this: A trillion dollars is the number 1 followed by 12 zeroes. Or we can think of it this way: One trillion $1 bills stacked one on top of the other would reach nearly 68,000 miles (about 109,400 kilometers) into the sky, or about a third of the way from the Earth to the moon.

Senate Republican leader Mitch McConnell has said that Americans have become desensitized to just how much money that is.

To put a trillion dollars in context, if we spend a million dollars every day since Jesus was born, we still wouldn't have spent a trillion. A million dollars a day for 2,000 years is only three-quarters of a trillion dollars.

Back in 1993, President Bill Clinton wanted a $30 billion jobs and investment package. He didn't get it. Just last year, President George W. Bush signed an emergency economic stimulus of $168 billion - a tally that seems paltry compared with the amount requested today. But consider this: If all of the financial market interventions, loans, guarantees, bailouts and rescues are approved, they will total more than $7 trillion. This simply means total absolute collapse of the financial house of cards.

Threat 7 - Brittle Economies

Dollar - Undependable World Currency

World experts in money markets like Warren Buffet and George Soros are betting on a major crash of the dollar in the near future. They think it will be greater than the Great Depression of the 1930s. With trade deficits of over 650 billion this year, America is placing its future in the hands of non-Americans. It is now, roughly 6.5 percent of the total economy. Their deficit is financed by the central banks of countries like China and Japan. In fact all the world banks are chock-full of US dollars, much more than they want or need for trade.

If the dollar collapses the whole world economy collapses because there is no alternative yet to the dollar. Right now if the dollar crashes so would the economies of China, Japan and dozens of other countries and much of their holdings are in American banks.

However, the supremacy of the dollar world wide is under a challenge by the Euro. For the time being the Euro is struggling and is not yet a safe bet to jump into instead of the dollar.

Right now, the US dollar is probably 40 per cent overvalued versus the Japanese yen or the Chinese Yuan. The fear in the short term is that some one may dump the dollar and start a dollar run.

> *So actually, human opulence means not these tin cars. Once it is dashed with another car, it is finished, no value. Human opulence means the society must have enough gold, enough jewelry, enough silk, enough grains, enough milk, enough vegetables, like that. That is opulent. That is opulence. Formerly a person was considered rich by two things: dhanyena dhanavan. How much grain stock he has got at his home. A big, big barn, filled with grains. Still in India, if I am going to give my daughter to some family, to see the family's opulence, I go to see the house, and if I see there are many, many barns' stock of grains and many cows, then it is very good.*
> *-Srila Prabhupada (Srimad-Bhagavatam 1.9.2 — Los Angeles, May 16, 1973)*

Just like the stock market, the first out is going to loose the least money and everyone else will be holding dollars at less value. What if some small Islamic country decides they have too many dollars and dumps $10 billion all at once? Panic will set in the rest of the world, and everyone will start getting out of the dollar leaving those holding dollars with half its present value.

What is saving the dollar is not faith in the dollar but the lack of an alternative.

UN: World Economy May Lose 51 Million Jobs

In January 2009, International Labor Organization (ILO), a United Nations Agency said in Geneva that up to 51 million jobs worldwide could disappear by the end of this year as a result of the economic slowdown that has turned into a global employment crisis.

The International Labor Organization (ILO) said that under its most optimistic scenario, this year would finish with 18 million more unemployed people than at the end of 2007, with a global unemployment rate of 6.1.

More realistically, it said 30 million more people could lose their jobs if financial turmoil persists through 2009, pushing up the world's unemployment to 6.5 percent, compared to 6.0 percent in 2008 and 5.7 percent in 2007.

In the worst-case economic scenario, the Global Employment Trends report said 51 million more jobs could be lost by the end of this year, creating a 7.1 percent global unemployment rate.

"If the recession deepens in 2009, as many forecasters expect, the global jobs crisis will worsen sharply," it said. "We can expect that for many of those who manage to keep a job, earnings and other conditions of employment will deteriorate."

Caterpillar, Sprint, Philips, Texas Instruments and ING are

We're entering a really fierce global recession. It's a very dangerous situation. The danger is that instead of having a few bad years, we'll have another lost decade.
- Kenneth S. Rogoff, Former Chief Economist, IMF

among the companies that have cut thousands of jobs in response to the financial crisis and economic downturn that has spread around the world.

The ILO's previous employment estimate, released in October, was that 20 million jobs would disappear by the end of 2009 as a result of the financial crisis.

Economic Earthquake - Devastation That Happens Within Minutes

Its a classic case of 1929 repeat. On 21st January 2008, known as Black Monday, investors in India lost Rs 6 trillion within minutes of the Indian Stock Exchange's opening in Mumbai. The authorities immediately suspended the trading for one hour. The sensex tumbled 2,029 points within minutes of start of trading.

This loss of Rs 6,54,887 crore came on top of over Rs 11 trillion loss suffered by investors at Dalal Street in the last six days.

Small investors were advised to stay away from the markets.

Investors' wealth - measured in terms of cumulative market capitalisation of all the listed companies - declined by a whopping Rs 18,40,173 crore.

As per information available on the Bombay Stock Exchange website, the total market capitalisation stood at Rs 59,53,525 crore at the end of the Black Monday's trading against Rs 71,38,810

> *So actual value, to keep cows, to have food grains or gold, jewelries, these are the signs of richness. But Kali-yuga is so cruel that if you have got gold, if you have got jewels, then government will take away. Dasyu-dharmabhih. Formerly there were ordinary plunderers, thieves. Now, according to Srimad-Bhagavatam, the government will be composed of organized thieves. That is meant: dasyu-dharmabhih, rajabhih. Government officer means organized thieves in every country. That will be the situation. So you cannot keep now. You have to be satisfied with these papers. That's all.*
> *-Srila Prabhupada*
> *(Srimad-Bhagavatam 1.8.21 — Mayapura, October 1, 1974)*

crore before the stock exchange began business on January 14.

The cause for this was attributed on concerns regarding the US economy going into recession.

2008 - The Cousin of 1929

Apart from the story of January 2008 in India, by October 2008, investors across the world lost more than $10 trillion - an amount more than 10 times of the entire investor wealth in India.

All 52 equity markets of the world suffered a loss of $10.5 trillion in 2008 as per a leading rating agency and financial data provider, Standard and Poors.

Indian stock market valuation nearly halved in 2008. 2009 is expected to be worse than its predecessor.

Tremors of An Economic Earthquake

Day When On Wall Street, It Rained The Bodies Of Men Jumping From Offices High Above.

In 1929, America was having an economic explosion. Immigrants were pouring in. There were more jobs than people. Farmers were leaving their fields for factories, making twice the income for half the labor. Politicians confidently portrayed a picture of an endless era of unprecedented prosperity. The prophets of gloom and doom were ignored as being fanatical crazies.

Fall is a beautiful time of year. A time of thanksgiving, a remembrance of God's blessing upon the birth of a Christian country. The leaves are in full bloom, ready to fall. It is a time for

I think we have more machinery of government than is necessary, too many parasites living on the labour of the industrious.

~ Thomas Jefferson

Sunday drives through the country without a thought of the winter to come. Splashes of color cover the hills and valleys. As the squirrels wisely gather food for a cold long winter, a nation is borrowing and spending because of a thriving economy that can promise only spring and summer.

A ship sails to England in the early part of October, full of wealthy entrepreneurs, a sign of absolute faith in a thriving American economy. While they were on their care–free vacation, enjoying the pleasure away from the stress of their jobs, a powerful economic tremor rippled through the United States. On October 24, 1929, 12,000,000 shares of common stocks traded in a single afternoon. By Monday, October 28th, the trading averages had dropped by 20 points. On Tuesday, October 29th, virtually all trades were to sell. It became 'A Nightmare On Wall Street.' Investors became panic–stricken, resulting in a huge economic land slide. AT&T was down a hundred points, General Electric, 90 points and General Motors, plummeted 150 points. Sixteen million shares were traded at a loss of 10 billion dollars.

This was equivalent to twice the amount of currency of the entire USA. Headlines proclaimed, Wall Street Crashes. Tens of millions of people's life savings became completely useless. Millionaires were reduced to the unemployed. On Wall Street, it rained the bodies of men jumping from their offices high above. When the ship returned full of happy–go–lucky entrepreneurs, they were worth the clothes on their backs. An economic winter had fallen upon America which would effect the entire earth. An ice age that would last four long years.

Simple And Healthy Economics

By Srila Prabhupada

Money is required for purchasing food, but the animals, they do not know that food can be purchased. They are searching after food. But we are civilized; we are searching after money. Money is required for purchasing food. Why don't you produce food directly? That is intelligence. You are getting money, very good. What is that money? A paper. You are being cheated. It is written there, "hundred dollars." But what is that hundred dollars? It is cheap of..., piece of paper only. But because we are so fool, we are accepting a piece of paper, hundred dollars, and the struggle for existence for

Dhanyena dhanavan. If you have got grain, then you are rich. And if you have got cows, then you are rich. This is the standard of Vedic richness. Dhanyena dhanavan gavayo dhanavan. They don't say, "Keep some papers and you become rich." All rascal, one thousand dollar I promise to pay, a piece of paper. Practical, we have got enough food grains. We have got enough... That is richness. What is use of paper? Even gold you have got, you have to exchange. And if you have grain, immediate food. Just boil with milk, and it is nectarean, param anna, immediately. Take some wood... collected from the wood and have fire, put the milk and the grains–oh, you'll get so nice food, nutritious, full of vitamin, and so easily made. It is practical. So tasteful, so nutritious, and don't require. If you simply boil little milk and little grain, whole day, so much sweet rice, you take– You don't require any more. And if you add little apples and fruits, oh, it is heavenly. Your whole day free from any food anxiety, and you can work. And you can work. You can chant Hare Krsna. Make this ideal life here. America has got good potency. We have got so much land here. We can have hundreds of New Vrindabans or farms like that. And people will be happy. And invite all the world, "Please come and live with us. Why you are suffering congestion, overpopulation? Welcome here.
-Srila Prabhupada (Room Conversation —June 28, 1976, New Vrindaban)

a piece of paper. Why don't you be intelligent — "Why shall I take the piece of paper? Give me food"? But that intelligence you have lost. Therefore my Guru Maharaja used to say the present human society is combination of cheaters and cheated, that's all. No intelligent person. Formerly money was gold and silver coins. It had some value. But what is the present currency? Simply piece of paper. Bunch of papers. During the last war the government failed in Germany, and these bunch of papers were thrown in the street. Nobody was caring. Nobody was caring.

So our civilization is based on that way. You require food. That's fact. Therefore Krsna says, annad bhavanti bhutani [Bg. 3.14]. You produce your food. Anywhere you can produce your food. The land is enough land. In Australia you have got enough land. In Africa you have enough land, uncultivated. No. They'll not produce food. They will produce coffee and tea and slaughter animals. This is their business. I understand that in your country animals are slaughtered and exported for trade. Why export? You produce your own food and be satisfied. Why you are after that piece of hundred dollars paper? Produce your own food and eat sumptuously, be healthy and chant Hare Krsna. This is civilization. This is civilization.

(Lecture, Bhagavad-gita 9.4 — Melbourne, April 22, 1976)

Cooked Up Books - Concealing The Financial Realities

On January 7, 2009, India Inc. woke up to a shocker of a life time - $1.6 billion Satyam Computers fraud. Chairman Ramalinga Raju and his family cooked up books and siphoned off money in

> <u>Headlines</u>
> *London, September 22, 2008: Satyam Computer Services Ltd., a leading global consulting and information technology services provider, has won the coveted Golden Peacock Global Award for Excellence in Corporate Governance for 2008.*
> *India, January 7, 2009: Rs. 7000 Crore Fraud in Satyam, Chairman Detained.*
> *(Only a mere 19 out of 4.700 listed firms whose shares are traded in India, have made their corporate governance ratings public.)*

what is being termed as India's biggest corporate fraud to date. By the end of the day, the fourth largest IT company lost a staggering Rs 10,000 crore in market capitalisation as investors reacted sharply and dumped shares, leaving an uncertain future for the company and its 53,000 employees. The entire stock market crashed.

Its unprecedented. Satyam's balance sheet as on Sep 30, 2008, carried an inflated (non-existent) cash and bank balances of Rs 5,040 crore (as against Rs 5,361 reflected in the books).

Satyam fraud clouds the corporate governance of India Inc. More skeletons are supposed to come out from corporate closets and it poses a big question over the credibility of auditors in general also.

Ramesh Damani, a financial expert, was quoted as saying, "I am actually a little less surprised at what was going on because I have

---

If one gets a diamond, he possesses something valuable. But in this civilization you are simply making plastic plates and plastic cups. Indeed, in Japan I have seen pasteboard homes. And everyone is thinking that he is advanced. Formerly people used to have golden and silver utensils, but now they have plastic ones, and still they are very proud to be so materially advanced. What is your position? You have a bunch of paper and think, "I am a millionaire." What is the value of that paper? Is that not cheating? However, if we possess gold or diamonds worth a million dollars, that is actual wealth. But we are educated in such a way that we think we are millionaires by paper only. As soon as there is some catastrophe, millions of such dollars could not buy bread. This actually happened in Germany; millions of marks could not purchase one piece of bread. All this is going on in the name of advancement of civilization, and the real purpose of life, God consciousness, is missing.
-Srila Prabhupada (Interview with the New York Times — September 2, 1972, New Vrindaban)

been in the markets long enough and know all manners of companies, not just in India but across the world, do some degree of cooking of books, and that is let's say 'accepted'."

Damani adds, " In fact a survey in the US that was conducted a couple of years back of CFOs, 70% of the CFOs said that they had always been pressurised to cook the books by the CEO, and a reasonable proportion of the 70% admitted to having cooked the books. And that is the US. So, the fact is that companies cook books."

When asked whether market fears were legitimate that many more companies were propping up their books if not cooking them,

Prabhupada: So one very important word is here: sadasvaih svarna-bhusitaih. Formerly the horses were used in military division. Horses, chariot, elephants and then infantry. So not one or two, but one division of military phalanx required sixty thousand horses. Aksauhini. So many horses, so many elephants, so many chariot, and so many infantry soldiers — that will compose one division of soldiers. So "so many" means the, I exactly remember now, sixty thousand horses. So all the horses, when they are required for procession or for going to the fight, were well-decorated with golden ornaments, svarna-bhusitaih. So just imagine the, all the saddles of the horse, if they are golden ornamented, how many ounces you will require to decorate the horse. And what is the price of gold now?
Danavir: One hundred and twenty-eight dollars an ounce.
Prabhupada: Just see, at least fifty ounce will be required to decorate one horse. And one ounce is $120. So what is the price of fifty ounce?
Devotees: Five thousand dollars.
Prabhupada: Such sixty-thousand horses, how much it comes? (laughter) Where is that gold? They are very much proud, advancement of material civilization, but instead of gold, we find plastic. (laughter) And the nonsense, they are very much proud of their wealth. Just see. Even they cannot decorate their wives.
-Srila Prabhupada (Srimad-Bhagavatam 1.9.2 — Los Angeles, May 16, 1973)

he replied, "It is a great question and if you ask me, off the record, I could name you 50 companies where I am not convinced about the quality of earnings coming through the reports that they do. Beginning this quarter, the market will examine, with a whole new microscope or a whole new magnifying glass, to see exactly what the quality of earnings is. Is it legitimate, is the bank balance legitimate, and there are lot of well-created, highly liquid counters where we always puzzle and scratch heads as to how they produce these results in an operating environment that is so non-conducive. Companies will inevitably have to face analysts who are more hostile, auditors who are more hostile, and inevitably, there will be a lot of companies that fall through the crack."

Delta and Northwest Bankruptcy - A Similar Tale.

The America's airline crisis took a stunning turn for the worse when Delta Air Lines Inc. and Northwest Airlines Corp. filed for bankruptcy in the face of massive losses in 2005.

Much of the problems of these airlines were caused by all the CFOs and MBAs hired to paint a rosy picture of earnings along with converting losses into profits through creative accounting.

The suited guys with absolutely no life experience, fresh off the MBA assembly line of Harvard, hired to replace the old-gen economists in the vain hope of increased efficiency.

Sure, it is all good, as long as the economy is coasting along. As soon as it hits a rough patch, it becomes necessary to lie, so that you may cover up the mess. And one lie leads to another, and another, and then the whole thing falls flat.

> It went to hell in a handbasket. I didn't think this would happen to me. It's just something that I don't think that people think is going to happen to them, is what it amounts to. It happens very quickly, too.
> -Barbara Harvey (A homeless living in car)

Threat 7 - Brittle Economies

Time To Live In Cars

Almost A Milliion US Homes Repossessed In 2008

Inventors of car thought of it as a means of transport. They never imagined that one day it will double up as home also. Well, That's happening now in America with thousands becoming homeless overnight and living in cars.

Hundreds of thousands are being forced into homelessness after being laid off. More than 2.3 million American homeowners faced foreclosure proceedings in 2008 with more than 860,000 properties actually repossessed by lenders. This was more than double the 2007 level. The worst is yet to come as consumers grapple with layoffs, shrinking investment portfolios and falling home prices.

U.S. home values fell by $3.3 trillion in 2008. Since the housing market's peak in 2006, homes across the US lost $6.1 trillion in value. Approximately 22 percent of all American homeowners are underwater and owe more on their mortgages than what their home is worth.

In UK, year 2008 saw repossession of some 35000 homes with 168,000 mortgage borrowers at least three months in arrears. This number is expected to skyrocket in 2009.

If you write something which you do not believe in, are you not cheating? That means cheating. You take word, you are giving a piece of paper, and it is written there, "one thousand dollars." That means you are cheating, in the name of God, he will accept you, that's all. If you say, "No, I don't want paper. Give me gold dollar," then you are finished. Your currency will be finished. Immediately there will be revolution, that "The government is cheating us." Actually it is cheating. What is the proof, value, of this paper, little paper? Simply "I promise to pay, governor and this..." But it is on trust only: "Yes, government will pay me." They'll never pay, but so long the government goes on, it will go on, that's all, cheating will go on. And as soon government fails, you throw in the street, no one will care for it.
-Srila Prabhupada (Garden Conversation — June 22, 1976, New Vrindaban)

Nowhere To Live, All of A Sudden

Barbara Harvey, a 67-year-old Californian lady, climbs into the back of her small Honda sport utility vehicle and snuggles with her two dogs, her head nestled on a pillow propped against the driver's seat.

She says she is forced to sleep in her car with her dogs after losing her job. She never thought she'd spend her golden years sleeping in her car in a parking lot. "This is my bed, my dogs," she said. "This is my life in this car right now."

Harvey was forced into homelessness this year after being laid off. She said that three-quarters of her income went to paying rent in Santa Barbara, where the median house in the scenic oceanfront city costs more than $1 million. She lost her house few months ago and had little savings as backup.

Harvey now works part time for $8 an hour, and she draws Social Security to help make ends meet. But she still cannot afford an apartment, and so every night she pulls into a gated parking lot to sleep in her car, along with other women who find themselves in a similar predicament.

There are 12 parking lots across Santa Barbara that have been set up to accommodate the growing middle-class homelessness. The lots open at 7 PM. and close at 7 AM. A growing number of senior citizens, women and middle-class families are living on the streets today.

She adds, "I see women sleeping on benches. It's heartbreaking. The way the economy is going, it's just amazing the people that are becoming homeless. It's hit the middle class. It's a tough existence. There are no showers or running water. I can't drink liquids after 7pm as the public baths close by then."

War - A Fall out of Economic Collapse

An economic collapse is a devastating breakdown of a national, regional, or territorial economy. It is essentially a severe economic depression characterised by a sharp increase in bankruptcy and unemployment. A full or near-full economic collapse is often quickly followed by months, years, or even decades of economic

Threat 7 - Brittle Economies

depression, social chaos, and civil unrest. Such crises have both been seen to afflict capitalist market economies and state controlled economies.

Today it feels like the summer of 1931. The world's two biggest financial institutions have had a heart attack. The global currency system is breaking down. The policy doctrines that got us into this mess are bankrupt. No world leader seems able to discern the problem, let alone forge a solution. The International Monetary Fund has abdicated into schizophrenia. All these does not forebode well for an already unstable world

Historically, the causes for war have always been economic in nature, no matter what the official reasons were. Economic disintegration and war go hand in hand, as both have a similar, imperial root.

If world economies continue to disintegrate and fall apart, war would be a real threat. History is a witness that bucks have been the basis of the great wars. Two world wars were fought to counteract British colonialism and their financial exploitation of the whole world. Hitler termed the British as 'Shopkeepers' nation." The Germans made better and cheaper products but all the world markets were forcefully occupied by the British. This led to the World Wars.

Modern word for unscrupulous colonials is corporations. Corporatisation is the modern way of colonizing the world. Today's world is getting ground under the corporate jackboot. These huge corporations make obscene profits from human misery and they want the world to remain in misery. They run our health care industry. They run our oil and gas companies. They run our bloated weapons industry. They run Wall Street and the major investment firms. They run our manufacturing firms. They also, ominously, run our government. World is simply not a safe place in the shadows of these greedy monsters. They want profits - when economy thrives and they want profits - when economy dies. Profits in a dying economy means war. That's the only way to go about it.

End of Modern Civilization and Alternative Future

Bank Runs And Currency Collapse

Prior to the 1800s, savers looking to keep their valuables in safekeeping depositories deposited gold coins and silver coins at goldsmiths, receiving in turn a note for their deposit. Once these notes became a trusted medium of exchange an early form of paper money was born, in the form of the goldsmiths' notes.

As the notes were used directly in trade, the goldsmiths observed that people would not usually redeem all their notes at the same time, and saw the opportunity to invest coin reserves in interest-bearing loans and bills. This left the goldsmiths with more notes on issue than reserves to pay them with. This generated income—a process that altered their role from passive guardians of bullion charging fees for safe storage, to interest-paying and earning banks. Thus 'Fractional-reserve banking' was born.

However, if creditors (note holders of gold originally deposited) lost faith in the ability of a bank to redeem (pay) their notes, many would try to redeem their notes at the same time. If in response a

Why this hypocrisy? In the schools, colleges, you are forbidding, "Don't talk of God," and on the bills you are writing, "In God We Trust." That means if the bill is not paid, don't be dissatisfied, you trust in God. (laughs) Although I'm giving you a piece of paper, don't hesitate to take it. Trust in God, it will be paid. They write, "I promise to pay," but people may not have faith in this word. Actually, I'm paying you hundred rupees — or a thousand rupees-worth currency note, but actually it is paper. But only on faith and trust I'm accepting it, it is one thousand dollars. That much. In last war, the Germany, marks note were thrown in the street. And the bunch of note, taken to the confectioner, "Give me a piece of bread," There is no bread; they throw away. It happened, actually. So these notes are accepted on the understanding that the government will pay. But time may be there when government may be not able to pay. And it has been practically experienced in the last war.
-Srila Prabhupada (Interview with Jackie Vaughn (Congressman) — July 12, 1976, Detroit)

bank could not raise enough funds by calling in loans or selling bills, it either went into insolvency or defaulted on its notes. Such a situation is called a bank run and has caused the demise of many banks.

The collapse of Washington Mutual bank in September 2008, the largest bank failure in history, is an example of a "silent run" on the bank, where depositors removed vast sums of money from the bank through electronic transfer.

In year 2008 we witnessed many currencies suddenly collapse. Iceland, Argentina, Hungary, Ukraine and others all saw a sharp fall in the value of their currency.

When a currency loses the confidence of its people, its fall becomes exponential, as has happened to the Zimbabwe dollar. In 1982 one US dollar equalled one Zimbabwe dollar. Today around Z$200,000 buys one US $1. During World War II, German mark was used for making Cigars. Rampant inflation, current account deficits, lower interest rates, these all contribute to the currency collapse. Most of the currencies in the world, including major ones, have no asset backing. Governments simply print money whenever they need it or a crisis hits them. This leads to inflation and when a currency gets completely discredited, it collapses. Today the US dollar, the world currency, is in real danger of collapsing.

Threat - 8

Growing Cruelty And Desensitization

We are the living graves of murdered beasts,
Slaughtered to satisfy our appetites.
We never pause to wonder at our feasts,
If animals like men could possibly have rights.
We pray on Sunday that we may have light,
To guide our footsteps on the paths we tread.
We are sick of war, we do not want to fight,
The thought of it now fills our hearts with dread,
And yet we gorge ourselves upon the dead.
Like carrion crows we live and feed on meat,
Regardless of the suffering and pain
We cause by doing so.
If thus we treat
Defenceless animals for sport or gain,
How can we hope in this world to attain
The Peace we say we are anxious for?
Thus cruelty begets its offspring—War.
~George Bernard Shaw

Cruelty can be described as indifference to suffering, and even positive pleasure in inflicting it. Sadism can also be related to this form of action or concept.

Cruel ways of inflicting suffering may involve violence, but violence is not necessary for an act to be cruel. For example, if another person is drowning and begging for help, and another person is able to help, but merely watches with disinterest or perhaps mischievous amusement, that person is being cruel. This trait is on the rise in global population today.

Total Lack of Reverence Towards Life

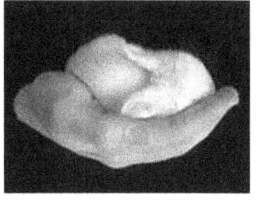

When a few birds get infected with bird-flu, we kill millions of them. When a few cows fall sick, we kill hundreds of thousands of them. This is cold blooded murder, this is holocaust and this is terrorism. In God's kingdom, all beings have a right to live and one has to pay dearly for killing even an ant unnecessarily.

In spite of the availability of so much food, billions of animals are mercilessly raised, transported and slaughtered every year. The reactions are equally severe for mankind. Human beings also get killed in riots, bombings and wars like the animals they kill. Time is coming when people will 'cull' a whole race or a country when it gets infected with a disease.

> *If you caught your kid raising cats in tiny boxes, forcing them to live in their own feces without clean air or sunlight, pulling their teeth and claws out with pliers to keep them from hurting each other, then skinning them alive to make collars to sell to friends, you'd rush him to a psychiatrist. But you support that very behaviour every time you buy meat, eggs, dairy or fur.* ~ Dan Piraro

Factory Farms - Hells on Earth

Cruelty has existed in human society since time immemorial but in modern times, it has become industrialized. Cruelty has taken the shape of a global industry and the world has never witnessed such institutionalization of barbarism. People always killed animals for food, entertainment or fur etc. but killing in mechanized industrial slaughterhouses is a modern invention. Animals were never transported thousands of miles for killing and neither existed global marketing networks in animal products.

Factory farming is the practice of raising farm animals in confinement at high stocking density, where a farm operates as a factory - a practice typical in industrial farming by agribusinesses.

Confinement at high stocking density is one part of a systematic effort to produce the highest output at the lowest cost by relying on economies of scale, modern machinery, biotechnology, and global trade. Confinement at high stocking density requires antibiotics and pesticides to mitigate the spread of disease and pestilence exacerbated by these crowded living conditions. There are differences in the way factory farming techniques are practiced around the world.

If we saw someone beating a puppy senseless with a stick on the street, we would most likely drop our backpack, run over, and knock the guy out. But if we never see it, it goes unnoticed and unpunished. The same goes with the meat industry.

Billions of animals are raised in appalling conditions that would have people thrown in jail if performed on dogs or cats, but farm animals are specifically excluded from Animal Welfare Acts which are supposed to exist in various countries. There's far too much information regarding animal treatment to give an accurate picture

"To kill cows means to end human civilization."
-Srila Prabhupada (Srimad Bhagavatam 1.4.9)

in just a few pages, but here are the most relevant facts behind the main sources of meat we consume.

Meat production, like any other industry, is one that is driven purely by profit. It exhibits complete disregard for humane animal treatment and the environment.

Milk or White Blood
Dairy Cows in Factory Farms

Regardless of where they live, all dairy cows must give birth in order to begin producing milk. Today, dairy cows are forced to have a calf every year. Like human beings, cows have a nine-month gestation period, and so giving birth every twelve months is physically demanding. The cows are also artificially re-impregnated while they are still lactating from their previous birthing, so their bodies are still producing milk during seven months of their nine-month pregnancy. With genetic manipulation and intensive production technologies, it is common for modern dairy cows to produce ten times more than they would produce naturally. As a result, the cows' bodies are under constant stress, and they are at risk for numerous health problems.

> *A nation can be judged by how it treats its animals.*
> *~Gandhi*

"Lord Christ says 'Thou shalt not kill'; why you are killing?" they give evidence that "Christ also ate meat sometimes." Sometimes Christ ate meat, that's all right, but did Christ say that "You maintain big, big slaughterhouse and go on eating meat?" There is no common sense even. Christ might have eaten. Sometimes he... If there was no, nothing available for eating, what could you do? That is another question. In great necessity, when there is no other food except taking meat... That time is coming. In this age, Kali-yuga, gradually food grains will be reduced. It is stated in the Srimad-Bhagavatam, Twelfth Canto. No rice, no wheat, no milk, no sugar will be available. One has to eat meat. This will be the condition. And maybe to eat the human flesh also. This sinful life is degrading so much so that they will become more and more sinful.
(Lecture, Bhagavad-gita 2.6 — London, August 6, 1973)

In developed countries, approximately half of the dairy cows suffer from mastitis, a bacterial infection of their udders. This is such a common and costly ailment that a dairy industry group, the National Mastitis Council, has been formed in several countries to specifically combat this disease. Other diseases, such as Bovine Leukemia Virus, Bovine Immunodeficiency Virus, and Johne's disease are also rampant on modern dairies, but they commonly go unnoticed because they are either difficult to detect or have a long incubation period. A cow eating a normal grass diet could not produce milk at the abnormal levels expected on modern dairies, and so today's dairy cows must be given high energy feeds. The unnaturally rich diet causes metabolic disorders including ketosis, which can be fatal, and laminitis, which causes lameness.

Another dairy industry disease caused by intensive milk production is "Milk Fever." This ailment is caused by calcium deficiency, and it occurs when milk secretion depletes calcium faster than it can be replenished in the blood.

In a healthy environment, cows would live in excess of twenty-five years, but in modern dairies, they are slaughtered after just three or four years. The abuse wreaked upon the bodies of dairy cows is so intense that the dairy industry also is a huge source of "downed animals" — animals who are so sick or injured that they are unable to walk or even stand. Investigators have documented downed animals routinely being beaten, dragged, or pushed with bulldozers in attempts to move them to slaughter.

Bovine Growth Hormone (BGH), a synthetic hormone, is now being injected into cows to get them to produce even more milk. Besides adversely affecting the cows' health, BGH also increases birth defects in their calves.

> Our inhumane treatment of livestock is becoming widespread and more and more barbaric... These creatures feel; they know pain. They suffer pain just as we humans feel pain.
> - Senator Robert Byrd

Calves born to dairy cows are separated from their mothers immediately after birth. The half that are born female are raised to replace older dairy cows in the milking herd. The other half of the calves are male and are slaughtered for meat. Most are killed for beef, with many millions ending up as veal.

The veal industry was created as a by-product of the dairy industry to take advantage of an abundant supply of unwanted male calves. Veal calves commonly live for eighteen to twenty weeks in wooden crates that are so small that they cannot turn around, stretch their legs, or even lie down comfortably. The calves are fed a liquid milk substitute, deficient in iron and fiber, which is designed to make the animals anemic, resulting in the light-colored flesh that is prized as veal. In addition to this high-priced veal, some calves are killed at just a few days old to be sold as low-grade veal.

Terrorism Eggs

There are approximately 4 billion egg laying hens in the world confined in battery cages — small wire cages stacked in tiers and lined up in rows inside warehouses. Hens are commonly packed four to a cage measuring just 16 inches wide. In this tiny space, the birds cannot stretch their wings or legs, and they cannot fulfill normal behavioral patterns or social needs. Constantly rubbing against the wire cages, they suffer from severe feather loss, and their bodies are covered with bruises and abrasions.

In order to reduce injuries resulting from excessive pecking — an aberrant behavior that occurs when the confined hens are bored and frustrated — practically all laying hens have part of their beaks cut off. Debeaking is a painful procedure that involves cutting through bone, cartilage, and soft tissue.

Laying more than 250 eggs per year each, laying hens' bodies are severely taxed. They suffer from "fatty liver syndrome" when their liver cells, which work overtime to produce the fat and protein for egg yolks, accumulate extra fat. They also suffer from what the industry calls 'cage layer fatigue,' and many become 'egg bound' and die when their bodies are too weak to pass another egg.

Osteoporosis is another common ailment afflicting egg laying hens, whose bodies lose more calcium to form egg shells than they can assimilate from their diets. Inadequate calcium contributes to broken bones, paralysis, and death.

After one year in egg production, the birds are classified as 'spent hens' and are sent off to slaughter. Their brittle, calcium-depleted bones often shatter during handling or at the slaughterhouse. They usually end up in soups, pot pies, or similar low-grade chicken meat products in which their bodies can be shredded to hide the bruises from consumers.

Disposing off of spent hens is particularly cruel. In a system called 'Jet-Pro', live birds are ground up and turned into 'Pellets. Also birds are routinely tossed alive into a wood-chipping machine to dispose them of .

After the hens finish with laying eggs, they may be 'force molted'. This process involves starving the hens for up to 18 days, keeping them in the dark, and denying them water to shock their bodies into another egg-laying cycle. Many die during this forced famine.

Male chicks are of no economic value, and they are discarded on the day they hatch — usually by the cheapest, most convenient

When there was too much animal killing, the incarnation of Lord Buddha was there to stop animal killing. In Buddhism there is no animal killing. Although they are now killing animals, but originally Buddha religion means non-violence. Also Lord Christ also said, "Thou shalt not kill." And Krsna says, ahimsa. So in no religion unnecessary killing of animals is allowed. Even in Mohammedans, they are also... Kurvani. Kurvani means they can kill animals in the Mosque. So everywhere animal killing is restricted.
- Prabhupada (Room Conversation with Professor Durckheim, June 19, 1974, Germany)

means available. Either these little cute creatures are thrown into trash cans by the thousands or groundup alive or put into shredders, alive. This can result in unspeakable horrors, as described by one research scientist who observed that "even after twenty seconds, there were only partly damaged animals with whole skulls". In other words, fully conscious chicks were partially ground up and left to slowly and agonizingly die. Eyewitness accounts at commercial hatcheries indicate similar horrors of chicks being slowly dismembered by machinery blades en route to trash bins or manure spreaders.

The Rescue - A Story

On May 23, 2001, investigators rescued eight hens, in dire need of immediate veterinary care, from a factory farm in Maryland, USA.

A hen, later named Jane, was found pinned by one wing in the wire bars of her cage, survived the amputation of her wing and enjoyed sunbathing, running through the grass, dustbathing, jumping onto her perch at night, and eating her favorite treat--grapes. Jane was free from the exploitation of the egg industry for six months before succumbing to cancer.

The hens, practically featherless and very despondent when rescued, were given a second chance at life. One year later, Jane's seven friends are alive and doing well--enjoying a virtual paradise

> *The factory farm attitude is exemplified by the ISE corporation, whose lawyer asserted that it is legally acceptable to dispose of live birds as if they were manure. When the judge asked, 'Isn't there a big distinction between manure and live animals?' ISE's lawyer responded, 'No, your honour.'*

compared to their former existence inside a factory farm. But this rescue is like a drop in a vast ocean. There are other 4 billion hens still suffering in battery cages all over the world.

On Assembly Lines - Dying Piece By Piece

Many beef cows are born and live on the range, foraging and fending for themselves for months or even years. They are not adequately protected against inclement weather, and they may die of dehydration or freeze to death. Injured, ill, or otherwise ailing animals do not receive necessary veterinary attention. One common malady afflicting beef cattle is called "cancer eye." Left untreated, the cancer eats away at the animal's eye and face, eventually producing a crater in the side of the animal's head.

Accustomed to roaming unimpeded and unconstrained, range cattle are frightened and confused when humans come to round them up. Terrified animals are often injured, some so severely that they become "downed" (unable to walk or even stand). These downed animals commonly suffer for days without receiving food, water or veterinary care, and many die of neglect. Others are dragged, beaten, and pushed with tractors on their way to slaughter.

Cattle all over the world are branded with hot iron brands. Needless to say, this practice is extremely traumatic and painful, and the animals bellow loudly as brands are burned into their skin. Beef cattle are also subjected to 'waddling,' another type of identification marking. This painful procedure entails cutting chunks out of the hide that hangs under the animals' necks.

In North America, most beef cattle spend the last few months of their lives at feedlots, crowded by the thousands into dusty,

This killing of animals is for the non-civilized society. They cannot... They do not know how to grow food. They were killing animals. When man is advanced in his knowledge and education, why they should kill? Especially in America, we see so many nice foodstuffs. Fruits, grains, milk. And from milk, you can get hundreds of nice preparations, all nutritious.
-Prabhupada (Room Conversation, July 5, 1975, Chicago)

manure-laden holding pens. The air is thick with harmful bacteria and particulate matter, and the animals are at a constant risk for respiratory disease. Feedlot cattle are routinely implanted with growth-promoting hormones, and they are fed unnaturally rich diets designed to fatten them quickly and profitably. Because cattle are biologically suited to eat a grass-based, high fiber diet, therefore concentrated feedlot rations contribute to metabolic disorders.

Cattle may be transported several times during their lifetimes, and they may travel hundreds or even thousands of miles during a single trip. Long journeys are very stressful and contribute to disease and even death. A distinct disease called "Shipping fever" is common and costs livestock producers as much as $3 billion a year around the globe.

Inside The Slaughter House

Slaughterhouses examplify hell on earth and may be manual or mechanized. Modern mechanized slaughterhouses kill 250-500 cows every hour. The high speed of the assembly line makes it increasingly difficult to treat animals with any semblance of humaneness. A Meat & Poultry article states, "Good handling is extremely difficult if equipment is 'maxed out' all the time. It is impossible to have a good attitude toward cattle if employees have to constantly overexert themselves, and thus transfer all that stress right down to the animals, just to keep up with the line."

Prior to being hung up by their back legs and bled to death, cattle are supposed to be rendered unconscious. One common practice is 'stunning' which is usually done by a mechanical blow to the head. However, the procedure is terribly imprecise, and inadequate stunning is inevitable. As a result, conscious animals are often hung upside down, kicking and struggling, while a slaughterhouse worker makes another attempt to render them unconscious.

This is detailed in an April 2001 Washington Post article, which describes typical slaughterplant conditions:

> The cattle were supposed to be dead before they got to Moreno. But too often they weren't.
> They blink. They make noises, he said softly. The head moves, the eyes

are wide and looking around. Still Moreno would cut. On bad days, he says, dozens of animals reached his station clearly alive and conscious. Some would survive as far as the tail cutter, the belly ripper, the hide puller. They die, said Moreno, piece by piece...

"In plants all over the United States, this happens on a daily basis," said Lester Friedlander, a veterinarian and formerly chief government inspector at a Pennsylvania hamburger plant. "I've seen it happen. And I've talked to other veterinarians. They feel it's out of control."

Boiling Alive - Are You Really That Hungry

After detailing the egg story, we shall examine the fate of birds meant for meat. These too are crowded by the thousands into huge, factory-like warehouses where they can barely move. Each chicken is given less than half a square foot of space, while turkeys are each given less than three square feet. Shortly after hatching, both chickens and turkeys have the ends of their beaks cut off, and turkeys also have the ends of their toes clipped off. These mutilations are performed without anesthesia, ostensibly to reduce injuries that result when stressed birds are driven to fighting.

Today's "broiler" (meat) chickens have been genetically altered to grow twice as fast and twice as large as their ancestors. Pushed beyond their biological limits, hundreds of millions of chickens die every year before reaching slaughter weight at 6 weeks of age. An industry journal explains that "broilers [chickens] now grow so rapidly that the heart and lungs are not developed well enough to support the remainder of the body, resulting in congestive heart failure and tremendous death losses. Modern broiler chickens also experience crippling leg disorders, as their legs are not capable of supporting their abnormally heavy bodies. Confined in unsanitary, disease-ridden factory farms, the birds also frequently succumb to heat, infectious diseases, and cancer.

Starvation, world hunger, cruelty, waste, wars -- we must make a statement against these things. Vegetarianism is my statement. And I think it's a strong one.
- Isaac Bashevis Singer, Nobel laureate and Holocaust survivor

Transport

Chickens and turkeys are taken to the slaughterhouse in crates stacked on the backs of open trucks. During transport, the birds are not protected from weather conditions, and a percentage of the birds are expected to die en route. Birds freeze to death in winter, or die from heat stress and suffocation in warm weather. It is "cheaper" for the industry to transport the birds in open crates without adequate protection, despite high mortality rates. Upon arrival at the slaughterhouse, the birds are either pulled individually from their crates, or the crates are lifted off the truck, often with a crane or forklift, and the birds are dumped onto a conveyor belt. As the birds are unloaded, some miss the conveyor belt and fall onto the ground. Slaughterhouse workers intent upon 'processing' thousands of birds every hour have neither the time nor the inclination to pick up individuals who fall through the cracks, and these birds suffer grim deaths. Some die after being crushed by machinery or vehicles operating near the unloading area, while others may die of starvation or exposure days, or even weeks, later.

Inside The Slaughterhouse

Birds inside the slaughterhouse suffer an equally gruesome fate. Upon entering the facility, fully conscious birds are hung by their feet from metal shackles on a moving rail. Many slaughterplants first stun the birds in an electrified water bath in order to immobilize them and expedite assembly line killing.

However, stunning procedures are often inadequate. Poultry slaughterhouses commonly set the electrical current lower than

> *tatas canu-dinam dharmah*
> *satyam saucam ksama daya*
> *kalena balina rajan*
> *nanksyaty ayur balam smrtih*
>
> Sukadeva Gosvami said: *Then, O King, religion, truthfulness, cleanliness, tolerance, mercy, duration of life, physical strength and memory will all diminish day by day because of the powerful influence of the age of Kali.*
> ~Srila Prabhupada (SB 12.2.1)

what is required to render the birds unconscious because of concerns that too much electricity would damage the carcasses and diminish their value.

After the shackled birds pass through the stunning tank, their throats are slashed, usually by a mechanical blade. Inevitably, the blade misses some birds, who may still be moving and struggling after improper stunning. Proceeding to the next station on the assembly line - the scalding tank - the birds are submerged in boiling hot water. Those missed by the killing blade are boiled alive.

Slaughterhouse: The Shocking Story of Greed, Cruelty and Barbarism

Every year, over 60 billion animals are slaughtered for human consumption worldwide.

As discussed earlier, in factory farms, millions of animals and birds are confined and tortured in hellish conditions, are deprived of sunlight, fresh air and natural food and the freedom to walk or fly. Thus we create an environment for the spread of virus and disease. And at the whiff of an infection, statutorily kill millions of them in the name of 'culling'.

Millions of cows and pigs who make it to the slaughterhouse alive are unable to walk off the trucks. Called "downers," a former slaughterhouse worker describes the customary welcome for these animals:

"... they beat him with pipes, kick them, hit them with pieces of

> *Practically there is no mercifulness now, daya. Formerly a man was very charitable, but here, at the present moment, where is the question of charity? He cannot maintain oneself. So these things are reducing. Therefore Vyasadeva thought it wise to give the Vedic knowledge in writings so that we can read, we can hear, and we can utilize, we can take benefit out of it.*
> *–Srila Prabhupada (Sunday Feast Lecture — Los Angeles, January 19, 1969)*

wood, stick them with knives. If he still won't move, you wrap the cable around his neck and drag them in with the hoist. You drag them while they're still alive." "And they stab cows in the butt to make 'em move. Break their tails. They beat them so bad. I've drug cows till their bones start breaking, while they were still alive. Bringing them around the corner and they get stuck up in the doorway, just pull them till their hide be ripped, till the blood just drip on the steel and concrete. Breaking their legs pulling them in. And the cow be crying with its tongue stuck out. They pull him till his neck just pop."

The Word 'Terrorist' Is A Misnomer,

Lot More Terrorists Are Around

Fur Trade

Approximately 23.5 million furbearing animals - raccoons, coyotes, bobcats, lynxes, opossums, nutria, beavers, muskrats, otters and others are killed each year by trappers around the world.

Despite the fur industry's attempts to downplay the role of trapping in fur production, it is estimated that more than half of all fur garments come from trapped animals.

2.7 million animals are harvested on fur "farms" in US alone. Many more millions are skinned in other parts of the world to cover the bodies of westerners. The killing of these creatures is especially ruthless so as not to cause damage to the skin.

So this is nature's law. You don't require to be sent to the slaughterhouse. You'll make your slaughterhouse at home. You'll kill your own child. Abortion. This is nature's law. ....If you kill, you must be killed.
Bhagavan: They kill the cow, which is a mother, and then sometimes they get the reaction back, when their mother kills them. -
Srila Prabhupada (Room Conversation, June 11, 1974, Paris)

Hunting

Every year, hundreds of thousands of animals like elephants, tigers, rhinos and other endangered species are killed by poachers to sell in black markets. Additionally hundreds of thousands are killed in 'canned hunts' or hunting of animals procured from captivity including zoos, to allow rich hunters the thrill of killing them.

In US federal land alone (more than half a billion acres), more than 200 million animals are killed every year. Hunting is permitted on 60% of US wildlife refuges, national forests and state parks.

Fishing

Overharvesting of oceans and seas has led to threatened populations of many fish and marine mammals. Millions of seals are killed every year because of competition with humans for remaining fish. Other marine predators are devastating the balances of new fish populations because previous prey is disappearing.

China's Graphic Skinning of Live Animals

China is a major exporter of fur for the western consumers. The skinning of animals is done without killing, while the animal is fully conscious. This is accomplished by either hanging the animal from one of the hind legs or by throwing it down on the floor. Several types of animals are reared in thousands of fur farms across China in most harrowing conditions. After skinning, the animal's body is thrown over a heap of bodies. The poor animal, covered with blood and completely deskinned, looks around and remains alive for a considerable period of time. Merciful death descends

When we kill the animals to eat them, they end up killing us because their flesh, which contains cholesterol and saturated fat, was never intended for human beings.
~Williams C. Roberts, M.D., editor of The American Journal of Cardiology

only after a long wait, sometime after many days. The beautiful furry animal is turned into a horrific living carcass.

The Horror of the Indian Meat and Leather Trade
Long Cruel Road To Slaughterhouse - The Painful Death March

For seven years, PETA India and its affiliates have conducted undercover investigations into the transport and slaughter conditions that are endured by the cows, buffaloes, sheep and goats who are used in the Indian meat and leather trade. The leather produced from the skins of these animals is exported throughout the world, including US and Europe.

The investigators have gathered graphic evidence of the widespread illegal abuse of these animals as well as evidence of unhygienic and dangerous conditions in slaughter facilities. The animals are subjected to cruelty that includes being crammed into lorries in such large numbers that many become severely injured when they are crushed or gouged by the horns of other animals. Many of them die en route. The evidence also reveals that most of the animals are dragged into abattoirs before they are cut open – often with dirty, blunt knives and in full view of one another – on floors that are covered with feces, blood, guts and urine. Some animals are even skinned and dismembered while they are still conscious.

Cow is considered a sacred animal in India and that cow slaughter is banned in most states though the ban is never followed. Cows and calves are bought under the false pretense that they will live out their lives in rural farms. They are marched to slaughter houses for days and crammed into lorries, causing many to suffocate in direct violation of the constitution of India. Animals that collapse from exhaustion or injury have their eyes smeared with chilly

The cow is not my mother? Who can live without milk? And who has not taken cow's milk? Immediately, in the morning, you require milk. And the animal, she's supplying milk, she's not mother? What is the sense? Mother-killing civilization. And they want to be happy. And periodically there is great war and wholesale massacre, reaction.
-Srila Prabhupada (Garden Conversation, June 14, 1976, Detroit)

peppers and tobacco and their tails broken in an effort to keep them moving.

Blatant Crime

India's own minimal animal protection laws regarding transport and slaughter are blatantly ignored, and although it claims to have an Animal Welfare Reform Programme, the Indian Council for Leather Exports (CLE) refuses to take any action to prevent leather-selling businesses from obtaining hides and skins from such abattoirs. Animals of all ages, including small calves, are killed and used in the leather trade.

The Supreme Court

PETA India has a case pending before the Indian Supreme Court against the Union of India, each state-level government and the Animal Welfare Board of India (AWBI) for their failure to enforce animal protection laws and for allowing the unnecessary and extreme suffering to animals who are used for leather and meat. The Court has publicly

> *Dog is untouchable according to Vedic literature, and they are being kept. And cows? Killed. And cruelty to animals means not to be cruel to the cats and dogs. And for the cows, "Oh, there is no question of cruelty. It has no soul. Kill him." This is your civilization, Dog civilization.*
> *One side they're advertising "Stop cruelty to animals," another side they're opening unrestricted slaughterhouse. Just see. Just like a gang of thieves gives a signboard, "Goodman and Company." So there are so many members of the society against cruelty to animals. But they are all meat-eaters.*
> *-Srila Prabhupada (Talk with Bob Cohen - February 27-29, 1972, Mayapura)*

expressed its shock at the evidence of cruelty that PETA India has submitted.

Major Retail Chains Ban Indian Leather Products

When PETA's campaign to alleviate the suffering of animals used for leather was first launched in 2000, about 40 major companies stated that they would not use leather sourced from Indian animals. An estimated US$68 million was reportedly lost by the Indian leather industry as a result of these companies' decisions not to support unlawful cruelty. The campaign also gained the support of celebrities all around the world, including His Holiness the Dalai Lama, Sir Paul McCartney, Pamela Anderson, Jackie Chan and others.

Recently, US retailer Liz Claiborne – which has annual sales of US$4.8 billion – has assured PETA US that it will not use leather from India. Kenneth Cole, another US retailer, which has annual sales of US$518 million – has also weighed in, giving its commitment to PETA US.

Increasing Cruelty Requiring Tougher Legislation

All over the world, torturing and killing of animals/humans is becoming increasingly common. Examples of cruelty cited below

> *Prabhupada: Now Kirtanananda was prosecuted because he is not killing cows.*
> *Brahmananda: By having them grow old, they were saying that "This is cruelty. You should kill them."*
> *Prabhupada: This is their civilization, that "You are not killing? You are cruel." Just see. Christ said, "Thou shall not kill." That is cruel. How can you pull on this civilization? But this is their religion. So what kind of persons they are?*
> *- Srila Prabhupada (Room Conversation - February 28, 1977, Mayapur)*

are everyday occurrences.

-Puppy found burned and bound with wires.

-Kitten's leg crushed after it was thrown from a balcony when a 17-year-old youth had an argument with his girlfriend. Another cat shot in the eye with a slug-gun pellet.

-Cat trapped by man, clubbed with a softball bat and dumped. Cat survived but badly injured, with an eye hanging out of its socket.

-Starving dog found with mouth taped shut and eyes hanging from sockets.

Most parts of the world have no felony animal-cruelty laws. Even where the laws exist, these are never enforced.

Cruelty Towards Animals Translates Into Crime Against Humanity

There appears to be a direct link between the way a person treats animals and the way he treats his fellow human beings.

US serial killer Dennis Rader admitted to police that before he ever started strangling humans, he killed dogs and cats, according to court records.

As a kid, George Bush, President of US, enjoyed putting firecrackers into frogs, throwing them in the air, and then watching them blow up. Should this be cause for alarm? How relevant is a man's childhood behavior to what he is like as an adult? Can we link this childhood behaviour of his with the heavy bloodshed and so called wars on terrorism during his tenure.

Cruelty to animals is a common precursor to later criminal violence. In fact, Bush's childhood friend, Terry Throckmorton, openly and laughingly admits, "We were terrible to animals." So how much importance should we attribute to this early behavior?

Is boy George's lack of empathy and cruelty not just childhood insensitivity, but rather a personality trait still present in the man?

If it were absolutely necessary to choose, I would rather be guilty of an immoral act than of a cruel one.
~Anatole France

If so, we have much to be concerned about. Do we really want a man who appears to be empathetically challenged to hold the most powerful position in America?

Dr. Vizard says, "Cruelty to animals, if accompanied by a sexual interest in animals, is a high-risk indicator of a future sex offender." Studies have shown that individuals who enjoy or are willing to inflict harm on animals are more likely to do so to humans. One of the known warning signs of certain psychopathologies, including antisocial personality disorder, is a history of torturing pets and small animals.

According to the New York Times: "the FBI has found that a history of cruelty to animals is one of the traits that regularly appears in its computer records of serial rapists and murderers, and the standard diagnostic and treatment manual for psychiatric and emotional disorders lists cruelty to animals as a diagnostic criterion for conduct disorders."

Alan R. Felthous reported in his paper "Aggression Against Cats, Dogs, and People" (1980) that: "A survey of psychiatric patients who had repeatedly tortured dogs and cats found all of them had high levels of aggression toward people as well, including one patient who had murdered a boy."

This is a commonly reproduced finding, and for this reason, violence towards animals is considered a serious warning sign of potential serious violence towards humans.

Animals Have A Soul, Animals Feel Just Like You Do

Those who claim that animals have no soul are the ones without soul. This is a completely nonsensical and absurd proposition that

animals have no soul. We eat, sleep, mate and defend and animals do the same, then where is the difference. Rather animals are more 'humane' than the human beings.

Take for example rats who are highly sociable beings - they communicate with each other at high-frequency sounds, play together, wrestle, and love sleeping curled up together. Much like us, if they do not have companionship, they can become lonely, anxious, depressed, and stressed.. They become attached to each other, love their own families, and easily bond with their human guardians, returning as much affection as is given to them. Many rats will even "groom" their human companion's hand and would appreciate a massage, a scratch behind the ears, or even a tickle in return. Recent studies by a neuroscientist at Bowling Green State University, suggest that when rats play or are playfully tickled, they make chirping sounds that are strikingly similar to human laughter. The rats he studied also bonded socially with the human tickler and even sought to be tickled more. Young rats have a marvelous sense of fun.

Male rats will snuggle up for a cuddle and find contentment curled up in a person's lap. Rats love seeing kind people and will often bounce around waiting to be noticed and picked up. Rats can bond with their human companions to the point that if they are suddenly given away to someone else or forgotten, they can pine to death.

It is estimated that each year, tens of millions of rats and mice are killed in experiments in laboratories. With the popularity of genetic engineering, the numbers are increasing.

Let's take another example of baboons. Like human parents, baboons tend to newborns around the clock. Babies stay close to

The animals of this world exist for their own reasons. They were not made for humans any more than black people were made for whites.
~ Alice Walker

their mothers, clinging to them as they forage for food and snuggling into their laps for a nap in the afternoon sun. Drawn to the nourishment and close contact provided by their mothers' milk, young baboons even have tantrums when their mothers attempt to wean them.

Young baboons love to play, and they show a joy in living. They spend carefree days swinging from vines, playing games of chase, and wrestling and tumbling with their friends. Female baboons remain in the group into which they were born, among their relatives, throughout their entire lives. Their social lives are centered on the network of family in which they live.

Baboons who are being used as "research tools" in the modern labs and are denied all that is natural to them. Crammed into barren metal cages, these naturally social beings suffer unbearable loneliness. Mother baboons, who fuss over and care attentively for their young in the wild, have their babies taken from them. Trapped in their tiny prisons, they are deprived of the ability to roam over long stretches of land.

Experimenters at Columbia University are causing strokes in baboons by removing their left eyeballs and using the empty eye sockets to clamp critical blood vessels to their brains; they are surgically implanting heavy pipes into the skulls of baboons to induce stress and study the connection between stress and menstrual cycles; and they are pumping nicotine and morphine into pregnant baboons and their fetuses.

Cruelty-Free, Humanely-Raised Meat?

Conditions of factory farms are so horrible that meat eaters are resorting to 'cruelty-free' meat which is an irony in itself. There is

Cruelty to dumb animals is one of the distinguishing vices of low and base minds. Wherever it is found, it is a certain mark of ignorance and meanness; a mark which all the external advantages of wealth, splendour, and nobility, cannot obliterate. It is consistent neither with learning nor true civility.
~William Jones

an emerging class called "ethical omnivores" – people who won't eat meat unless it is 'humanely' raised.

Two recent books - Fast Food Nation - a book that describes many horrific aspects of food meat/dairy production, and Dominion, in which a former speechwriter for President Bush describes how profit-margin-obsession and the separation of farming from the average consumer's life has led to consumers supporting horrifically cruel conditions for farm animals.

There is a growing number of "ethical omnivores" - people who eat meat but only if it's been raised humanely in a "cruelty-free" way (or at least less cruel than standard meat/dairy farm practice). The growing number of these ethical omnivores has led to the opening of new ground in what was previously a no-man's land between carnivores and vegetarians, and given rise to numerous farms who sell free-range, cage-free, or humanely raised products.

But all this humaneness is about making mistreated, starved, mutilated, abused, and confined animals slightly less mistreated, starved, mutilated, abused, and confined. May be something is better than nothing.

Animal Testing - Millions Live In Agony, Only To Die In Vain

As many as 320 million animals are experimented on and killed in laboratories around the world every year. Experimentation means things like pumping chemicals into rats' stomachs, hacking muscle tissue from dogs' thighs, and putting baby monkeys in isolation chambers far from their mothers.

Animal experimentation is a multibillion-dollar industry fueled by massive public funding and involving a complex web of corporate, government, and university laboratories, cage and food manufacturers, and animal breeders, dealers, and transporters.

> *Ask the experimenters why they experiment on animals, and the answer is: 'Because the animals are like us.' Ask the experimenters why it is morally OK to experiment on animals, and the answer is: 'Because the animals are not like us.' Animal experimentation rests on a logical contradiction.*
> *–Professor Charles R. Magel*

The industry and its people profit because animals, who cannot defend themselves against abuse, are legally imprisoned and exploited.

Fortunately for animals in laboratories, there are people who care. Some of them work in labs, and when they witness abuse, they call PETA. Thanks to these courageous whistleblowers, PETA's undercover investigators and caseworkers, who sift through reams of scientific and government documents, have exposed what goes on behind laboratory doors.

Animal Experimentation Is Unnecessary

Medical Research on animals accounts for only 2% of medical advances in this century. Atleast 10 billion dollars are poured into animal experiments every year around the world.

Draize Test

Rabbits are routinely blinded by having various products forced into their eyes by many companies today. This is called Draize Test. The Draize test does not guarantee human safety but protects companies from potential lawsuits by their customers. Their necks are stuck in wooden or metal traps, their eyes are kept open by clips and for days or weeks, harmful chemicals are poured in their

> *So without being devotee a man will become cruel, cruel, cruel, cruel, cruel, in this way go to hell. And devotee cannot tolerate. We have studied in the life of Lord Jesus Christ. When he saw that in the Jewish synagogue the birds were being killed, he became shocked. He therefore left. Jes... He inaugurated the Christian religion. Perhaps you know. He was shocked by this animal-killing. And therefore his first commandment is "Thou shall not kill." But the foolish Christians, instead of following his instruction, they are opening daily slaughterhouses.*
> Srila Prabhupada (Srimad-Bhagavatam 7.9.52 — Vrndavana, April 7, 1976)

eyes. Due to struggling to get free, they suffer broken necks and turn blind. Most of them die soon after.

Life in a Laboratory
Auschwitz, Dachau and the Gulag Camps Still Exist

Life in a laboratory is deprivation, isolation, misery and horrible pain.

Chimpanzees, in their natural homes, are never separated from their families and troops. They spend hours together every day, grooming each other and making soft nests for sleeping each night. They are loving and protective parents, and baby chimps will live close to their mothers for many years. But in a laboratory, chimpanzees are caged alone. There are no families, no companions, no grooming, no nests. There are only cold, hard steel bars and loneliness that goes on for so many years that most chimpanzees sink into depression, eventually losing their minds.

On top of the deprivation, there are the experiments. Animals are infected with diseases that they would never normally contract–tiny mice grow tumors as large as their own bodies, kittens are purposely blinded, rats are made to suffer seizures. Experimenters force-feed 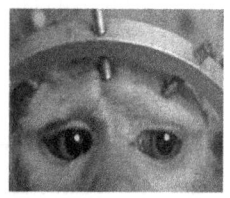 chemicals to animals, conduct repeated surgeries on them, implant wires in their brains, crush their spines, and much more. Think of what it would be like to endure this and then be dumped back into a cage, usually without any painkillers. Video footage from inside laboratories shows that animals cower in fear every time someone walks by their cages. They don't know if they will be dragged from their prison cells for an injection, blood withdrawal, a painful procedure or surgery, or death. Often animals see other animals killed right in front of them.

PETA documented at University of North Carolina,

> "... all beings have beliefs, desires, perception, memory, and a sense of the future and are to be considered "subjects-of-a-life" and have intrinsic value."

experimenters killing mice by cutting off their heads with scissors. There are no happy animals inside laboratories.

Animals are blinded, dropped in boiling water, burnt on hot plates, frozen in dry ice. They are allowed to bleed by exposing the carotid artery or by incision through the jugular vein. Electrodes are implanted in the brain to stimulate pain centres; they are subjected to huge doses of radiation and then forced to run on a treadmill to see how long they can survive. They are deafened, mutilated, exposed to infection, and driven mad. Babies are removed from their mothers to study the effects of deprivation. Free-ranging creatures are confined for years in small cages or, worse, in harnessed chairs. They are starved or forced to inhale carcinogenics or toxic material, till they die. Auschwitz, Dachau and the Gulag camps are still a reality for animals.

Entertainment Animals

The Circus

Since 1990, captive elephants have killed more than 300 people. The degree of suffering and cruelty of training techniques is clear when naturally peaceful elephants attack humans.

Marine Parks

Killer whales and dolphins live only 25% of their natural life expectancy when captive. Normally they swim dozens of miles in the wild and suffer stress-induced disease and ailments when kept in small pools and forced to perform tricks.

Dog Races

Up to 50,000 greyhounds are killed a year or sent to experimentation when they are no longer profitable for the racing industry.

Some rascals put forward the theory that an animal has no soul or is something like dead stone. In this way they rationalize that there is no sin in animal killing. Actually animals are not dead stone, but the killers of animals are stone-hearted. Consequently no reason or philosophy appeals to them. They continue keeping slaughterhouses and killing animals.
-Srila Prabhupada (Srimad-Bhagavatam 4.26.9)

Cruelty in the KFC Slaughterhouse - A Case Study

US fast food giants are taking over the world. They can be found in every nook and corner of every city in the world.

PETA's undercover investigation into a Moorefield, West Virginia, slaughterhouse that was named KFC's "Supplier of the Year" found workers who were stomping on chickens, kicking them,  and violently slamming them against the floors and walls. Workers also ripped the animals' beaks off, twisted their heads off, spat tobacco into their eyes and mouths, spray-painted their faces, and squeezed their bodies so hard that the birds expelled feces—all while the chickens were still alive.

More than 850 million chickens are killed for its restaurants each year. There is a campaign called "Boycott KFC" pledge which is going around and enrolling members.

Whiteners Used In Pink Milk

Like humans, cows give milk for their babies. They are therefore regularly artificially inseminated and given hormones to produce 100 pounds of milk a day. This is ten times more than they would produce naturally. As a result, a huge percentage of dairy cows suffer from mastitis, a bacterial infection of the udders. Since this milk is still considered drinkable, the blood and pus from their infections, along with massive quantities of antibiotics, end up in the milk on supermarket shelves. Many times milk turns pink due to presence of blood. This milk is turned natural white by adding whitening chemicals.

Foie gras Cruelty

The controversial production of foie gras (the liver of a duck or a goose that has been specially fattened) involves force-feeding birds

Of all the animals, man is the only one that is cruel. He is the only one that inflicts pain for the pleasure of doing it.
~Mark Twain

more food than they would eat in the wild, and much more than they would voluntarily eat domestically. The feed, usually corn boiled with fat (to facilitate ingestion), deposits large amounts of fat in the liver, thereby producing the buttery consistency in the flesh.

At the start of production, a bird might be fed a dry weight of 250 grams of food per day, and up to 1,000 grams (in dry weight) by the end of the process. The actual amount of food force-fed is much greater, since the birds are fed a mash whose composition is about 53% dry and 47% liquid.

The feed is administered using a funnel fitted with a long tube (20–30 cm long), which forces the feed into the animal's esophagus. Modern systems usually use a tube fed by a pneumatic pump. Many times during feeding, bird's esophagus gets damaged which causes injury or deaths.

Zoosadism

Zoosadism refers to torturing of animals for entertainment purposes.

Cat Burning

Cat burning was a form of zoosadistic entertainment in European countries and it continues in some form or another by inflicting cruelty on cats. In this form of entertainment, people would gather dozens of cats in a net and hoist them high into the air from a special bundle onto a bonfire. The assembled people would "shriek with laughter as the animals, howling with pain,

> *mrgostra-khara-markakhu-*
> *sarisrp khaga-maksikah*
> *atmanah putravat pasyet*
> *tair esam antaram kiyat*
>
> One should treat animals such as deer, camels, asses, monkeys, mice, snakes, birds and flies exactly like one's own son. How little difference there actually is between children and these innocent animals. (Srimad Bhagavatam 7.14.9)

were singed, roasted, and finally carbonized." Sometimes a fox was burned.

Bull Fighting

More than 40,000 bulls are killed every year in bloody bullfights around the world. For 'entertainment', the animals are tortured over the course of an hour, speared in their backs before finally dying from blood loss and exhaustion.

Bullfighting is criticized by many animal rights activists, referring to it as a cruel or barbaric blood sport, in which the bull

Srila Prabhupada: some of the Christian people say, "We believe that animals have no soul." That is not correct. They believe animals have no soul because they want to eat the animals, but actually animals do have a soul.

Mike Robinson: How do you know that the animal has a soul?

Srila Prabhupada: You can know, also. Here is the scientific proof: the animal eats, you eat; the animal sleeps, you sleep; the animal has sex, you have sex; the animal also defends, you also defend. Then what is the difference between you and the animal? How can you say that you have a soul but the animal doesn't?

Mike Robinson: I can see that completely. But the Christian scriptures say...

Srila Prabhupada: Don't bring in any scriptures; this is a commonsense topic. Try to understand. The animal is eating, you are eating; the animal is sleeping, you are sleeping; the animal is defending, you are defending; the animal is having sex, you are having sex; the animals have children, you have children; they have a living place, you have a living place. If the animal's body is cut, there is blood; if your body is cut, there is blood. So, all these similarities are there. Now, why do you deny this one similarity, the presence of the soul? This is not logical. You have studied logic? In logic there is something called analogy. Analogy means drawing a conclusion by finding many points of similarity. If there are so many points of similarity between human beings and animals, why deny one similarity? That is not logic. That is not science.

-Srila Prabhupada (SSR, Reincarnation and Beyond)

suffers severe stress and a slow, torturous death.

Bull fighting includes horrors like prolonged and profuse bleeding caused by horse-mounted lancers, the charging by the bull of a blindfolded, armored horse who is "sometimes doped up, and unaware of the proximity of the bull", the placing of  barbed darts by banderilleros, followed by the matador's fatal sword thrust. These procedures are a normal part of bullfighting and death is rarely instantaneous. Then there are various failed attempts at killing the animal before it lies down.

Occasionally, if the public or the matador believe that bull has fought bravely, they may petition the president of the plaza to grant the bull an indulto. This is when the bull's life is spared and allowed to leave the ring alive and return to the ranch where it came from. However, few bulls survive the trip back to the ranch. With no veterinarian services at the plaza, most bulls die either while awaiting transportation or days later after arriving at their original ranch. Death is due to dehydration, infection of the wounds and loss of blood sustained during the fight.

Holocaust - Everyday And In Every Corner

Meat and dairy industries have no consideration for sick, diseased or disabled animals and they suffer unspeakable abuse and neglect at production facilities, stockyards and slaughterhouses.

Under current law, most sick, diseased or disabled animals are still sent to slaughter for human food—in spite of their tortured

Vegetarians have the best diet. They have the lowest rates of coronary disease of any group in the country... they have a fraction of our heart attack rate and they have only 40 percent of our cancer rate. On the average, they outlive other people by about six years now."
~William Castelli, M.D.,
Director, Framingham Heart Study, the longest-running epidemiological study in medical history.

condition. Sadly, even sick and suffering animals spell profit to the meat and leather industry. Profit, not humane considerations, guides industry practice. From the industry perspective, there is no financial gain in euthanizing a suffering animal, but if that animal can be dragged, pushed or prodded onto into the slaughterhouse, a profit can be made. Because of this simple economic fact, there is little doubt that the abuse of such animals is widespread across the world.

Following the discovery of Bovine Spongiform Encephalopathy (BSE)—also known as "mad cow disease"— the governments took modest measures to curtail the slaughter of sick cattle for human consumption. The result was that sick animals were left to die, piled atop one another for hours or even days without food, water or veterinary care.

In early 2008, video documentation exposed California slaughterhouse workers using shock prods, chains, high pressure hoses and even forklifts to move suffering, bellowing, and injured cattle into the slaughterhouse.

> *You have become mad and you are engaged in doing all forbidden things which you should not do. You are doing that. And why you are doing that? Nunam pramattah kurute vikarma [SB 5.5.4]. Why? Yad indriya-pritaya aprnoti. Simply for sense gratification. Simply for sense gratification. I have seen one hotel man in Calcutta. He cut the throat of a chicken, and the chicken, half-cut, it was flapping and jumping. The child of the hotel man, he was crying, and the hotel man was laughing. He was taking pleasure, "Oh, how this chicken, half-cut throat, and how he is jumping... Why you are crying? Why you are crying?" And in Western countries I think students are sometimes taken to slaughterhouse to see. Is it a fact? Yes. You see. They take pleasure. Doing something sinful, they take pleasure. For pleasure's sake they do that.*
> Srila Prabhupada (Srimad-Bhagavatam 3.25.16 — Bombay, November 16, 1974)

Eating Fish Alive

In some restaurants, fish are actually eaten alive — eviscerated, filleted, and delivered to the serving table. The eyes are covered so that the fishes will not see and react to diners reaching for parts of their bodies.

One article, written by Hodding Carter, describes eating a live fish in gruesome detail: "We each reached in with our chopsticks. The fish buckled... Now, as it slowly died, would it feel each piece of its body lifted away and hungrily masticated?"

Grilling Birds Alive

In some South East Asian countries and China, restaurants have a large grill in which live birds are thrown in. Customers choose their bird for grilling. The birds, before getting roasted, go round and round until collapse from exhaustion. Customers watch this 'spectacle' and then dine.

Eating Destruction - Meat Diet Endangering Planet

Animal products based diet is leading to widespread environmental destruction, resource depletion and a global health crisis unparalleled in human history.

Dietary advice on the subject of global warming and environmental health was never as definitive as it is today. The United Nations has called on governments and individuals to open their eyes to climate change, calling it "the most serious challenge facing the human race." More than any other factor, how we meet that challenge will depend on what we eat.

Factory Farming - Highest Carbon Footprints

According to a 2006 UN-sponsored report titled "Livestock's Long Shadow," animal factory farming plays a major role in every

> *On the street, in your front, if somebody's being killed, nobody will take care; he'll go on. There is no mercifulness. Even the mother has no mercifulness, killing the child. This is Kali-yuga.*
> *-Srila Prabhupada (Srimad-Bhagavatam 7.6.3 -Toronto, June 19, 1976)*

aspect of environmental collapse, from ozone depletion to ocean dead zones.

Factory farms, which hold tens of thousands of animals per facility in windowless warehouses, are responsible for more than 18 percent of greenhouse gas emissions worldwide. Emissions from industrial farming are not just caused by cow burps. They are also caused by the one billion tons of waste (including 64 percent of ammonia emissions, the primary producer of acid rain) produced by suffering animals held in extreme confinement.

Containing high levels of hormones and pesticides, this untreated toxic waste is converted into concentrated liquid sewage, known as "slurry." Stored in vast 25-million-gallon lagoons, this endlessly increasing waste releases gases into the atmosphere before it is used to fertilize feed crops. The leading cause of soil and groundwater contamination, lagoon breaches and fertilizer spills are increasingly common.

Even as these animal farms produce more emissions than transportation, they are also responsible for a majority of emissions produced by all transportation functions. Most food animals travel hundreds of thousands of miles in their lifetimes as they are transported between various  operations such as stockyards and slaughterhouses. Maintaining the support industries of factory farming also takes a toll on local environments. Planting, fertilizing, irrigating and harvesting feed crops, continually pumping water and sewage, running packing plants and slaughterhouses, (which kill 250 cows an hour), all rely on heavy machinery and fossil fuel consumption.

If anyone wants to save the planet, all they have to do is just stop eating meat. That's the single most important thing you could do. It's staggering when you think about it. Vegetarianism takes care of so many things in one shot: ecology, famine, cruelty.
- *Sir Paul McCartney*

Meat Eaters Devouring Forests, Destroying Ecosystems

About a fifth of the world's land is used for grazing meat animals -twice the area used for growing crops. Because of the deforestation, soil erosion and desertification meat industry causes, it is fundamentally unsustainable and has an extremely negative impact on the environment. Thirty percent of the earth's land is now occupied by livestock, with another 33 percent devoted to GMO feed crops, and this number is expanding every year. Seventy percent of previously forested land in the Amazon has been converted into cropland and pastures, destroying biodiversity, introducing carcinogenic pesticides, and playing a primary role in pushing species toward extinction at a rate 500 times of that we ought to be experiencing according to models based on fossil records.

So this is our program. Let the cows live. We take sufficient milk. We are getting milk, one thousand pounds. One thousand pounds daily in our, one center, New Vrindaban, Virginia. So we are making various preparations from the milk, and they are very happy, and the cows are also happy. So this is one of our programs, to stop killing this important animal. And the flesh-eaters may wait a little until the cow dies. Then he gets the opportunity. Why there should be slaughterhouse maintained? As you are one of the leading citizens of Paris, we appeal to you to take up this consideration seriously. Why we should maintain slaughterhouse? If we want to eat the flesh, let us wait till the death. And there will be death. There is no doubt about it. So why they should maintain slaughterhouse? And this is most cruelty. A animal which is giving milk, so important foodstuff, and that is being killed, it does not suit any moral sense of any human being.
Srila Prabhupada (Room Conversation with Monsieur Mesman, Chief of Law House of Paris — June 11, 1974, Paris)

Right now we raise about 40 billion animals for food. Inevitably, intensive animal agriculture depletes valuable natural resources. Instead of being eaten by people, the vast majority of grain harvested is fed to farm animals. This wasteful and inefficient practice has forced agribusiness to exploit vast stretches of land. Forests, wetlands, and other natural ecosystems and wildlife habitats have been decimated and turned into crop and grazing land. Scarce fossil fuels, groundwater, and topsoil resources which took millenium to develop are now disappearing. Of all agricultural land in the United States, 80-87% is now used to raise animals for food.

The space equivalent to seven football fields is being destroyed in rainforests every minute; 55 sq. feet of rainforest is needed to produce a quarter-pound burger.

50 million acres of tropical forest in Latin America alone have been cut down for livestock production since 1970. In Canada also, local wilderness is being destroyed for more and more grazing land for livestock.

Grave Threat To Water Supply

In the context of the global water supply, the impact of animal agriculture threatens utter catastrophe. Every kilo of beef requires 16,000 liters of water to produce, according to the Institute for Water Education. This means a single person can save more water simply by not eating a pound of beef than they could by not showering for an entire year. Factory farming is responsible for 37 percent of pesticide contamination, 50 percent of antibiotic contamination and one-third of the nitrogen and phosphorus loads found in freshwater. Nearly half of all water consumed in the US is used to raise animals for food.

Poisoning water is bad enough, but depleting the supply is suicidal. The majority of the earth's water is now used to support animal agriculture, and much of it cannot be reclaimed.

New Fatal Diseases

Many of the worst human diseases — BSE, TB, avian flu, West Nile virus, bluetongue— are associated with animals of modern meat industry which are kept in crammed, unhygienic conditions.

Unprecedented Pollution

The animals raised for food in the US alone produce 130 times the excrement of the entire human population on Earth, at a rate of 86,600 pounds per second. Only a sixth of this excrement is used as fertilizer; the rest is just dumped into lakes and rivers, untreated. Slaughterhouse runoff is killing millions of fish, and is the main reason why 35% of Earth's rivers and streams are "impaired". In countries with concentrated animal agriculture, the waterways have become rife with a bacteria called pfiesteria. In addition to killing fish, pfiesteria causes open sores, nausea, memory loss, fatigue and disorientation in humans. Even groundwater, which takes thousands of years to restore, is being contaminated. For example, the aquifer under the San Bernadino Dairy Preserve in southern California contains more nitrates and other pollutants than water coming from sewage treatment plants.

But it's not only fresh water sources that are at risk; ocean waters are also imperiled. Dead zones, vast stretches of costal waters in which nothing can live, are created by untreated hormone, nitrate and antibiotic laden slaughterhouse waste seeping into the soil, groundwater and rivers before contaminating the ocean. According to the EPA, In USA, 35,000 miles of rivers in 22 states and groundwater in 17 states has been permanently contaminated by industrial farm waste.

One pig factory farm produces raw waste equivalent to that of a city of 120000 people -- except unlike a city, it doesn't have a waste treatment facility. Its raw wastes are dumped straight into surrounding rivers and lakes.

Massive Energy Requirements

Raising animals for food requires more than one-third of all raw materials and fossil fuels used in the United States. Producing a single hamburger patty uses enough fossil fuels to drive a small car 20 miles.

... we prefer our own [human] species over others for arbitrary reasons, just as racists and sexists prefer their race or sex over others.

Meat production requires 10-20 times more energy per edible tonne than grain production.

Meat Eating - Cause For World Hunger & Criminal Waste of Grains

There is plenty of food. It is just not reaching human stomachs. Of the 2.13bn tonnes consumed in 2008, only 1.01bn, according to the UN's Food and Agriculture Organisation (FAO), reached people.

The great food recession is sweeping the world faster than the credit crunch. The price of rice has risen by three-quarters in the past year, that of wheat by 130%. There are food crises in 37 countries. One hundred million people, according to the World Bank, could be pushed into deeper poverty by the high prices. But at 2.1bn tonnes, last year's global grain harvest broke all records. It beat the previous year's by almost 5%. If hunger can strike now, what will happen if harvests decline?

While 100 million tonnes of food will be diverted this year to feed cars, 760 million tonnes will be snatched from the mouths of humans to feed animals. This could cover the global food deficit 14 times. If we care about hunger, we have to eat less meat.

Traditionally, most societies have eaten meat until recently - for special occasions. Meat as staple diet is unknown in any traditional culture.

It is depressing to consider that throughout the last big famine in Ethiopia, that country was exporting desperately needed soy to Europe to feed to farmed animals. The same relationship held true throughout the famine in Somalia in the early 1990's. The same relationship holds between Latin America and the United States today. As just one example, two-thirds of the agriculturally productive land in Central America is devoted to raising farmed animals, almost all of whom are exported or eaten by the wealthy

One million animals are eaten every hour in the US alone.
The average meat eater consumes 90 animals a year.
Every year, ten billion animals are slaughtered in North America alone for meat consumption.

few in these countries. Animals in the US are fed 70% of the nation's corn, wheat, and other grains.

The world's cattle alone consume a quantity of food equal to the caloric needs of 8.7 billion people -- more than the entire human population on Earth. Meanwhile, the UN says that 800 million people are suffering from "nutritional deficiency" (i.e. they're starving).

A meat based diet requires seven times more land than a plant-based diet -- that is, the amount of land to feed one meat-eater can be used to feed seven vegetarians.

Really, it comes down to this: generating meat for human consumption requires vast amounts of land that could be used to feed people, and is therefore withholding food from millions of people who are starving.

Increasing Meat Consumption - Decreasing Survival Possibilities

Despite these horrifying statistics, global production of meat is **projected to double in the next 10 years**.

Average American is already consuming more than 200 pounds of meat per year and rest of the world is trying to follow in their footsteps. In an immediate sense, adopting a meat-free diet may be the most rewarding and effective step an individual can take to help save the planet.

Viewing any animals as commodities has had a profoundly negative impact on understanding the world we live in. There is no more important task at hand than combating the false notion that the entire natural world is economically quantifiable or exists simply for our purposes alone.

An animal, an ocean, a forest, a species...and humanity are not separate, but intimately connected in every way. **The world consumes 240 billion kilos of meat each year.** But more than 75

> *Well-planned vegan diets are appropriate for all stages of life cycle, including during pregnancy, lactation, infancy, childhood, and adolescence.*
> *- The American Dietetic Association's position paper on vegetarianism*

per cent of what is fed to an animal is lost through metabolism or inedible parts such as bones.

Bleak Future

The UN and OIE estimate that in coming decades there will be billions of additional consumers in developing countries eating meat factory farmed in developing countries, but currently only about 40 out of the around 200 countries in the world have the capacity to adequately respond to a health crisis originating from animal disease (such as avian flu, West Nile virus, bluetongue, and foot and mouth disease).

Widespread use of antibiotics increases the chance of a pandemic resistant to known measures, which is exacerbated by a globally distributed food system. Decreased genetic diversity increases the chance of a food crisis.

Many people may gladly recycle paper and aluminum cans or take the subway rather than drive to work, they get home and cook up a steak for dinner, unaware that the environmental damage caused to produce that steak far outweighs their other environmental efforts.

We have to make our choice now.... steak on our platter or our very survival.

Story of Pigs - Four Legged and Two Legged

Pigs are sentient being and they have a soul, irrespective of what so-called religious leaders may claim. A recent incident which took place in Andhra Pradesh, South India, substantiates this point.

A tiny pig was found circumambulating dhwaja sthambam (holy pillar) of various temples. Temple priests tried to shoo away the pig but it refused to budge. The news attracted local media and crowds arrived on the scene. The pig was given a statewide coverage. Next day, the pig took bath in Godavari (a river considered holy) and again started the devotional chore. It was also reported to be

> *"A single person can save more water simply by not eating a pound of beef than they could by not showering for an entire year."*

Threat 8 - Growing Cruelty and Desensitization

putting its head inside the vermilion (kumkum) container as the regular devotees do. Owner of the pig said that it went missing from his herd few days ago and he noticed it only through media. The pig owner also said that there were no temples around where he lived and also that the pig never got exposed to any temple atmosphere.

Now look at the facts how pigs get treated in modern slaughterhouses and factory farms.

With corporate hog factories replacing traditional hog farms, pigs raised for food are being treated more as inanimate tools of production than as living, feeling animals. From beginning to end, this system is a nightmare from which the animals have no escape, and it all starts with the breeding sows.

Modern breeding sows are treated like piglet-making machines. Living a continuous cycle of impregnation and birth, each sow has more than 20 piglets per year. After being impregnated, the sows are confined in gestation crates – small metal pens just 2 feet wide that prevent sows from turning around or even lying down comfortably. At the end of their four-month pregnancies, they are transferred to similarly cramped farrowing crates to give birth. With barely enough room to stand up and lie down and no straw or other type of bedding to speak of, many suffer from sores on their shoulders and knees.

Numerous research studies conducted over the last 25 years have pointed to physical and psychological maladies experienced by sows in confinement. The unnatural flooring and lack of exercise causes obesity and crippling leg disorders, while the deprived environment produces neurotic coping behaviors such as repetitive bar biting and sham chewing (chewing nothing).

Approximately 105 million pigs are raised and slaughtered in the U.S. every year and another 800 million worldwide. As babies, they are subjected to painful mutilations without anesthesia or pain relievers. Their tails are cut off to minimize tail biting, an aberrant behavior that occurs when these highly-intelligent animals are kept in deprived factory farm environments. In addition, notches are taken out of the piglets' ears for identification. By two to three weeks of age, 10% of the piglets will have died. Those who survive are taken away from their mothers and crowded into pens with metal bars and concrete floors. A headline from National Hog Farmer magazine (from North America) advises, "Crowding Pigs Pays...", and this is exemplified by the intense overcrowding in every stage of hog confinement systems. Pigs will live this way, packed into giant, warehouse-like sheds, until they reach a slaughter weight of 250 pounds at 6 months old.

The air inside hog factories is so polluted with dust, dander and noxious gases from the animals' waste that workers who are exposed for just a few hours per day are at high risk for bronchitis, asthma, sinusitis, organic dust toxic syndrome (ODTS) and acute respiratory distress syndrome (ARDS). Unlike these workers, the pigs have no escape from this toxic air, and roughly half of all pigs that die between weaning and slaughter succumb to respiratory disease.

Poor air quality, extreme close-quarters confinement and unsanitary living conditions combine to make diseases such as porcine reproductive and respiratory syndrome (PRRS), swine influenza virus (SIV) and salmonellosis a serious threat to animal welfare.

In addition to their direct effects on animal health, several viruses are known to suppress pigs' immune systems, leading to greater risk from opportunistic bacteria which further degrade health and result in on-farm deaths. These viral infections frequently go undiagnosed because they are masked by the overlying bacterial disease and testing is expensive.

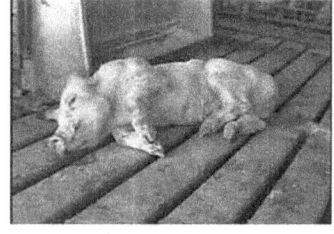

The overcrowding and confinement is unnatural and stress-producing since pigs are actually very clean animals. If they are given sufficient space, pigs are careful not to soil the areas where they sleep or eat. But in factory farms, they are forced to live in their own feces, urine and vomit and even amid the corpses of other pigs.

In addition to overcrowded housing, sows and pigs also endure extreme crowding in transportation, resulting in rampant suffering and deaths.

Wingless Vultures And Two Legged Jackals Eating Rotten Carcasses

There's a growing amount of evidence that a meat-based diet actually quite unhealthy for people. The filthy and unsanitary conditions of slaughterhouses contaminate almost all meats that we eat. Increasingly, meat covered with feces, abscesses, tumors, hair, and maggots has moved into the human food system. Most of the slaughterhouses are infested with cockroaches and rats and condemned meat is taken out of trash barrels and returned to production lines.

"Never doubt that a small group of thoughtful, committed people can change the world. Indeed, it is the only thing that ever has"
- Margaret Mead

Testimonials from USDA Inspectors and slaughterhouse workers.

Following are the extracts from affidavits by USDA inspectors. This is the condition of modern slaughterhouses in developed countries. This is the beef that is now passing federal inspection. What to speak of slaughterhouses in the third world!

"Rats were all over the coolers at night, running on top of meat and gnawing at it ... We saw fecal contamination get through -- up to one-foot smears -- as well as flukes (liver parasites), grubs (wormlike fly larvae that burrow into the cow's skin and work their way through the animal's body), abscesses (encapsulated infections filled with pus), (hide) hair, and ingesta (partially digested food found in the stomach or esophagus)" ... "Manure, hair, hide, metal, and chewing tobacco regularly contaminate products... Cows are slaughtered that have been dead on arrival, some so long they are ice-cold."
"Insects have a feast. Rodent infestation and cockroaches up to two inches long have been prevalent. There are pools of urine on the viscera table that regularly contacts products. The company sprinkled the floor with anti-maggot solution, but the drains are so often stopped up, filthy water splashes

on the carcasses even if they don't fall off the rail..."

"Red meat animals and poultry that were dead on arrival were hidden from us and hung up to be butchered. ... Severed heads from cancer eye cattle were switched to smaller carcasses before inspection so less meat would be condemned. ... Up to 25 percent of slaughtered chicken on the inspection line was covered with feces, bile, and ingesta. ... In one enforcement action at a single facility, we retained six tons of ground pork with rust which was bound for a school lunch program in Indiana, 14,000 pounds of chicken speckled with metal flakes, 5,000 pounds of rancid chicken necks, and 721 pounds of green chicken that made employees gag from the smell. Rancid meat had been smoked to cover foul odor, or marinated and breaded to disguise slime and smell. ... Chickens and hams were soaked in chlorine baths to remove slime and odor and red dye was added to beef to make it appear fresh."

'With the advent of modern slaughter technologies,' said former USDA microbiologist Gerald Kuester, 'there are about fifty points during processing where cross-contamination can occur. At the end of the line, the birds are no cleaner than if they had been dipped into a toilet.'

With one hamburger containing meat from as many as one hundred different animals, one infected animal can cross-contaminate sixteen tons of beef. And because the grinding process creates a much larger surface area for the bacteria to inhabit than a cut of beef, they find hamburger meat especially hospitable.

In 1991, a USDA microbiologist and leading authority on a bacteria called 'Campylobacter' found the bacteria present in 98 percent of store-bought chickens. According to the National Academy of Sciences, studies of market-ready chickens found Campylobacter on up to 82 percent. And in a survey of fifty brand-name broilers in Georgia, a government researcher found 90 percent contaminated with Campylobacter. Even Food Safety Review, the USDA's own publication, reported that "heavily contaminated flocks may result in a contamination rate of 100 percent for finished products." And again, even with chlorine and the other "improvements" in place, Campylobacter was found on up to 100 percent of the chickens coming out of the chill tank.

Millions Of Baby Seals - Clubbed To Death Every Year

Every year in Canada during the spring time, fishermen gather to the shores of Newfoundland to begin a cruel slaughter of seals for their pelts. This year, the horrific Canadian seal slaughter has begun -- 325,000 baby seals to be killed this season alone, 95% of them less than 4 weeks old.

Shockingly, the annual cull is subsidized and therefore supported by the Canadian government.

Nonsensical & Insane Government

Because seals are known to eat cod, the Canadian government claims that by lowering the seal population the cod population will rise. However, they have overlooked key aspects of this theory: only 3% of a seal's diet consists of cod, and other animals eat cod. Although the amount of cod that Harp seals eat may be debatable, no matter what the numbers are, the fact of the matter agreed by all credible scientists and biologists is that the seals didn't cause the fishery collapse.

Even US Government Rejects This Insanity

An excerpt from US Congress Resolution 33 is as follows:

Whereas the fishing and sealing industries in Canada continue to justify the expanded seal hunt on the grounds that the seals in the Northwest Atlantic are preventing the recovery of cod stocks, despite the lack of any credible scientific evidence to support this claim;

Whereas two Canadian Government marine scientists reported in 1994 that the true cause of cod depletion in the North Atlantic was over-fishing, and the consensus among the international scientific community is that seals are not responsible for the collapse of cod stocks.

Senseless Cruelty

While there are regulations as to how to perform the seal cull, there are never enough people enforcing them. Over the past year,

IFAW (International Fund for Animal Welfare) documented 660 violations of the laws in this area in just one season. The sealers were found 79% of the time clubbing the seals without checking to see if the animals were dead before skinning them.

When an independent group of veterinarians examined the skulls of killed seals, 42% were found to have little or no fracture, suggesting a high possibility that they were conscious when skinned. Often these conscious and skinless seals are thrown onto heaps of others to rot and die. Live seals are also brutally hooked by sealers and dragged across the ice onto ships or other locations where they will then be killed and skinned, though not necessarily in that order.

Another US Resolution

US Congress Resolution 33, 109th Congress, 1st Session, dated February 1, 2005 summarizes the facts:

Whereas the veterinary report [conducted by an independent team of veterinarians invited by IFAW to observe the hunt] concluded that as many as 42 percent of the seals studied were likely skinned while alive and conscious;

Whereas the commercial slaughter of seals in the Northwest Atlantic is inherently cruel, whether the killing is conducted by clubbing or by shooting;

Whereas many seals are shot in the course of the hunt, but escape beneath the ice where they die slowly and are never recovered, and these seals are not counted in official kill statistics, making the actual kill level far higher than the level that is reported;

Time To Stop This Insanity

Its time for Canadian government to understand that killing for the pleasure of killing is no good. Canada is not going to starve even if these innocent seal babies ate up all their fish. God has provided food for all living beings and they should not poke their sinister nose into God's affairs, conducted perfectly through the agency of material nature.

War Crimes

Baked Alive In Hot Sun, Drinking Blood of Fellow Prisoners

During war in Afghanistan, "Death by container" had been a cheap means of mass murder used by both the Taliban and the Northern Alliance for several years. Abandoned freight containers - international standard size, 40 feet by 8 feet by 8 feet- litter the roads of Afghanistan, rusting reminders of the many tons of aid that have poured into the country over the past 20 years. It was reputedly a savage Uzbek general who first saw the container's potential as a killing machine in 1997. After a Taliban assault on Mazar-e Sharif had been repulsed, the general -according to a subsequent U.N. report-killed some 1,250 Taliban by leaving them in containers in the desert sun. When the containers were opened, it was found the inmates had been grilled black. When the Taliban took Mazar-e Sharif in 1998, they in turn killed several hundred enemies in the same fashion.

"Afghan Massacre: The Convoy of Death," a documentary film that has received significant screenings in Europe was produced and directed by Irish filmmaker and former BBC producer Jamie Doran. The film tells the story of thousands of prisoners who surrendered to the US military's Afghan allies after the siege of Kunduz. According to the film, some three thousand of the prisoners were forced into sealed containers and loaded onto trucks for transport to Sheberghan prison. When the prisoners began shouting for air, U.S.-allied Afghan soldiers fired directly into the truck, killing many of them. The rest suffered through an appalling road trip lasting up to four days, so thirsty they clawed at the skin of their fellow prisoners as they licked perspiration and even drank blood from open wounds.

Witnesses say that when the trucks arrived and soldiers opened the containers, most of the people inside were dead. They also say US Special Forces re-directed the containers carrying the living and dead into the desert and stood by as survivors were shot and buried. Now, up to three thousand bodies lie buried in a mass grave.

Great World War 2008
42 Million Babies Killed

In year 2008 alone, nearly 42 million babies were killed in the womb all over the world. Put simply, per day, 115,000 babies were killed in 2008. This translated into 80 babies every minute. By the time you finish reading these passages on abortion, hundreds of unborn babies, lying in supposedly secure womb of their mothers would be brutally done to death. And let us not forget that most of these murders are not caused by medical exigencies.

In most parts of the world, abortion had been an illegal practice and only in last few decades, it gained legal status. Prior to 1973, it was illegal in the US as well but a historic case in the US Supreme Court, Roe vs Wade, changed all that.

The Silent Scream

The Silent Scream is a 1984 video about abortion directed and filmed by Dr. Bernard Nathanson. The film depicts the abortion process via ultrasound and vividly shows an abortion taking place on the fetus. In detail, the fetus is described as appearing to make outcries of pain and agony during the process. The video has been shown at the White House also on the request of President Ronald Reagan.

> *Marshall Foch, he was in charge of the French centers. So there were many refugees from Belgium, most women and children. They came to France. And in charge was Marshall Foch. So this Mr. MacPherson, he told me that "We were officers. We informed that so many refugees have come from Belgium. What to do." Then Marshall became very angry. You see. He became very... "What can I do? In this battlefield?" So it was ordered that they should be killed. So actually it so happened that all these women and children, they were assembled together, and four guns from four sides, they were blown up. You see. Their own Allies.*
>
> *So these things take place in war, sometimes. There is no international law, no humanitarian... Everything goes on. Everything. Similarly, the point is that as people act, hook and crook, everything, for satisfying the senses, gaining some material profit.*
>
> *-Srila Prabhupada (Lecture - Bombay, December 26, 1972*

Following gruesome methods are generally used:
Saline Abortions - Gruesome, Painful
Saline abortions are one of the most brutal and inhumane medical procedures performed today. Saline abortion causes horrific suffering for unborn babies and poses great dangers to women's health.

In a saline abortion procedure, the abortionist injects a long needle through the wall of the uterus and removes the amniotic fluid which provides a safe and nutritious environment for the developing child. It is replaced with a hypertonic saline (salt) solution which is toxic to the unborn child. Within one to one-and-one-half hours, the baby's heart stops beating. The corrosive effect of the salt solution often burns and strips away the outer layer of the baby's skin. The mother soon delivers a burned, shriveled and dead baby.

Dilation And Evacuation Abortion (D&E)
Slow And Painful Death, Live Babies Cut Into Pieces
In this horrid method, the women's cervix is dilated, which is a two or three day process requiring two trips to the abortionist, forceps are inserted through the enlarged cervix into the uterus. The body parts of the baby are grasped at random with a large, long toothed grasping clamp. With the large, long toothed grasping clamp, the abortionist twists the limbs and body parts from the unborn baby — and pulls them from the baby — and pulls the body parts out of the vaginal canal. The head is then crushed in order to remove it through the vaginal canal. The body parts must be reassembled outside of the mother's body to be sure all was removed from the womb. If some body parts are missing, then the abortionist must continue to search for the missing body parts and retrieve them. At a gestational age of twenty weeks, the mother can feel her baby kick. The toughest part of the dilation and evacuation abortion is extracting the baby's head. The head of a baby is floats freely inside the uterine cavity. The skull pieces must then be

Right now we raise about 40 billion animals for food.

extracted. Some abortionists have reported that on bad days, a little face may come out and stare back at you. No anesthetic is administered to the unborn child.

Dilation and Curettage (D&C)

In this technique, the cervix is dilated or stretched to permit insertion of a loop-shaped steel knife in order to scrape the wall of the uterus. This cuts the baby's body into pieces and cuts the placenta from the uterine wall. Bleeding is sometimes considerable.

Methotrexate & Misoprostol

Two drugs that were developed for cancer (methotrexate) and ulcer (misoprostol) treatment are now being used in combination to kill babies. Methotrexate is used to poison the baby and then Misoprostol empties the uterus of the baby. Methotrexate is a chemotherapy drug with the potential for serious toxicity, which can result in the death of the mother as well as the baby.

Partial Birth Abortions

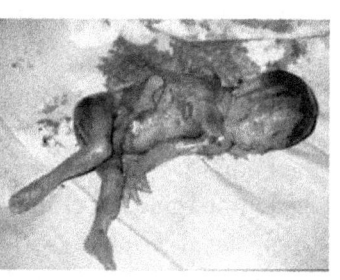

A partial-birth abortion is the killing of a baby seconds before birth. The abortionist turns the baby around and pulls the boy or girl out of the womb feet first. "Delivery" is stopped when just the top of the baby's head is the only part of the baby still within the birth canal. The abortionist then uses scissors to puncture the back of the baby's head at the base of the skull, inserts a suction tube and sucks the baby's brains out. After the baby's head is collapsed, "delivery" is completed.

In 1996, US Congress passed a federal law, the Partial-birth Abortion Act, to outlaw this inhumane, barbaric assassination of defenseless babies but President Bill Clinton vetoed the measure.

Prostaglandin

Prostaglandin are hormones which assist the birth process.

Abortion is the ultimate form of child abuse.

Injecting concentrations of them into the amniotic sac induces violent labor and premature birth of a child usually too young to survive. Oftentimes salt or another toxin is first injected to assure that the baby will be delivered dead, since some babies have been delivered alive. Serious side-effects and complications from prostaglandin use, including cardiac arrest and rupture of the uterus are possible.

Hysterotomy

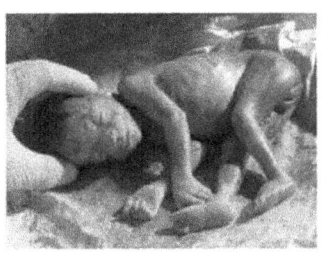

Similar to the Cesarean Section, this method is generally used if the salt poisoning or prostaglandin methods fail. Sometimes babies are born alive during this procedure which raises questions as to how and when the infants are killed and by whom. Some infants who are attended to after a hysterotomy have been known to survive and were subsequently accepted by their natural mothers, or placed in adoptive homes.

This method offers the highest risk to the health of the mother. The risk of mortality from hysterotomy is two times greater than risk from D&E.

Civilized Cannibalism
Foetophagy: Aborted Foetus as Food.

Cooked Human Foetuses for $100! This is a story of what is happening in Taiwan, China and many other parts of the world where the aborted human foetuses are being eaten as food. This "dish" is so popular in places like Taiwan that hospitals sell these aborted foetuses for between $50 to $79 a piece. In hotels, spices are applied to these foetuses and then they are cooked in an oven or on a barbecue and placed on a platter before being brought to the dining table.

> *Equal rights for women....and unborn women. Fully half of the babies aborted are women.*

A report released by the Eastern Express in Hong Kong mentions that human foetuses are being served in restaurants in China, and are being smuggled into Hong Kong.

Cooked in soup or mixed with minced pork, many believe human foetuses to be highly nutritious and delicious.

With hundreds of millions of pregnancies aborted every year, this trend is only expected to grow. This is alarming in view of the fact that abortion is widely practiced in China. Forced abortion under the Chinese birth control policy means possibly hundreds of thousands of pregnancies are terminated each year.

Women in Tibet have long reported cases of forced abortion under often terrifying, painful, and unhygienic conditions.

Benefitting financially from human body parts is a well established practice in China. Organs are regularly cut out of prisoners who have been executed. These are highly saleable being "fresh" and from persons not suffering from sickness. There have been reported cases of organs being cut out of prisoners on their way to the execution ground. Such attacks have been carried out without anaesthetic or sterilisation.

However repugnant, immoral, and outrageous the practice, there does not appear to be a statute forbidding the eating of human unborn babies.

Eating Live Monkey Brains

In parts of Europe and Asia, eating the monkey's brain out of his opened skull is supposed to arouse sex drive.

They have a table with a hole in the middle, called monkey table. It splits down in the center where the monkey's neck is locked, so that the head is above the table and the body underneath it.

Then a man comes and hammers and chips away the top of the

monkeys head. The customers then apply salt and stir the monkey brain, turning it into a soup, all this while the monkey is fully conscious.

Reportedly many types of brains and testicles are eaten - that of bear, owl, jackals etc. Looks like there is nothing that human beings will not eat, alive or dead.

Another popular method of eating monkey brain is by cutting the skull and pouring boiling oil into it to cook it.

Then there are restaurants where they serve 'drunk shrimp', which is drowned in brandy while you wait, and served and eaten while still alive. Also there is cheese lobster, where the cheese is mixed into a part boiled lobsters guts - as it is served the arms and eyes are still moving.

Torture In Modern Society

Torture is widely practiced worldwide. Amnesty International received reports of torture or cruel, inhuman or degrading treatment or punishment in more than 150 countries during the four year period from 1997 to 2000. These accusations concerned acts against political prisoners in 70 countries and other prisoners and detainees in more than 130 countries. State torture has been extensively documented and studied, often as part of efforts at collective memory and reconciliation in societies that have experienced a change in government. Surveys of torture survivors reveal that torture is not aimed primarily at the extraction of information. Its real aim is to break down the victim's personality and identity. When applied indiscriminately, torture is used as a tool of repression and deterrence against dissent and community empowerment.

Thou Shalt Not Kill

-By Srila Prabhupada

The Srimad-Bhagavatam states that any bona fide preacher of God consciousness must have the qualities of titiksa (tolerance) and karuna (compassion). In the character of Lord Jesus Christ we find both these qualities. He was so tolerant that even while he was being crucified, he didn't condemn anyone. And he was so compassionate that he prayed to God to forgive the very persons who were trying to kill him. (Of course, they could not actually kill him. But they were thinking that he could be killed, so they were committing a great offense.) As Christ was being crucified he prayed, "Father, forgive them. They know not what they are doing."

A preacher of God consciousness is a friend to all living beings. Lord Jesus Christ exemplified this by teaching, "Thou shalt not kill." But the Christians like to misinterpret this instruction. They think the animals have no soul, and therefore they think they can freely kill billions of innocent animals in the slaughterhouses.  So although there are many persons who profess to be Christians, it would be very difficult to find one who strictly follows the instructions of Lord Jesus Christ.

A Vaisnava is unhappy to see the suffering of others. Therefore, Lord Jesus Christ agreed to be crucified — to free others from their suffering. But his followers are so unfaithful that they have decided, "Let Christ suffer for us, and we'll go on committing sin." They love Christ so much that they think, "My dear Christ, we are very weak. We cannot give up our sinful activities. So you please suffer for us."

Jesus Christ taught, "Thou shalt not kill." But his followers have now decided, "Let us kill anyway," and they open big, modern, scientific slaughterhouses. "If there is any sin, Christ will suffer for us." This is a most abominable conclusion.

Christ can take the sufferings for the previous sins of his devotees. But first they have to be sane: "Why should I put Jesus Christ into suffering for my sins? Let me stop my sinful activities."

Suppose a man — the favorite son of his father — commits a murder. And suppose he thinks, "If there is any punishment coming, my father can suffer for me." Will the law allow it? When the murderer is arrested and says, "No, no. You can release me and arrest my father; I am his pet son," will the police officials comply with that fool's request? He committed the murder, but he thinks his father should suffer the punishment! Is that a sane proposal? "No. You have committed the murder; you must be hanged." Similarly, when you commit sinful activities, you must suffer — not Jesus Christ. This is God's law. -*Srila Prabhupada (Science of Self-realization)*

Section-VIII

The Alternative Future
Deindustrial or Post-industrial Society

The Next Industrial Revolution.

From An Extractive, Polluting, Single-use "Cradle To Grave" System To Everlasting Economics Of Renewable Cradle to Cradle system.

End of Modern Civilization and Alternative Future

Our present way of life is brutally destructive. Destructive to us as an individual, family and community and to the creation at large. In order to have better, happier lives, a total rethinking is required.

When man used to do natural work (farming and related activities) he could do the same repetitive work day after day-generation after generation. After the Industrial Revolution when man switched over to an artificial lifestyle, he began a never ending process of making new machines, new things, new products- a process which can only end with the complete destruction of environment or planet itself.

We need just a few things to live and we are busy manufacturing thousands. Trapped in this artificial civilization, we miss out on life altogether. We fail to appreciate the creation and the creator - we don't know what it is to truly behold a flower, we don't know what it is to spend a day by a river meditating, we don't know what it is to pick up a piece of a rotten wood in a forest and discover a whole city of insects and fungi thriving on it. We are so disconnected with nature and its creator. In fact, for many people, the only time they remotely appreciate nature is when they put a 'nature' wallpaper on their desktop.

U.N. World Conference on Sustainable Development was held in August 2002 in Johannesburg, South Africa. Two major areas

A new ethic in the use of material resources must be developed which will result in a style of life compatible with the coming age of scarcity.
~Mankind At The Turning Point, Mesarovic and Pestal, 1974

were discussed:

1) The overriding need for rich countries to put poor countries on a global welfare system called a 'redistribution of assets';

2) Our current way of life -- Industrial Civilization -- is not sustainable and must be dramatically changed.

Over 100 Presidents, Prime Ministers and other high-ranking officials attended the meeting and overwhelmingly voted to make our civilization more sustainable. Their very presence at this conference strongly imprinted a sense of need for a shift.

Meanwhile the need for the change of direction gets ever more urgent. Modern civilization is something like cancer in the human body. At the beginning the symptoms are not very acute and it can pass off like something as minor as cold. As the cancer progresses it starts to reveal ever more serious effects, but by the time the victim does pay attention it is very often too late. The longer the failure to treat it, the greater the risk of it proving fatal.

Every year, every day and every hour that we fail to take the action needed to change our course similarly increases the risks of civilizational fatality.

All we need to do is make small, real changes in our lives and the world around us, rather than engage in big dangerous plans for the end of the world.

Ideal Human Civilization

Following excerpt from Srimad Bhagavatam, a Vedic text, describes a city in ancient India, 5000 years ago. Purport is by Srila Prabhupada.

sarvartu-sarva-vibhava-
punya-vrksa-latasramaih
udyanopavanaramair

The British Government in India constitutes a struggle between the Modern Civilisation, which is the Kingdom of Satan, and the Ancient Civilisation, which is the Kingdom of God. The one is the God of War, the other is the God of Love.
-Mahatma Gandhi

vrta-padmakara-sriyam

The city of Dvarakapuri was filled with the opulences of all seasons. There were hermitages, orchards, flower gardens, parks and reservoirs of water breeding lotus flowers all over.

PURPORT

Perfection of human civilization is made possible by utilizing the gifts of nature in their own way. As we find herewith in the description of its opulence, Dvaraka was surrounded by flower gardens and fruit orchards along with reservoirs of water and growing lotuses. There is no mention of mills and factories supported by slaughterhouses, which are the necessary paraphernalia of the modern metropolis. The propensity to utilize nature's own gifts is still there, even in the heart of modern civilized man. The leaders of modern civilization select their own residential quarters in a place where there are such naturally beautiful gardens and reservoirs of water, but they leave the common men to reside in congested areas without parks and gardens. Herein of course we find a different description of the city of Dvaraka. It is understood that the whole dhama, or residential quarter, was surrounded by such gardens and parks with reservoirs of water where lotuses grew. It is understood that all the people depended on nature's gifts of fruits and flowers without industrial enterprises promoting filthy huts and slums for residential quarters. Advancement of civilization is estimated not on the growth of mills and factories to deteriorate the finer instincts of the human being, but on developing the potent spiritual instincts of human beings and giving them a chance to go back to Godhead. Development of factories and mills is called ugra-karma, or pungent activities, and such activities deteriorate the finer sentiments of the human being and society to form a dungeon of demons.

We find herein the mention of pious trees which produce seasonal flowers and fruits. The impious trees are useless jungles only, and they can only be used to supply fuels. In the modern civilization such impious trees are planted on the sides of roads. Human energy should be properly utilized in developing the finer senses for spiritual

Today, in the midst of this devastated, chaotic, and unhappy world, mankind has a fresh opportunity to reject selfish, materialistic living and to begin to tread the Lighted Way. The moment that humanity shows its willingness to do this, then the stability and peace will come. ~Mesarovic

understanding, in which lies the solution of life. Fruits, flowers, beautiful gardens, parks and reservoirs of water with ducks and swans playing in the midst of lotus flowers, and cows giving sufficient milk and butter are essential for developing the finer tissues of the human body. As against this, the dungeons of mines, factories and workshops develop demoniac propensities in the working class. The vested interests flourish at the cost of the working class, and consequently there are severe clashes between them in so many ways. The description of Dvaraka-dhama is the ideal of human civilization.
- Srimad Bhagavatam 1.11.12 (copyright BBT)

Tradition Is Our Treasure - Let's Preserve
Traditional Alert Saved Andaman Tribes

Preserving tradition helps in survival of the species. Moving away from tradition is moving towards annihilation. Humanity today has to re-explore its roots and plan going back to the basics.

In December 2004, a disastrous tidal wave struck several countries in Indian ocean. Thousands died and many thousands went missing in the massive tidal wave, called tsunami. But the indigenous people on the Andaman and Nicobar islands are thought to have escaped the calamity, thanks to the traditional warning systems that interpret bird and marine animal behaviour.

According to the director of the Anthropological Survey of India, V. R. Rao, no casualties were reported among five tribes – the Jarwas, Onges, Shompens, Sentenelese and Great Andamanese. He believes this is because the tribal people fled for safety at the first indications — such as changes in bird calls — that something was wrong.

The conception of worldly opulence was formerly based mainly on natural resources such as jewels, marble, silk, ivory, gold and silver. The advancement of economic development was not based on big motorcars. Advancement of human civilization depends not on industrial enterprises, but on possession of natural wealth and natural food, which is all supplied by the Supreme Personality of Godhead so that we may save time for self-realization and success in the human form of body. -Srila Prabhupada (Srimad Bhagavatam 4.9.62)

According to a related BBC Online news story, wildlife officials in Sri Lanka reported that despite the large loss of human life, there were no reported animal deaths. It is thought that animals moved to safer ground having sensed vibrations or changes in air pressure in advance of the waves' arrival. In contrast to all this, modern civilized man suffered most in the hands of furious waves. So in a survival test, we are scoring rather low.

Human tradition, coming down since time immemorial, has a lot to offer and has answers to many a predicaments facing us today.

The Alternative Future - 1

A World Based On Proper Understanding Of Self

(A Radical Re-envisioning Of Ourselves And Our Lives)

Who Am I - A Question In Need of Answers

Root Of All Evil - Forgetfulness Of Who We Really Are

Glitter of industrialization has covered us, i.e.., our souls from our vision. Rediscovering our identity will make a holistic relationship with the environment possible.

Understanding the difference between our temporary material identity and our true spiritual identity is the key to solving the environmental crisis. The foundation for an environmentally healthy planet is a science of consciousness that incorporates knowledge of the soul.

"DO YOU HAVE THE ROOT OF ALL EVIL ?...."

Over the last few years, research into consciousness has at last become accepted within the academic community. As John Searle puts it, raising the subject of consciousness in cognitive science discussions is no longer considered to be 'bad taste', causing graduate students to "roll their eyes at the ceiling and assume expressions of mild disgust."

The Gita offers a simple solution to environmental anomalies, linking our problems directly to our lack of spiritual culture and values. Forgetfulness of our spiritual nature is making us overuse the technology to meet the exaggerated demands of the senses, leading to global crises of different sorts.

If the world is ever to become free from the threat of environmental annihilation, we shall have to undertake a thorough reexamination of the materialistic assumptions underlying not only our picture of nature but our conception of our very selves.

Alternative Future 1 - A World Based on Proper Understanding of Self

Ideas Have Consequences

Adolf Hitler had ideas that he expressed in a book entitled "Mein Kampf." Karl Marx had ideas that he expressed in "Das Kapital." Both sets of ideas have had enormous consequences for human history.

Our world crises have their roots in incorrect and imperfect idea of the self and the universe. When we understand our true spiritual nature, our unlimited urge to consume things and to produce things for consumption can be curbed. The natural result will be a better environment in which to pursue spiritual growth instead of excessive economic growth.

The theologian Jürgen Moltmann wrote that the "alienation of nature brought about by human beings can never be overcome until men find a new understanding of themselves and a new interpretation of their world in the framework of nature."

With a deep, spiritual change of heart, a permanent change of goals and values, environmental reform would take place as a by-product, almost automatically.

> *The basic principle of this modern civilization is wrong. Everyone, the so-called advanced scientists, so-called advanced philosopher or politician, everyone is thinking that "I am this body." So on the basic principle they're wrong. Therefore the so-called advancement of civilization is wrong. It's... At one point mathematical calculation, if you have done mistake in one point... Two plus two equal two. Why if you have made up three, the mistake, then the whole calculation will be mistaken. The balance, it will never tally. Similarly, our present civilization... Not present; it is always there. Now it is very strong bodily conception of life, so the basic principle is wrong. Therefore whatever we are advancing, that is wrong. Parabhava, defeat. That is stated in the Srimad-Bhagavatam. Basic principle is wrong, abodha, ignorance.*
> *- Srila Prabhupada*
> *(Lecture, Srimad-Bhagavatam - Los Angeles, December 9, 1973)*

From Consumption Crazy Society To A Self-realization Centered Society

If the conscious self is factually supernatural in origin, and if this knowledge were firmly integrated into our educational and cultural institutions, society would probably be much more directed toward self-realization than it is today. The overwhelming impetus toward the domination and exploitation of matter that underlies today's industrial civilization and culminates in environmental catastrophe would certainly be lessened.

In the words of Grandon Harris: Our honeymoon with the planet Earth is over. We must take our marriage with the earth seriously. We cannot divorce it, but it can divorce us!

This seriousness, as opposed to frivolousness, comes from understanding our real identity as spirit souls and not as Darwinian monkeys. From a monkey, hardly any seriousness can be expected.

Following verses from Bhagavad-gita illustrate these points.

kamopabhoga-parama, etavad iti niscitah

They believe that to gratify the senses is the prime necessity of human civilization (Bg 16.11). This verse of Bhagavad-gita tells us that those who mistake their identities or those who fail to understand who they are, they tread the path of sense aggrandizement. All the world crises are an outcome of this viewpoint.

Another verse (Bg 2.62) sums up the our consumeristic civilization:

dhyayato visayan pumsah
sangas tesupajayate
sangat sanjayate kamah
kamat krodho 'bhijayate

While contemplating the objects of the senses, a person develops attachment for them, and from such attachment lust develops, and from lust anger arises.

This verse of Bhagavad-gita tells us that by contemplating the objects of the senses one becomes attached to them and ultimately ends up frustrated and bewildered. Industrialized society in particular has as its cornerstone the need to stimulate consumption, to constantly fuel economic growth. To this end, it constantly encourages us to meditate on the objects of our senses. With individuals' desires massively outstripping their abilities to meet their aspirations, it is hardly any surprise that we create ongoing frustration and extreme egotism, which result in environmental, social, and cultural devastation.

Text 4.22, 'yadrccha-labha-santusto' describes that by practicing bhakti-yoga, one is satisfied with gain which comes of its own accord and one attains a taste for simple living and high thinking. In other words, developing love for God automatically moderates one's appetite for material things by enriching one's life spiritually.

Tapping Into The Deep Spiritual Reservoirs of Humanity

Humanity is on a "spiral to suicide" and the environmental discourses of academia often suggest an 'end-of-the-pipeline approach'. Mary Evelyn Tucker echoes this misgiving. "We're all concerned about simply rhetorical statements or a superficial approach that is not going to tap into the deep spiritual reservoirs of people. A spiritual change of heart could only offer a solution towards this 'much talked about and little done for' crisis."

Humanity's Absorption In Superficialities

In the last few decades people have become far more concerned about external factors such as the possession of consumer goods, celebrity status, image, and power rather than the development of what is an interior life. It wasn't long ago that people were measured by the internal traits of virtue and morality, and it was the person who exhibited character and acted honorably who was held in high esteem. This kind of life was built upon contemplation of what

A beast does not know that he is a beast, and the nearer a man gets to being a beast, the less he knows it.
~George McDonald

might be called the "good life." After long deliberation, an individual then disciplined himself in those virtues most valued.

Paul reminds us of the dangers of over-emphasizing personality ethics as opposed to character ethics when he writes, "Their destiny is destruction, their god is their stomach, and their glory is in their shame. Their mind is on earthly things."

The world is in crisis because we're conditioned to see the earth and its resources and creatures as things to be exploited unlimitedly for personal gratification. And this is so because we have forgotten our connection with God.

A World Afflicted With The 'Skin Disease'

Today's world is divided on the basis of skin. Everybody identifies with the body and therefore great divisions like white, black, colored, Hindu, Muslim etc. exist. But these are all based on the skin or body which is just a temporary dress.

Srila Prabhupada explains this, "We all have some 'skin disease,' which is the body, and therefore we are suffering. Because we have become such rascals, we are thinking, 'I am this body.' The more we are in the bodily conception, the more we suffer."

Srila Prabhupada adds, "Presently so many "ism's" are being developed according to the bodily conception—nationalism, communism, socialism, communalism and so on. In Calcutta during the 1947 Hindu-Muslim riots, there was more suffering because everyone was thinking, "I am a Hindu" or "I am a Muslim." But, if one is advanced in Krishna consciousness, he will not fight according to such conceptions. Because people are being educated to become more body conscious, their sufferings are increasing. If we reduce the bodily conception, suffering will also be reduced."

A poem written by an African Shakespeare further illustrates this mood:

Dear white fella,
Couple things you should know:
When I was born, I black
When I grow up, I black,
When I go in sun, I black

Alternative Future 1 - A World Based on Proper Understanding of Self

When I cold, I black
When I scared, I black
When I sick, I black,
And when I die, I still black.

You, white fella,
When you born, you pink
When you grow up, you white
When you go in sun, you red
When you cold, you blue
When you scared, you yellow
When you sick, you green
And when you die, you grey.
And you have the damned nerve to call me colored?

Science Is Ill-equipped To Explain About Soul

Some scientists are already beginning to question whether materialistic principles are really adequate to explain basic features of human existence-such as consciousness. For example, John C. Eccles, a Nobel-prize-winning neurobiologist, states, "The ultimate problem relates to the origin of the self, how each of us as a self-conscious being comes to exist as a unique self associated with a brain. This is the mystery of personal existence." Eccles said that "the uniqueness each of us experiences can be sufficiently explained only by recourse to some supernatural origin."

Consequences of Forgetfulness of Our Identity As Spirit Soul

-Never ending clashes between nations, states, ethnic groups, religious groups, tribes.

- The overwhelming impetus toward the domination and exploitation of matter

- Overly scientific-technological relationship with the earth instead of a spiritual "intimacy" with the earth.

-Madness for material enjoyment and misdirecting of life energies.

-Missing the purpose of human existence and a life of material dissatisfaction.

-Humanity's progress towards destruction, on individual and collective levels, due to material bewilderment.

What Is Soul

The "soul" is defined as a non-material, eternal spiritual entity present within any living being. The symptom of the presence of the soul within a body is consciousness. The soul continues to exist after the destruction of the body and it existed prior to the creation of the body. The material body develops, changes and produces by-products [offspring] because of the presence of the soul within. The material body deteriorates in due cause of time and when it is no longer a suitable residence for the soul it is forced to leave the body. This is known as death.

Any material body inhabited by a soul will undergo changes. It will be created, it will grow, it will produce by-products [offspring], it will dwindle and ultimately it will die.

Soul Is Higher Energy

There exists, within this material universe, three types of energies: gross material, subtle material and spiritual. The gross material energy consists of earth, water, fire, air and ether [defined as the "space" within the universe]. The subtle material energy consists of mind, intelligence and false-ego [defined as the identification of the body as the self]. The spiritual energy consists of the soul [the individual living entity] and the Supersoul.

Nature of Soul

The soul is eternal, it has no birth and it never dies. The soul is the "person within the body", or "the ghost in the machine". At

> *In the Vedic literature it is said that "One who is in the bodily concept of life, he is nothing more than an animal." Therefore at the present moment, without knowledge of the self, the whole world is going on under the bodily concept of life. The bodily concept of life is there amongst the animals. The cats and dogs, they are very proud of becoming a big cat or big dog. Similarly, if a man also becomes similarly proud that "I am big American," "big German," "big," what is the difference? But that is actually going on, and therefore they are fighting like cats and dogs.*
> *-Srila Prabhupada (Lecture - Germany, June 16, 1974)*

the time of "death" the soul leaves the body and is transferred to its next mother's womb according to its accumulated karma which literally means actions.

Proof of Soul In The Body

Presence of Consciousness or Life

The presence of the soul in any living entity is indicated by consciousness. Although we cannot actually see the soul, we can see its symptoms. We cannot "see" electricity but when we see an illuminated light bulb we can see the symptom of the presence of electricity. Similarly when we see consciousness we see the symptom of the soul.

Life or consciousness is the symptom of the soul. There is no other explanation of consciousness available. No one has been able to show that life or consciousness can be generated from matter. And there are many inconsistencies which cannot be explained within the present framework, without considering the existence of the soul.

Out-of-Body Experiences (OBE)

An out-of-body experience (OBE) is an experience that typically involves a sensation of floating outside of one's body and in some cases, perceiving one's physical body from a place outside one's body (autoscopy). Scientists still know little about this phenomenon. One in ten has an out-of-body experience at some time in his/her life. OBEs are often part of the near-death experience, and reportedly may also lead to astral projection. Those who have experienced OBEs sometimes claim to have observed details which were unknown to them beforehand

In some cases the phenomenon appears to occur spontaneously; in others it is associated with a physical or mental trauma or a dream-like state.

There is a large body of data relating to out-of-body experiences where a person leaves the body and observe what is happening to his or her body from a different perspective. A large body of evidence is certainly there and it requires scientific study. Unless there are two separate entities, the body and the soul, out-of-body experiences would be impossible. This is a compelling proof of the existence of the soul.

Near-Death Experience (NDE)

Near-death experience (NDE) refers to an observation by a person by 'floating' out of body in a life threatening situation. In some cases of automobile accidents, heart attacks or prolonged surgeries a victim 'almost' dies but after a while his or her consciousness returns and he or she accurately describes the sequence of events, even complex surgical procedures applied on them.

About near-death experience one thing is certain -- they do exist. Thousands of people have actually perceived similar sensations while close to death. One of the first things the experiencer notices is being outside his body.

The 'experiencer' finds himself floating in the air looking down on the activity below. If this is a hospital room, he will see the doctors and nurses working on his lifeless body. The doctors' conversations is remembered and the tools they are using is identified by the experiencer after he is brought back to life.

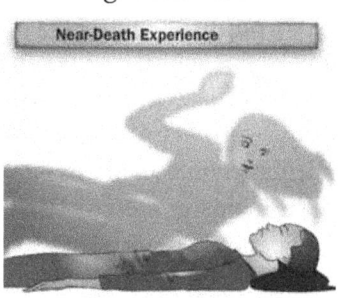

In other cases, the experiencer leaves the location of his lifeless body and visits other places and/or people. Upon being brought back to life the experiencer will remember in detail the conversations and events seen while being out of body. Many of these conversations and events will later be verified by those whom the experiencer visited while being out of body.

This phenomenon also proves the presence of soul within the body.

Past Life Memories

There are many verifiable accounts of past life experiences. This is another area currently outside the boundaries of science but it should be studied by science. Turning a blind eye is dogmatic and unscientific. If there was no soul, no entity that continued from one life to the next, there could be no memory of "past lives". This is another strong proof of the existence of the soul.

So it is a theory suitable for study using the currently accepted "scientific method". Thousands of past life cases have been recorded and many of them have been verified by the critics and media. During past three decades, Dr. Stevenson, an authority on this subject, has collected about 3000 cases that showed evidences indicating that people have remembered their past lives. Stevenson concentrates his efforts on children because their stories are far less likely to be tainted than those of adults who claim to have memories of former lives.

The case history of Sukla Gupta, a little girl from West Bengal is one of 3000 in the files of Dr. Stevenson. When Sukla was a year and half old and barely able to talk, she used to cradle a pillow and address it "Minu, Minu." Sukla over the next three years also recalled her previous life events, which indicated Minu to be her daughter in her previous life. Sukla was the daughter of a railway worker in Kampa, a village in West Bengal. Sukla often talked not only about her daughter, Minu but also about her husband, the father of Minu. She also talked about his younger brothers Khetu and Karuna.

> *The condition of not knowing anything about the spirit soul is called tamas. This material world is also generally called tamas because ninety-nine percent of its living entities are ignorant of their identity as soul. Almost everyone is thinking that he is this body; he has no information of the spirit soul. Guided by this misconception, one always thinks, "This is my body, and anything in relationship with this body is mine." For such misguided living entities, sex life is the background of material existence. Actually, the conditioned souls, in ignorance in this material world, are simply guided by sex life, and as soon as they get the opportunity for sex life, they become attached to so-called home, motherland, children, wealth and opulence. As these attachments increase, moha, or the illusion of the bodily concept of life, also increases. Thus the idea that 'I am this body, and everything belonging to this body is mine" also increases, and as the whole world is put into moha, sectarian societies, families and nationalities are created, and they fight with one another.*
> *~Srila Prabhupada (Srimad Bhagavatam 3.20.18)*

They all lived, she said, at Rathtala in Bhatpara. Sukla's family, the Guptas, knew little about Bhatpara, that it was a city about 11 miles south. But, they had never heard of a place called Rathtala, nor of people Sukla had named.

Yet Sukla developed a desire to go there, and she insisted that if her parents didn't take her she would go alone. K.N.Sen Gupta, Sukla's father, talked about the matter with some friends. He also mentioned it to one of his railway co-workers, S.C.Pal, an assistant station master. Pal lived near Bhatpara and had two cousins there. Through his cousins he learned that Bhatpara indeed had a district called Rathtala. He also learned of a man there named Khetu. Khetu had a sister in law named Mana who died several years before, in 1948, leaving behind an infant daughter named Minu. SenGupta decided to investigate further. With the consent of that family, he arranged for a visit to Rathtala. Sukla said that she could show the way to the house. So in 1959, when Sukla was about five, Sen Gupta and five other members of his family journeyed with her to Bhatpara.

When they arrived, Sukla took the lead. Avoiding possible wrong turns, she brought them straight to the house of Amritlal Chakravarty, her supposed father in law in her past life. As the party approached, Chakravarty happened to be out on the street. When Sukla saw him, she looked down shyly, following the usual custom for a young woman in the presence of older male relative. But when Sukla went to enter the house she was confused. She didn't seem to be at the right entrance. Her confusion however made sense. After the death of Mana (Sukla's name in her previous life), the entrance had been moved from the main street to an ally on the side. And the party soon found that Sukla recognized not only the house, but also the people in it, including those she said were her mother in law, her brother in law, her husband and her daughter. In side house, Sukla found herself in room with some 20 to 30 people. When she was asked, can you point out your husband, she correctly indicated Chakravarty.

This and many more such incidents are indicative of something serious and some serious need to recognize and study the science of soul.

Past Life Regressions

Past life regression is a technique that uses hypnosis to recover what most practitioners believe are memories of past lives or incarnations. Past life regression is typically undertaken either in pursuit of a spiritual experience, or in a psychotherapeutic setting.

Past-life regression practitioners use hypnosis and suggestion to promote recall in their patients, using a series of questions designed to elicit statements and memories about the past life's history and identity.

Descriptions of past lives have been found to be extremely elaborate, with vivid, detailed descriptions. Many times the subjects have talked in foreign languages in centuries old accent, without any prior knowledge of that language. This confirms their presence in those times. Also many persons have given accurate, elaborate and intimate historical accounts without any prior knowledge in that field.

In the Eastern traditions, this is a very old concept. But in West, Past life regression has been developed since the 1950s by psychologists, psychiatrists and mediums.

This is another indication that we are a soul, we change our bodies and we continue to live after our body is finished.

Inability of Chemicals To Produce Life

Evolutionists are claiming that life came from chemicals but they are unable to manufacture a single mosquito in laboratory. If indeed life is not due to soul and it is due to chemicals, then why not they inject some chemicals to revive a dead scientist. Science today can synthesize any chemical. So this is an open challenge to the scientific community - revive a dead person by injecting some chemicals or accept that the soul has left the body and now nothing can be done.

They have to show that living entities can be produced by a combination of chemicals. The resulting living entities must be able to exhibit the symptoms of the presence of the soul, i.e., consciousness, and undergo the transformations of growth, change, production of by-products [offspring], dwindling and death. Common sense and day-to-day observation proves that life comes from life and not from chemicals. All living beings are caused, or born from "parents", i.e.., other living entities.

Unless there is a soul present within matter it will not go through the cycle of birth, growth, production of by-products, dwindling and death. This cycle is a symptom of the presence of the soul. The soul is placed within matter by other living being and then the body develops.

Therefore, birth of life with touch of another life and invincibility of death are two confirmations of soul.

Ghost Sightings

Once again modern science fails to explain the ghost phenomenon. Over the centuries, millions of people have experienced ghosts. Out of these millions, even if one case is accepted by the science, then the question would arise about the presence of soul which is not destroyed at the time of death.

A poll conducted in 2003 showed that more than half of adults in the United States believe in ghosts and spirits. There are thousands of haunted locations around the world. Discovery channel has made hundreds of TV episodes on ghost sightings and haunted houses.

Vedic literatures present a scientific explanation on the ghost riddle. A ghost is a soul with just subtle body, consisting of mind, intelligence and ego. A person alive has both subtle and gross body. Subtle body is like inner wear for the soul and gross body is like an outer wear.

Normally when a person dies, the soul transmigrates into another gross body. But in specific cases of suicides, traumatic deaths or excessively indulgent lives, the soul is not awarded a gross body and it has to live in subtle body for a certain period of time.

Due to subtle body, the ghost feels all the urges like hunger and thirst, but lacking a gross body, he is unable to satisfy them. Therefore he tries to occupy another person's body.

If accepted, ghost phenomena would be another proof for the presence of soul.

Bhagavad-gita : Timeless Science of Consciousness

Bhagavad-gita has no parallel as far as science of soul is concerned. Any curious reader will have all his or her questions on mystery of life answered herein. Apart from Bhagavad-gita, all other standard scriptures of the world testify to the presence of soul within the body.

Lamentation on Passing Away

While lamenting over the passing away of a loved one, we say, "Such and such person has left us or gone away." Now the body is lying right there, where has the person gone?

It means the real person was different from the body and though the body is lying there, real person, the soul has gone and therefore we are wailing.

Try To Answer This Simple Question

We say, this is 'my pen'. We never say 'I pen', because me and the pen are different and I possess the pen. Similarly we say 'my shirt' and never say 'I shirt'. This is because me and the shirt are different and I own the shirt.

Similarly we say 'my body' and never 'I body'. This proves that me and my body are different and I possess the body.

Then who is that 'I'?

Am I this head or face ? No, it is 'my' head or 'my' face. Am I this chest ? No, it is my chest. Am I this arm or leg? No, it is 'my' arm or leg. All the parts of my body—indeed, my entire body—is mine. But who am I, the owner of the body ?

If we reflect on this question, we can immediately come to the understanding that we are not our body; rather we are conscious of it, we possess it just like any other external possession.

I am a spirit soul, possessing this body. This is a common sense conclusion.

Examples To Understand Soul Body Relationship

How the soul lives in body can be understood from the following analogies.

Driver In The Car

Bhagavad gita compares the body to a car and the soul within to a driver. *"bhramayan sarva-bhutani yantra-rudhani mayaya"*. Because of the driver, car moves and because of the soul, body moves. A car without a driver and body without a soul are useless.

 Simply by taking care of the car, servicing, washing or filling gas, the driver can not be satisfied. Similarly no amount of bodily care can comfort the soul. Soul can only be satisfied by the process of spiritual communion with the Supreme Soul.

Tenant In The House

Body is like a house and spirit soul is like its resident. Just as one stays in a cheap or expensive house according to one's paying  capacity, a soul lives in a superior (human or above) or inferior (animal or below) body according to his karma or previous actions.

Death is like leaving one house to enter another. The resident (soul) is not destroyed, simply the house is changed.

Person In The Dress

"As a person puts on new garments, giving up old ones, the soul similarly accepts new material bodies, giving up the old and useless ones. (Bhagavad-gita 2.22)

Body has been compared to a garment. Simply washing and ironing garments can not make a person happy. Dress requires to be cared for, but the person inside the dress is more important. Similarly body needs to be cared for but the soul, the person inside is more important. Body is only an external covering for the soul.

We wear two types of outfits - inner and outer. Same way, the soul is covered with two bodies - subtle and gross. Subtle body consists of mind, intelligence and ego. Gross body is composed of

---

First we have to study, "Am I this body, or am I something within this body?" Unfortunately, this subject is not taught in any school, college, or university. Everyone is thinking, "I am this body." For example, in this country people everywhere are thinking, "I am South African, they are Indian, they are Greek," and so on. Actually, everyone in the whole world is in the bodily conception of life. Krsna consciousness starts when one is above this bodily conception.
-Srila Prabhupada (SSR : Meditation and the Self Within)

earth, water, air, fire and ether.

Bird In The Cage

Body can also be compared to a cage and the spirit soul to a bird encaged within. Cleansing and washing of cage is required, but to feed the bird is more important. Modern civilization is simply busy polishing the cage (body) without any information of the starving bird (the soul). No matter how much we paint and shine the cage, the bird inside will starve and die. Similarly, no matter how much we take care of the material body, the soul will starve and we can not be happy and peaceful. This is the reason we find the least happy people in most advanced countries.

Our On Stage Roles and Off Stage Real Identity

Our daily lives can be compared to acting in a play. We have become so absorbed with our temporary roles in this play that we have completely forgotten our true offstage identities. Someone is taking the part of our parent, another person is acting as our lover, another as our friend or foe, but actually it is all simply a performance; our real identities are something else. Our very bodies are nothing more than costumes, but out of illusion we identify ourselves with them and try to relate to others on the basis of these costumes. The resulting relationships are not false; they are real, but they are temporary and therefore illusory. When the curtain falls on our play—when death comes—all the different relationships we have cultivated during our lives will be finished, and our real self, an individually conscious spirit soul, will be transferred to a new situation.

Great Traditions, Great Thinkers Believed In Soul

What do Gandhi, Plato, Napoleon, Socrates, Benjamin Franklin, Johann Wolfgang Goethe, Ralph Waldo Emerson, Henry David Thoreau, Charles Dickens, Leo Tolstoy, Jack London, Herman Hesse, Isaac Bashevis Singer, Richard Bach and George Harrison have in common - they all believed in immortality of soul and its transmigration from one body to another. Arthur

Schopenhauer, the great nineteenth-century German philosopher once observed, "Were an Asiatic to ask me for a definition of Europe, I should be forced to answer him: It is that part of the world which is haunted by the incredible delusion that man was created out of nothing, and that his present birth is his first entrance into life."

But today, influenced by materialistic science's refusal to consider the existence of a nonmaterial conscious self, people tend to identify exclusively with the body and mind. They therefore tend to exploit matter for the purpose of continually increasing their bodily satisfaction. Expressed through today's urban-industrial civilization, this exploitation is causing environmental decay of unprecedented global proportions.

Plato, for example, believed in the immortality of the human soul. To him, the soul was an entity that was fundamentally distinct from the body although it could be and often was affected by its association with the body, being dragged down by what he called "the leaden weights of becoming." The soul was simple, not composite, and thus not liable to dissolution as were material things; further, it had the power of self-movement, again in contrast to material things. Ideally the soul should rule and guide the body, and it could ensure that this situation persisted by seeing that the bodily appetites were indulged to the minimum extent necessary for the continuance of life. The true philosopher, as Plato put it in the Phaedo, made his life a practice for death because he knew that after death the soul would be free of bodily ties and would return

I stood on a tower in the wet,
And New Year and Old Year met,
And winds were roaring and blowing:
And I said, "O years, that meet in tears,
Have ye aught that is worth the knowing?
Science enough and exploring,
Wanderers coming and going,
Matter enough for deploring,
But aught that is worth the knowing?"
~Alfred Tennyson

to its native element.

Many eminent men of science have stated that life is not reducible to chemistry and physics. These include Alfred Wallace (co-author of Charles Darwin's first publication on evolution); Thomas H. Huxley (a contemporary of Darwin's who championed Darwin's evolutionary theory); and Nobel physicists Niels Bohr and Eugene Wigner. The eminent mathematician John von Neumann has shown how quantum mechanics implies that the consciousness of the observer (he called it the "abstract ego") is distinct from all aspects of the observer's body and brain. This concept of an "abstract ego" corresponds to the irreducible nonmaterial entity called jivatma (soul) by Lord Krishna in Bhagavad-gita.

The Gita (2.20, 2.17) offers extensive information about the nature of the nonmaterial particle that imparts the symptoms of life to the material body: "For the soul there is neither birth nor death at any time. He has not come into being, does not come into being, and will not come into being. He is unborn, eternal, ever-existing, and primeval. He is not slain when the body is slain.... That which pervades the entire body you should know to be indestructible. No one is able to destroy that imperishable soul."

Ignorance of our true identity as eternal spirit souls is sapping the vitality from our existence. Only a spiritual paradigm can help us check the imbalance of values in life and achieve real unity and peace in the world.

Everyone is thinking, "I am this body, and everything, whatever we find in this world, that is to be enjoyed by me." This is the mistake of civilization. The knowledge is: "Everything belongs to God. I can take only whatever He gives me, kindly allows."
-Srila Prabhupada (Bhagavad-gita 2.9 -- London, August 15, 1973)

End of Modern Civilization and Alternative Future

The Alternative Future - 2

Ecology of The Mind
Chanting of Holy Name

Prayer And Spirituality

Chant For Change

 *There is not in the world a kind of life more sweet and delightful than that of a continual conversation with God.*
~Brother Lawrence

B efore the onset of materialism and all the problems associated with it, people led a devout and religious life and material progress was assigned a secondary place in life. Primary goal of life was considered to be the attainment of the kingdom of God. No doubt they had their share of problems but the terms like global warming, rising oceans, lethal pollution levels, pesticides in food chain and nuclear threat were unheard of. There were weapons and wars but not nuclear and hydrogen bombs which can destroy the Earth several hundred times over. Neither was the fear of biological and chemical weapons falling in the hands of terrorists, threatening to wipe out entire nations. Wars at best were localized and concept of world wars engulfing the entire planet and killing hundreds of millions was unknown.

Then there came a time when people started adopting materialistic ways of life and these earthly years came to be considered all in all. Sense gratification began to occupy the supreme position in life. This, in short, marked the beginning of present times we live in.

In this chapter, we wish to point out a practice of prayers which was prevalent all over the world, irrespective of the denomination one belonged to. Reverting back to this noble practice will impact the consciousness of the people and the change will reflect externally in world affairs.

Environmental Cleansing Begin From Within

The only way to a clean environment would be to start from the inside, deep within us. We have materialistic dust in our hearts and we need to clear it away. If we don't start cleaning from the inside then all the legislation or conferences will have no effect because people will go back to the same unclean habits. Our dormant love for God and for one another has turned into lust due to material association. We must transform this lust into love by practicing mantra meditation. That is the most effective way to restore the environment to its natural condition.

Japa Yoga - A Universal & Timeless Tool To Change The World, Change The Life....One Bead At A Time

Since time immemorial, in every continent and in every major organized and pagan religion, followers have used a string of beads to chant repetitive, uplifting sonic phrases to help create a sense of calm and purpose in life. Known commonly as Mantra Beads, this is an ancient tool that we can use to bring harmony in the opposing energies within body, mind, intellect and innermost spiritual nature.

Since the earliest of times, people have used pebbles or a string of knots or beads on a cord to keep track of prayers offered to God. Virtually every major religious tradition in the world uses some form of prayer beads. Over two-thirds of the world's population employ prayer beads as part of their religious practices. Prayer beads have a variety of forms and meanings, but the basic purpose is the same: to assist the worshiper in reciting and counting specific prayers or incantations.

Beads have long been linked with the act of prayer. The English word bead is derived from the Anglo-Saxon words bidden (to pray) and bede (prayer).

Get a job, make some money, work till you're sixty, then move to Florida and die. Have you ever had that uneasy feeling that there must be something more to life than this? Most of us have at one time or another. Yet, each morning we trudge wearily through ever-growing traffic to take part in the daily grind. Then one day we wake up to the realization that our time here is almost up.
~Daniel Quinn

Prayer is a time-tested formula to protect the mind from the poisons of the world like anger, hatred, jealousy, attachment, ignorance, delusion, pride and greed. When you are ready to allow the noisy world to fade into the background of your mind...pick up your mala (beads) and fill your mind with blessedness through the recitation of sacred Mantras. When entering a state of prayer, one can awaken innate goodness, kindness, serenity, all virtues, joy, and a peaceful heart.

Prayer beads are traditionally used to keep count of the repetitions of prayers or chants and they allow one to keep track of how many prayers have been said with a minimal amount of conscious effort, which in turn allows greater attention to be paid to the prayers themselves. Of course its main function is to engage the sense of touch which leads to better concentration and less distraction.

Prayer Beads - A History

The rosary was introduced to Europe by the crusaders, who took it from the Arabs, who in turn took it from Tibetan monks and the yoga masters of India. (Bertelsmann; 1976)

This timeless practice of chanting on beads, originating in Vedic tradition thousands of years ago, spread all over the world. Marco Polo, visiting the King of Malabar in the thirteenth century, found that monarch employed a rosary of 104 precious stones to count his prayers. St. Francis Xavier and his companions were equally astonished to see that rosaries were universally familiar to the Buddhists of Japan. Among the monks of the Greek Church we hear of the kombologion, or komboschoinion, a cord with a hundred knots used to count genuflexions and signs of the cross. Similarly, beside the mummy of a Christian ascetic, of the fourth century, recently disinterred in Egypt, was found a sort of cribbage-board with holes, 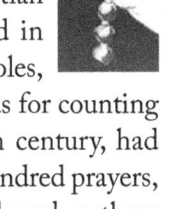 which has generally been thought to be an apparatus for counting prayers. A certain Paul the Hermit, in the fourth century, had imposed upon himself the task of repeating three hundred prayers, according to a set form, every day. To do this, he gathered up three hundred pebbles and threw one away as each prayer was finished. It is probable that other ascetics who also numbered their prayers by hundreds adopted some similar expedient.

Archeologists have unearthed beads made more than 40,000 years ago made of grooved pebbles, bones, and teeth. The ancient Egyptians, whose use of beads goes back to 3200 BCE, called them sha-sha (luck).

Procedure for Praying on Japa Yoga Beads

Mantras are often repeated hundreds or even thousands of times. One mantra is usually said for every bead, turning the thumb clockwise around each bead, though some traditions or practices may call for counterclockwise or specific finger usage. When arriving at the head bead, one turns the beads around and then goes back in the same direction.

If more than 108 repetitions are to be done, then sometimes in Tibetan traditions grains of rice are counted out before the chanting begins and one grain is placed in a bowl for each 108 repetitions. Each time a full mala of repetitions has been completed, one grain of rice is removed from the bowl. Often, practitioners add extra counters to their malas, usually in strings of ten. These may be positioned differently depending on the tradition; for example some traditions place these strings after every 10th bead. This is an alternative way to keep track of large numbers, sometimes going into the hundreds of thousands, and even millions.

The 109th bead on a mala is called the sumeru, bindu, stupa, or guru bead. Counting should always begin with a bead next to the sumeru. In the Hindu, Vedic tradition, if more than one mala of repetitions is to be done, one changes directions when reaching the sumeru rather than crossing it. The sumeru thus becomes the static point on the mala.

To be able to fill leisure intelligently is the last product of civilization, and at present very few people have reached this level.
~ Bertrand Russell

Many believe that when one uses a mala many times in this way, it takes on the energy of the mantra that is being chanted. For this reason sometimes it is common to chant only one particular mantra with a particular mala.

There are numerous explanations why there are 108 beads, with the number 108 bearing special religious significance in a number of Hindu and Buddhist traditions.

Procedure In Hinduism

Hindu tradition holds that the correct way to use a mala is with the right hand, with the thumb flicking one bead to the next, and with the mala draped over the middle finger. The index finger represents false ego and propensity to criticize, the great impediments to self-realization, so it is considered best avoided when chanting on a mala.

Generally, the rosary or Mala used for Japa contains 108 beads. A man breathes 21, 600 times every day. If one does 200 Malas of Japa, it becomes 21,600; thereby, he does one Japa for every breath. If he does 200 Malas of Japa every day, that amounts to remembrance of God throughout the day.

In Vedic tradition, many followers chant 16 malas (ie.,16x108) of Maha-mantra *(hare krishna hare krishna krishna krishna hare hare/ hare rama hare rama rama rama hare hare)* which has 16 names of God in it. Thereby it works out close to 27000 names, well above the 21,600 mark. Of course chanting that many mantras does not take the whole day, but just 1.5 to 2 hours. The Meru (the central bead in the Mala) denotes that you have done your Japa 108 times. This also denotes that every time you come to the Meru bead, you have gone one step further on the spiritual path and crossed over one obstacle. A portion of your ignorance is removed. A rosary or mala is a whip to goad us to do Japa meditation.

I envy them, those monks of old; Their books they read, and their beads they told.
~ G. P. R. James

Uses for Prayer Beads

There are three widely accepted uses for prayer beads:

1. Repetition of the same devotion a set (usually large) number of times. This is the earliest form of prayer beads (the japa mala) and the earliest Christian form (the prayer rope). This is also the type in use by the Baháʼí Faith

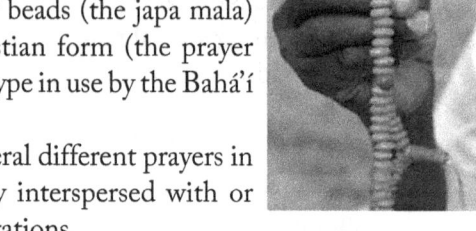

2. Repetition of several different prayers in some pattern, possibly interspersed with or accompanied by meditations.

3. Meditation on a series of spiritual themes, e.g. Islam.

Chanting of Holy Names And Prayer Beads In Various Traditions

Baháí Faith

Baháís recite the phrase "Alláh-u-Abhá", a form of the Greatest Name, 95 times per day, sometimes using prayer beads. Baha'i prayer beads often are made from wood, stone or pearls.

There are two main types of Baha'i prayer beads. One consists of 95 beads, often with the first 19 distinguished by size, color or some other means, and will often have five additional beads that are strung below. The other main type has 19 beads strung with the addition of five beads below. This counts Alláh-u-Abhá 95 times.

Buddhism

Prayer beads, or Japa Malas are also used in many forms of Mahayana Buddhism, often with a lesser number of beads (usually a divisor of 108). In Pure Land Buddhism, for instance, 27 bead rosaries are common. In China such rosaries are named "Shu-Zhu" (Counting Beads); in Japan, "Juzu". These shorter rosaries are sometimes called 'prostration rosaries', because they are easier to hold when enumerating repeated prostrations. In Tibetan Buddhism, often larger malas are used of, for example, 111 beads:

> *Whatever you ask for in prayer with faith, you will receive.*
> *~ Matthew 21:12-22*

when counting, they calculate one mala as 100 mantras, and the 11 additional beads are taken as extra to compensate for errors.

Each school of Buddhism has their own style of Juzu. Some are small for the wrist and others are large. The beads may be made of crystal, Bodhi tree wood, bamboo, coral or any number of materials. The number of beads may vary but the most common denominator is one hundred and eight. One hundred and eight represents the one hundred and eight earthly desires.

On the Buddhist rosary, the three beads directly above the base bead represent the Three Refuges: Homage to the Buddha, Homage to the Dharma and Homage to the Sangha.

Christianity

The Desert Fathers (third to fifth century) used knotted ropes to count prayers, typically the Jesus Prayer ('Lord Jesus Christ, Son of God, have mercy on me, a sinner'). The invention is attributed to St. Anthony or his associate St Pachomius in the fourth century.

Roman Catholics and Anglicans use the Rosary as prayer beads. The Rosary (its name comes from the Latin 'rosarium,' meaning rose garden), is an important and traditional devotion of the Roman Catholic Church, combining prayer and meditation in sequences (called 'decades') of an 'Our Father', ten 'Hail Marys', and a 'Glory Be to the Father', as well as a number of other prayers (such as the Apostle's Creed and the Hail Holy Queen) at the beginning and end. Traditionally a complete Rosary involved the completion of fifteen decades, but John Paul II added an additional five.

Roman Catholics also use prayer beads to pray chaplets. Eastern Christians use loops of knotted wool (or occasionally of beads), called chotki or komvoschinon to pray the Jesus Prayer. Although among the Orthodox, their use is mainly restricted to monks and bishops, being less common among laity or secular clergy. Among Russian Old Believers, a prayer rope made of leather, called lestovka,

When we pray to God we must be seeking nothing – nothing.
~Saint Francis of Assisi

is more common, although this type is no longer commonly used now by the Russian Orthodox Church. According to the Catholic Encyclopedia, "The rosary is conferred upon the Greek Orthodox monk as a part of his investiture with the full monastic habit, as the second step in the monastic life, and is called his 'spiritual sword'."

In the mid-1980s Anglican prayer beads or "Christian prayer beads" were developed in the Episcopal Church. They have since been adopted by some Protestants. The set consists of 33 beads (representing the 33 years of the life of Christ) arranged in four groupings of symbolic significance. Many Anglo-Catholics use the Catholic rosary in addition to or instead of Anglican prayer beads.

Pearls of Life

The contemporary Pearls of Life, invented by Martin Lönnebo, Bishop Emeritus of the Linköping Diocese of the Swedish Lutheran Church, is a set of 18 beads, some round and some elongated, arranged in an irregular pattern. Each one has its own significance as a stimulus and reminder for meditation, although they can also be used for repetitive prayer.

The mantra that is used most commonly in the Christian tradition is *Maranatha*, which means in Aramaic "Our Lord come."

Paternosters

In Monastic Houses, monks were expected to pray the Psalms daily in Latin, the liturgical language of the Roman Catholic Church. In some Houses, lay brothers who did not understand Latin or who were illiterate were required to say the Lord's Prayer a certain number of times per day while meditating on the Mysteries of the Incarnation of Christ. Since there were 150 Psalms, this could number up to 150 times per day. To count these repetitions, they used beads strung upon a cord and this set of prayer beads became commonly known as a Paternoster, which is the Latin for 'Our Father'. Lay people adopted this practice as a form of popular worship. The Paternoster could be of various lengths, but was often

> *Pray, and let God worry.*
> *--Martin Luther*

made up of 5 'decades' of 10 beads, which when performed three times made up 150 prayers. Other Paternosters, most notably those used by lay persons, may have had only 10 beads, and may have also been highly ornamented. As the Rosary (ring of flowers) incorporating the Hail Mary prayer became more common, it was often still referred to as a Paternoster.

Hinduism

The earliest use of prayer beads can be traced to Hinduism, where they are called japa mala. Japa is the repeating of the name of a deity or a mantra. Mala means 'garland' or 'wreath.'

Japa malas are used for repetition of a mantra, for other forms of sadhana (spiritual exercise), and as an aid to meditation. The most common malas have 108 beads. The most common materials used for making the beads are Rudraksha seeds (used by Shaivites) and Tulasi stem (used by Vaishnavites).

Islam

In Islam, prayer beads are referred to as Misbaha or Tasbih or Subha, and contain 99 beads, corresponding to the 99 Names of Allah. Sometimes only 33 beads are used, in which case one would cycle through them 3 times to equal 99. Use of the misbaha to count prayers and recitations is an evolution of Muhammad's practice of using the fingers of his right hand to keep track. While in pretty wide use today, some adherents of Wahhabism shun them as an intolerable innovation, preferring to stick to the exact method believed to have been used by the Prophet.

They are most commonly made of wooden beads, but also of olive seeds, ivory, pearls or plastic.

The beads in general use are said to be often made of the sacred clay of Mecca or Medina.

Some believe that evil spirits do not like dangling objects, making the tassel effective in warding off the evil eye. For those with 33 or 66 beads they may repeat the words of the call to prayer, 'Allahu akbar (God is great) and 'La Ilaha ila Allah wa Mohamadun rasul Allah' (There is only one God and Mohammed is his prophet).

Pilgrims travelling to Mecca for Haj often buy beads there as gifts for their families. Beads made from the clay of the holy cities of Mecca and Medina are particularly prized.

Sikhism
Sikhs use a prayer string made of wool with 99 knots rather than beads.

Judaism
Through prayer and contemplation, the Jewish mystical tradition envisions contemplative spiritual transformation. Kabbalah references a variety of meditative practices with the intent to connect with God in daily life and also to seek stillness within from time to time.

Jewish practices include meditation on portions of the Torah, visualization of the Hebrew letters 'Ribbono shel Olam' (Master of the Universe) chanting mantras from the Torah or Talmud, and contemplating the names of God.

Sufism
Sufism is the Islamic mystical tradition that teaches the concept of relinquishment of the ego and surrender to God in love. Repetition of the divine name, Allah, and meditation on verses from the Koran lead the practitioner to God consciousness and self discovery.

African Masai and Native American Yaqui
Almost all traditional societies use the beads in their various religious ceremonies. In Africa, extremely bright and colorful beads are used. Traditions in these societies have been handed down since time immemorial. This shows that beads have been integral part of human culture since earliest times.

Non-denominational
In his book, 'Simply Pray', Erik Walker Wikstrom offers a modern prayer practice that can be customized to meet individual spiritual needs. Using a set of 28 beads as a frame of reference, the practice includes centering and entering-in prayers, breath prayers and prayers of Naming, Knowing, Listening and Loving.

Beads are known as 'Chotki' in the Greek Orthodox tradition. Among the Japanese, especially elaborate systems of counting exist. One apparatus is described as capable of registering 36,736 prayers or repetitions.

Alexander Von Humboldt is also quoted as finding prayer beads, called Quipos, among the native Peruvians.

Smaller Ring-type Rosaries, Credit Card Sized Rosaries

These rosaries, especially the smaller ring-type, have since become known as soldiers' rosaries, because they were often taken into battle by soldiers, most notably during WWI. These single-decade Rosary variations can be worn as a ring or carried easily and are still popular. A rosary ring is a ring worn around the finger with 10 indentations and a cross on the surface, representing one decade of a rosary. This is often worn as jewelry, and used through the day. Some ring Rosaries use a small bearing on the inside of the ring to permit easy turning. A finger Rosary is similar to a ring, but is a bit larger. Rosaries like these are used by rotating them on a finger while praying. Credit card-sized Rosaries have also appeared, especially among members of militaries, where holes or bumps represent the prayers and the persons praying move their fingers along the bumps to count prayers.

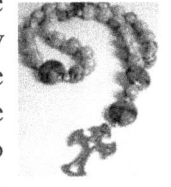

Physical and Psychological Benefits of Mantra Meditation

Apart from the spiritual significance, chanting of mantras using japa mala seems to have a calming effect on the heart. The chanting might be viewed as a health practice as well as a religious practice.

To investigate, the researchers measured the breathing rates of 23 adults while they prayed a mantra on beads. For comparison, the researchers also measured the study participants' respiration during free talking, and during spontaneous and controlled slow breathing exercises.

When the participants breathed spontaneously, their respiratory rate was about 14 breaths per minute, which slowed down to almost 6 breaths per minute during chanting session.

A slow respiration rate of 6 breaths per minute has generally favorable effects on cardiovascular and respiratory function. This indicates that these methods could stabilize the respiratory rate, lower the heartbeats and calm down the mind.

During mantra meditation, the amount of adrenaline being

released into the blood goes down. While meditating, our cortisol level drops and stays low for hours afterward. Cortisol is known as the stress hormone although there are several stress hormones, including adrenaline. But cortisol is one of the most important. It is present in our blood in small amounts all the time, but when we experience stress, our body produces quite a bit of it, and in high amounts, it has unhealthy and unpleasant effects. Getting it out of our blood stream, in contrast, has healthy and pleasant effects.

A high level of cortisol makes our body store extra fat in our abdomen and makes us crave fattening foods with extra intensity. The Journal of the American Dietetic Association reported that stress in general is a "primary predictor of relapse and overeating." And they concluded that meditation is an effective method for managing the kind of stress that causes weight gain.

Another ingredient of our bloodstream that changes during meditation is lactate. Lactate drops nearly four times as fast while meditating as it does when we just lie down and rest quietly. And the lactate stays lower afterwards. Lactate is a by-product of burning blood sugar, and when there is a lot of it in the blood stream, it tends to produce feelings of anxiety.

After meditating, our reaction to stressful events changes. Events that would normally make us feel stressed (or irritated) don't make us feel as stressed, and our feelings of stress don't last as long. In one study for example, the researchers showed a film to people. This was a gruesome film that normally makes people feel stressed and increases their heart rate.

The researchers measured meditators and nonmeditators. Here's what they found: the meditators' heart rates didn't climb as high and returned to normal faster than the nonmeditators. Some of the meditators in this study were new to meditation. They also experienced less stress than nonmeditators, showing that mantra meditation doesn't require a long time before it starts having an effect.

In another experiment, researchers blasted people with loud, annoying sounds. The meditators' bodies reacted with significantly less stress than the nonmeditators.

Think about this simple effect. If we meditate, the body will react less intensely to stressful events. Think about what would happen as this effect accumulates day after day. It could explain most of the health effects of meditation. Stress hormones can be destructive. In occasional doses, they aren't very harmful. In fact, in small amounts, they are necessary. But when your body produces a lot of stress hormones often, it is bad for your heart and bad for your immune system. And those are two things that lead to two diseases that kill the most people - heart disease and cancer. Here is a "medicine" for these two deadly diseases, but nobody has a patent on it.

We are each motivated by different things. Some might just chant to feel more calm. Others might look at it from a purely financial standpoint: Meditation is a good investment because health problems are expensive.

Mantra Meditation mellows our body and mind. Herbert Benson, one of the most prolific meditation researchers, wrote, "During meditation, the individual's mental patterns change so that he breaks free of what is called 'worry cycles.' These are unproductive grooves or circuits that cause the mind to play' over and over again, almost involuntarily, the same anxieties or uncreative, health-impairing thoughts."

It also increases your alertness. During mantra meditation, blood-flow to the brain increases while the body relaxes. Aginine-vasopressin (AVP - a harmone) increases four hundred percent during meditation. AVP is sometimes given in synthetic form to people to reverse the mental dullness of old age because it increases alertness.

Mantra meditation is relaxing and yet it increases alertness. It increases blood flow to the brain. It is unusual in that way. It is a unique state, unlike other states we are used to. In a sleeping state, you are relaxed but less alert. In a very alert waking state, you are less relaxed. But here is a state that produces alertness and deep relaxation at the same time.

Meditators also sleep better than non-meditators. Not getting enough quality sleep in itself is a source of excess stress hormones. And according to those who study the subject, a large percentage of us are chronically sleep-deprived.

Meditators are more effective in the world. It makes them more relaxed and less reactive to stressful events, so better at dealing with people, better at handling conflict. It also improves their health, and everyone knows that you are more effective in the world healthy than unhealthy.

The owner of a Detroit manufacturing company started a meditation experiment at his firm, and enrolled fifty-two out of his one hundred employees to meditate twenty minutes before work and twenty minutes at work on company time. The owner, R.W. Montgomery, says, "Over the next three years, absenteeism fell by 85%, productivity rose 120%, quality control rose 240%, injuries dropped 70%, sick days fell by 16%, and profit soared 320%."

What Happens During Mantra Meditation

In many of the studies on meditation, researchers have one group meditate for twenty minutes while another group simply sits quietly for same amount of time. The physical effects are dramatically different. Sitting quietly hardly changes a thing. Meditating causes all kinds of changes in the body.

During mantra meditation, we rest our mind on a single mantra. Sitting quietly, on the other hand, allows our thoughts to roam. David Barlow, the director of the Center for Stress and Anxiety Disorders at the State University of New York, says, "If we were somehow able to build a thought recorder, what we would record would be just about every kind of thought imaginable...but for the most part, fleeting."

What happens, according to the researcher, Mihaly Csikszentmihalyi, is that the thoughts bounce around randomly until something catches our attention, and what often catches the attention is something that bothers you. The mind stops roaming and sticks on the disturbing thought. That's one reason why it can be so unrelaxing to just sit quietly.

Holy Name - Connecting With The Guiding Spirit In Life

Chanting the Holy Name brings self-awareness and the realization that nothing in life is permanent and so attachment to anything is futile. The ultimate aim is to connect with the Supreme Reality and cultivate compassion and loving kindness to bring about the cessation of one's own suffering and to extend inner peace and love to others.

Chanting of the Holy Name awakens the mind to a more spiritual plane. Such contemplation and recitation is like a ladder that leads to God's presence. But also, at the same time, Holy Name is non-different from God because God is the absolute reality and there is no difference between Him and His name, form, abode, pastimes and paraphernalia.

In Holy Name - Unification of All Faiths, Unification of Mankind

Reverence for Holy Name of God is the common thread running through all religions of the world. Holy Name provides a common ground for unification of all faiths, unification of mankind.

God has an unlimited variety of names. Some of them—like Jehovah, Krishna, Adonai, Buddha and Allah—are familiar to us, while the names like Rama or Narsimha may be less so. However, whatever name of God we may accept, we are enjoined by all scriptures to chant it for spiritual purification.

The special design of the Hare Krishna chant makes it easy to repeat and pleasant to hear. Spoken or sung, by yourself or in a group, Hare Krishna invariably produces a joyful state of spiritual awareness—Krishna consciousness.

Chinese religions

One name of God in China is 'Shangdi' (literally King Above). He was a supreme deity worshipped in ancient China. It is also used to refer to the Christian god in the Standard Mandarin Union Version of the Bible.

Another name is 'Shen' (lit. God, spirit, or deity). It was adopted by Protestant missionaries in China to refer to the Christian god. Another name is Zhu or Tian Zhu (lit. Lord or Lord in Heaven). It is translated from the English word, "Lord".

Vedic Tradition or Hinduism

Krishna is venerated as the Supreme God, svayam bhagavan and His shakti, or manifestations thereof is called Radha. Krishna is considered the Supreme Personality of Godhead.

Impersonally God is addressed as Brahman, Bhagavan, Ishvara, and Paramatma but personal names of God are Krishna, Rama, Visnu etc.

Chief of all mantras in called Mahamantra or the Great Chant: *hare krishna hare krishna krishna krishna hare hare / hare rama hare rama rama rama hare hare.*

World's oldest scriptures, the Vedas state, "Chant the holy name, chant the holy name, chant the holy name of the Lord. In this age of quarrel there is no other way, no other way, no other way to attain spiritual enlightenment." (Brhan-naradiya Purana)

Vishnu is seen as Para Brahman within Vaishnava traditions, and the Vishnu Sahasranama enumerates 1000 names of Vishnu, each name eulogizing one of His countless great attributes. The names of Vishnu's Dasavatara in particular are considered divine names.

Sikhism

There are multiple names for God in Sikhism. Some of the popular names for God in Sikhism are:

'Ek Omkar' meaning One Creator.

'Satnam' meaning True Name, some are of the opinion that this is a name for God in itself.

'Bhagat Vachhal' means Lover of His devotees. 'Hari' meaning Glowing, Shining, Vitalising, the Lord who takes away all our miseries. 'Govinda' means the Lord who gives pleasure to the senses and cows. 'Bhagavan' refers to the Lord or the Supreme Being.

God according to Guru Nanak has endless number of virtues; takes on innumerable forms; and can be called by an infinite number of names, thus "Your Names are so many, and Your Forms are endless. No one can tell how many Glorious Virtues You have."

Jainism

There are no direct names of God in Jainism, as this religion is nontheistic. Gods do not figure into its philosophy. However, Mahavir and other 'prophets' or 'perfected beings' are known as

Tirthankar (literally one who becomes enlightened). Most common mantra chanted is : Namo Arihantânam Namo Siddhânam Namo Âyariyânam Namo Uvajjhâyanam.

Buddhism

Lord Buddha declared, "All who sincerely call upon my name will come to me after death, and I will take them to Paradise." (Vows of Amida Buddha 18)

Theravada Buddhism is nontheistic. Gods do not figure into its philosophy. In Tibetan Buddhism, the Adi-Buddha is conceived of as the eternal aspects of Buddha-nature, such as wisdom and compassion. The most popular mantra is 'om mani padme hum'.

In Jodo Shinshu, the largest sect of Buddhism in Japan, calling upon the name of Amida Buddha is considered to open the believer to the infinite.

Religions in Classical Antiquity

Pharaonic Egypt

'Aten' is the earliest name of a supreme being associated with monotheistic thought, being the solar divinity which Akhenaten had declared the only god of the state cult, as part of his wholesale absolutist reforms. This threatened the position of the various temple priesthoods, which had the old polytheism restored immediately after his death.

Roman Religion

Latin prominently used an abstract word for god, 'Deus' (hence deity and, from its adjective divinus, divinity). The epithet Deus Optimus Maximus, means "Best and Greatest God", was later adopted in Christianity.

Semitic Religions

Judaism

In the Hebrew scriptures (i.e. the Law Torah, plus the Prophets and the Holy Writings) name of God is considered sacred and, out of deep respect for the name, Jews do not say it. (Exodus 20:7). The most important and most often written name of God in Judaism is the Tetragrammaton, the four-letter name of God, "YHWH or Yahweh". Modern Christians have adopted pronunciations such as "Yahweh", "Yahveh" and "Jehovah".

Christianity

Saint Paul said, "Everyone who calls upon the name of the Lord will be saved" (Romans 10.13). King David preached, "From the rising of the sun to its setting, the name of the Lord is to be praised" (Psalms 113.3). Holy Bible says, "Our Father, Who art in Heaven, Hallowed be Thy Name."

Yahweh is a common vocalization of God's personal name based on the Hebrew tetragrammaton. Also some other names for God used by Christians are Father, Lord, Heavenly Father, or the Holy Trinity.

'Jehovah', an English rendering of the tetragrammaton, the four Hebrew letters used by Bible writers to represent the personal name of the supreme deity, is found in Tyndale's Bible, in the King James Bible, and in many other translations from that time period onward.

Jesus (Iesus, Yeshua, Joshua, or Yehoshûa) is a Hebraic personal name meaning "Yahweh saves/helps/is salvation". Christ means "the anointed" in Greek. Khristos is the Greek equivalent of the Hebrew word Messiah.

Another term used is 'King of Kings' or 'Lord of Lords' and Lord of the Hosts. Other names used by Christians include Father/Abba, 'Most High' and the Hebrew names Elohim, El-Shaddai, and Adonai. "Abba/Father" is the most common term used for the creator within Christianity, because it was the name Jesus Christ himself used to refer to God.

Islam

Muhammed counseled, "Glorify the name of your Lord, the most high" (Koran 87.2). Allah is the most frequently used name of God in Islam. It is an Arabic word meaning "the god", and was used in polytheistic pre-Islamic Arabia to refer to the supreme God above all of the "other gods" and idols; a concept similar to that found in many polytheistic societies. The word Allah is a linguistic cognate of the Hebrew word Eloah and a translation of the English word "God".

A well established Islamic tradition enumerates 99 names of God, each representing certain attributes or descriptions of God; in which God is seen as being the source and maximum extent of each name's meaning. The names Ar-Rahman and Ar-Raheem are the most frequently mentioned in the Qur'an, both meaning the "Most Merciful", but with different emphasis' of meaning, either of which are also often translated as the "Most Compassionate" or the "Most Beneficent".

Besides these Arabic names, Muslims of non-Arab origins may also sometimes use other names of their own languages which refer to God, such 'Khoda' in Persian language which has the same Indo-European root as god.

Bahá'í Faith

Bahais refer to God using the local word for God in whatever language it is being spoken. Bahais often, in prayers, refer to God by titles and attributes, such as the Mighty, the All-Powerful, the Merciful, the Ever-Forgiving, the Most Generous, the All-Wise, the Incomparable, the Gracious, the Helper, the All-Glorious, the Omniscient. Since the languages in which the Bahá'í Faith was first authored were Arabic and Persian, the term Allah and other names are used in some specific contexts, even by non-Arabic speakers.

Other Traditions

Xwedê is the term used for God in the Yazidi religion and in Kurdish.

Abraxas is a god uniting the dualistic concepts in Gnosticism.
Cao Dai is the name of God in Caodaism.

Japanese Religions

Tenri-o-no-Mikoto is the principal name of God in Tenrikyo sect. Tenri-o-no-Mikoto is also called Tsukihi, Oyagami, and Kami.

Tenchi-Kane-no-Kami is the name of God in Konkokyo sect.
Mioya-Ookami is the name of God in the PL Kyodan sect.

Zoroastrianism

Ahura Mazda "Lord of Light" or "Lord Wisdom" is the name of the supreme benevolent god in Zoroastrianism. Zoroastrians today may refer to Ahura-Mazda as 'Ormazd,' a short form of the original term.

Awe And Reverence For The Holy Name

All world religions consider the Holy Name of God to be worthy of utmost awe and reverence.

It is common to regard the written name of one's God as deserving of respect; it ought not, for instance, be stepped upon or dirtied, or made common slang in such a way as to show disrespect.

Vedic Tradition

In vedic system, Holy Name of God is supposed to be chanted always irrespective of what one is doing. There are no hard and fast rules for chanting the Holy Name of God. Just like a medicine taken accidentally also benefits a patient, similarly the Holy Name chanted casually or inattentively also benefits the chanter. *Kirtaniya sada hari* - lord Hari should always be glorified. Many hindus take bath before chanting on beads or entering a temple. Holy scriptures containing the Names of God or prayer rosaries are never thrown away but disposed of respectfully in a holy water body or under a holy tree.

Also it is considered to be auspicious to name people after God's Names.

Judaism

Most observant Jews forbid discarding holy objects, including any document with a name of God written on it. Once written, the name must be preserved indefinitely. This leads to several noteworthy practices:

Commonplace materials are written with an intentionally abbreviated form of the name. For instance, a Jewish letter-writer may substitute "G-d" for the name God. Thus, the letter may be discarded along with ordinary trash.

Copies of the Torah are, like most scriptures, heavily used during worship services, and will eventually become worn out. Since they may not be disposed of in any way, including by burning, they are removed, traditionally to the synagogue attic. There they remain until they are buried.

All religious texts that include the name of God are buried.

Islam

In Islam, the name (or any names) of God is generally treated with the utmost respect. It is referred to in many verses of the Qur'an that the real believers respect the name of God very deeply. (e.g. 33/35, 57/16, 59/21, 7/180, 17/107, 17/109, 2/45, 21/90, 23/2) On the other hand the condition is openly stressed by prohibiting people from unnecessary swearing using the name of Allah. (e.g. 24/53, 68/, 63/2, 58/14, 58/16, 2/224) Thus the mention of the name of God is expected to be done so reverently.

Christianity

In Christianity, God's name may not "be used in vain" (Ten Commandments), which is commonly interpreted to mean that it is wrong to curse while making reference to God. Also in relation to oath taking, the command is to hold true to those commands made 'in God's name'. (Jesus also makes it clear that a Christian should hold true to all their words - cf Matthew 5:37)

Christians capitalize all references to God in writing, including pronouns. (eg.,"The Lord, He is God, Holy is His Name.")

More pious swearers try to substitute the blasphemy against holy names with minced oaths like Jeez! instead of Jesus! or Judas Priest! instead of Jesus Christ!.

Traditionally, when a copy of the Bible is worn out, the book is burned, not simply thrown away.

Mahamantra - The Great Chant

By Srila Prabhupada

This transcendental vibration of chanting of *"Hare Krsna, Hare Krsna, Krsna Krsna , Hare Hare/ Hare Rama, Hare Rama, Rama Rama, Hare Hare"* is the sublime method of reviving our Krsna consciousness. As living spiritual souls we are all originally Krsna conscious entities, but due to our association with matter since time immemorial, our consciousness is now polluted by the material atmosphere.

In this polluted concept of life, we are trying to exploit the resources of material nature, but actually we are becoming more and more entangled in her complexities. This illusion is called maya -- our hard struggle for existence for winning over the stringent laws of material nature.

This illusory struggle against material nature can at once be stopped by the revival of our Krsna consciousness. Krsna consciousness is not an artificial imposition on the mind. It is the original energy of the living entity. When we hear the transcendental vibration, this consciousness is revived, and therefore the process of chanting Hare Krsna is recommended by authorities for this age.

By practical experience, also, we can perceive that by chanting this maha-mantra, or "the great chanting for deliverance," one can at once feel transcendental ecstasy from the spiritual stratum. When one is actually on the plane of spiritual understanding, surpassing the stages of sense, mind, and intelligence, one is situated on the transcendental plane.

This chanting of *Hare Krsna, Hare Krsna, Krsna Krsna , Hare Hare/ Hare Rama, Hare Rama, Rama Rama, Hare Hare* is directly enacted from the spiritual platform, surpassing all lower stages of consciousness, namely sensual, mental, and intellectual. There is no need to understand the language of the mantra, nor is there any need of mental speculation, nor any intellectual adjustment for chanting this maha-mantra. It springs automatically from the spiritual platform, and as such anyone can take part in this transcendental sound vibration without any previous qualification and dance in ecstasy. We have seen it practically -- even a child can take part in the chanting, or even a dog can take part in it.

The chanting should be heard, however, from the lips of a pure devotee of the Lord, so that the immediate effect can be achieved. As far as possible, chanting from the lips of nondevotees should be avoided. Milk touched by the lips of a serpent has poisonous effects.

The word Hara is a form of addressing the energy of the Lord. Both Krsna and Rama are forms of directly addressing the Lord, and they mean "the highest pleasure." Hara is the supreme pleasure potency of the Lord. This potency, addressed as Hare, helps us in reaching the Supreme Lord.

The material energy, known as maya, is also one of the multipotencies of the Lord. The living entities are described as an energy that is superior to matter. When the superior energy is in contact with inferior energy, it becomes an incompatible situation. But when the marginal potency is in contact with the supreme spiritual potency, Hara, it becomes the happy, normal condition of the living entity.

The three words -- namely Hare, Krsna, and Rama -- are the transcendental seeds of the maha-mantra, and the chanting is the spiritual call for the Lord and His internal energy, Hara, for giving protection to the conditioned souls. The chanting is exactly like genuine crying by the child for his mother. Mother Hara helps in achieving the grace of the supreme father Hari, or Krsna, and the Lord reveals Himself to such sincere devotees.

Therefore no other means of spiritual realization is as effective in this age as chanting the maha-mantra: Hare Krsna, Hare Krsna, Krsna Krsna , Hare Hare/ Hare Rama, Hare Rama, Rama Rama, Hare Hare. *(HDG. A.C.Bhaktivedanta Swami Prabhupada)*

Why Chant Hare Krishna or The Holy Name

Chanting Hare Krishna awakens love of God and brings liberation as a side benefit along the way. When we chant Hare Krishna, we automatically develop knowledge and detachment. It gets us out of the endless cycle of birth and death and it is the most effective means of self-realization in the present Age of Quarrel. Nothing else works nearly as well.

Also chanting of Hare Krishna cleanses the heart of all illusions and misunderstandings and we become free from all anxieties. It brings us to self-realization—and shows us how to act as a self-realized soul. It keeps us ever mindful of God, the reservoir of pleasure. The beauty of chanting is that there are no hard and fast rules and you can chant anywhere, any time, under any circumstances.

God and His Holy Name are non-different. Therefore God Himself is fully present in the transcendental sound of His name. And the more we chant, the more we realize Him. All other prayers and mantras are included in the chanting of the Holy Name. So just by chanting the Holy Name, we get the benefit of all the prayers and mantras.

Chanting purifies not only us but every living entity around us. Therefore whoever hears the chanting gets spiritual benefit. A person thus chanting develops all good qualities. One can chant Hare Krishna softly for personal meditation or loudly with family or friends. Both ways it works. Great souls in the past chanted the Holy Names of God, therefore we should do also. Holy Name is free. It never costs us any money. Chanting Hare Krishna brings the highest states of ecstasy. There are no previous qualifications needed for chanting. Young or old, educated or fool, rich or poor, anyone can chant—from any race, any religion, or any country of the world.

Even if we don't understand the language of the mantra, it works anyway just as a medicine works whether we understand the composition or not. Chanting the Holy Name brings relief from all miseries. Chanting is easy. When the best way is also the easiest, why make life hard for yourself?

Chanting invokes spiritual peace—for you and for those around you. When we chant, God Himself becomes pleased. When you chant, God dances on your tongue.

By chanting, we return to the Kingdom of God, the eternal abode of full happiness and knowledge. Chanting Hare Krishna frees us from the reactions of all past karma. Chanting Krishna's name even once, purely and sincerely, can free you from the reactions of more karma than we could possibly incur. Moreover chanting Hare Krishna counteracts the sinful atmosphere of Kali-yuga, the present Age of Hypocrisy and Quarrel.

By chanting Hare Krishna we can relish at every step the full nectar that's the real thirst of the soul. The more we chant Hare Krishna, the better it gets. To conclude, If we look through all the Vedic scriptures, you'll find nothing higher than the chanting of Hare Krishna. Hare Krishna, Hare Krishna, Krishna Krishna, Hare Hare/ Hare Rama, Hare Rama, Rama Rama, Hare Hare.

How to Chant

There are no hard-and-fast rules for chanting Hare Krsna. The most wonderful thing about mantra meditation is that one may chant anywhere-at home, at work, driving in the car, or riding on the bus or subway. And one may chant at any time.

There are two basic types of chanting. Personal meditation, where one chants alone on beads, is called japa. When one chants in responsive fashion with others, this is called kirtana. Kirtana is usually accompanied by musical instruments and clapping. Both forms of chanting are recommended and beneficial.

To perform the first type of meditation, one needs only a set of japa beads. To meditate with the beads, hold them in your right hand. Hold the first bead with your thumb and middle finger and chant the complete maha-mantra-Hare Krsna, Hare Krsna, Krsna Krsna, Hare Hare/ Hare Rama, Hare Rama, Rama Rama, Hare Hare. Then go to the next bead, holding it with the same two fingers, again chanting the entire mantra. Then go on to the next bead and then the next, continuing in this way until you have chanted on all 108 beads and have come to the Krsna bead. You have now completed "one round" of chanting. Do not chant on the Krsna bead, but turn the beads around and chant on them in the opposite direction, one after another. Chanting on beads is especially helpful, for it engages the sense of touch in the meditative process and helps you concentrate even more on the sound of the mantra.

Holy Name can be chanted indoors, but you can chant just as comfortably walking along the beach or hiking in the mountains. Just bring your beads along with you. If you chant sitting down, you should assume a comfortable position (preferably not lying down or slouching, for there's always the tendency to fall asleep). You can chant as loudly or as softly as you like, but it's important to pronounce the mantra clearly and loudly enough to hear yourself. The mind may have a tendency to wander off to other matters when you chant, for the mind is flickering and unsteady, always looking for something new and pleasurable to absorb itself in. If your mind wanders (to anything except Krsna and things related to Him), gently bring it back to the transcendental sound vibration. It won't be difficult, because the mind is easily satisfied when absorbed in the divine sound of the Lord's holy names (unlike other meditational practices, where one may be asked to fix his mind on "nothing" or "the void").

One may chant japa at any time, but the Vedic literatures note that certain hours of the day are most auspicious for performing spiritual activities. The early morning hours just before and after sunrise are generally a time of stillness and quietude, excellently suited to contemplative chanting. Many people find it especially helpful to set aside a certain amount of time at the same time each day for chanting. Start with one or two "rounds" a day, and gradually increase the number until you reach sixteen, the recommended minimum for serious chanters.

हरे कृष्ण हरे कृष्ण
कृष्ण कृष्ण हरे हरे
हरे राम हरे राम
राम राम हरे हरे

While japa is a form of meditation involving you, your beads, and the Supreme Lord, kirtana, on the other hand, is a form of group meditation, where one sings the mantra, sometimes accompanied by musical instruments. We may have seen a kirtana party chanting on the streets of your city, for the Hare Krishna devotees frequently perform this type of chanting to demonstrate the process and allow as many people as possible to benefit from hearing the holy names.

One may hold a kirtana at home with family or friends, with one person leading the chanting and the others responding. Kirtana is more of a supercharged meditational process, where in addition to hearing oneself chant, one also benefits by hearing the chanting of others. Musical instruments are nice, but not necessary. One may sing the mantra to any melody and clap his hands. Children can sing along as well and make spiritual advancement. You can get the whole family together every evening for chanting.

In order to realize the full efficacy of the Holy Name, following mantra (called Pancha-tattva mantra or mantra to invoke God in five features) can be chanted audibly once before beginning each round: *jaya sri krishna chaitanya prabhu nityananda / sri advaita gadadhara srivas adi gaura bhakta vrinda.*

The sounds of the material world are boring, hackneyed and monotonous, but chanting is an ever-increasingly refreshing experience. Make a test yourself. Try chanting some word or phrase for even five minutes. If you chant "Coca-Cola" over and over again, even for a few minutes, it becomes practically unbearable. There's no pleasure in it. But the sound of Krsna's names is transcendental, and as one chants he wants to chant more and more.

Mantra & Environment
Mantra Meditation - Addressing The Root Cause of World Crisis

Much of environmental policy to date has not really been designed to 'solve' problems but rather lo hide, dilute or delay emissions or to dispose of them further away. When highly toxic materials are thrown into the sea in 'safe' containers, this is just a way of delaying by a couple of decades their free release. Similarly in its 1974 Guidelines for Action To Reduce Emissions of Sulphur Oxides recommended 'the confinement of high polluting fuels to large installations equipped with tall chimneys". Such policies may have been undertaken in the belief that substances can be diluted into concentrations that are harmless. Today we know that this is not true. Some substances have no safe threshold level, others may be reconcentrated in the food chains or by other natural processes.

The most cynical way of 'solving' waste disposal problems is the dumping of hazardous wastes in countries where such disposal is cheaper or where control is, for various reasons, less rigorous.

Different types of policy instrument, taxes, subsidies, regulations, information, emission standards or marketable emission permits etc. are all external measures which try to deal with the issue while leaving the cause intact.

Adoption of policies like famous "polluters pay principle' which explicitly states that the use (or degradation) of environmental resources should be reflected in the final price of the product concerned, thereby, in the ideal case, informing the consumer of the cost to the environment and reducing demand when appropriate. In practice, however, the effective use of price mechanisms for environmental purposes is rare.

When policies were introduced to reduce emissions of Sulphur in one country so that companies had to convert to low-sulphur oil, then instead of leading to an increase in the desulphurization of oil we simply caused its relocation since high sulphur oil became relatively cheaper and was burnt somewhere else.

Thus we an see that the whole hype of environmentalism is just going about in circles unless we opt for a fundamental change, change in consciousness, change in the way we think, feel and will.

And that is made possible by chanting. Chanting is a source of nonmaterial satisfaction. When we chant, our insatiable urge to consume is sated and we are satisfied with a simpler life. A simpler life is easier on natural resources and a less polluting one at the same time.

Therefore let us 'Chant for Change.'

The Alternative Future - 3

Holy Cow!

Land & Cow Subsistence

Cow-slaughter and man-slaughter are in my opinion the two sides of the same coin.
~Gandhi

Allama Iqbal, a 19th century scholar once remarked, "Ancient civilizations of Greece, Egypt and Rome have all disappeared from this world, but the elements of Indian civilization still continue. Although world-events have been inimical to India for centuries, there is something in Indian civilization which has withstood these onslaughts." Similarly Gandhi described European civilization as a 'nine day wonder" while praising Indian civilization to be founded on a solid footing.

It is a fact that many civilizations have come and gone but vedic civilization continues, at least in traces, till today. India has survived the onslaught of centuries of invasion and colonization. The culture still lives on, even thriving in some pockets.

What is the reason for sustainability of Indian culture? How come the vedic tradition has survived the onslaught of time. One  important reason for this is their ability to harmonize their living with the laws of nature and God. And an important part of that balancing act is interweaving every aspect of their existence with cows and bulls.

However strange it may sound to an average Westerner or a person steeped in western ideas, Vedas, the greatest repository of knowledge, crown the bovine species with the loving title of mother. Just as a mother provides all necessities to her children, similarly in Vedic tradition, mother cow provides all necessities to the human society. Human society reciprocates this services by protecting, serving, worshiping, adoring and glorifying her. Bull is regarded as symbol of religion and father because bull produces grains by ploughing the fields.

In the natural plan of Vedic living, human society depends on cows for its requirements of economic prosperity, food production, soil fertility, nutrition, healthcare, fuel supply, transport, spiritual well-being, sustainable development, individual and social peace, higher consciousness, development of human qualities, performance of religious duties, environmental protection, ecological preservation, advancement of art & culture, cottage industry etc.

In the universal scheme of creation, fate of species called humans has been attached to that of another, namely cows, to an absolute and overwhelming degree. This implies that welfare and well-being of cows means progress and prosperity of humans and neglect and mistreatment of cows means degradation and ruin of humans. Many of the maladies staring in the face of human society today can be traced to this factor – humanity distancing itself from protection and service to cows.

The cow is now forced to trek the path of disgrace and death. Today a dead cow fetches more money than a living one.

Cow & Economic Prosperity

Centuries ago, there were no industries in India but still she was considered to be one of the richest countries in the world. This attracted the attention of the invaders. There was untold amount of wealth in India. Prosperity and affluence was widespread. This was due to India's focus on agriculture and cow protection. As its focus shifted to industry, especially in post-independence era, India was reduced to severe poverty. Industries helped a few to become billionaires, but condition of masses considerably deteriorated.

People left clean and healthy village life and migrated to cities to live in slums and work is hellish factories. Industrial life offered no security as any time these factories would lock out. Then they would have no where to go.

In Sanskrit literatures, cow is referred to as 'kamadhenu', the bestower of all desirable things. For centuries, land and cows were

Cow protection to me is one of the most wonderful phenomena in the human evolution. ~ Gandhi

the standard measure of wealth. Even today in some parts of the world, people keep their investment in cows. A family is considered rich if it owns hundreds of cows.

Cows are indispensable, first and foremost, for their milk. Every drop of milk can be put to good use. Srila Prabhupada explains the utility of milk, the wonder food :

"Milk is so nice that it cannot be wasted, even a drop. First of all you get milk, that is the Indian system. So there is a big milk pan, and as soon as the milk is drawn it is put into the pan. The pan is in the fire. So as much as you like, drink milk, children, elderly persons. Then at night, when there is no demand for milk, it is converted into yogurt, not wasted. Whatever balance milk is there is converted into yogurt. Then in daytime also you take yogurt, as much as you like. If it is not all consumed, then it is stored in a pot. Then when that pot is enough stored, then you churn it. Churn it, and you get butter and Buttermilk. So again you take buttermilk with chapati and everything, not a single drop is lost. Then the butter, you melt it, convert into ghee and store it, it will stay for years. So not a drop of milk can be wasted. And this butter, because in the village they are eating so many milk products, they do not require butter or ghee. Maybe little, so that is stored. They go to the city. The city men they require, especially. Ghee is very important thing in the city. So they purchase. So in exchange of that money, whatever they want, they purchase in the city and come back. By simply maintaining the cows, their economic problem is solved. Simply maintaining the cows. And to maintain cow there is no difficulty. The boys.... Just like Krishna, as boy, was taking the cows, the calves, in the fields. They are grazing here and there, and coming back they're giving milk. Only one attendant required to take them into the pasturing ground and bring them back home. You don't require to give them food even. Simply take care, they give milk, and with milk you make so many preparations."s *(Garden*

Mother cow is in many ways better than the mother who gave us birth. Mother provides milk for a year or two, mother cow gives milk for the whole life
~ Gandhi

Conversation, June 10, 1976, Los Angeles)

Every inch of cow, whether living or dead, is meant for the good of humanity. Even urine and stool of cow are put to good use. In Indian villages, house flooring and walls are smeared with cow dung and cow dung patties are used as fuel. It has been scientifically proven that cow dung and urine have antiseptic properties. Goddess of wealth, Lakshmi is said to reside in cow dung. When cows graze, they fertilize the fields by their excrements. Besides on an average, a cow gives birth to ten calves in her life time. Cow is the lifeline of two million villages and two billion villagers in the third World.

In the book 'When Histories Collide', the author calculates that the milk from a cow gives 480 lb of digestible dry matter content in a year. In contrast, eating a cow only gives 48 lb of digestible dry matter. Milking cows thus does seem to be around 10 times more productive, in just one year. When taken for her full life, it works out hundreds of times more. This perhaps gives a scientific, secular and common sense explanation for why Hinduism and other religious traditions prohibit eating beef. It is rational for people to avoid eating an animal that, if kept alive, can render so much service.

When dead, her hide, bones, hooves, horns and everything else is put to use.

An average cow's contribution in her lifetime comes to thousands of dollars. Cow represents sound economics. Recent meltdowns have put question marks on the sustainability of our colossal globalized economy. Going back to land and cows would mean moving out of a 'house of cards' economy.

Cow & Soil Fertility

World's soil is in danger. Death of soil is death of civilization. Bad soil is bad for global health. All over the world, more than seven and a half million acres of soil has been degraded. That's larger than the U.S. and Canada combined. What remains is ailing as a result of compaction, erosion and salination making it near impossible to plant and adding to greenhouse gases and air pollution. Soil degradation is putting the future of the global population is at risk according to a National Geographic article by Charles Mann.

Civil unrest in Latin America, Asia and Africa have been attributed to a lack of food and affordable food as a result of poor soil. *Currently, only 11-percent of the world's land feeds six billion people.* Experts estimate that by 2030 the Earth's population will reach 8.3 billion. Farmers will need to increase food production by 40-percent. But not much soil remains. Scientists don't know much and don't care either about this critical resource.

One solution to this grave problem would be switching over to cow based farming.

Many organic farmers are reviving age old practices of cow dung fertilizers and cow urine pesticides. Popularly known as zero-budget farming and bio-dynamic farming, it is being practiced on thousands of acres across India with great success. When nourished by mother cow, soil remains fertile for thousands and millions of years but when scorched by chemicals, it dies in 3-4 decades.

There is perfect cooperation in nature's plan. We take the grains, fruits and vegetables. Cow takes the stems, chaff and whatever else is leftover. We feed the cow with these by-products and cow in turn feeds our crops.

In an experiment at the Dairy Research Institute, Ellinbank, Victoria, effects of dairy cow manure on soil fertility was observed. In the soil, extractable soil P (Olsen) was 32mg/kg. After 60 days of application, extractable soil P increased to 61mg/kg. Extractable soil K (Colwell) almost doubled from 642 mg/kg to 1226 mg/kg in manure treated soils.

Cows return significant quantities of nutrients to pastures through dung and urine. Up to 65% of the phosphorus (P) eaten in the diet is returned in faeces while approximately 11% and 79% of the consumed potassium (K) is returned in dung and urine respectively (Haynes and Williams, 1993). These nutrients contribute to soil fertility.

When I see a cow, it is not an animal to eat; it is a poem of pity for me and I worship it and I shall defend its worship against the whole world. ~ Gandhi

In another experiment in Kerala, India, a manure prepared with fermented cow dung, enriched with groundnut cake and neem cake was effective in improving soil quality and enhancing microbial status. In this Indian State, famous for black pepper farming, black pepper often suffers from poor growth and wilt disease. This has been linked to the intensive application of chemicals, resulting in imbalances in soil micro-flora and fauna and spread of diseases like quick wilt and slow wilt. These problems can be alleviated by improving soil fertility and soil microbial status using fermented cow dung, enriched with groundnut cake and neem cake.

Cow & Human Nutrition

The UN estimates that there are approximately 1000 million (1 billion) starving/undernourished people in the world. This is a scandal for humanity when we consider that more than half of the grains produce goes for meat and fuel production.

Milk is a complete food. In India, even now there are thousands of ascetics who simply live on milk. They do not eat anything else and are quite healthy. Our mother feeds us milk for few months but cow feeds us milk for the whole life. Srila Prabhupada explains this: "just like milk is the essence of the blood. The milk is nothing, but it is cow's blood transformed. Just like mother's milk. The mother's milk, wherefrom it comes? It comes from the blood, but transformed in such a way that it becomes nutritious to the child, tasteful to the child. Similarly, cow's milk also, a most nutritious and valuable food. *(Lecture on Bhagavad-gita 7.3, Montreal, June 3, 1968).* He further adds, "So from the cows, the milk. And from the milk we can make hundreds of vitaminous foodstuff, hundreds. They're all palatable. So such a nice animal, faithful, peaceful, and beneficial. After taking milk from it, if we kill, does it look very well? Even after the death, the cows supply the skin for your shoes. It is so beneficial. You see. Even after death. While living, he gives you nice milk. You cannot reject milk from the human society. As soon as there is a child born, milk immediately required. Old man, milk is life. Diseased person, milk is life. Invalid, milk is life. So therefore Krishna is teaching by His practical demonstration how

He loves this innocent animal, cow. So human society should develop brahminical culture on the basis of protecting cows. *(Lecture , Los Angeles, December 4, 1968).*

Many doctors blame cow's milk for various diseases. But real culprit is our modern dairy practices. Cows are overloaded with hormones, antibiotics and bio-feeds. They are fed groundup cows. A vegetarian animal is fed cannibalistic diet. Milk is extracted, processed and distributed in most unnatural manner and therefore it leads to ill-health. But when we talk of a mother cow giving milk out of affection for its calf, living in natural surroundings, that milk is as good as or better than our mother's milk.

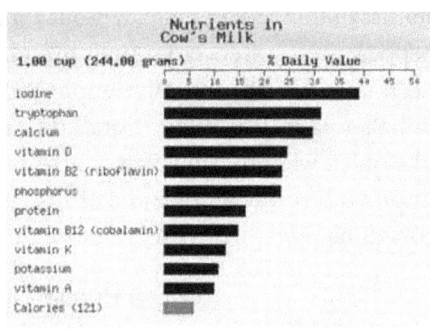

Cow's milk, the basis for all other dairy products, promotes strong bones by being a very good source of vitamin D and calcium, and a good source of vitamin K--three nutrients essential to bone health. In addition, cow's milk is a very good source of iodine, a mineral essential for thyroid function; and a very good source of riboflavin and good source of vitamin B12, two B vitamins that are necessary for cardiovascular health and energy production.

Cow's milk is also a good source of vitamin A, a critical nutrient for immune function, and potassium, a nutrient important for cardiovascular health.

Milk produced by grass fed cows also contains a beneficial fatty acid called conjugated linoleic acid (CLA). Researchers who conducted animal studies with CLA found that this fatty acid inhibits several types of cancer in mice. In vitro (test tube) studies indicate this compound kills human skin cancer, colorectal cancer and breast-cancer cells. Other research on CLA suggests that this beneficial fat may also help lower cholesterol and prevent atherosclerosis.

Recently "Monocaprin" contained in milk and milk products is reported to possess excellent microbicidal properties and useful against transmitted diseases in Humans

According to Ayurveda, the cow ghee (clarified butter) is believed to be the best food for human health and brain. It has much nutritive qualities and is an ideal diet for the heart patients, who suffer from the cholesterol issues. Cow ghee enhances physical and mental strength and vitality, detoxifies, enhances eyesight, maintains the health of muscles and tendons and keeps the bones stout and flexible.

Curd is another byproduct of cow milk. In Sanskrit the curd is called Dadhi. The ancient Ayurveda specialists like Charaka and Sushruta have described the qualities and usefulness of curd. It is useful in many diseases and it has been described as a tonic. It prevents premature aging, cures diarrhea, dysentery and chronic colitis.

Cow & Energy

Reliance on fossil fuels has largely developed in the last 200 years. Before that, most energy was renewable – animal and human muscle, wood, some wind and water power. The harnessing of new sources of energy, especially coal, about 250 years ago was crucial to the industrial revolution and all that followed.

The world economy is hooked on fossil fuels: oil, gas, and coal. This dependency cannot last. All these fuels were formed millions of year ago and once used up cannot be replaced. But before industrial revolution, practically all the energy used was renewable.

For millennia animals have been harnessed to pull carts, carry loads, transport people, haul water, trash harvests, plough, puddle and weed crop fields etc. **Even today, more than half the world's population depends on animal power** for much of its energy. Draught animals operate on more than 50% of the planet's cultivated areas. In the mid 1990s work by draught animals was estimated to be equivalent to a fossil fuel replacement value of

> *The cow to me is a sermon on pity.*
> *~Gandhi*

US$ 16 billion. Estimates of the number of animals used for power applications range from 300 million upwards. Oxen are the most frequently used animals and ploughing is the most common function. Almost all species of domestic quadruped are used, however, in a variety of agricultural and transport roles. In agriculture positive effects are seen to be higher crop output, better returns to labour, increased cash income and improved food security.

Despite motorization on all fronts the use of ox is still often more economic than the use of machinery and vehicles, especially in small scale agriculture and in remote areas. Animals are produced and maintained locally and don't require the infrastructure needed for motorization. Where the value of machinery needs to be depreciated over time, that of animals can appreciate because of growth.

Ox power represents a sustainable and renewable resource of energy.

In terms of agriculture, ox power creates a lighter footprint on the earth than a tractor, which tends to compact the soil. Also in terms of the environment, it takes far less resources to produce a team of oxen than a tractor. How many mining operations and how many factories does it require to produce even one tractor? How many drilling and refining operations does it take to fuel it? The "factory" that produces an ox is a cow. For "fuel" the oxen can eat grass and grain which they themselves produce.

And, we should not underestimate the level of benefit that oxen can provide. With the exception of the cultures of the Americas, practically every materially advanced civilization before the crusades – including China, India, the Middle East, North Africa and Europe – relied on oxen to be the engine for agriculture, local transport, grinding grains and even building. Many of the great projects of ancient times were all accomplished without the incredible level of pollution it would take to recreate such structures today.

Srila Prabhupada advises, "Petrol is required for [long-distance]

Cow protection is the gift of Hinduism to the world. ~ Gandhi

transport, but if you are localized, there is no question of [such] transport. You don't require petrol.... The oxen will solve the problem of transport."

The tractor is a real sore point in agriculture. Tractors are expensive to operate. This expense partly explains why hundreds of thousands of small farms collapse every year. But ox power, though slower, is far more efficient.

Oxen cost far less than tractors to maintain, provide free fertilizer, preserve precious topsoil, and don't foul the atmosphere with carbon monoxide. Bovine waste, when mixed in the traditional way with straw, is the world's best fertilizer. And when the animal dies, its skin can be processed into leather.

Turning to Gandhi for inspiration, we find that a key requirement for building peace is to provide full employment by emphasizing localized production for localized markets. Gandhi stressed that everything which can be produced locally should be, even if the local economy is less efficient at its production.

Since time immemorial, cows have provided many essential services to humanity for very little maintenance. They're an inseparable part of God's efficient system for human civilization.

Dr. Vandana Shiva, an ecologist, comments on India's recent cattle policy while calling it a policy of ecocide of indigenous cattle breeds and a policy of genocide for India's small farmers: "The traditional approach to livestock is based on diversity, decentralisation, sustainability and equity. Our cattle are not just milk machines or meat machines. They are sentient beings who serve human communities through their multidimensional role in agriculture."

"On the other hand," continues Shiva, " externally driven projects, programmes and policies emerging from industrial societies treat cattle as one-dimensional machines which are maintained with capital intensive and environmentally intensive inputs and which provide a single output - either milk or meat. Polices based on this

Man through the cow is enjoined to realize his identity with all that lives. ~ Gandhi

approach are characterised by monocultures, concentration and centralisation, non-sustainability and inequality."

Thus, whether we like it or not, when fossil fuels bid us good bye, world will have to revert back to bull power for fulfilling its energy requirements.

Cow & Healthcare

Indian science of medicine, known as Ayurveda, describes thousands of medicines based on cow products like milk, curd, ghee, cow urine and cow dung. Called 'Pancha-gavya', these traditional medicines are gaining popularity and many incurable diseases are getting cured with these medicines. Ayurvedic health care is holistic and it aims at physical, mental and spiritual well-being.

Global Health Care Alternative

Considering the fact that more than 70% of the global population do not have access to modern health care, panchagavya can play an important role in improving global health. Pharmaceutical giants are making obscene profits out of people's miseries. How many can afford such treatment? Panchagavya presents, on the grassroot level, a very practical alternative to corporate health care. Last year, out of $600 billion spent on health care worldwide, more than half was spent in the US alone, which is just 4% of the world's population. Many third world countries are trying to imitate US healthcare systems with disastrous results.

Cow Urine

Cow urine is antifungal, antibacterial, antibiotic, antiallergic, and antimicrobial. There is a great demand for it in India, especially among cancer patients. Milk is around Rs 15-20 a litre where as cow urine is selling Rs 30-40 a litre. There are two US Patents on Gomutra Ark (Cow Urine Distillate): US Patent 6410059 25-06-2002 and US Patent 6896907 24-05-2005. From constipation to cancer, diarrhea to diabetes, advocates of cow urine are offering to cure nearly everything.

Ayurveda says that the main cause of diseases is the imbalance of three elements Air (Vata), Bile (Pitta), Mucous (kapha). Cow urine balances these three elements, 'Samya dosharogata' meaning when three elements are in balance, there are no diseases.

A herbal preparation popular in Nigeria is based on cow's urine and some herbs and is called Cow urine concoction (CUC). Over fifty chemical compounds have been identified in CUC. It's major pharmacological actions include anticonvulsant and hypoglycemic effects.

Cow urine works wonders in recuperating dead cells, especially the cancerous ones. So it is being used in the treatment of cancer with considerable success.

Since ages, Indian women have applied cow urine in their hairs to get rid of lice.

For The Critics of Cow Urine

If urine of mare can be used, why not cow urine. Premarin is the commercial name for compound drug which is isolated from mare's urine. It is manufactured by Wyeth Pharmaceuticals and has been marketed since 1942. Premarin is a form of hormone replacement therapy. Arabs used camel urine to treat ailments also.

Saying goes, one living being's food is poison for another. What cow rejects can be perfectly useful for humans. All things excreted from all bodies are harmful or waste, since they are rejected. That is perfectly all right. But that are bad for just that body not for all. Why do we accept oxygen that excretes from plants and why plants take our excreta as manure? It is a natural law that living beings depend upon each other. Hogs relish human excreta and become plump on that.

What to speak of cow urine, all over world cities are opting for recycling sewage for drinking water purposes.

Panchagavya - The Plant Tea

The ayurvedic literature (Charak Samhita, Sushrut, Gud Nigrah) suggests a number of pharmacological application of the substances obtained from panchagavya. A systematic research is being carried out on chemical nature, biological activity, pharmacology, microbiology and pharmaceutical aspects and mechanism of bioactive compounds in Panchagavya.

Panchagavya has reference in Vrkshayurveda (Vrksha means

plants and ayurveda means health system) also. The texts on Vrkshayurveda are systematizations of the practices the farmers followed at field level, placed in a theoretical framework and it defined certain plant growth stimulants; among them Panchagavya was an important one that enhanced the biological efficiency of crop plants and the quality of fruits and vegetables (Natarajan, 2002). The Panchagavya products show excellent agricultural applications. A formulation derived from cow urine and leaves of neem is an excellent pesticide and insect repellent. The cow is an inseparable part of the farming community.

Rishi Krishi, a system of Agriculture practiced in Maharashtra India is using Amrit pani (prepared by mixing 20 kg cow dung, 0.125 kg butter, ½ kg honey, ¼ kg ghee) and kept over night to treat seeds and for spraying on field crops to maintain soil fertility and crop yield (Pathak and Ram, 2002). Individually or system as a whole, biogas slurry with Panchagavya combination is adjudged as the best organic nutritional practice for the sustainability of maize – sunflower – greengram system by its overall performance on growth, productivity and quality of crops, the soil health and economics (Somasundaram, 2003).

Apart from health, it has great significance in vedic rituals. It is one of the important offerings made to yajna, the sacrificial fire. Intake of panchagavya purifies the consciousness.

Cow & Housing

In mud houses in India, cow dung is used to line flooring and walls. It is mixed in mud for construction purposes to repel insects and pests from burrowing in the walls. In cold places cow dung is used for wall linings for thermal insulation. Cow dung is an excellent mosquito repellent also. It was used extensively in Indian railways to seal smoke boxes on steam locomotives.

Cow & Fuel Supply

Cow dung is an excellent fuel. It helps preserve world's fossil fuel reserves. It is odorless and burns without scorching, giving a slow, even heat. A housewife can count on leaving her pots unattended all day or return any time to a preheated griddle for short-order cooking. To replace dung with coal would cost India $1.5 billion per year.

Cow dung is used extensively to produce biogas, an excellent form of renewable energy which can be used for cooking, lighting or running of vehicles. There are perhaps hundreds of thousands of biogas (called gobar gas) plants in India. A biogas plant is designed in the following way.

A sealed water-tight circular pit, normally about ten feet deep, is made of concrete to which cow manure is added regularly. Alternate materials may be used for constructing this pit as desired. A wall is built across the middle of the pit, extending from the bottom almost to the top.

The manure is mixed with water in the intake basin which flows through the piping to the bottom of the left side. This side of the cylinder gradually fills and overflows to the right side. When both sides of the cylinder are full, the manure effluent flows out from the bottom of the right side each time more raw manure is added to the left.

Manure residue from the decomposition process comes out in a concentrated form and it is an excellent fertilizer.

The concoction produces methane which rises to the top and collects under a large metal dome. As the gas builds pressure it is routed via a rubber tube. The methane gas thus produced is literally free. After the initial construction expense, there are no running expenses, other than adding manure .

Cow & Transport

The world cattle population is close to one billion out of which over 200 million indigenous cows reside in India. This accounts for one-fifth of the world's cattle population. In recent years, some economists have come to agree that cow is essential to the world's economy. Cows are a great natural resource. They eat only grass - which grows everywhere - and generates more power than all of the generating plants in developing countries. Many developing countries runs on bullock power. In India, some 15 million bullock carts move approximately 15 billion tons of goods across the nation.

Newer studies in energetics have shown that bullocks do two-thirds of the work on the average farm in developing countries. Electricity and fossil fuels account for only 10%. Bullocks not only pull heavy loads, but also grind the sugarcane and turn the oil presses. In India itself, converting from bullocks to machinery would cost an estimated $300 billion plus maintenance and replacement costs.

Agricultural is still the mainstay of developing economies. Cow breeding and cow preservation are integral to it. 75 per cent of Indians live in villages and despite the compulsions of modernisation, tractors are not suitable for small land holdings unlike in the US and UK. In US the land available to each person is around 14 acre; in India it is around 0.70 acre. A tractor consumes diesel, creates pollution, doesn't eat grass nor produces dung for manure. So for Indian conditions ploughing is still ideal. Even Albert Einstein, in a letter to Sir CV Raman, wrote: "Tell the people of India, that if they want to survive and show the world path to survive, then they should forget about tractor and preserve their ancient tradition of ploughing."

Cow & Spiritual Well-being

The cow symbolizes Earth, the nourisher, the ever-giving kind mother. The cow represents life and the sustenance of life. The cow is so generous, taking nothing but grass and chaff and giving the most valuable of foods in return. It gives and gives milk just as the liberated souls bestow spiritual knowledge. The cow is so vital to life, the virtual sustainer of life for the mankind. The cow is a symbol of grace and abundance. Veneration for the cow instills in human beings the virtues of gentleness, receptivity and connection with nature.

Many holy books mention milk; Bible contains references to the land of milk and honey. In the Quran, there is a request to wonder on milk as follows: 'And surely in the livestock there is a lesson for you, We give you to drink of that which is in their bellies from the midst of digested food and blood, pure milk palatable for the drinkers.'(16-The Honeybee, 66). The Ramadhan fast is traditionally broken with a glass of milk and dates.

Cow & Development of Human Qualities

Serene by temperament, herbivorous by diet, the very appearance of a white cow evokes a sense of piety. Srila Prabhupada explains this phenomenon, "The body can be maintained by any kind of foodstuff, but cow's milk is particularly essential for developing the finer tissues of the human brain so that one can understand the intricacies of transcendental knowledge. A civilized man is expected to live on foodstuffs comprising fruits, vegetables, grains, sugar and milk. The bull helps in the agricultural process of producing grain, etc., and thus in one sense the bull is the father of humankind, whereas the cow is the mother, for she supplies milk to human society. A civilized man is therefore expected to give all protection to the bulls and cows." (SB 3.5.7)

Srila Prabhupada further says, "If we really want to cultivate the human spirit in society we must have first-class intelligent men to guide the society, and to develop the finer tissues of our brains we must assimilate vitamin values from milk. Devotees worship Lord Sri Krsna by addressing Him as the well-wisher of the brahmanas and the cows. The most intelligent class of men, who have perfectly attained knowledge in spiritual values, are called the brahmanas. No society can improve in transcendental knowledge without the guidance of such first-class men, and no brain can assimilate the subtle form of knowledge without fine brain tissues. For such important brain tissues we require a sufficient quantity of milk and milk preparations. Ultimately, we need to protect the cow to derive the highest benefit from this important animal. The protection of cows, therefore, is not merely a religious sentiment but a means to secure the highest benefit for human society. (Light of Bhagavata 27)

Cow & World Peace

We can expect peace only as long as our cows come back home. We can remain in peace only as long as we let other living beings live in peace. If we are not willing to spare peace, we should not expect to live in peace also. Those who clamor for peace should know that animals have as much right to exist in God's creation as we have. Human wrongs can never undermine animal rights.

Srila Prabhupada explains, "The bull is the emblem of the moral principle, and the cow is the representative of the earth. When the bull and the cow are in a joyful mood, it is to be understood that the people of the world are also in a joyful mood. The reason is that the bull helps production of grains in the agricultural field, and the cow delivers milk, the miracle of aggregate food values. The human society, therefore, maintains these two important animals very carefully so that they can wander everywhere in cheerfulness. But at the present moment in this age of Kali both the bull and the cow are now being slaughtered and eaten up as foodstuff by a class of men who do not know the brahminical culture. The bull and the cow can be protected for the good of all human society simply by the spreading of brahminical culture as the topmost perfection of all cultural affairs. By advancement of such culture, the morale of society is properly maintained, and so peace and prosperity are also attained without extraneous effort." (Srimad Bhagavatam 1.16.18)

Srila Prabhupada adds, "The next symptom of the age of Kali is the distressed condition of the cow. Milking the cow means drawing the principles of religion in a liquid form. The great rishis and munis (sages) would live only on milk. Srila Sukadeva Gosvami would go to a householder while he was milking a cow, and he would simply take a little quantity of it for subsistence. Even fifty years ago, no one would deprive a sadhu of a quart or two of milk, and every householder would give milk like water. For a Sanatanist (a follower of Vedic principles) it is the duty of every householder to have cows and bulls as household paraphernalia, not only for drinking milk, but also for deriving religious principles. The Sanatanist worships cows on religious principles and respects brahmanas. The cow's milk is required for the sacrificial fire, and by performing sacrifices the householder can be happy. The cow's calf not only is beautiful to look at, but also gives satisfaction to the cow, and so she delivers as much milk as possible. But in the Kali-yuga, the calves are separated from the cows as early as possible for purposes which may not be mentioned in these pages of Srimad-Bhagavatam. The cow stands with tears in her eyes, the sudra milkman draws milk from the cow artificially, and when there is no milk the cow is sent to be slaughtered. These greatly sinful acts are responsible for all the troubles in present society. People do not know what they are doing in the name of economic development. The influence of Kali will keep them in the darkness of ignorance. Despite all endeavors for peace and prosperity, they must try to see the cows and the bulls happy in all respects. Foolish people do not know how one earns happiness by making the cows and bulls happy, but it is a fact by the law of nature. Let us take it from the authority of Srimad-Bhagavatam and adopt the principles for the total happiness of humanity. (SB 1.17.3)

Srila Prabhupada further continues, "Panca-gavya, the five products received from the cow, namely milk, yogurt, ghee, cow dung and cow urine, are required in all ritualistic ceremonies performed according to the Vedic directions. Cow urine and cow dung are uncontaminated, and since even the urine and dung of a cow are important, we can just imagine how important this animal is for human civilization. Therefore the Supreme Personality of Godhead, Krsna, directly advocates go-raksya, the protection of cows. Civilized men who follow the system of varnasrama, especially those of the vaisya class, who engage in agriculture and trade, must give protection to the cows. Unfortunately, because people in Kali-yuga are mandah, all bad, and sumanda-matayah, misled by false conceptions of life, they are killing cows in the thousands. Therefore they are unfortunate in spiritual consciousness, and nature disturbs them in so many ways, especially through incurable diseases like cancer and through frequent wars among nations. As long as human society continues to allow cows to be regularly killed in slaughterhouses, there cannot be any question of peace and prosperity." (SB 8.8.11)

> *The central fact of Hinduism is cow protection.*
> *~ Gandhi*

Cow & Sustainable Development

Development and progress of world today is like progress of moths into fire. We are running at great speed but we are on the wrong road. We are too busy with speedometer to see the milestone. Vedic India presents an ideal example of sustainable development wherein perfect harmony exists between nature, mankind, other life forms and God. Vedic text, Srimad Bhagavatam presents a picture of Cow based sustainable development five thousand years ago during the rule of Pandava dynasty.

Srila Prabhupada says, "So Maharaja Yudhisthira was so pious that during his reign time, kamam vavarsa parjanyah [SB 1.10.4]. There was regular rainfall and everything was produced nicely. Sarva-kama-dugha mahi. Sarva-kama. The, another side is that you don't require industries, factories. You don't require. If you have got land and cow, then everything is complete. This is basic principle of Vedic civilization. Have some land. Have some cows. Dhanyena dhanavan gavayah dhanavan. Not industry. There is no need of industry. Because you want some food, nice food, nice milk, nice fruit, that will be produced by nature. You cannot manufacture all these things in the factory. So therefore at the present moment, the big, big factories, they are the activities of the asuras (demons), ugra-karma. All the people are dragged in the city, industrial area, to engage them in the produce of iron bars, big, big iron bars, Tata iron industry, and so many other industry. Capitalists, they have drawn all the innocent people from the village. And they think that "We are getting fat salary." But what is the use of fat salary? One side you get fat salary; another side you have to purchase three rupees a kilo rice. Finish your salary. This is going on. Let them produce their own food. Let him have some land. Let him produce his own food. Let there be cows. Let cows become happy.

Now here is very important word, that *payasodhasvatir muda, udhasvatir muda*. They were very jolly because they can understand whether they are going to be killed or not. Because they have got, they're animal, they have got sense. I have seen in your country, almost all cows are crying. Because in the beginning, all the calves are taken away and slaughtered in their presence. Perhaps you know. So what is the position of the cow? I have seen when we purchase cows, the calves are already taken away. The cow was crying, regular tears were gliding down. So they can understand that... Who cannot understand? Suppose if you are taken in the concentrated camp? Just like the Germans did. What is the meaning of concentrated...? That he'll be killed after some days. So how can you be happy? If you are already informed, condemned to death, and kept in a concentration camp, will you be happy? Similarly, when these people take these cows to the slaughterhouse, animal stock room, godown, they understand. Very recently, about few years ago, some..., that animal stock store was some way or other broken and all the cows began to... Perhaps you know. It was published in the... And they were shot down. Shot to death. They were fleeing like anything, that "We shall save ourselves."

So if the cows are not happy, if they are always afraid, that "This rascal will kill us at any moment," then how they can be happy? There was no such thing. Therefore it is said: muda. Muda. Happy. And as soon as the cows are happy, you not only get sufficient milk, but the pasturing ground, I mean to say, ground, becomes moist with milk. So much milk supplied. Here it is stated, payasa udhasvatir muda. Yes. There is another description. Formerly, Krsna's cows, when they were passing on, the whole road will be moistened with milk. Milk supply was so sufficient. Simply manufacture butter, milk products, dahi... Distribute. Krsna was distributing amongst the monkeys even: "Take," the monkey, "come on."

So by Krsna's grace if we actually become dharmic, follow Krsna, the milk supply will be so profuse that everyone, even the animals can take the butter and yogurt. That is wanted. That is civilization. Produce sufficient quantity of grains, let the milk, cows, supply sufficient quantity of milk. All economic question solved. There is no use of industry. No use of man's going fifty miles to work. No, there is no need. Simply land and cows. Here is the statement. Kamam parjanyah, vavarsa parjanyah sarva-kama-dugha. Everything you'll get from the land. Even luxury articles. What can be more luxurious article than the jewels? The jewels are also produced. The medicine is produced, the minerals are produced, gold is produced, diamond is produced from the earth. Sarva-kama-dugha. You get everything. Make your civilization very perfect, very luxurious simply by satisfying Krsna. This is Krsna consciousness movement." *(Srimad-Bhagavatam 1.10.4 -- Mayapura, June 19, 1973)*

Cow & Environmental Protection

Vedic culture's concern for nature and life in general is reflected in an attitude of reverence towards the cow. Cow represents the Vedic values of selfless service, strength, dignity, and non-violence. For these reasons, although not all Hindus are vegetarian, they traditionally abstain from eating beef.

Vedic seers could see into the future... to our time when we would feed cows ground up cows and make mad cow disease... a time when mankind would be all bad... they saw us abusing everything...from our fellow creatures to nature all around us.

Africans for thousands of years used cow dung cakes as fuel. 18th and 19th century missionaries taught them to give up this 'uncivilized' practice. People turned to forests for fuel and in no time the continent went bald.

The cow dung is an important source of producing non-conventional energy. It is a substitute for firewood and electricity. As a result, the forests can be conserved and their faunal wealth can be enriched.

Every single aspect of cow protection interweaves with the protection of our environment. In fact, care for cow represents care for life and nature in general. The cow is central to our life and bio-diversity. Cow protection has a great potential in poverty alleviation and employment generation. It deserves full support at all levels.

Cow & Higher Consciousness

Cow milk nourishes human brain. Body can be maintained by any kind of food but to develop higher faculties, we require cow's milk. Human beings have a higher function to discharge and that requires finer brain tissues.

Srila Prabhupada says, "Those who are animal killers, their brain is dull as stone. They cannot understand any thing. Therefore meat-eating should be stopped. In order to revive the finer tissues of the brain to understand subtle things, one must give up meat-eating." *(Bhagavad-gita 2.18 - London, August 24, 1973)*

Srila Prabhupada further adds, "The brahmana cannot take any other food except it is made of milk preparation. That develops the finer tissues of the brain. You can understand in subtle matters, in philosophy, in spiritual science. Just like in a scientific college, not ordinary man can understand the scientific intricacies. They require some preliminary qualification to enter into the scientific college. They require some preliminary qualification to enter into the law college, in the postgraduate classes. Similarly, to understand the subtle or finer implications of spiritual science, one has to become a first class human being. (Lecture - *Los Angeles, December 4, 1968)*

End of Modern Civilization and Alternative Future

The Alternative Future - 4

From Cold-blooded, Cruel Agriculture To Enlightened Agriculture

Back To Agrarian Base

Access to land means access to self-sufficiency, which means access to life. Land is primal, everything else is based upon it, even culture. - Jensen

Alternative Future 4 - Enlightened Agriculture

Mainstay of any civilization has been its agriculture. It thrives and survives on agriculture, because food is all that matters, first and foremost. Two other essential ingredients, water and air are of course free. Industries are artificial and they sap the vitality of human beings and nature. They deplete all resources, human, environmental and natural. Industries are a short run drama and a drama does not last forever. Next few decades will see the sad ending of this drama when the curtain of realities falls over it. Agriculture is real life. Drama is for few hours and real life is forever.

Modern industrial agriculture is a form of molesting earth. Humanity is set to pay a big price for this crime. Lesser and lesser number of people are showing any interest in agriculture. Unscrupulous profit crazy corporations are taking over small farms. These corporations have only one relationship with Earth - that of exploitation & profiteering. All this can not last forever. We are taking food for granted, we are taking God's nature for granted. Its not going to work. Something has to change and something will change, whether we like it or not.

Agriculture is still the occupation of almost 50% of the world's population, but the numbers vary from less than 3% in industrialized countries to over 60% in Third World countries.

Legacy of 'Development'

Some traditional societies believed that the land does not belong to them but to their ancestors and their descendants and that it was their duty to hand it on in as good condition as they received it. What kind of land or planet or environment are we preparing for handing over to the next generation? We will hand over a legacy of an Earth, turned into a toxic waste dump.

If we study the life of a typical villager in any traditional community, we would find him living with his wife and a few children in a thatched hut with mud walls and a dirt floor. He has a couple of cows, a well and some land. He may have never gone beyond two or three villages, but he is happy. He lives to a ripe old age, doesn't get many diseases, works honestly in the fields, and has enough milk and grains to eat. With his extra produce, beyond what he needs to maintain his family, he may trade for clothing, jewelry and other items. In other words, he lives a very simple life. And he has sufficient time in hand to cultivate art, culture and to nurture tradition, in a crime and stress free environment. Now this 'backward and undeveloped' community needs to be developed and science and technology need to be introduced in their lives. Soon they will be a 'developed' lot with pollution, crime, stress, life-style diseases, family breakdown, drugs, violence, prostitution and financial meltdowns. This is what we are doing in the name of progress and development.

Subsistence Farming To Commercial Farming - A History

From early times, people created ingenious systems of ploughing, seeding, irrigation and harvesting. For example, in the Middle East, the American Southwest and Mexico, the Nile Valley, and South Asia, we find distinct agricultural systems, suited to local condition. Subsistence farming basically means farming for the purpose of self-survival whereas commercial farming means growing crops primarily for trade.

Modern agriculture finds its roots in industrial revolution that started in 18th and 19th century in Europe. This was the beginning of the demise of local and self-sufficient agriculture. Industrial revolution gave rise to market economy which set in motion a process that is even now destroying traditional village economies and the environment.

In the village communities of many areas of medieval Europe, land was managed in ways that were not very destructive to the environment. Out of numerous such healthy practices, one was three-field system wherein the peasants divided their farmland into three fields, one for winter crops, one for summer crops, and one to remain fallow. The use of the fields was rotated each year. A second part of the system, in order to prevent soil exhaustion, was to use different crops that took different nutrients from the soil. The winter crop typically would consist of winter wheat or rye, and the spring crop would be either spring wheat or legumes (beans or peas). The greater variety of crops provided people with a more balanced diet. Also an advantage of legumes is that they take nitrogen out of the air rather than the soil, and when buried, actually replenish the soil with nitrogen (the Romans referred to this as "green manuring"). Pastures, forests, and water resources were held in common, and their use was carefully regulated by village councils.

It was all set to change with the introduction of cash crops. Inland communities with little access to markets had practiced traditional agriculture that aimed to feed, clothe, and reproduce the family. This form of subsistence farming was far more ecologically sensitive than farming for the market would later be. After clearing forest trees by cutting or burning, farmers used small lots for crops for just a few years, rotating corn, beans, and squash between three fields. Those fields then lay fallow (unused) or served as pastureland for up to eight years, then reverted to forest while a new lot was cleared for the growing of crops. Such methods worked effectively to preserve soil nutrients.

Single-crop fields were more vulnerable to pests including insects, squirrels, and crows. Deforestation altered the climate resulting in colder springs, warmer summers, and earlier frosts. Planters, slaves, and small farmers all suffered from changes in the disease environment. As the aedes mosquito found breeding grounds in new ditches and reservoirs, populous towns endured epidemics of yellow fever and malaria.

Construction of roads and canals that provided backcountry easier access to markets. The transportation and market revolutions altered the environment in two kinds of ways. Direct consequences included disruptions to the fragile ecosystems of rivers and lakes

Produce your own food and eat sumptuously, be healthy and chant Hare Krsna. This is civilization. This is civilization.
-Srila Prabhupada (Lecture, Bhagavad-gita 9.4 — Melbourne, April 22, 1976)

by canal and dam construction and the burning of vast quantities of firewood aboard new steamboats. Indirect consequences were perhaps more profound. New forms of transportation helped create new regions and economic zones.

The impact of the new methods of commercial agriculture on European ecology was profound. Inhabitants came to perceive of their physical surroundings in basically capitalist terms. Natural resources increasingly were viewed as commodities, articles of value capable of being exchanged for other goods or money. Though ecological consequences varied according to region, every colony touched by the growing commercialisation suffered deforestation, epidemics, soil exhaustion, and decreasing numbers of wild animals. Market forces would continue to transform the European environment. Trees were cut to expand farmland and pasture and to supply fuel and raw materials for factories. Deforestation resulted in a drier landscape more vulnerable to erosion from high winds. Beaver, fox, and lynx had grown scarce as trappers and traders sought valuable pelts.

Elsewhere, Colonial agriculture was carried out not only to feed the colonists but also to produce cash crops and to supply food for the home country. This meant cultivation of such crops as sugar, cotton, tobacco, and tea and production of animal products such as wool and hides. From the 17th to the 19th century the slave trade provided needed laborers, replacing natives killed by unaccustomed hard labor in unfavorable climates and substituting for imported Europeans on colonial plantations that required a larger labor force than the colony could provide. Slaves from Africa worked, for instance, in the Caribbean area on sugar plantations and in North America on indigo and cotton plantations.

Beginning Of Industrial Agriculture

Like any monoculture (an agricultural system dominated by a single crop), single-crop fields promoted the development of soil toxins and the rapid multiplication of parasites. With access to better transportation, farmers began to participate in the market economy in new ways, beyond raising cash crops, that the landscape could not long sustain.

Alternative Future 4 - Enlightened Agriculture

The eventual ecological decline of farms helped set the stage for early industrialization, which in turn created new environmental challenges. As farms faltered, many landless sons and daughters turned to wage labor in new factories including textile mills and sawmills. This new source of cheap labor, combined with the introduction of the power loom fueled an explosive textile industry. Sawmills also expanded, depleting forests. Construction of dams for the new industries altered the ecology of rivers in which fish, including salmon, were blocked from upstream spawning grounds. By the late 18th century, the signs of modern industrial pollution were already evident. As textile mills turned to steam power, burning coal, smoke blackened the skies over fast-growing cities.

The real onset of industrialization would have to await the railroad and textile boom of the Early nineteenth century.

During the 18th century, England, faced with a shortage of wood, had switched to coal as an energy source for industry. Carolyn Merchant says, "Whereas the medieval economy had been based on organic and renewable energy sources-wood, water, and wind- the emerging capitalist economy taking shape over most of western Europe was based not only on the nonrenewable energy source-coal-but on an inorganic economic core-metals: iron, copper, silver, gold, tin, and mercury-the refining and processing of which ultimately depended on and further depleted the forests".

The interaction between mankind and the environment was reciprocal: short-term effects on weather and longer-term climatic change, had profound consequences for medieval economies, societies, and cultures.

This un-ecofriendly science-based civilizational model that originated a few centuries ago in Europe would eventually spread all over the world in the form of 'American dream' and threaten the very existence of life on this planet. We can clearly see this happening now.

When tillage begins, other arts follow. The farmers, therefore, are the founders of human civilization.
~Daniel Webster

History of Chemical Fertilizers

First introduction of chemical fertilizers in agriculture can be traced to the theories of nineteenth-century German chemist Baron Justus von Liebig, who in 1840 published an essay entitled "Chemistry in Its Application to Agriculture and Physiology." His idea was that when a living plant is incinerated and all its organic matter destroyed, the mineral salts remaining in the ashes will contain all that's required for its growth (basically potash, nitrates, and phosphates.) Other scientists and agriculturalists concluded that simply adding these chemicals to the soil would maintain its fertility.

Although this conclusion apparently oversimplified ages of agricultural practice, the observable results were impressive. Artificial fertilizers composed of the above chemicals and calcium oxide (lime) produced good initial crops—which seemed to verify Liebig's experiments. This apparent breakthrough led to the astronomical fertilizer production now so lucrative for the chemical industry. Typically, whenever a farmer has a soil test made on his fields, if the laboratory report indicates deficiencies of phosphate, lime, and so on, he receives a formula of chemicals. He then adds them to the soil to correct the imbalance. Here we have the basis of the prevalent belief that "you get out of the soil what you put into it."

However, this conclusion came into question a few years ago, when the French agricultural bulletin "Nature et Progres" disclosed a startling experiment. A researcher reported that every month for one year, he had monitored two identical soils—one to which only fermented compost had been added, and one to which an organic mixture rich in phosphorus had been added. At the end of the year, the first sample contained one-third more phosphorus than the second sample, the one to which phosphorus had originally been added.

Thus, soil itself can produce phosphorus without any external supply of this mineral. The researcher called it "a miracle of the living soil!" One wonders where the phosphorus in the first sample came from, since none was added before or during the experiment.

After all, chemists have learned that it's impossible to create new elements or transform one element into another (that is, to alter an element's atomic structure) simply by chemical reactions. At the same time, many scientists still believe that all reactions occurring in nature are in fact simply chemical—or, in other words, that life comes from chemicals. The fact is that life generates chemicals and not vice versa.

This conclusion was proven in another experiment by chemist, Albrecht von Herzeele, who demonstrated that seeds sprouted in distilled water, with nothing added but air, increased their content of elements like sulphur, calcium, and magnesium (although the law of conservation of matter holds that this is impossible). This experiment proved that plants can continuously create matter as well as absorb matter from soil, water, and air. Von Herzeele claimed that plants could also transmute or change one element into another (such as phosphorus into sulphur, and so on).

Agricultural Chemicals - Leftover War Explosives

Then came the war and the war ended sooner than expected, resulting in stock piling of war explosive, mostly compounds of nitrogen and phosphorus. Global approach to agriculture modified in the light of industrialization. New seeds were developed and war surplus chemicals were converted into compounds called chemical fertilizers. The seeds, popularly called Green revolution seeds or miracle seeds, were developed to consume these synthetic chemical fertilizers. Thus monoculture came into being at the

> *Why don't you get your eatables from the land? Therefore it is said, sarva-kama-dughā mahī. You can get all the necessities of your life from land. So dughā means produce. You can produce your food. Some land should be producing the foodstuff for the animals, and some land should be used for the production of your foodstuffs, grains, fruits, flowers, and take milk. Why should you kill these innocent animals? You take. You keep them mudā, happy, and you get so much milk that it will moist, it will make wet the ground. This is civilization. This is civilization.*
> *-Srila Prabhupada*

expense of agro biodiversity and water resource crunch.

To understand its long run impacts, we take up the case of India, an agrarian economy till date. Four decades into the green revolution, the situation is pathetic; soil in general has become humus deficient, excessively hard and bears no pores for holding air and moisture. This soil no longer harbours the beneficial microbes but the pathogens and pest eggs, requiring excessive use of synthetic pesticides. The impacts of these chemical fertilizers and synthetic pesticides are well observable. Use of chemical fertilizers especially nitrogen fertilizers invites more pests and leads to further usage of pesticides. The disastrous consequences of the use of these pesticides over several decades are now clearly observable. There is a rise of resistance in the pest species at the expense of the beneficial organisms like the beneficial insects (honey bee) and scavenging birds (vultures). Reports of crop failure are also linked to the changes in natural status of the soil. Reports of occurrence of agricultural pesticides in underground water (bottled water and soft drinks) are certainly due to their excessive applications and non-degradation. There are various reports of people in villages dying after consuming water from shallow tube wells in India. (Chakulia, Balasore, 2005).

One may argue that such chemicals are, after all, also a part of nature, and that scientists are simply using them in a more advantageous way. However, studies indicate that prolonged use of chemical fertilizers designed to increase soil nitrates creates an artificial dependence on the chemical itself: the chemical fertilizers kill the myriad microorganisms and earthworms in the soil that naturally produce such nitrates.

Initially there may be "bumper" crops, if climatic conditions are good; but eventually the soil loses fertility. And the long-range leaching effect can be disastrous. Wes Buchele, Professor of Agricultural Engineering at Iowa State University, describes the situation in no uncertain terms. "We've lost one-half of the country's topsoil since we started farming here."

There ought to be a shift in approach to the whole practice of agriculture at the moment.

Green Revolution Becoming A Yellow Nightmare

Green revolution was introduced in India and some other developing countries in the early sixties to meet the food deficit. But the aftermath of this revolution is disastrous as we have seen already. The soil, devoid of humus has lost its water holding ability, pests have acquired resistance against pesticides. Indian paddy fields are adding large amounts of methane, a green house gas, into the atmosphere. Food chain and water table are contaminated with pesticides.

The environmental deterioration, food and water contaminations demand a paradigm shift from chemical to organic agriculture. With the growing demand of food, diminishing arable land holdings and exodus of the agrarian community from villages to towns abandoning agriculture, only organic farming will not suffice. An integrated new approach of sustainable agriculture is required where soil fertility, crop yield and pest management are

> *Just like here in this Letchmore Heath there are so many, so much land lying vacant. You produce you own food. Why you are going to London, to the factories? There is no need. This is wrong civilization. Here is land. You produce your food. If you produce your food, there is no need of going hundred miles, fifty miles on your motorcycle or motor to earn your livelihood. Why? There is no need.*
>
> *Then you require petrol. And petrol there is scarcity. Then you require so many parts, so many. That means you are making the whole thing complicated unnecessarily. Unnecessarily. There is no need. Simply you keep to the land and produce your food, and the cows are there. They will supply you milk. Then where is your economic problems. If you have sufficient grains, sufficient vegetables, sufficient milk from the land where you are living, where your economic problem? Why you should go to other place?*
>
> *That is Vedic civilization. Everyone should remain in the spot and produce everything as he requires, and God will help you. Because you can produce from the land anywhere. The rainfall is there. If you have got land and the rainfall is regular, then you can produce anything.*
> *- Srila Prabhupada*

taken care of together with the environmental protection.

Albert Howard explains the nature of soil fertility in his classic book, "An agricultural Testament" as follows, "The nature of soil fertility can be understood only when it is considered in relation to Nature's round. To study soil fertility we have to know the natural working system and to adopt methods of investigation in strict relation to such a subject. We must look at soil fertility as we would study a business where the profit and loss account must be taken along with the balance sheet, the standing of the concern, and the method of management. So it is with soil fertility." According to him, a fertile soil is one which has humus in abundance. If the soil is deficient in humus, the volume of pore space is reduced, the aeration of the soil is impeded, there is insufficient organic matter for the soil population, the soil machinery runs down, the supply of oxygen, water and dissolved salts needed by the root hairs is reduced, the synthesis of carbohydrates and proteins in the green leaf proceeds at a lower tempo; growth is affected.

Agriculture - A Journey From The Noblest Profession To The Most Hazardous Industry

Agriculture ranks among the most hazardous industries as per the United States National Institute for Occupational Safety and Health (NIOSH). Farmers are at high risk for fatal and nonfatal injuries, work-related lung diseases, noise-induced hearing loss, skin diseases, and certain cancers associated with chemical use and prolonged sun exposure. Farming is one of the few industries in which the families (who often share the work and live on the premises) are also at risk for injuries, illness, and death. In an average year, 516 workers die doing farm work in the U.S. (1992-2005). Of these deaths, 101 are caused by tractor overturns. Every day, about 243 agricultural workers suffer lost-work-time injuries, and about 5% of these result in permanent impairment.

Agriculture is the most dangerous industry for young workers, accounting for 42% of all work-related fatalities of young workers in the U.S. between 1992 and 2000. Unlike other industries, half the young victims in agriculture were under age 15. For young agricultural workers aged 15–17, the risk of fatal injury is four times the risk for young workers in other workplaces. Agricultural work exposes young workers to safety hazards such as machinery, confined spaces, work at elevations, and work around livestock.

An estimated 1.26 million children and adolescents under 20 years of age resided on farms in 2004, with about 699,000 of these youth performing work on the farms. In addition to the youth who live on farms, an additional 337,000 children and adolescents were hired to work on U.S. farms in 2004. On average, 103 children are killed annually on farms (1990-1996). Approximately 40 percent of these deaths were work-related. In 2004, an estimated 27,600 children and adolescents were injured on farms; 8,100 of these injuries were due to farm work.

This is the outcome of industrialization of agriculture which until few decades back, was regarded as the noblest profession.

Solution - Depatent Life

Another controversial issue is the patent protection given to companies that develop new types of seed using genetic engineering. Since companies have intellectual ownership of their seeds, they have the power to dictate terms and conditions of their patented product. *Currently, ten seed companies control over two-thirds of the global seed sales.* Vandana Shiva, an environmentalist, argues that these companies are guilty of biopiracy by patenting life and exploiting organisms for profit. Farmers using patented seed are restricted from saving seed for subsequent plantings, which forces farmers to buy new seed every year. Since seed saving is a traditional practice for many farmers in both developing and developed countries, GMO seeds legally bind farmers to change their seed saving practices.

Solution - Healthy Agronomic Practices

Pesticide use has increased since 1950 to 2.5 million tons annually worldwide, yet crop loss due to pests has remained relatively constant. The World Health Organization estimated in 1992 that 3 million pesticide poisonings occur annually, causing 220,000 deaths. Pesticide resistance in the pest population is leading to a condition termed the 'pesticide treadmill' in which pest resistance warrants the development of a new pesticide. Giving up good agronomic practices such as crop rotation has landed us in a vicious cycle.

Solution - Free Agriculture From Clutches of Meat

Livestock production occupies 70% of all land used for agriculture, or 30% of the land surface of the planet. It is one of the largest sources of greenhouse gases, responsible for 18% of the world's greenhouse gas emissions as measured in CO_2 equivalents. By comparison, all transportation emits 13.5% of the CO_2. It produces 65% of human-related nitrous oxide (which has 296 times the global warming potential of CO_2,) and 37% of all human-induced methane (which is 23 times as warming as CO_2). It also generates 64% of the ammonia, which contributes to acid rain and acidification of ecosystems. Livestock expansion is cited as a key factor driving deforestation, in the Amazon basin 70% of previously forested area is now occupied by pastures and the remainder used for feedcrops. Through deforestation and land degradation, livestock is also driving reductions in biodiversity. Thus livestock meant for meat are one of the most significant contributors to today's most serious environmental problems.

Solution - Environmentally Sound Traditional Agricultural Systems

There are many remarkable cases of environmentally sound traditional agricultural systems which have been developed over a long historical period.

For example, land surrounding the Hagmataneh hill in Hamadan, Iran, with over 5000 years of agricultural history, does not show any sign of degradation, whereas other sites in the same district where modern methods are in practice, have degraded. Similarly, in the territory of San Francisco Pichátaro, an indigenous community of Central Mexico, with at least 4000 years of agricultural history, no sign of land degradation is visible.

There is a growing and urgent need to realign agricultural processes with natural process, so that they can work complementarily instead of against one another. In these integrated systems, agriculture will be more successful, environmental degradation will be lessened, and more of an opportunity will exist to preserve the landscape. In the same vein, the principles of sustainable and organic agriculture, as well as specific practice of Community Supported Agriculture and vegetarianism are all alternatives to conventional agriculture which embrace the tenets of bioregionalism and environmental conservationism.

Modern technology and High Yield Variety (HYV) seeds significantly outperform traditional varieties in the presence of adequate irrigation, pesticides, and fertilizers. But as our earth's resources deplete and the availability of these inputs come into question, importance of traditional technologies and traditional seeds increases.

The first Western scientist to demonstrate the real importance of life activities in agriculture was Sir Albert Howard, who at the turn of the century was the imperial botanist to the Indian government. Beginning in Pusa, Bengal, and continuing for forty years in other parts of the subcontinent, Howard managed several experimental agricultural stations. His famous book An Agricultural Testament (1943) inspired a surgeon named J. I. Rodale to begin the organic farming movement in the United States, during the early 1940s. By following the ancient methods of Indian farmers—who regularly aerated the soil, used no artificial fertilizers or pesticides, and returned accumulated cow manure and compost to the land—Howard virtually eliminated disease from both soil and animals. Also, he managed dairy cows and kept oxen for plowing. He wrote, "With no chemical help from science, and by observation alone, he [the Indian farmer] has in the course of ages adjusted his methods of agriculture to the conservation of soil fertility in a most remarkable manner... For countless ages he has been able to maintain the present standard of fertility."

Solution - Disengage Food From Oil

Since the 1940s, agriculture has dramatically increased its productivity, due largely to the use of petrochemical derived pesticides, fertilizers, and increased mechanization (the so-called Green Revolution). Between 1950 and 1984, the Green Revolution transformed agriculture around the globe. However, every energy unit delivered in food grown using modern techniques requires over ten energy units to produce and deliver. The vast majority of this energy input comes from fossil fuel sources. Because of modern agriculture's current heavy reliance on petrochemicals and mechanization, there are warnings that the ever decreasing supply of oil (the dramatic nature of which is known as peak oil) will inflict major damage on the modern industrial agriculture system, and could cause large food shortages.

Modern or industrialized agriculture is dependent on petroleum in two fundamental ways: 1) cultivation - to get the crop from seed to harvest and 2) transport - to get the harvest from the farm to the consumer's refrigerator. It takes approximately 400 gallons of oil a year per citizen in developed countries to fuel the tractors, combines and other equipment used on farms for cultivation or 17 percent of the those nations' total energy use. Oil and natural gas are also the building blocks of the fertilizers, pesticides and herbicides used on farms. Petroleum is also providing the energy required to process food before it reaches the market. It takes the energy equivalent of a gallon of gasoline to produce a two-pound bag of breakfast cereal. And that still does not count the energy needed to transport that cereal to market; it is the transport of processed foods and crops that consumes the most oil. The kiwi from New Zealand, the asparagus from Argentina, the melons and broccoli from Guatemala, the organic lettuce from California - most food items on the US consumer's plate travel average of 1,500 miles just to get there.

Oil shortages could interrupt this food supply. The consumer's growing awareness of this vulnerability is one of several factors fueling current interest in organic agriculture and other sustainable farming methods. Some farmers using modern organic-farming methods reporting yields as high as those available from conventional farming (but without the use of fossil-fuel-intensive artificial fertilizers or pesticides. However, the reconditioning of soil to restore nutrients lost during the use of monoculture agriculture techniques made possible by petroleum-based technology will take time.

Alternative Future 4 - Enlightened Agriculture

Solution - Locavores, Eating Local Food

The dependence on oil and vulnerability of the food supply has also led to the creation of a conscious consumption movement in which consumers count the "food miles" a food product has traveled. The Leopold Center for Sustainable Agriculture defines a food mile as: "...the distance food travels from where it is grown or raised to where it is ultimately purchased by the consumer or end-user."

In a comparison of locally-grown food and long-distance food, researchers at the Leopold Center found that local food traveled an average of 44.6 miles to reach its destination compared with 1,546 miles for conventionally-grown and shipped food.

Consumers in the new local food movement who count food miles call themselves "locavores"; they advocate a return to a locally-based food system where food comes from as close as possible. In addition to the "locavore" movement, concern over dependence on oil-based agriculture has also dramatically increased interest in home and community gardening.

Solution - Food For Food, Not For Fuel

Farmers have also begun raising crops such as corn (maize) for non-food use in an effort to help mitigate peak oil. This has contributed to a 130% rise in wheat prices recently, and has been indicated as a possible precursor to serious social unrest in developing countries. Such situations would be exacerbated in the event of future rises in food and fuel costs, factors which have already impacted the ability of charitable donors to send food aid to starving populations.

In 2007, higher incentives for farmers to grow non-food biofuel crops combined with other factors such as over-development of former farm lands, rising transportation costs, climate change, growing meat consumption in China and India, caused food shortages in Asia, the Middle East, Africa, and Mexico, as well as increase in food prices around the globe. As of December 2007, 37 countries faced food crises, and 20 had imposed some sort of food-price controls. Some of these shortages resulted in food riots and even deadly stampedes.

Solution - Revival of Small Farms

One national advertisement by a US farm machinery manufacturer depicts the historical development of farming techniques, leading up to the phenomenal modern harvests. The first illustration shows a single man in a corner of a field cutting small amounts of grain by hand with a scythe. He represents the earliest, "primitive" farming methods. The second illustration shows a man driving a horse-drawn machine, indicating how much more could be accomplished using animals. The third illustration pictures an early tractor in operation, and the series ends with a photograph of a giant, modern tractor silhouetted against a blue sky and endless fields of perfectly cut grain. The tractor is replete with a wrap-around windshield, radio, air conditioning, and padded dash.

But if the first illustration were expanded beyond the close-up of the lone man in one corner of the field, we would see a whole field of men working together with scythes, very much as they still gather bundles of grain in parts of India and other developing countries. In America the process of urbanization has brought nearly all the descendants of those people who formerly worked in the fields with scythes, horses, and oxen into an economic dependence upon a comparatively small number of farmers using sophisticated machinery. Unscrupulous business practices by food processing conglomerates, inflated living costs, a scarcity of honest labor, bad weather, an exodus of young people to the cities, and the high cost of machinery and artificial fertilizers have forced many owners of

> *Bhagavan:* Now they have... the other day in the paper that India exploded its first atomic bomb.
> *Prabhupada:* Yes, and therefore yet it has become very great.
> *Yogesvara:* Now its in the top six.
> *Prabhupada:* But there is no food. Never mind, you starve, but get your atom bomb. That's all. This is civilization. There was a cartoon. Somebody approached some politician, and he said, "Yes, I know there is food problem. So I cannot say what can I do for you, but from next week, you will have television." This is their program, "From next week you will have television." As if television will minimize my hunger. This is the civilization.

smaller farms to exploit the land for as much yield as possible, as soon as possible, as often as possible. Yet the numbers of farms going out of business indicate that it still costs too much to produce too little.

The latest federal Agriculture Department figures show that between 1954 and 1974 the United States farm population dropped more than 50%—until today only about 10 million people (out of a nation of more than 260 million) live on farms. In addition, although the total farmland remained at about one billion acres, the number of farms dropped almost 42%. In fact, since the 1940s the number of farms has decreased by three million, and it continues to drop by two thousand per week. Clearly, "agribusiness" is gobbling up the small- and medium-size farms.

Solution - Organics

Organic agriculture is a production system that sustains the health of soils, ecosystems and people. It relies on ecological processes, biodiversity and cycles adapted to local conditions, rather than the use of inputs with adverse effects. Organic agriculture combines tradition, innovation and science to benefit the shared environment and promote fair relationships and a good quality of life for all involved.

Organic farming relies on crop rotation, green manure, compost, biological pest control, to maintain soil productivity and control pests, excluding or strictly limiting the use of synthetic fertilizers and synthetic pesticides, plant growth regulators, livestock feed additives, and genetically modified organisms. Since 1990 the market for organic products has grown at a rapid pace, averaging 20-25 percent per year to reach $33 billion in 2005. This demand has driven a similar increase in organically managed farmland. Approximately 306,000 square kilometers (30.6 million hectares) worldwide are now farmed organically, representing approximately 2% of total world farmland. In addition, as of 2005 organic wild products are farmed on approximately 62 million hectares.

Organic agricultural methods are internationally regulated and legally enforced by many nations, based in large part on the standards set by the International Federation of Organic Agriculture

Movements (IFOAM), an international umbrella organization for organic organizations established in 1972.

Solution - Isavasya (God-centered) Farming

By Rupanuga dasa

A God-centered farming conception is relevant because it forms the basis for a workable agricultural life-style which includes a strict consideration of the ecological balance between humans, animals, the land, and God. Although sophisticated modern farmers might concede that the success of their endeavors, including their use of innovative machinery, depends in the end on "acts of Providence or God," or at least upon chance, the Isavasya (God-centered) farmer considers that long-range production and ecological balance require actual God consciousness. Therefore, even today in many parts of India, farmers make a point of gratefully offering God a portion of the crop in the form of prasada, or vegetarian food preparations. These offerings are often part of community celebrations in which the members of the community or village meet, especially in the morning and evening, to chant God's holy names and dance.

This God-centered attitude does not reflect a "primitive" agrarian culture or mentality of a distant Indian sect, but about a life-style that's in real harmony with the ideals of sustainable living. In fact, some of the most successful of the modern farm communities are based expressly upon isavasya principles.

Members of the International Society for Krishna Consciousness (ISKCON) say that farm communities of theirs don't use technological prowess to try to outwit natural laws. Rather, community members try to do their work in a God-conscious way. "Success cannot come by working at your own risk," says one follower, "You may get good results for a while, but lasting success depends on how conscious you are of your relationship with the actual proprietor of nature."

Gradually, we have to become aware that God is always present—in every place and at every moment. As we learn this art of being conscious of God's presence, we will naturally develop a devotional, serving attitude toward everyone, including humans, plants, and animals. Then we will see all living beings as spiritually equal, because all living beings are equally related with God. Thus, in one sense, returning to the land, to vegetarianism, to nonviolence, to herbal medicine, and to ecological concern—returning to nature—necessitates returning to God consciousness, our natural consciousness. The age-old Vedic literatures describe that consciousness, in clear-cut, scientific terms.

In fact, in most instances the work of scientists like Howard, Kervran, Baranger, and Hauschka echoes these Vedic conclusions. Howard, for example, simply rediscovered ancient, biologically sound, and ecologically balanced agrarian practices based upon Vedic principles. And Hauschka's assertion that life is not a combination of elements, that instead it "precedes" matter and "originates in a preexistent spiritual cosmos," tells us what the Vedic literatures said thousands of years ago. The Bhagavad-gita, the essence of the Vedas, verifies that individual life is never created or destroyed, but that it is moving (transmigrating) among temporary bodies sustained by God, the original life.

The Alternative Future - 5

From Artificial Necessities To Basics of Life

*Civilization is a limitless multiplication of
unnecessary necessities.
~Mark Twain*

Alternative Future 5 - From Artificial Necessities To Basics of Life

Throwing Money On Questionable Nonessentials

The world is afflicted with scourge of poverty and hunger. Millions are out there without a grain in their mouth and a thread on their bodies. And here we are spending more than half of world's money on defence. Countries with severe droughts have no money to buy food but they have enough money to buy weapons. Half of world's grain production is going for meat and fuel industry. The world is suffering not due to scarcity of resources but misallocation and mismanagement of resources.

Take the example of America where all the world's wealth lands up. While Americans are still reeling from the nearly one trillion dollars which Congress gave to bail out shady bankers and investment firms on Wall Street, and the "common man" frets about how to afford essentials like home mortgages and food on the table, they are simultaneously throwing money away for morally questionable, even reprehensible nonessentials to which—according to traditional religious or spiritual values—it shouldn't go.

For instance, Americans' addiction to drugs and alcohol costs their economy an estimated 276 billion dollars each year in lost productivity, health care expenditures, substance-abuse related crime and motor vehicle crashes, etc. Each American pays nearly $1,000 for the damages of addiction.

According to Frank Rich, author of "Naked Capitalists: There's No Business like Porn," Americans spend between 10 and 14 billion dollars on pornography annually, and while it's impossible to estimate how much hard-earned cash is surrendered to prostitution, prostitution is a huge, multi-billion business.

A study by economist Ben Scafidi of Georgia State University found that divorce and out-of-wedlock childbearing, traditionally discouraged by the world's religious scriptures, cost U.S. taxpayers more than 112 billion dollars each year. The "average" divorce in

America costs state and federal governments $30,000 in direct and indirect costs.

Besides the suffering it wreaks, child abuse is also expensive to deal with in America. Prevent Child Abuse America, an agency, cited research by John Holton and Ching-Tung Wang, Ph.D.s, that by a conservative estimate, the cost related to child abuse and neglect in America was 103.8 billion dollars in 2007 alone. Other forms of abuse are costly as well. According to the National Coalition Against Domestic Violence, an estimated 1.3 million American women are victims of physical assault by an intimate partner each year. The cost of this ungodly violence exceeds $5.8 billion each year.

> *The basic principle of economic development is centered on land and cows. The necessities of human society are food grains, fruits, milk, minerals, clothing, wood, etc. One requires all these items to fulfill the material needs of the body. During the regime of Maharaja Yudhisthira, all over the world there were regulated rainfalls. Rainfalls are not in the control of the human being. The heavenly King Indradeva is the controller of rains, and he is the servant of the Lord. When the Lord is obeyed by the king and the people under the king's administration, there are regulated rains from the horizon, and these rains are the causes of all varieties of production on the land. Not only do regulated rains help ample production of grains and fruits, but when they combine with astronomical influences there is ample production of valuable stones and pearls. Grains and vegetables can sumptuously feed a man and animals, and a fatty cow delivers enough milk to supply a man sumptuously with vigor and vitality. If there is enough milk, enough grains, enough fruit, enough cotton, enough silk and enough jewels, then why do the people need cinemas, houses of prostitution, slaughterhouses, etc.? What is the need of an artificial luxurious life of cinema, cars, radio, flesh and hotels? Has this civilization produced anything but quarreling individually and nationally? Has this civilization enhanced the cause of equality and fraternity by sending thousands of men into a hellish factory and the war fields at the whims of a particular man?*
> *-Srila Prabhupada (SB 1.10.4)*

In a 1998 report, the Justice Department estimated the annual cost of crime to victims at $450 billion a year, about $4,500 per household. But that cost skyrockets further when they pay to imprison criminals. Indeed, the Pew Center estimated that another $44 billion dollars is spent annually to jail America's 2.3 million prisoners. It's a sad fact that the United States locks up over 1% of its population behind bars, far more than any other nation, in both raw numbers and even ratio to population, and this includes countries with questionable human rights records like China and Iran. Such wide-scale incarceration of fellow human beings—who are largely minorities—suggests a spiritual and moral vacuum, the karma for which hits them squarely in their pockets.

Americans also throw big bucks into unhealthy habits like cigarette smoking, too. Economist Justin Trogdon, Ph.D. concluded, "Reducing the number of smokers in the U.S. could save taxpayers billions of dollars in Medicare costs," If all Medicare beneficiaries quit smoking, taxpayers would save $10 billion.

While many of the above are considered sinful, or border-line sinful, by religions, there is a slew of vain non-essentials that Americans lavish their money on. They squander about 637 billion dollars on legal gambling annually and fork out about $17.2 billion dollars each year on video games. They cough up $35 billion on cosmetics, $13 billion on plastic surgery, $122.9 billion to deal with rampant epidemic of obesity, $112 billion on junk food, untold billions on viagra and the like, the list goes on and on.

Perhaps tough economic times will give them a chance to re-scrutinize their values. When their power gets cut off, either by the power company for failure to pay bill, or by a hurricane like Ike, will they read scripture in the candlelight and learn to live a little more simply, and a little more righteously? It's worth considering. Maybe there will be a silver lining in world's economic woes. *(By Sarva Dasa for Houston Chronicle)*

People don't like the true and simple; they like fairy tales and humbug.
~Edmond Jules

Who says spirituality, religion and our pockets are not related?

Living Gently

Rampant blind materialism lies at the root of world crisis. We are recklessly dealing with our environment and our fellow living beings. To lead such kind of life is nothing short of mass insanity. The solution lies at turning our face towards spiritual development, once again.

Its heartening to see that several influential environmental organizations in the world, though secular by constitution, are echoing this theme.

Once such forum is the Worldwatch Institute, an independent research organization that works for an environmentally sustainable and socially just society, in which the needs of all people are met without threatening the health of the natural environment or the well-being of future generations.

Alan Durning of Worldwatch Institute writes, "In a fragile biosphere, the ultimate fate of humanity may depend on whether we can cultivate a deeper sense of self-restraint, founded on a widespread ethic of limiting consumption and finding non-material enrichment...Those who seek to rise to this environmental challenge may find encouragement in the body of human wisdom passed down from antiquity. To seek out sufficiency is to follow the path of voluntary simplicity preached by all the sages from Buddha to Mohammed. Typical of these pronouncements is this passage from the Bible: "What shall it profit a man if he shall gain the whole world and lose his own soul?"

Allen adds,"....action is needed to restrain the excesses of advertising, to curb the shopping culture, and to revitalize household and community economies as human-scale alternatives to the high consumption lifestyle. There could be many more people ready to begin saying "enough"....After all, much of what we consume is wasted or unwanted in the first place. How much of the packaging that wraps products we consume each year -- 162 pounds per capita in the United States -- would we rather not see? ...How many of the unsolicited sales pitches each American receives each day in the mail -- 37 percent of all mail -- are nothing but bothersome junk? How much of the advertising in our morning newspaper -- covering 65 percent of the newsprint in American paper -- would we not gladly see left out?"

Allen continues, "How many of the miles we drive -- almost 6,000 a year a piece in the United States -- would we not happily give up if livable neighborhoods were closer to work, a variety of local merchants closer to home, streets safe to walk and bicycle, and public transit easier and faster?

> *In the human society, they have created problem. Nobody knows where to eat. These hotels means, increase of number of hotels means that people have no place to live. They have no fixed place to live. Today in this hotel, the next day, another hotel. The so many restaurants means people have no fixed place where to eat. The solution... In India still, because they are not so materially advanced, even the poorest man has got some certain fixed up place, his cottage, he has got his wife, he has got his child, and he works, whatever he can do. He lives peacefully still, in the village, although he hasn't got very gorgeous dress and motorcar. But he's peaceful. You'll find still. And sometimes, say, about ten years ago, I was in Ahmedabad. I saw one poor man, he was pulling cart, hand cart...we call thela, in India. So the thela, in that cart there was sufficient load. So one side of the thela there was the wife, and the other side was the husband, and they had a little child, and that child was put up on the load. You see? And they were pulling. That means the husband and wife, working as God has given them to work. So they're working, taking care of the child. So after earning money, they'll go home. They have got a little cottage, and the wife will cook, the husband will eat, and they're peaceful. They're peaceful. It doesn't matter whether first-class eating, second-class... It doesn't matter. But still, they have got a home, and there they live peacefully. The wife cooks for the husband, and the husband eats, and the child is also taken care. It is not killed. There is peaceful. Peacefulness there is.*
> *But here, the advanced civilization, the mother is killing the child, abortion. You see? Still, it is called advancement.*
> *-Srila Prabhupada (Srimad-Bhagavatam 1.16.23 -- Hawaii, January 19, 1974)*

Keith C. Heidorn sums this up when he defines 'Living Gently' as a voluntary manner of living which pursues a positive, satisfying life that is considerate, noble and easily managed and that seeks to produce as small an impact on the environment as possible. It is a lifestyle chosen not only for personal satisfaction, but also for the good of our fellow inhabitants of Planet Earth: animals, humans and plants. It involves frugality but goes beyond.

Downshifting or Voluntary Simplicity

In the U.S. there are 1,000 cars for every 1,000 adults.
In Germany, it's 550 cars for every 1,000 adults.
In India, there are four cars for every 1,000 adults.
Let us take a look at other figures

Within the developed world, North Americans annually consume about 340 Gigajoules per person (GJ/person), whereas Europeans consume 150 GJ/person of commercial energy. Most of the rest of the world consumes about 60 GJ/person, and India and China consume 10 and 30 GJ/person, respectively.

So technically it is possible to live with less resources and lesser damage to the environment. When one voluntarily decides to consume less, it is called voluntary simplicity. Voluntary simplicity means doing/having/living more with less - more time, more meaning, more joy, satisfaction, relationships, community; less money, less material possessions, less stress, competition, isolation. Voluntary simplicity is a growing movement of people who have realized that happiness and fulfillment do not lie in having more money, or new and bigger things.

So in this type of lifestyle individuals consciously choose to minimize the 'more-is-better' pursuit of wealth and consumption. Adherents choose simple living for a variety of reasons, including spirituality, health, increase in 'quality time' for family and friends, stress reduction, conservation, social justice or anti-consumerism,

What we call progress is the exchange of one nuisance for another nuisance. ~Henry Havelock Ellis

while others choose to live more simply for reasons of personal taste or personal economy.

Simple living as a concept is distinguished from those living in forced poverty, as it is a voluntary lifestyle choice. Although asceticism resembles voluntary simplicity, proponents of simple living are not all ascetics. The term "downshifting" is often used to describe the act of moving from a lifestyle of greater consumption towards a lifestyle based on voluntary simplicity.

The act of voluntary simplicity or cultivation of detachment has been the focal point of all religious teachings. In human history, there have been countless souls who led a life of selflessness, dedication and voluntary simplicity. These personalities are respected, revered and remembered even today.

Also known as downshifting, many today are deciding to reduce their incomes and place family, friends and contentment above money in determining their life goals.

Voluntary Simplicity - A True Story

Fast Track Fast Food To Slow Track Slow Food Life

As the following article shows, there is a movement toward "Voluntary Creative Simplicity." It appeared in The Sun on January 2, 2008.

How We Went From $42,000 To $6,500 And Lived To Tell About It!

By L. Kevin & Donna Philippe-Johnson

As a middle class American, it's been difficult for me to understand how we are supposed to make a living when there are so many things working against us. How can we go on day after day with the rising cost of food, fuel, utilities, car insurance, taxes and health care, while dealing with the insecurity of unemployment? In the past, whenever I considered these things, I felt a hopeless sense of impending doom in the pit of my stomach. There is so much talk about how to solve these issues, but nothing ever seems to stop the downward spiral of struggle and stress that millions of folks are experiencing.

Like many working people, my life went along fine during the 1980s. I had a good paying job ($42,000 a year) and though I didn't enjoy the kind of work I was doing as an industrial draftsman, receiving a steady paycheck every week kept me going without much complaint. But then came the Gulf War in the 1990s and after that point I faced nine layoffs over the span of 10 years. By the time September 11 happened, I hadn't been able to maintain steady employment in the petrochemical industry for over a decade. I would work about three or four months, then back again to the unemployment line.

It was at this point that I realized that something was wrong. The life strategy I had grown up to believe in was no longer working and there didn't seem to be any answers. Obviously no one was going to get me out of this, so I decided I needed to take matters into my own hands and figure out a way to redefine my basic approach to living.

Lucky for me, I have an adventurous wife. She was on the same page with me and was willing to make some drastic changes in our lifestyle. As a committed team, we decided to figure out another way to survive despite these uncertain, hard economic times. Since we didn't have a lot of money and because it was getting harder to find steady employment, we decided to rethink our basic values in order to create a life for ourselves where we could be independent and free of needing a career or a full-time job.

> *This is called jagat. Everything is going on. Your motorcar is going on. You are going on. We have a big city, especially in Europe, America, simply going on. This way, this... Whoosh, whoosh, whoosh. No rest. This is called jagat. Where he is going on? You have heard Rabindranath Tagore, poet Tagore. He wrote one article that "When I was in London I saw the people are walking very fast, the cars are going very fast. But I was thinking that 'This England is a small island; they may not fall down in the sea.'" (laughter) If you let loose your dog, it will go on this way, this way, this way, this way, this way. (laughter) This is jagat, going on. Going on, but condition: "You cannot go beyond this." Just like these so-called scientists are going to the moon planet and coming back -- because conditioned. You have to remain where you are placed by your karma.*
> - **Srila Prabhupada** *(Lecture, London, August 16, 1971)*

Alternative Future 5 - From Artificial Necessities To Basics of Life

And for us, that meant first and foremost, moving to the country. If we were going to be poor, we thought, at least it would be better to be poor in the country. That way we could grow our own food and reduce our expenses. Eventually we discovered that there were others who felt the same way we did. Today there is a small, but growing movement in this country towards a lifestyle we call "Voluntary Creative Simplicity."

We decided to start over, to shake loose from all the things holding us down. We got rid of all the stuff we didn't need and worked on paying off debt. Then canceling our credit cards and using cash, we followed an efficient financial plan that taught how to track every penny. By doing this we were able eventually to save a little bit of money.

Also, we wanted to be strong and healthy to do the work required for this basic lifestyle so we changed our eating habits. We broke away from the standard American fast food, pre-packaged supermarket diet in favor of organically grown whole grains, raw fruits and vegetables, fermented dairy, nuts, seeds and sprouts and eliminated all junk foods and prescription drugs. We started exercising regularly by walking, practicing yoga, and gardening. Since we no longer wanted to pay health insurance premiums, we decided to start a special savings account ($1,000) just for emergency first-aid treatment. And of course we got rid of the cell phone, cable television and Internet bills and greatly minimized

> *"Any child born into the hugely consumptionist way of life so common in the industrial world will have an impact that is, on average, many times more destructive than that of a child born in the developing world"*
> ~*Albert Gore*

our use of air conditioning. The beginning of the path to the simple life was a process of elimination in every aspect of our lives.

Eventually we found 2-1/2 acres of land, 35 miles out of the city. Inspired by our new vision, one summer we said goodbye to the city, permanently moved out to our new place and set up a dome tent to live in. We happily lived in our tent that summer while clearing the land and constructing a rustic 10' by 12' room with a sleeping loft. We did this on a "pay-as-you-go" plan, hauling all the materials in the back of our old pickup truck. Never having built anything before, we worked hard and gained the skill of building our own shelter.

As the tiny outbuilding took shape, next came the installation of an underground cistern for collecting rainwater, and finally, the construction of our three-room (500 square foot) cabin. Since we had to borrow $9,000 to purchase the property, I continued to take whatever jobs I could find (drafting, clerk work, courier, dishwasher, bakery assistant, etc.) while Donna (my wife!) stayed busy working on our organic garden, planting fruit trees and composting. She enjoys learning about native plants and healing herbs that she can grow.

Over the next few years, while working toward our goals of self-reliance and independence, we became stronger, healthier and more confident in our ability to rely on our own skills. It was quite an empowering experience. We learned how to build things, grow our own food, take responsibility for our own health, and best of all, we learned how to laugh and have fun again. The simple joys and true pleasures of fresh, home-grown food, watching everything grow and prosper in harmony, working with our own hands and

> *Nobody learns to smoke from the very birth. He has to eat something. He drinks milk, the child. He doesn't say, "Give me a cigarette," but you have learned it by bad association. This is called anartha, unnecessary things in life. These things you have not learnt from the beginning of your life but by bad association. So if you engage yourself in devotional service, then these things will disappear automatically.*
> -Srila Prabhupada (Bhagavad-gita 7.1 -- Nairobi, October 27, 1975)

spending quality time together replaced all of the costly false values that had occupied our time before.

Gradually we paid off the land, finished the cabin and succeeded in minimizing our basic utility costs. We began to notice that our expenses were decreasing as the quality of our life was increasing. As long as we stayed home and didn't travel to a steady job we really didn't need very much money. The lifestyle of voluntary creative simplicity was resulting in compounding efficiency and improvement in every area of our lives.

Soon, we saw the proof of the inefficiency of working a full-time job. After figuring in the work-related expenses of one job, I realized that my take home pay was only $3 an hour! At that point I was convinced that it was far more cost effective to stay home, grow our own food, split our own firewood and bake our own bread than it was to travel to a job day after day. Yet we still needed some form of income.

Though we had reduced the amount we needed to around $540 a month (way below the poverty level in America), we still had to find a way to generate that income without relying on full-time employment. Once we had succeeded in drastically reducing the amount of money we needed, I knew it would be easy to earn this income by working odd jobs such as building rustic furniture, playing guitar for tips, simple carpentry, part-time drafting, office work, plumbing, etc. However, there was one thing I really loved to do...bake handmade whole-grain sourdough bread in an outdoor wood-fired clay oven! I had always shared my bread with friends and family, but it never really occurred to me to do it as a way to earn extra money.

We soon discovered that there was no authentic, handmade sourdough bread being produced in our area, and little by little, people began asking if they could trade or buy from us. Within a year we had enough bread customers to generate the supplemental income needed to meet our modest expenses. And now there is

> *The dying process begins the minute we are born, but it accelerates during dinner parties.* ~Carol Matthau

even more demand and a waiting list of neighbors and friends who want our bread regularly. They know our bread is special because the organic wheat is freshly hand milled, the loaves are lovingly made entirely by hand and baked in our outdoor clay oven.

While the key to the lifestyle of voluntary simplicity, is "thinking small," many people still believe the opposite is true-"bigger is better." For example, people often tell us we should invest in a commercial bakery and produce more sourdough bread. But in order to expand and make a career out of baking and selling bread, we would have to go into debt to purchase commercial mixers, freezers and large ovens, work longer hours and face the mountain of bureaucratic permits, codes, fees and restrictions. As a result, the simple, authentic handmade artisan bread that our customers love would have to be sacrificed in favor of expanding volume and making more money. Everybody loses but the bankers and the bureaucrats.
We would fall right back in the same old trap, getting into debt and sacrificing our freedom and quality of life for a job. This is an example of compounding inefficiency.

The downfall of many people who would like to break the bonds of stress and financial enslavement to the system is their tendency to think too big. But we must realize that this has been programmed into us by the industrial society and loan institutions, all attempting to excite and feed our insatiable desires. Friends, it takes a lot of mindful awareness to break free of all these traps. It also requires an ability to improvise and adapt towards an alternative

True freedom is in the minimum of needs.
~Diogenes

model. The lifestyle of voluntary simplicity is one option and the resulting benefits are transformational.

The point I'm making is this: many of us can no longer think in terms of having a lifetime career anymore. For whatever reason, things are changing in this country. Outsourcing and cheaper labor costs in other countries will continue to eliminate jobs in the United States. And though the opportunity still exists to work, we must understand that it may be only temporary. While continuing to

> *In the name of civilization, we have increased so many unwanted things, unnecessarily. This is called anartha. Artha means which is substance. So just like we can give so many examples. At least, in, two hundred years ago in India, there was no industry. I think I am correct. Yes. But people were so happy. They did not have to go two hundred miles or five hundred miles away from home and for earning livelihood. In Europe and America, I see people are going for earning their livelihood by aeroplane, daily passengers. I've seen. From Vancouver, they were coming to Montreal and other places. Five hundred miles. At least fifty miles, one must go. In New York, many people are coming from distant place, Long Islands, crossing the sea, and then again bus, again... Anartha, simply unnecessary. People... Canakya Pandita says that "Who is happy?" He says, "The man who does not go out of home, and who is not a debtor he is happy." Very simple thing. Who does not go out of home, and he's not a debtor, he's happy. So now we see everyone is out of home, and everyone is a great debtor. So how you can be happy? In America the bank canvasses that "You take money, you purchase motorcar, you purchase your house, and, as soon as you get your salary, you give me." That's all. Finished. You take the card... American... What is it called? Am-card? Yes.*
> *Syamasundara: Bankamericard.*
> *Prabhupada: "Bank-card" or something. "Bank-rupt." (laughter) You see? So you take the card and you purchase whatever you like. And deposit your money in the bank. Then again, you are without any money. Simply that card. That's all.*
> *Srila Prabhupada (Srimad-Bhagavatam 1.2.18 -- Vrndavana, October 29, 1972)*

work at a job or career one should be wise and set up a plan to survive without steady employment for certain periods of time if necessary.

This could mean storing some supplies, purchasing a piece of property where a small shelter, tent or tipi can be erected if necessary, or getting out of the city and into the country where one can provide food for themselves. My old Grandpa used to say, "all the troubles in this country began when people stopped growing their own food." And he was right. The younglings of this modern age don't even know what real food is, much less how to grow or prepare it! This has to change. (That's another reason we promote sourdough bread baking. It is time to start a "slow-food" movement).

Thinking small is one of the most intelligent and powerful things one can do. Consciously reducing one's life down to the simple basics is the secret to happiness. And it is so easy. What is the solution? This is our advice, especially to young people:

"Don't get in debt, don't think in terms of a career (work at a job for one reason only, to get paid so you can buy a place to live and grow some food), live in a small shelter, unload unnecessary stuff, reduce monthly expenses, extract yourself from the enslavement of modern technological materialism, stay healthy by exercising, eat a simple, wholesome diet, develop some practical skills, practice your art or trade and serve your local community. Teach your children to value true pleasures. Real wealth is perishable: food, health, trees, flowers, herbs, healthy soil, clean water, fresh air, friends and art. Learn to value and appreciate these above all else."

Alternative Future 5 - From Artificial Necessities To Basics of Life

Of course we realize that everyone has to creatively work out their own unique plan according to their particular circumstances, especially if there are children to raise. (We have six grown children.) But with "small thinking," so many opportunities open up and the more one can release, the more freedom there is to experience with each passing year.

If someone would have suggested to us ten years ago that there was a way for the two of us to live on much less, build our own little hut, buy our freedom, give up steady employment, work fewer hours, become happy, healthy, debt free, self-reliant, and live fearlessly without health insurance, I would have told them they were crazy. This has been an incredible, radical journey for us, but now we know from first hand experience that with vision, patience, self-discipline and courage, it is possible to create such a reality.

Creative voluntary simplicity expands faster than inflation for those who can do it, rather than waste time and energy thinking too big and chasing after more money to find happiness and security.

> *Have some small cottage, and grow your own food grains, vegetables, and have your cow's milk. Get nice foodstuff, save time. Why should you go in the city, hundred miles in car and again hundred miles come back and take unnecessary trouble? Stick to this spot and grow your own food, your own cloth, and live peacefully, save time, chant Hare Krsna. Very nice program. This is actual life. What is this nonsense life, big, big cities and always people busy? If he wants to see one friend, he has to go thirty miles. If he has to see a physician, he has to go fifty miles. If he has to go to work, another hundred miles. So what is this life? This is not life. Be satisfied. The devotee's life should be yavad artha-prayojanam. We require material necessities as much as it is required, no artificial life. That is spiritual life. Simply increasing artificial life, even for shaving, a big machine is required. What is this? Simply wasting time. Devil's workshop. Make life very simple. And simple living, high thinking, and always conscious to go back to home, back to Krsna. That is life. Not this life, that simply machine, machine, machine, machine.*
> *-Srila Prabhupada (Srimad-Bhagavatam 6.1.49 -- New Orleans Farm, August 1, 1975)*

End of Modern Civilization and Alternative Future

The Alternative Future - 6

Living on Mother Nature's Gifts

Exploitation of Nature vs. Cooperation With Nature

God writes the gospel not in the Bible alone, but on trees and flowers and clouds and stars. ~Martin Luther

Alternative Future 6 - Living on Mother Nature's Gifts

All The World Issues Stem From Our Disregard for Nature and Natural Living

Modern techno-scientific institution has lost concern for God and nature. The nature that was seen as a handiwork of God, to be revered, cooperated and preserved, has became a subject to be dominated and made a slave. Sir Francis Bacon (1561-1626), one of the founders of the modern scientific method, viewed nature as a mysterious, wild woman, something to be exploited and plundered and that "scientists with their new mechanical devices had to torture nature's secrets out of her."

Francis Bacon set forth the empirical method. Bacon was the first to formulate a clear theory of the inductive procedure - to make experiments and to draw general conclusions from them, to be tested in further experiments - and he became extremely influential by vigorously advocating the new method. He boldly attacked traditional schools of thought and developed a veritable passion for scientific experimentation.

The "Baconian spirit" profoundly changed the nature and purpose of the scientific quest. From the time of the ancients the goals of science had been wisdom, understanding the natural order and living in harmony with it. Since Bacon, the goal of science has been knowledge that can be used to dominate and control nature, and today both science and technology are used predominantly for purposes that are profoundly antiecological.

Nature, in his view, had to be "hounded in her wanderings", "bound into service", and made a "slave". She was to be "put in constraint", and the aim of the scientist was to "torture nature's secrets from her".

The ancient concept of the earth as a nurturing mother was radically transformed in Bacon's writings, and it disappeared completely as the Scientific Revolution proceeded to replace the organic view of nature with the metaphor of the world as the machine.

In 1626 Bacon wrote a utopian novel, The New Atlantis. It depicts a mythical land, Bensalem, to which he sailed, that was located somewhere off the western coast of the continent of America. He recounts the description by one of its wise men, of its system of experimentation, and of its method of recognition for inventions and inventors. The best and brightest of Bensalem's citizens attend a college called Salomon's House, in which scientific experiments are conducted in Baconian method in order to understand and conquer nature, and to apply the collected knowledge to the betterment of society. In this novel, Bacon listed some of the inventions he could foresee: "The prolongation of life ... means to convey sound in trunks and pipes in strange lines and

> *ime jana-padah svrddhah supakvausadhi-virudhah*
> *vanadri-nady-udanvanto hy edhante tava viksitaih*
> "All these cities and villages are flourishing in all respects because the herbs and grains are in abundance, the trees are full of fruits, the rivers are flowing, the hills are full of minerals and the oceans full of wealth. And this is all due to Your glancing over them."
> **Prabhupada:** This is Vedic civilization. There is mention of so many things, that "The grains are in abundance and the trees are full of fruits. The rivers are flowing nicely. The hills are full of minerals and the ocean full of wealth." So where is the scarcity? There is no mention that slaughterhouse is flourishing, industry is flourishing. No such mention. There are all nonsense things they have created. Therefore problems are there. If you depend on God's creation, then there is no scarcity, simply ananda. If the trees are full of fruits, if you have got sufficient grains and... Because there is sufficient grains, there is sufficient grass also. The animals, the cows, they will eat the grass. You'll eat the grains, the fruits. And the animal will help you, the bulls will help you to produce grains. And he will partake little, what you throw away.
> -Srila Prabhupada (Srimad-Bhagavatam 1.8.40 -- Los Angeles, May 2, 1973)

distances ... flying in the air ... ships and boats for going under water." Also in the list: "instruments of destruction as of war and poison" and "engines of war, stronger and more violent, exceeding our greatest cannons."

Well, three centuries later, Baconianism has become a reality. Science and technology have come to play a primary role in people's lives and spiritual quest has been assigned a secondary place. The consequences have been devastating. Individuals and cultures have been stripped of inner meaning and the external world (including the global ecology) has been rendered into a set of things, mere resources. Consequently the world of modernity has been built on an illusion: the illusion that only half of reality matters: the external, objective, measurable part. The cry 'no more myths' has led to the abandonment of any possibility of further development and to the 'disenchantment' of self and the world. Historian Lewis Mumford says, "Whatever their adhesion to the outward ceremonies of the Church... more and more people began to act as if their happiness, their prosperity, their salvation were to be achieved on the earth alone, by means they themselves would if possible command."

Every decade is further seeing the degradation of human spirit and further rise of materialism. Thus even greater thrust has been laid into building the machines Bacon envisioned, vastly increasing human ability to exploit the earth's resources.

Almost two millenia ago, Pliny (A.D. 23-79) urged us to cooperate with nature for our own good. The words that he wrote in his work called 'Natural History', deserve a mention, "For it is upon her surface, in fact, that she has presented us with these substances, equally with the cereals, bounteous and ever ready, as she is, in supplying us with all things for our benefit! It is what is concealed from our view, what is sunk far beneath her surface,

"Three or four hundred years ago science turned towards reductionism, the idea that we can understand everything around us and inside ourselves solely in terms of matter acting according to simple physical laws. This paradigm gave human society increased ability to exploit matter. But this viewpoint has cost us a lot - a planet threatened with ruination, and depletion of the human spirit."

objects, in fact, of no rapid formation, that urge us to our ruin, that send us to the very depths of hell. As the mind ranges in vague speculation, let us only consider, proceeding through all ages, as these operations are, when will be the end of thus exhausting the earth, and to what point will avarice finally penetrate! How innocent, how happy, how truly delightful even would life be, if we were to desire nothing but what is to be found upon the face of the earth; in a word, nothing but what is provided ready to our hands!"

Attitude Towards Nature - Need For Change

There is a growing understanding that addressing the global crisis facing humanity will require new methods for knowing, understanding, and valuing the world. Narrow, disciplinary, mechanistic, and reductionist perceptions of reality are proving inadequate for addressing the complex, interconnected problems of the current age. The currently dominant worldview of scientific materialism, which views the cosmos as a vast machine composed of independent, externally related pieces, promotes fragmentation in our thinking and perception. The materialist view of natural

> *Simply, wherever you go, (makes traffic noise) "sonh, sonh, sonh, sonh," and "gonh, gonh, gonh, gonh, gonh." Up in the sky, "gonh, gonh, gonh, gonh," and in the street, "sonh, sonh..." And then, when digging, "gut-gut-gut-gut-gut-gut-gut-gut-gut!" (laughter) Is it not? Don't you feel botheration. But they are thinking, "Oh, America is very much advanced in machine." And when there is that garbage truck? "Ghon-ghon-ghon-ghon-ghon-ghon-ghon-ghon-ghon!" (laughter) So many sounds are going on, always. Eh? Of course, you have got very nice city, nice roads everywhere. But this trouble... You have created so many troubles. And there are news that one lady was a patient. She became mad by the sounds. And I think they are thinking very seriously how to stop all these sounds. Is it not? ...We are creating a civilization which is so much painful, but we are thinking that we are advanced. This is illusion.*
> *-Srila Prabhupada (Room Conversation - December 21, 1970, Surat)*

systems as commodities to be exploited coupled with the ethos of consumerism and social Darwinism has encouraged widespread destruction of our natural life support systems. The cancerous spread of nihilism and dehumanization are driving the decay and disintegration of techno-industrial culture.

In Vedic literatures like Bhagavad-gita, material nature has been described as God's inferior energy and living entity, the soul as God's superior nature. Vedic literature do not approve the idea that life can originate from chemicals and neither does empirical science has any proof to support this idea. By portraying life forms to mere biological machines, science has done tremendous damage. This godless perspective lies at the heart of all the maladies including environmental ones. True God consciousness inspires one to treat environment as one of God's manifestations and act responsibly towards it. Godless worldview has produced an extremely callous attitude towards life, ecology and world resources.

Ideas or thoughts do manifest as our destiny as reflected in the adage, "Sow a thought to reap an act, sow an act and reap a habit, sow a habit and reap a character, sow a character and reap a destiny." Therefore flawed paradigms of humanity are costing us dearly now.

Nature vs Industry : Mother vs Witch

Srila Prabhupada explains in his Srimad Bhagavatam purports, "It is understood that in the past people depended on nature's gifts of fruits and flowers without industrial enterprises promoting filthy slums for residential quarters. Advancement of civilization is not established on the growth of mills and factories to deteriorate the finer instincts of the human being; it rests on developing the potent spiritual instincts of humanity."

Daybreak is one of the greatest disadvantages of living under the solar system: It means having to get up almost the very minute you go to bed, And bathe and shave and scrub industriously at your molar system And catch a train and go to the office or factory.
~Ogden Nash

Living by Nature's Gifts

After several centuries, the Industrial Revolution has left a legacy of dissatisfaction, conflict, and pollution. Best course would be to stay away from the factory, live in harmony with the earth, and make our goals spiritual, not material.

Following are some more extracts from the teachings of Srila Prabhupada on this subject.

Gigantic Industrial enterprises" Srila Prabhupada says, "are products of a godless civilization, and they cause the destruction of the noble aims of human life."

"The more we go on increasing such troublesome industries," the more we "squeeze the vital energy out of the human being" and "the more there will be unrest and dissatisfaction of the people in general, although a few only can live lavishly by exploitation." (SB 1.8.40)

"The productive energy of the laborer is misused when he is occupied by industrial enterprises.... The production of machines and machine tools increases the artificial living fashion of a class of vested interests and keeps thousands of men in starvation and unrest.

> *There is one instance. Not very long ago, say, about two hundred years ago there was a big zamindar. He was known as king in Krishnanagar. So he was charitably disposed. He went to a brahmana and asked him — he was a great learned scholar — "Can I help you any way?" And the pandit replied, "No. I don't require your help. I am quite satisfied." "How you are satisfied?" "Oh, my, these students, they bring some rice. So my wife boils that, and I have got this tamarind tree. I take some leaves and prepare some juice out of it. That is sufficient." So he was satisfied. That's all. But he was a learned scholar. Similarly, Canakya Pandit... You have perhaps heard. He was the greatest politician. He was prime minister of India. He was living in a cottage and just giving instruction. So that is India's Vedic civilization. Everyone is satisfied, self-sufficient. And now in your country, oh, you have to attend office fifty miles off.*
> *-Srila Prabhupada (Room Conversation - December 21, 1970, Surat)*

This should not be the standard of civilization." (SB 1.9.6)

Terrible Industrial Enterprises

"'Factory' is another name for hell. At night, hellishly engaged persons take advantage of wine and women to satisfy their tired senses, but they are not even able to have sound sleep, because their various mental speculative plans constantly interrupt their sleep." (SB 3.9.10)

"The dungeons of mines, factories, and workshops develop demoniac propensities in the working class." Meanwhile, "the vested interests flourish at the cost of the working class, and consequently there are severe clashes between them in so many ways." (SB 1.11.12)

"Manufacture of the 'necessities of life' in factories and workshops, excessively prominent in the Age of Kali, the age of the machine, is the summit of the quality of darkness." Why? "Because factually there is no necessity for the commodities manufactured." (SB 2.5.30)

"What is the need of an artificial luxurious life of cinema, cars, radio, flesh, and hotels? Has this civilization produced anything but quarreling individually and nationally? Has this civilization enhanced the cause of equality and fraternity by sending thousands of men into a hellish factory and the war fields at the whims of a particular man?" (SB 1.10.4)

"The real problem is how to get free from the bondage of birth, death, and old age. Attaining this freedom, and not inventing unnecessary necessities, is the basic principle of Vedic civilization...."The modern materialistic civilization is just the opposite of the ideal civilization. Every day the so-called leaders of modern society invent something contributing to a cumbersome way of life that implicates people more and more" in the cycle of birth and death." (SB 7.14.5)

"Now people are very busy trying to find petroleum in the midst of the ocean. They are very anxious to make provisions for the future petroleum supply, but they do not make any attempts to ameliorate the conditions of birth, old age, disease, and death." (SB 4.28.12)

"The materialists ... think that they are advancing. But according to Bhagavad-gita they are unintelligent and devoid of all sense. They try to enjoy this material world to the utmost limit and

> *Those who have got my books, you will see that how much profusely the earth was producing during the time of Maharaja Yudhisthira, because the executive head of the state was a pious, so how nature was helping. Nature was helping. Now India there is scarcity, scarcity of foodstuff. But the same India was producing so much grains, even during British time, that many thousands and thousand tons of rice were being exported from India to other countries. You see? That I have seen. I have seen. My maternal uncle was very rich man by simply exporting rice to the foreign countries. Yes. Spices... And old history you will find that India, they had got their own ships for exporting spices to Greece and other countries of Europe. The history is there. And they were supplying muslin cloth, even just before the British period, Muslim period. So India's export, export, I mean to say, status was far greater than other countries. And these spices and other export attracted persons from Europe, that Vasco de Gama, and the Columbus also wanted to go, but he fortunately came to America. You see? All these Europeans and the Britishers went and established their supremacy. So India was so rich. But now how that India has become so poor? The same land is there. Why? Because they have lost that old culture, God consciousness. You see? And at least my calculation is that, that a state, a secular state... Secular state means he has no... Here in America you have got state religion. You have got state religion. But in India there is no state religion. Every country has state religion. Even Pakistan, it has divided. It is now a part of India. But they have also their state religion. But unfortunately India has no state religion. That means deliberately they are trying to disconnect with God relation, godly relation. But in the same India... You just read the history, five thousand years before, how much profusely the nature was supplying. So nature can give you anything. After all, it is the nature that supplies your necessities, not the industry. Industry simply transformed in a different way, and a certain class make profit out of it. Industry does not mean really economic improvement. Real economic improvement means what you produce from the land. That requires God help. Without raw materials, even your industry cannot go on.*
> -Srila Prabhupada *(Lecture, Bhagavad-gita, New York, April 1, 1966)*

therefore always engage in inventing something for sense gratification. Such materialistic inventions are considered to be advancement of human civilization, but the result is that people grow more and more violent and more and more cruel." (BG 16.9)

Human Society Should Depend On Natural Gifts

"According to Vedic economics, one is considered to be a rich man by the strength of his store of grains and cows. With only these two things, cows and grain, humanity can solve its eating problem.... All other things but these two are artificial necessities created by man to kill his valuable life at the human level and waste his time in things which are not needed." (SB 3.2.29)

"If we have sufficient grains, fruits, vegetables, and herbs, then what is the necessity of running a slaughterhouse and killing poor animals? A man need not kill an animal if he has sufficient grains and vegetables to eat. The flow of river waters fertilizes the field, and there is more than what we need. Minerals are produced in the hills, and jewels in the ocean. If human civilization has sufficient grains, minerals, jewels, water, milk, etc., then why should it hanker after terrible industrial enterprises at the cost of the labor of some unfortunate men?" (SB 1.8.40)

"Advancement of human civilization depends not on industrial enterprises but on possession of natural wealth and natural food, which is all supplied by the Supreme Personality of Godhead so that we may save time for self-realization and success in the human form of body." (SB 4.9.62)

Srila Prabhupada cites the example of Lord Krishna's ancient city of Dvaraka. "Dvaraka was surrounded by flower gardens and fruit orchards along with reservoirs of water and growing lotuses. There is no mention of mills and factories supported by slaughterhouses, which are the necessary paraphernalia of the modern metropolis....

"It is understood that the whole dhama, or residential quarter, was surrounded by gardens and parks with reservoirs of water where lotuses grew ... All the people depended on nature's gifts of fruits and flowers without industrial enterprises promoting filthy huts and slums for residential quarters." (SB 1.11.12)

Demoniac Civilization

"The natural gifts such as grains and vegetables, fruits, rivers, the hills of jewels and minerals, and the seas full of pearls are supplied by the order of the Supreme, and as He desires, material nature produces them in abundance or restricts them at times. The natural law is that the human being may take advantage of these godly gifts by nature and flourish on them without being captivated by the exploitative motive of lording it over material Nature." (SB 1.8.40)

"All these natural gifts are dependent on the mercy of the Lord. What we need, therefore, is to be obedient to the laws of the Lord and achieve the perfection of human life by devotional service." (SB 1.8.40)

"Everyone is acting under the influence of material nature, and only fools think they can improve upon what God has created." (SB 7.14.7)

"The prosperity of humanity does not depend on a demoniac civilization that has no culture and no knowledge but only gigantic skyscrapers and huge automobiles always rushing down the highways. The products of nature are sufficient." (SB 5.16.24)

"Ample food grains can be produced through agricultural enterprises, and profuse supplies of milk, yogurt, and ghee can be arranged through cow protection. Abundant honey can be obtained if the forests are protected.

"Unfortunately, in modern civilization, men are busy killing the cows that are the source of yogurt, milk, and ghee, they are cutting down all the trees that supply honey, and they are opening factories to manufacture nuts, bolts, automobiles, and wine instead of engaging in agriculture. How can the people be happy? They must suffer from all the misery of materialism. Their bodies become wrinkled and gradually deteriorate until they become almost like dwarves, and a bad odor emanates from their bodies because of unclean perspiration from eating all kinds of nasty things. This is not human civilization." (SB 5.16.25)

A Higher Goal of Life

"Advancement of civilization is estimated not on the growth of mills and factories to deteriorate the finer instincts of the human being, but on developing the potent spiritual instincts of human beings and giving them a chance to go back to Godhead.... Human energy should be properly utilized in developing the finer senses for spiritual understanding, in which lies the solution of life." (SB 1.11.12)

"Nature already has an arrangement to feed us," Srila Prabhupada says. "The Lord has provided food for both the elephant and the ant....

"Therefore one who is intelligent should not work very hard for material comforts. Rather, one should save his energy for advancing in Krishna consciousness." (SB 7.14.14)

"Demons are very much interested in advancing a plan by which people will labor hard like cats, dogs, and hogs, but Krishna's devotees want to teach Krishna consciousness so that people will be satisfied with plain living and Krishna conscious advancement." (SB 9.24.59)

"The sufferings of human society are due to a polluted aim of life, namely lording it over the material resources. The more human society engages in the exploitation of undeveloped material resources for sense gratification, the more it will be entrapped by the illusory, material energy of the Lord, and thus the distress of the world will be intensified instead of diminished." (SB 2.2.37)

"Advancement of human civilization must be towards the goal of establishing our lost relationship with God, which is not possible in any form of life other than the human. One must realize the nullity of the material phenomenon, considering it a passing phantasmagoria, and must endeavor to make a solution to the miseries of life. Self-complacence with a polished type of animal civilization geared to sense gratification is delusion, and such a 'civilization' is not worthy of the name." (SB 2.2.4)

"The materialistic advancement of civilization ... ultimately ends in wars and scarcity. The transcendentalist is specifically warned to be fixed in mind, so that even if there is difficulty in plain living and high thinking he will not budge even an inch from his stark determination." (SB 2.2.3)

"All human society is meant to worship Lord Visnu [God]. At the present moment, however, human society does not know that this is the ultimate goal or perfection of life. Therefore instead of worshiping Lord Visnu, people have been educated to worship matter.

"According to the direction of modern society, men think they can advance in civilization by manipulating matter to build skyscrapers, big roads, automobiles and so on. Such a civilization must certainly be called materialistic because its people do not know the goal of life.

"The goal of life is to reach Visnu, but instead of reaching Visnu, people are bewildered by the external manifestation of the material energy. Therefore progress in material advancement is blind, and the leaders of such material advancement are also blind. They are leading their followers in the wrong way." (SB 5.1.14)

"Life is never made comfortable by artificial needs, but by plain living and high thinking." (SB 2.2.37)

The Blind Man And the Lame Man Together

"At the present moment, India may be compared to the lame man and the Western countries to the blind man. For the past two thousand years India has been subjugated by the rule of foreigners, and the legs of progress have been broken. In the Western countries the eyes of the people have become blind due to the dazzling glitter of material opulence.

"The blind man of the Western countries and the lame man of India should combine together," Srila Prabhupada says. "Then the lame man of India can walk with the help of the Westerner, and the blind Westerner can see with the help of the lame man. In short, the material advancement of the Western countries and the spiritual assets of India should combine for the elevation of all human society." (SB 4.25.15)

"One who understands the purpose of Krishna, the Supreme Personality of Godhead, should seriously understand the importance of the Krishna consciousness movement and seriously take part in it. One should not endeavor for ugra-karma, or unnecessary work for sense gratification." (SB 9.24.59)

THE AUTHOR

Dr. Sahadeva dasa (Sanjay Shah) is a monk in vaisnava tradition. Coming from a prominent family of Rajasthan, India, he graduated in commerce from St.Xaviers College, Kolkata and then went on to complete his CA (Chartered Accountancy) and ICWA (Cost and works Accountancy) with national ranks. Later he received his doctorate.

Since last two decades, he is leading a monk's life and he has made serving God and humanity as his life's mission. He is also the president of ISKCON Secunderabad center. His areas of work include research in Vedic and contemporary thought, Corporate and educational training, social work and counselling, travelling in India and aborad, writing books and of course, practicing spiritual life and spreading awareness about the same.

He is also an accomplished musician, composer, singer, instruments player and sound engineer. He has more than a dozen albums to his credit so far. (SoulMelodies.com) His varied interests include alternative holistic living, Vedic studies, social criticism, environment, linguistics, history, art & crafts, nature studies, web technologies etc.

Many of his books have been acclaimed internationally.

OTHER BOOKS BY THE AUTHOR

This unique book by the author examines the lifeline of modern living - petroleum. In our veins today, what flows is petroleum. Every aspect of our life, from food to transport to housing, its all petroleum based. Either its petroleum or its nothing. Our existence is draped in layers of petroleum. This book is a bible on the subject and covers every conceivable aspect of it, from its strategic importance to future prospects. Then the book goes on to delineate important strategic solutions to an unprecedented crisis thats coming our way.

Pages-330, www.OilCrisisSolutions.com

For a copy, write to: soulscienceuniversity@gmail.com

Food is our common ground, a universal experience. But there is trouble with our food. Traditional societies had good food but we have just good table manners. A disease tsunami is sweeping the world. Humanity is dying out. This is the result of our deep ignorance about our food. If you don't have good health, the other things like food, housing, transportation, education and recreation don't mean much. This books lists out major killer foods of our industrial civilization and how to escape them.

Pages 276, www.FoodcrisisSolutions.com

For a copy, write to: soulscienceuniversity@gmail.com

This landmark book on cow protection delineates various aspects of cow sciences as presented by the timeless voice of an old civilization, Vedas. This book goes on to prove that the cow will be the making or breaking point for humanity, however strange it may sound. Science of cow protection needs to be researched further and more attention needs to be given to this area. Most of the challenges staring in the face of mankind can be traced to our neglect in this area.

Pages-136, www.cowism.com

For a copy, write to: soulscienceuniversity@gmail.com

This book discusses the vital role of cows in peace and progress of human society. Among other things, it also addresses the modern ecological concerns. It emphasizes the point that 'eCOWlogy' is the original God made ecology. For all the challenges facing mankind today, mother cow stands out as the single answer.

Living with cow is living on nature's income instead of squandering her capital. In the universal scheme of creation, fate of humans has been attached to that cows, to an absolute and overwhelming degree.

Pages-144, www.cowism.com

For a copy, write to: soulscienceuniversity@gmail.com

This book deals with the internal lives of the cows and contains true stories from around the world. Cow is a very sober animal and does not wag its tail as often as a dog. This does not mean dog is good and cow is food. All animals including the dog should be loved and cared for. But cow especially has a serious significance for human existence in this world. Talk about cows' feelings is often brushed off as fluffy and sentimental but this book proves it otherwise.

Pages 136, www.cowism.com

For a copy, write to: soulscienceuniversity@gmail.com

If humanity and the planet have to survive, we have to replace our present day economic model. It's a fossil fuel based, car-centred, energy inefficient model and promotes over exploitation of natural resources, encourages a throwaway society, creates social injustice and is not viable any longer.

This book presents an alternative economic system for the 21st Century. This is an economics which works for the people and the Planet.

Pages 136, www.cowism.com

For a copy, write to: soulscienceuniversity@gmail.com

www.ingramcontent.com/pod-product-compliance
Lightning Source LLC
Chambersburg PA
CBHW071643090426
42738CB00009B/1416